The Gulf Conflict and International Relations

The Gulf War of 1991 reflected and made many changes in relations between states. Its repercussions continue, both in regional tension, in domestic and international discussions about the role of the United Nations and justifications for the use of force, and in perceptions about the realities of bringing to bear apparent political and military strength.

Ken Matthews has made use of the analytical and forensic tools of the discipline of international relations to help the undergraduate to understand the Gulf conflict, rather than merely provide a chronological narrative of events. he examines the war and its build up from a number of different perspectives, in order to give the student a more rounded view. By making a number of 'lateral cuts' through the crisis, the book illustrates important aspects of international relations via an analysis of events in the Gulf.

This book should become required reading for all undergraduates of international relations because its examination of the relations between states is relevant to the so called new world order. It will also prove valuable for those interested in the analysis of international crises and the future role of the UN, as well as for students of the Middle East.

Ken Matthews is a Senior Lecturer in International Relations at the School of International Studies and Law, Coventry University.

The Gulf Conflict and International Relations

Ken Matthews

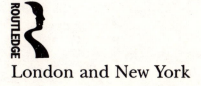

London and New York

First published 1993
by Routledge
11 New Fetter Lane, London EC4P 4EE

Simultaneously published in the USA and Canada
by Routledge
29 West 35th Street, New York, NY 10001

Typeset in Baskerville by EPPP Group at Routledge
from the author's disks
Printed and bound in Great Britain by
T.J.Press (Padstow) Ltd, Padstow, Cornwall

British Library Cataloguing in Publication Data

A catalogue record for this book is available from the
British Library

Library of Congress Cataloging in Publication Data

Matthews, Ken, 1938-
  The Gulf Conflict and international relations / Ken
  Matthews.
  p. cm.
  Includes bibliographical references and index.
  ISBN 0–415–07518–1 : $49.95. – ISBN 0–415–07519–X
  (pbk.) : $17.95
  1. Persian Gulf War, 1991. 2. Middle East – Politics
  and government – 1979- I. Title.
  DS79.M376 1993
  956.704'42–dc20

                                        92–47343
                                        CIP

ISBN 0-415-07518-1   0-415-07519-X (Pb)

There are three people to whom I would like to dedicate this book: Michael Banks for giving me the opportunity to study international relations at the London School of Economics, to Chris Hill for his friendship, and to them both for the intellectual stimulation they provided me rather late in my life, and finally to my wife, Janet, for her unfailing encouragement and unstinting support. This book is a less than adequate recognition of my debt to them.

Contents

List of figures ix

List of tables xi

Introduction: the Middle East and the study of international relations 1

1 The Middle East in historical context 12

2 Crisis: the provocation and the protagonists 33

3 The United Nations and the Gulf conflict 69

4 The diplomacy of crisis 91

5 The Gulf conflict and international law 126

6 The laws of war and the Gulf conflict 149

7 Morality and the Gulf conflict 170

8 The economic dimension of the Gulf conflict 191

9 War, strategy and the Gulf conflict 215

10 The aftermath 252

    Appendices 281
  I Gazetteer of states involved in the Gulf crisis 282
 II Chronology of the Gulf conflict 294
III Maps 301
IV Documents 306
 V Statistics of the Gulf War 313

    Notes 317
    Index 326

Figures

2.1 Reasons for the Iraqi invasion   45
4.1 Reasons for the US response   100
4.2 The structure of international crises   101
4.3 The structure of the Gulf crisis   102
9.1 Matrix of possible outcomes in the Gulf conflict   222

ERRATUM

The publishers wish to point out that the diagrams for figures 2.1 and 4.1 have become transposed by mistake. The figure number 2.1 and caption on page 45 refer to the diagram on page 100; and the figure number 4.1 and caption on page 100 refer to the diagram on page 45.

Tables

8.1 Breakdown of oil price per barrel, 1973   197
8.2 Percentage composition of world energy
    consumption, 1979-84   198
8.3 Top twenty producers of crude oil, 1988   199
8.4 Top twenty exporters of crude oil, 1988   200
9.1 Iraqi outcome priorities for the Gulf crisis   220
9.2 US/Coalition outcome priorities for the Gulf crisis   224
9.3 Key stages in the Gulf conflict, 1990–1   228

The Middle East and the Study of International Relations

The book is written from an international-relations perspective. Thus it is not a history of the Gulf conflict; it does not trace the events chronologically from beginning to end. What it aims to do is to take a series of 'lateral slices' through the conflict examining the crisis from different analytical perspectives. The objective is to provide a more rounded understanding of the conflict and per- haps provide a basis for the reader – student or interested layman – for further investigation. Each of the chapters could, and no doubt will in time, provide the subject for a whole book. Mean- while perhaps this book can in a single volume set the conflict as a whole in an overtly international relations perspective.

The historian's claim that events cannot be understood until decades, if not centuries, have intervened to lend 'historical perspective' to our judgements has some validity when applied to the problem of assessing where the events we study fit into the broad sweep of history. Even then 'historical perspective' does vary according to the times from which historical events are viewed, so the perspective of time by no means guarantees the discovery of 'historical truth' even if such a thing exists. But it is possible to gain some real, even if not ultimate, understanding of what happened by applying some of the insights of political science and the academic study of international relations. This can be done on the one hand without waiting for decades to elapse and on the other without resorting to 'instant journalism'.

There is another justification for attempting to produce a reasonably analytical examination of the crisis even at this relatively early stage after the actual events. It would be a plausible claim to say that the events relating to the Gulf crisis, both the relatively brief period of the military conflict itself and the four months or so of pre-conflict diplomacy, were the most publicly and continuously 'analysed' international events of recent times, if not all time. In that process a vast amount of 'expertise' was brought in to help process and digest the information flowing through the ether. Of course there are some who claim, not without justification, that there was considerably more analysis than information, and perhaps even more analysis than the information could support, and thus a danger of the medium overwhelming the message. Certainly one can note the idea of war as a 'media event' with distaste; but notwithstanding the reservations of some journalists concerning the access to 'real' information, the Gulf crisis was probably the most public crisis we have experienced.

The point is that the analysis during the crisis, however 'instant', utilised a vast array of academics and researchers from universities, polytechnics and international institutes, and these analysts brought directly to the public discussion of these events their academic tools of analysis from political science and international relations. So daily, in the press and broadcasting media, there were discussions about usually abstruse and even arcane subjects such as military strategy, crisis diplomacy, the international laws of warfare, the nature of 'holy war', the notion of the 'just war', the efficacy of economic sanctions, the meaning of the rhetoric of classical Arabic and so forth. There might be some value in bringing some of that disparate analysis together into one volume for both, student and interested general reader.

EXPLAINING AND UNDERSTANDING EVENTS

Crises and wars occur as a result of decisions taken by individuals and groups of individuals in positions of power.[1] Thus, explaining events like crises and wars entails an investigation of the immediate context in which those decisions are made as well as some examination of the historical and structural context in which events take place. Events are the product of contingent factors, historical factors and structural factors. These latter have the effect of limiting what action can be taken or is likely to be taken at any one time. Structural and historical factors do not determine what happens. They merely set the context within which subsequent events take place and set the outer limits to the range of options that are presented to decision-makers. It is the contingent factors that determine which of those options is chosen.

The role of the individual in explaining human affairs is always a problematical area in the study of the social sciences. The central question, put in the baldest terms, is whether individuals make history or history makes individuals. This underlying question for our purposes in explaining wars concerns the freedom of choice individuals have in making public decisions and policies. Are individuals, like Saddam Hussein or President Bush, essentially products of their environment and historical context or do they control the circumstances in which they make decisions?

These issues have practical as well as theoretical significance because if the view is taken that individual behaviour is essentially determined by structural factors (i.e. that individuals are merely the agents of historical and structural forces – perhaps now rapidly going out of fashion with the demise of Marxism-Leninism) then those individuals cannot be held entirely responsible (morally or politically) for those actions. So paradoxically the notion of 'orientalism' (a set of prejudices which are said to predetermine western attitudes to the Middle East – see below for further discussion of this phenomenon), when applied as a measure of criticism to the western reaction to the Gulf crisis, can be said to absolve individual decision-makers of responsibility for the decisions they made because they were merely prisoners of an intellectual or psychological paradigm outside of which, by definition, they cannot act. In any case the notion of 'freedom of action' in the context of political decision-making needs to be addressed with caution since most decisions are the result of constraints caused by the acceptability or otherwise of the consequences of other courses of action.

The stance taken by this study is that any combination of historical and structural factors presents a series of propensities within which individuals have freedom of action. At the peripheries of that set of propensities there exist areas of ambiguity where there can be conflict for supremacy between 'structural propensity' and 'individual freedom of action'. It is in this area that scope exists for individuals to change the environment and to some extent act outside of the range of propensities.[2] In any case, in circumstances of what might be called *structural flux*, the situation will be more difficult to define. There will be an increase in uncertainty and complexity; the 'pattern of propensities', as it were, will be more fluid, more chaotic, and thus the scope for individual freedom of action greater. In these circumstances there may be scope for individual actions/decisions actually to change the structure or perhaps influence the structural change that is already taking place.

An illustration of this point is the problem of explaining the profound changes that have been taking place in Eastern Europe and the Soviet Union over the past half decade. The question arises as to whether these events are the result of the decisions and political skill of one man (Mikhail Gorbachev with the help of his advisers) or the culmination of structural/historical forces in which, for example, it could be said that Marxism-Leninism has reached the limits of its own internal contradictions. After all, Nikita Krushchev attempted similar reforms in the late 1950s and early 1960s and failed – was it because the structural conditions in the Soviet system were then not yet right for reform or because he was not as politically skilled as Gorbachev? Perhaps it was a question of creating the conditions for counter-revolution. It is ironic that one has to revert to the language of Marxism to explain its demise. These examples demonstrate the need to consult both structural and contingent factors in attempting to explain events. After all it was Lenin, with all his Marxist baggage of historical determinism, who conceded the importance of the right individual being available to give history 'a helping hand' towards its preordained destiny.

The political scientist talks of 'structural' factors in which he includes historical events which are the precursors if not causes of contemporary events. These historical events have happened and cannot be ignored; the contemporary decision-maker cannot do anything about the past which has to be accepted as 'given' and in this sense the past is a contemporary 'fact' over which the decision-maker has no control. What has happened in the past can lead to opportunities for action in the present or entail constraints on action in the present. Most often decision-makers are faced with the consequences of actions taken in the past not only by other people but also by the decision-makers themselves. So the past represents one aspect of the 'structure' within which decision-makers have to act. The other dimension of structure is that whole network of interactions between states – their goals and expectations, their interests and style of action, their power and their weakness, their alliances and antagonisms, their perceptions and misperceptions and so on.

Structural factors then will predispose a state (or the government of a state) to act in a particular way when faced with a particular situation. It is not that a decision cannot be taken which is contrary to that predispostion; it is that there will be costs entailed in so doing. Thus in explaining why the major members of the UN Coalition (notably the United States) found themselves at war with Iraq, both structural and contingent factors have to be consulted and some judgement made about the extent of their interaction and their relative signficance. Insofar as this book aims to explain the crisis and the war, it will attempt to elucidate the interactions between structural and contingent factors. Some of the chapters will be concerned with describing the nature of those structures. For example, Chapters 1 and 2 deal with the historical and contemporary structures of the Middle East and the structural relationship between the Middle East and 'the west'. Chapter 5 examines both historical and contemporary international legal structures within which the conflict took place. Those chapters (e.g. Chapters 4 and 9) that deal with the dynamics of crisis and war will attempt to illuminate the processes of relations between states – that is, not only what happens but how it happens and why.

Such concerns for issues of methodology are usually dismissed by the more 'pragmatic' as philosophical navel-gazing which clouds the real issues and contributes little to actual understanding. That is not in fact the case, because issues of methodology are always relevant to the status of the knowledge we think we have about the world – though it can be conceded that it is possible to become preoccupied with such issues at the expense of operating in the 'real' world. However, in this case these issues become directly relevant since the 'credentials' of political science and the analytical approach to understanding human affairs are called into question specifically when related to events in the Middle East. The issue was raised in arguments that took place during the Gulf crisis which suggested that 'western' attitudes to events in the Gulf, and in particular the western propensity to respond with military force, were determined by the European imperialist past and that the Iraqis and those in the Arab world who supported them were motivated by their colonial experience at the hands of their former European masters. This is part of a more general thesis that these attitudes have persisted in the 'post-colonial' period in the form of 'neocolonialism', a term used to describe a condition of economic and cultural dependence.[3]

Specifically these arguments emerged in media discussion of events during the crisis firstly in the school of the mainly 'left-wing anti-war lobby', whose claim was that western policy towards the crisis was driven by what might be called 'the habit of imperialism'. This was held to be a combination of the remnants of old-style European imperialist thinking and newer-style (essentially American) neo-imperialism of the multinational companies and American military power (often seen as an agent of American economic power). The second manifestation of these ideas during the crisis was in the apparent problem of understanding Iraqi diplomacy and in particular of the attempt to penetrate the barrage of Arabic rhetoric that constantly emanated from Baghdad Radio; and in attempting to reconcile the apparent contradictions in the Iraqi government's policy pronouncements and its actual diplomatic behaviour – that is, to try to make some sense of the apparent inconsistency between what the Iraqis said and what they did. There was a prevalent idea that there was some inherent 'inscrutability' in the Arab way of diplomacy which was somehow beyond the powers of western diplomatists and commentators to penetrate and which thus they were bound to misinterpret. This is a characteristic of a certain type of thinking among some western individuals who hold anti-imperialist, and even anti-western, views but who nevertheless subscribe to the 'impenetrability' thesis of non-western cultures – a sort of 'perverse orientalism'.

Much of the argumentation about neo-colonialism is Marxist in origin but is part of a much wider thesis which is effectively articulated by Edward Said in the notion of 'orientalism'.[4] Put simply this thesis suggests that contemporary 'western' attitudes to the Middle East are determined by a 'mind set' dominated by stereotypical thinking, fantasies about the nature of the Middle East, the desert, Islam and the 'Arab mind' (and body) which was moulded by the earliest travellers in the region such as Richard Burton and Charles Doughty, and subsequently elaborated and reinforced by the imperialist attitudes of the European colonial period in the nineteenth and twentieth centuries, and even further enhanced by the continued domination in economic, political and cultural terms after the Second World War. The argument is that 'orientalism' now infests the whole western concern with the Middle East from diplomacy to big business to academic 'expertise' in Middle Eastern studies, learned institutions and so on.

But the thesis does not stop at western attitudes. It goes on to assert the existence of what might be called a 'reverse' orientalism; the idea that the peoples of the Middle East themselves have been so 'socialised', indoctrinated, undermined by persistent assumptions of their own inferiority, and browbeaten by cultural, economic, political and miltary onslaughts (not to say the defection of most of their intellectual elites to 'western' ways) that they themselves have adopted the assumptions of orientalism and thus the roles and behaviours it ascribes to them.[5] The upshot of this of course is that even indigenous Middle Eastern writers who themselves adopt some of the western critique of Middle Eastern politics, society and international relations, can be dismissed as being fatally subverted by the insidious frame of reference of orientalism.

It is important that this issue is drawn attention to, though the fundamental problem of which it is a manifestation cannot be 'solved'. In fact the problem is recognised and addressed by the very social and political sciences which Said condemns where it is referred to as 'ethnocentrism' and more generally in philosophy (and in particular the philosophy of the social sciences) as the problem of 'relativism'.[6] It is a very complex issue and this is not an appropriate medium in which to mount an exhaustive examination of the problems it raises. However, there are a number of forms of relativism, but they all in one way or another address the problem of whether it is possible to use the cultural and conceptual 'apparatus' of one society objectively to understand the structures and behaviours of another society which has a different cultural and conceptual apparatus.

This can apply for example to anthropology and the problem of whether social scientists from scientific, post-industrial revolution societies can form an objective understanding of 'primitive', pre-scientific societies which still have intact a conceptual edifice for understanding the world about them based upon witchcraft. It can apply to the conventional historian in, say, the twentieth century attempting to understand behaviour of people in his own country five hundred years ago when images of how the world works were so different. Of course, it can apply to contemporary analysts in international relations or comparative political science with the problem of whether academics, as well as decision-makers themselves, can accurately interpret the meanings of the declarations and actions of foreign-policy decision-makers of states with a different set of cultural, religious and ideological assumptions.

Such considerations raise intractable problems for the under-standing of human behaviour. Ultimately, of course, it is unlikely that different cultural systems will agree entirely in their respective interpretations of the world. There is an element of circularity here since cultural systems are defined by a particular edifice of beliefs and concepts that determine how the world is interpreted. To the extent that a cultural system interprets the world in a way consonant with another cultural system it loses its particularity. This issue has a special significance in the problems of under-standing relations between states and is even more relevant in situations of conflict and dispute. If there are intrinsic obstacles preventing different cultural systems accurately interpreting each others' behaviour then this is a particularly dangerous phenom-enon in situations of possible war. If there is a likelihood of misunderstanding and misinterpretation of behaviour then there is a likelihood of wars occurring unintentionally or by accident. Indeed there is a large body of literature in international relations that considers the consequences of misperception between states in dispute; some of it holds that misperception is the most com-mon cause of war.[7] Insofar as cultural differences and ethno-centrism are significant factors in misperception, they will be important to our understanding of the Gulf War.

This is relevant to another feature of the contemporary world which has a bearing on relations between the 'west' and the 'Middle East' – that is, the apparently inexorable diffusion of European/American cultural values throughout the world and the competition this sets in train between local indigenous ways of life and the insidious penetration of these societies by western values – and it is perhaps the least desirable aspects of western values that seem to attract local peoples. This is an aspect of what has come to be known as cultural imperialism in which the peoples of these countries are seduced by the popular culture and consumerism of the west aided by advertising of the multinational companies and socialised into desiring their products. The elites of these societies are 'captured' by the wealth and power of western countries, so that they have a greater loyalty to these 'alien' values than they do to their own peoples and their own cultural traditions.

The international political dimension of this 'cultural hege-mony' of western traditions, political and philosophical ideas, ways of life and interpretations of the world are profound and have been particularly prevalent in the Middle East. The so-called 'fundamentalist' Islamic revolution in Iran and the subsequent spread of its ideas throughout the region is a reaction to the domination of western values. The taking of American diplomats as hostages by the Iranian authorities in 1979 was a breach of one of the fundamental principles of western diplomatic practice – the immunity and inviolability of diplomatic representatives. Such action can be seen as an act of resentment against the fact that the very 'international system' within which all states have to operate is itself the product of 'western' (European) political philosophy.

Thus it is important to recognise that the problem of 'cultural relativism' has both theoretical and practical significance for the study of international relations in general and for the study of the Middle East in particular (especially the problems of gaining some perspective on the Gulf crisis). Moreover, western cultural hegemony and increasing diffusion is, and will continue to be, a problem in international relations, including western relations with the Middle East. Other non-western cultures that have perhaps had a different historical relationship with Europe have fared better in maintaining their own cultural integrity. For example, Japan and China have perhaps been selective in their choice of which western values to accept and which not to. Japan has exploited western capitalistic economic and technological values rather spectacularly and has easily accepted western consumerism. It must be said that it is highly probable that this has not been done without cost to other aspects of Japanese culture which have yet to become manifest. China on the other hand seems to have incorporated Marxism, a product of European political and philosophical thought, and little else, though it seems that democracy, another product of western thought and history, is vying to replace it. The issues of cultural diffusion, cultural diplomacy, cultural imperialism and other manifestations of the conflict and competition between diverse value systems, will become more prevalent in an international system which has become perhaps 'more fluid' after the breakdown of the Cold War system. The Cold War grew at the same time as the process of decolonization and its domination of the international system has had the effect of 'suffocating' the freer expression or regrowth of local, indigenous cultural systems that might have happened as a consequence of decolonisation.

As an analyst that operates from an overtly 'international

relationist' perspective I make reference to these phenomena not with any normative or prescriptive intent but merely to acknowledge their existence and their significance. Said's exegesis is comprehensive, erudite, elegantly written, masterly: the rage it expresses, however, is ultimately unappeasable. Even Said himself does not offer us a mechanism for escaping the confines of our orientalism. His book is a guide to the measure of our culpability, but it offers us no key to our salvation in this matter.

Indeed, it is not intended as an insult to say that Said comes near to hypocrisy. Being a Lebanese American he operates in both camps as it were – or neither? He speaks as a passionate advocate of the Arab/Islamic world, but his analysis and methodology is an impressive manifestation of that very western 'orientation' (occidentation?) he condemns. The author of this present book finds himself with the same dilemma; having drawn attention to the problems raised by orientialism the question arises as to whether the phenomenon precludes the possibility of any valuable understanding of the Gulf crisis emerging from his analysis? Whilst the limitations of the analytical approach must be acknowledged, so must the quagmires of 'cultural relativism' at all costs be avoided. With all its limitations the analytical approach must hold out a better prospect for understanding what happens in the world than a blind adherence to the idea of cultural hermeticism. All we can hope is that recognition of our propensity for ethnocentrism will in some measure be a guard against it distorting too much our perceptions or our capacity for applying reason to our understanding of the relations between states.

THE STRUCTURE OF THE BOOK

Having set out the intellectual perspective within which this book is written, finally I would like to present an outline survey of what follows. Chapter 1, as has been indicated, sets down both the historical background of the Middle East and illustrates the contemporary complexities of the social, political, religious and cultural structures of the region. Chapter 2 considers the background to the Gulf crisis itself, examines the sources of Iraq's motivations for invading Kuwait, the conditions that made it possible and the sources of the various responses to that event. Chapter 3 considers the role of the United Nations in the crisis, the operation of the Security Council; it analyses the voting and the resolutions it passed, as well as the motivations and interests of the major actors in the Security Council. Chapter 4 discusses the structure of crisis, the processes of coercive diplomacy and the mechanisms and principles of crisis management. In arriving at an explanation for the failure of crisis management to prevent war, the emphasis will be placed upon the structural and cognitive factors which determined the actions of the respective sides.

Chapter 5 examines the international legal context of the crisis, the legal validity of Iraqi territorial claims against Kuwait and the legal dimensions of the UN involvement in the crisis. Chapter 6 applies the laws of war to the conduct of the war by both sides and examines particular cases where the laws of war are held to have been breached. Chapter 7 considers the relevance and application of the principles of the 'just war' to the Gulf conflict and considers some of the moral arguments raised against the war. Chapter 8 examines the economic context of the conflict, the importance of the oil economy in explaining yet another Middle Eastern war but in particular considers the contention that it was essentially 'an oil war'. Chapter 9 analyses the war phase itself, the complexities of calculations in the face of war, the respective military strategies of the two sides and examines some of the strategic features of the war. Chapter 10 discusses some of the consequences of the war in the Middle East and the international system as a whole.

Chapter 1

The Middle East in historical context

THE 'MIDDLE EAST' DEFINED

The Middle East is a construction of the European mind. In intellectual and cultural terms, as has already been observed in the idea of 'orientalism', the Middle East is a product of the European imperial and bourgeois imagination. What might be termed the 'politics of exotica' describes the whole ethos of nineteenth-century European exploration, not only of the Middle East but of much of the globe. The era of exploration was financed very often by European governments for political/imperial reasons, but the incentive for the individual explorers and travellers themselves was a fascination with the 'exotic', with alien peoples and their cultures, customs and languages.[1] Thus the foundations of the European conception of the Middle East is based upon the accounts of these European travellers – in many ways these accounts 'defined' the Middle East in cultural terms.

But of course the very term 'Middle East' is essentially a geographical term and only has meaning when it is used in a relativistic way. The reference point of that relativity is Europe. It refers to a region which is east of Europe but not so far east as India or China. It is perhaps alone of the 'regions' of the world (themselves fabrications) in being referred to almost exclusively in terms of geography rather than a specific and unique designation. There is the 'Far East', but that can be broken down into South-East Asia, the East Indies, the Indian subcontinent, Indo-China – all of which terms include reference to a named continent or named region. The Middle East is merely that region which is in the European mind mid-way between Europe and India or Europe and China.

The Middle East is also defined politically in European terms. The 'importance' of the Middle East globally has been gauged in terms of European interests. It occupied a geostrategic position vital to European imperial power. Territorially it straddled the land access to Britain's Indian empire. Its strategic importance to Europe was considerably enhanced, of course, with the building by the Frenchman, de Lesseps, of the Suez Canal in 1869, which gave vital sea access to India in the nineteenth and early twentieth centuries and later, even in the post-colonial period, represented Europe's 'lifeline' in terms of international trade and post-colonial defence commitments. In the Suez crisis of 1956 the Canal fulfilled Ernest Renan's prediction to de Lesseps in 1885 when he said, 'You have marked out a great battlefield for the future'. This geostrategic signficance of the Middle East was enhanced in the post-1945 growth of the Cold War, in which, in addition to its importance in relation to the 'Far East', the region became a theatre of superpower rivalry and always a dangerous theatre for potential superpower military conflict.

The importance of the Middle East to European interests has also been defined in economic terms. The region was the site of the discovery of the world's largest reserves of oil, which of course became one of the major sources of the European and American 'second industrial revolution' – that is, the revolution in the late nineteenth century based upon organic chemistry (the chemistry of carbon compounds), as well as the source of power for the revolution in transport produced by the internal combustion engine and of the development of the automobile – the symbol of so many key facets of contemporary 'western civilisation', both functional (freedom, enterprise and individual autonomy) and dysfunctional (congestion, concrete landscape, air pollution and environmental damage).

Even the major problem of the Middle East in the post-Second World War era, the Arab–Israeli conflict, is the consequence of a 'displacement' of a European problem. The Israeli state, formed in 1948, is a Euro-American construction which was given its vital impetus by the Nazi atrocities of the Second World War fashioning a climate of opinion which made it impossible for the victorious powers to resist the Jewish claims for a homeland in Palestine. From the Arab point of view the Jewish homeland was imposed upon the region as a solution to an essentially European problem and a salving of the European conscience. Clearly there is not the space here for an extensive analysis of the Arab–Israeli dispute or of the validity of the respective territorial claims. The fact of the matter is that the establishment of the Jewish state (with or without justification) by dictat, has been the major source of instability in the region since 1948.

Thus it can be seen that the Middle East in the contemporary international system in a sense is seen in terms of European (in its widest sense) interests, conflict and aspirations. It is not seen in terms of the nature, development and aspirations of the peoples of the Middle East themselves. European relations with Middle Eastern states have not been for their own sake but have usually been developed by reference to relations between the European states themselves and even by reference to the constellation of political forces within their own domestic constituencies. In the nineteenth and early twentieth centuries the Middle East was merely the object of intra-European imperial rivalry; in the post-war world the significance of the area has been defined in terms of the Cold War rivalry between the United States and the Soviet Union. Even within this context American policy towards the region has been determined almost as much by reference to the strength of the Jewish lobby in the American electorate as to its ideological and strategic competition with the Soviet Union. So the Middle East has largely been a theatre for the playing out of interests and conflicts of external powers. The states and peoples of the area have been seen as objects of the diplomacy and conflict between external states rather than participants in the international system.

Having said all this is not to make any value judgement about that state of affairs or to say that it could have been or should have been any different. International politics are complex and all inter-state relationships are reducible to issues of perceived self-interest. We are not really concerned with whether this state of affairs is a good or a bad thing. What we have to do is to note the facts of these relationships and then consider how they help us better to understand contemporary events – in this case the crisis and war in the Gulf of 1990–1.

THE STRUCTURAL COMPLEXITIES OF THE MIDDLE EAST

It is ironic perhaps that the overriding declared aspiration of the peoples of the Middle East is unity – yet its overwhelming characteristics are division, tension and schism. It is only possible in this context to give an indication of this complexity by drawing attention to the intricate network of 'cross-cutting cleavages' operating across the region.

The Islamic diaspora

Though Islam is the overwhelmingly dominant religion in the Middle East, it is not confined to that region. Historically Islam spread wide and deep into Asia and Africa. In Asia it spread into the very heart of the continent as well as to its peripheries. Islam is the dominant religion of the central Asian republics of the former Soviet Union, of Afghanistan, Pakistan, Bangladesh (formerly East Pakistan), Malaysia and Indonesia, and of a large minority of the population in India. The whole of North and Saharan Africa is predominantly Islamic, with large minority Islamic populations in some West African and East African states. The only Islamic presence of any significance in the Americas is in the formerly British, French and Dutch Guianas (now Guyana, French Guiana and Surinam), where indented Indian labourers were imported from the Indian subcontinent during the early part of this century. However, the existence of Islamic societies outside of the Middle East means that states in the region may feel particular attachments to some of these non-Arab, non-Middle Eastern countries and in turn these countries often have particular views on, and interests in, Middle Eastern problems such as Palestine. Hence the particular significance of the stance taken on the Gulf crisis by such states as Pakistan, Indonesia and Malaysia. For example, the mujahedin, the Islamic anti-government guerrillas in Afghanistan, sent a detachment of fighters to join the UN Coalition forces, but the Afghan government did not.

An added dimension of the expansion of Islam is the movement of Muslim peoples that has taken place from the Muslim world to the European countries. This has occurred as a result essentially of the economic migration of peoples from the former colonial territories, especially of Britain and France, and from those Muslim countries closest to Europe. Hence the United Kingdom has been the destination of Muslims from Pakistan, India and Bangladesh, and France has been the recipient of peoples from its former North African colonial territories, especially Algeria and Morocco. Germany on the other hand has been the main destination of Muslim migrants from Turkey (see Appendix 1). The point to be made here is that increasingly these Muslim minorities in European states may feel themselves to have particular interests, expressed in terms of religious or cultural values, which may be at variance with those of their countries of residence or adoption, particularly in circumstances of foreign policy or military conflict with Muslim countries. In Britain the effects on the Muslim community of the *fatwa* issued by the Iranian religious leader Ayatollah Khomeini, condemning to death the British writer Salman Rushdie, is a case in point – as of course was the Gulf War, where many Muslims in Europe felt conflicting loyalties. This is part of the general problem of conflict between the demands for loyalty by the state and demands for loyalty by global proselytising political or religious ideologies and is bound to be a continuing global phenomenon with increasing movement of peoples across national and cultural boundaries

Islamic schism

The major religious schism in the Islamic world is that between the Shi'a and Sunni sects. Though a complex body of doctrinal differences has developed between the two groups, the origins of the split lie in political rivalries surrounding the legitimacy of the succession to the Prophet.[2] The Shi'a constitute about 20 per cent of the total world Muslim population and about 40 per cent of that in the Middle East.[3] The majority of these are in Iran. The rivalry of the two sects is significant given that it may give rise to conflicting loyalties since the schism transcends political boundaries. The majority of Shi'as are in Iran, yet the Shi'a holy city is Karbala in Iraq (the Sunni holy city is Mecca in Saudi Arabia). The Shi'a sect tends to be rather more extreme and revolutionary in its doctrine and thus the Iranians are suspected of subverting the majority Shi'a of southern Iraq and fomenting unrest against the Sunni dominated government in Baghdad. The government of Afaz Assad in Syria is Alawite, a Shi'a sub-sect, ruling over a predominantly Sunni population which thus partly explains Syria's pro-Iranian stance in the Iran–Iraq war even despite the fact that it ostensibly subscribes to the same political ideology as the Iraqi leadership – that of Ba'athism.

Ethnicity

It is also important to recognise that the Middle East contains non-Arabs as well as Arabs and that these play an important role in Middle Eastern politics. Of course, the major non-Arab, non-Islamic state is Israel, and the large underlying question that has lain behind Middle Eastern politics for the whole of the post-war period is whether it is possible in the long term for a non-Arab, non-Islamic state to co-exist with Arab, Islamic states in the very centre of the region. It is difficult to set aside the issue of territory since it is at the heart of the problem; but the question does arise as to whether even from a cultural/religious viewpoint it is possible for the two cultural systems to co-exist. That will be the future test of the 'Israeli experiment' even when and if a *modus vivendi* is achieved on the question of a Palestinian territory.

The major non-Arab Islamic states in the region are Iran and Turkey. Iran has occupied an ambivalent position in Middle Eastern politics partly because of its geography, partly because of its history, both pre-modern and contemporary, and partly because of its role in Islamic politics. Iran has a language, culture and history distinct and separate from that of the Arab nations, and both sides are keen to emphasise that distinction. Geographically it occupies an area of transition between the Middle Eastern world and the Asian world. It has a key and legitimate role to play in the security structure of the Gulf region which puts it in contention with the other Gulf states, notably Iraq and Saudi Arabia. For a long period during the 1960s and 1970s under the leadership of the Shah Muhammed Reza Pahlavi, Iran acted as a western, particularly American, 'agent of influence and interests' in the region. Indeed at one time Iran was seen, at least by its own advocates, as the model for secularising, modernising and westernisng Islamic states.

The third element of ambivalence of Iran's role in the Middle East is of course the fact that it is the centre for the Shi'a sect in the Islamic world and as such perhaps acts as a potential focus of loyalty for Shi'a minorities in many of the Arab countries of the region. After the overthrow of the Shah in 1979 Iran became the source and driving force of the Islamic fundamentalist revival – a development that posed a potential threat to established governments in the Middle East, especially those which have secularist aspirations for their countries. So Iran has moved from being a target (and perhaps source) of hostility for the Arabs because of its American 'client' status in the 1960s and 1970s to one of hostility because of its revolutionary fundamentalist ideology in the 1980s and 1990s.

Turkey is the other non-Arab Islamic state in the Middle East. Modern–day Turkey is the successor to the imperial Ottoman system which at its height included what is now Greece, Albania, Yugoslavia, Hungary, Romania, Bulgaria, Moldavia, the Black Sea territories of the former Soviet Union, Iraq, Syria, Lebanon, Jordan, Israel, the eastern shores of the Red Sea, Egypt, Libya, Tunisia and Algeria. Turkey was, after the dissolution of the Ottoman empire, the first of the Islamic states to secularise, under the leadership of Kemal Mustapha Attaturk, who aspired to modernise his country on the pattern of the European states. Indeed Turkey has now perhaps become the model more acceptable than Iran for those secular forces in the other Middle Eastern states who would like to bring about such a revolution in their own societies.

Turkey also occupies a position which may be regarded as 'pivotal' or 'ambivalent', depending on which perspective is used. As an Islamic state Turkey looks to the Middle East, and having borders with Syria, Iraq and Iran she clearly has important interests in the region not only politically but also economically, in particular relating to resources (water and oil). But also as a secular, 'westernised' state Turkey looks west to Europe, indeed with ambitions to become a member of the European Community. That claim to be European is based not only upon the secular nature of her society but also on the important role Turkey has played in the Cold War as an important member of NATO, effectively constituting the southern flank of NATO's military strategy against the Soviet Union. However, in the post-Soviet world Turkey now finds the tension caused by the contrary pulls of 'west' and 'east' enhanced. The ambivalence of her position on the cultural transition between Europe and Asia and her pivotal geostrategic position are both reinforced by the rebirth of the Central Asian republics. The changed political geography of the region means that Turkey has to exert its own influence in the area and further its own interests in the face of competition from other interested parties such as Iran. Added to this is the potential to be drawn into the Balkan conflicts in order to protect Muslims against Serbian aggrandisement, possibly even at the expense of her relations with Western Europe. Turkey's foreign–policy environment has become immensely more complicated in the wake of the fall of Soviet communism.

The largest group of non-Arab, non-state Islamic people in the region is the Kurds, who occupy a large area which consists of adjacent areas of Turkey, Syria, Iraq and Iran. A source of dissent under both Ottoman and British/French occupation of these areas, the Kurds have long claimed autonomous status and aspired to have their own state. Their attempt to declare their own state in 1945 prompted joint action by these states to put down the move. Autonomy has been opposed systematically by whoever has exercised authority over them; they have been repressed by all four governments because to concede their right to secede would entail losing large areas of territory and the resources contained in it – notably oil. Hence the clamour for a Kurdish autonomous zone even confined within Iraq after the Gulf War has not met with great enthusiasm from Turkey and the other states with a 'Kurdish problem'. The most recent and brutal acts of repression have been conducted by Saddam Hussein's Ba'athist regime in Iraq. Largely Sunni Muslims, the Kurds have not been integrated within the Sunni communities of any of these states; on the whole they tend towards secularism.

Fundamentalism versus secularism

Another major fault line running through the whole of the Middle East is that between those forces that want to retain and emphasise orthodox Islam as the major and unchallenged social and political authority in society and those that want a measure of secularism in which there is a separation of religious authority and political authority, with the former being subordinate to the latter. Many Middle Eastern states have achieved a measure of secularisation, either in fact or in effect, but both within and between states the issue of secularism continues to be a controversial one. The revival of orthodoxy received a large measure of reinforcement with the Islamic revolution in Iran in 1979, which has become the focus not only of Shi'a fundamentalism but of a more general return to Islamic orthodoxy and a rejection of secular and western aspirations. This has exacerbated conflicts within many Middle Eastern states between governments who very often recognise the importance of secularisation as a necessary concomitant of economic modernisation and their populations which are vulnerable to the anti-secular, anti-western rhetoric of the fundamentalists both within and outside of their societies. Egypt is the most successful example of a Middle Eastern state which has been able both to foster Arab nationalism and to establish a 'modernising secularist Islam'.[4]

The secularism to which Islamic orthodoxy and fundamentalism has been opposed is of two sorts – both of European origin. One was the secularism represented by Marxism-Leninism (not only secular but actually atheistic) and the philosophy of dialectical materialism. The credentials of such a challenge to Islam have diminished considerably during the past half decade with the collapse of the Soviet state and its sustaining ideology. The other major and continuing challenge to Islamic orthodoxy and fundamentalism comes from western consumerism; though the other arm of this form of secularism, that of liberal democracy, may be less of a challenge to the sway of Islam.

It seems likely that the contradiction between Islam and contemporary western consumerism is irresolvable. Thus another tension exists in the region, and it may very well exist within the psyche of individuals, between the desire for the spiritual consolation and guidance that Islam provides and the desire for a westernised consumerist life style that is the incentive for the secularist movement in the Arab world as well as the basis for the whole global international economy. Moreover, in the post-communist era there is little alternative focus of economic philosophy that can provide even a fig leaf of a rival to western-style consumerism. The choice between the two is stark and inevitable. It is clear that orthodoxy and fundamentalism cannot deliver 'the goods' – which of course have been defined by western, developed, industrial, consumer-oriented societies. For example, the continuing conflict within the Iranian regime is a direct manifestation of this tension, and Iran's current attempt at a rapprochment with western states is an implicit recognition that its future policies must emphasise the need to reintegrate the Iranian economy into the world economy and that the compromises must be made by the Islamic fundamentalist ideology. It is a measure of the strength of the 'requirements of the system' that 'autarky' is not an option for states in the contemporary world – sooner or later states have to conform to the requirements of the system. This is another sense in which a state is almost as much a manifestation of the perceptions of others as of the state itself. (see later in this chapter the discussion of the nature of the state in the Middle East).

Whether Islam can assume the sort of role that Christianity has assumed in western secular societies remains in doubt. Some hold that the secularisation that has taken place in the Middle East is in fact only apparent and superficial; that Islam is in essence 'secularisation-resistant'.[5] The extent to which Islam is 'secular-resistant' and the extent to which orthodox or fundamentalist Islam makes further gains in the Middle East will be a measure of the extent to which states in the region can become 'modernised'. It is conceivable that the next great ideological confrontation in the world will be between western liberal-democratic, market-oriented states and Islam. Islamic fundamentalism, like Soviet Marxism-Leninism, is a proselytising ideology – one that aspires to become the world system. As such its continued existence as a political as well as a spiritual authority depends upon its ability to confront the political orthodoxy of the western world. It is chilling to realise that the Balkan crisis of 1991–2 has the potential for converting that ideological polarisation between the 'Christian' west and the Islamic east into an overt and violent conflict.

Pan-Arabism versus statism

Charismatic leaders[6] like Saddam Hussein can appeal to the peoples of other Arabs states over the heads of their leaders on two grounds. One on the ground of Islam, Islamic unity and orthodoxy; secondly on grounds of pan-Arabism, Arab nationalism and Arab brotherhood. The reason why there will not be Arab unity on the grand pan-Arab scale is that unity based on ideology gives rise to the question of whose interpretation of the orthodoxy is the correct one; and since there is unlikely to be any agreement on this where it conflicts with current individual state interests, there is no real prospect of Arab unity. This applies also to Iraqi and Syrian Ba'athism; and also to the Islamic faith itself, which as we have seen, is riven with different sects.

An extensive discussion of what constitutes a nation would not be appropriate in this context.[7] It is obviously a very complex phenomenon, but an underlying question is whether a common language and a common religion are sufficient to ensure the existence of a nation, particularly when the geographical spread of these charactersistics is so large and gives rise to widely differing historical experiences, even though it might be possible to speak of an Arabic 'culture' and an Arab 'civilisation'. There are two major factors which have stimulated and reinforced the ideology of pan-Arabism in the contemporary world. One is the common experience of colonialism, under first Ottoman and then French and British rule; the other is the creation and existence of Israel in the midst of the Arab world. Both of these factors emphasise common enemies – colonialism (and later neo-colonialism) and Zionism. Thus it is negative factors (i.e. what they universally oppose) that 'unite' Arabs rather than positive and integrative factors. Moreover aspirations to pan-Arabism do not sit happily with the brutal and intrusive exercise of state power within many Arab countries. Of course, the whole post-colonial nation-state building process that is a characteristic of all former territories of the European empires, pulls strongly against a declared integrationist pan-Arab ideology. A pertinent case in point is the apparent incompatibility of the demand for an individual Palestinian state and the aspirations of Palestinians for pan-Arab unity.

Conservatism versus radicalism

The divisions between 'conservative' and 'radical' regimes in the Middle East overlap but do not neatly coincide with the divisions between fundamentalism and secularism. The conservative/radical spectrum is a political one rather than a religious one. The conservative regimes are those monarchies, sultanates and emirates composed of dynastic families established in either the colonial or pre-colonial periods. They exercise absolute and autocratic power which is, however, often tempered by a degree of paternalism. With the exception of Yemen, all of the states of the Arabian peninsular fall into this category – Saudi Arabia, Kuwait, Bahrain, Oman, Qatar and the United Arab Emirates. All have a vested interest in maintaining political traditionalism together with a strong degree of Islamic orthodoxy. They are anti-secular whilst maintaining strong links with the secular west and indeed are the main source and the main object of western support in the Arab world. These regimes are vulnerable on these very issues: they are vulnerable to the local forces of secularism which criticises the tendency for these families themselves to benefit from the freedoms of the western world whilst denying them to their own populations, and for maintaining a large and increasing disparity between the fabulously wealthy and the poor in their own countries – though it must be said that the oil wealth that most of them possess has enabled a universal public amenities structure of health, education and housing to be established. They are vulnerable to the forces of Islamic fundamentalism from Iran and they are vulnerable to the forces of political radicalism which call for a revolution from below and the establishment of socialist government.

The odd man out in this conservative category is Jordan, which is secular but also traditionalist in the sense that it is ruled by a monarch, King Hussein of the Hashemite dynasty, but has a degree of constitutionality which includes a parliamentary assembly. However, the operation of these political institutions is in effect subject to the absolute power of the King. But even within the category of traditonalism there is a schism between the Hashemites and the Saudis based upon long-standing tribal rivalries. Indeed it has been pointed out that one dimension of the Gulf conflict was that if Saddam Hussein had succeeded in holding on to Kuwait, his power would have been such that the Saudis of the south might well have been replaced by the Hashemites of the north[8] as a sort of legitimising façade for a new 'Saddamism' that no doubt would have followed an Iraqi victory.

The radical states are usually secular (Iran is a clear exception), run by revolutionary regimes, often dominated by the military or in which the military are important actors, in which socialism in one form or another and Arab nationalism are declared objectives and in which Islam is often used as a tool of the state. The major radical states are Iraq, Syria, Libya (Iran is radical but not in the sense of being socialist or Arab nationalist), Yemen and Algeria.

Pro-west versus pro-Soviet

Given the proximity of the Gulf War to the end of the Cold War and the fact that many of the alignments in the Middle East relate to the Cold War period, this category has been an important feature of these cross-cutting cleavages in the region. The unambiguously pro-western Arab states have been the 'Arabs of the south', that is Saudi Arabia and the Gulf states. The Gulf region has been a vital strategic, as well as economic, western interest during the Cold War. The unambiguously and consistently anti-western states have been Syria and Libya, both of whom have had very close relationships with the Soviet Union. Also at the pro-Soviet end of the spectrum, though perhaps not quite so extreme, have been Algeria and Yemen. Basically anti-western, but perhaps more pragmatic than ideological, Iraq has been courted by both the west and the Soviet Union and certainly benefited from the support, tacit and material, of both sides in the war against Iran, since both sides in the Cold War had an interest in stemming the spread of revolutionary Islamic fundamentalism.

Iran itself was, before the Islamic revolution in 1979, a major western client state in the region, but since the revolution it has achieved 'pariah' status in the eyes of both the Soviet Union and the United States. It is a measure of the end of the Cold War that all these previously anti-western states are now taking rapid action to revise and regularise their relations with the western powers. The stance of both Syria and Iran during the Gulf crisis was a manifestation of that movement and the post-war release of western hostages in the Lebanon is a continuing demonstration of the need for these countries to be reintegrated into normal diplomatic and economic intercourse with the west.

Jordan and Egypt have assumed rather more complex positions in the east–west conflict. Jordan is fundamentally pro-western but of course is the front line state in the Arab–Israeli dispute and thus conflicts with US and other western approaches to the problem of Palestine. As such Jordan finds itself allying with radical formerly pro-Soviet states on this issue. Egypt is the most populous and influential of all the Arab states and has been a prime target of both Soviet and western influence in the Middle East. Egypt was the first Soviet 'success' during the mid-1950s in its 'diplomatic offensive' to win friends and influence in the Third World. However, since the death of Nasser in 1970 relations with the Soviet Union have progressively deteriorated and the United States has replaced the Soviet Union as Egypt's major extra-regional ally.

Rich versus poor

A continuing source of disaffection between some of the Arab states is the great disparity between those which have vast wealth as a result of oil deposits and those which have virtually no economic resources at all. The major oil producers are Saudi Arabia, Iraq, the Gulf states, Iran and, outside of the 'central area', Libya. However, the most resentment is between those states like Jordan and Syria on the one hand and the traditionalist but western-oriented states of the south on the other.

This section has drawn attention to what have been called the 'cross-cutting cleavages' in the Middle Eastern region which go towards explaining the tensions and divisions within the region, and also sets a context for understanding the schism between the Middle East as a whole and 'the west'.

THE NATURE OF THE STATE IN THE MIDDLE EAST

The contemporary concept of the state is a European phenomenon and the modern international system of nation-states is in essence a European construction. The particular form of political organisation we now know as the nation-state arose out of the constellation of political and military forces in Europe during the seventeenth century – most conventional accounts date its origins back to the Treaty of Westphalia of 1648.[9] The subsequent dominance of European states over the global system was brought about by linked phenomena of the nineteenth century – the technological advances entailed by the industrial revolution in Europe and the wave of imperial expansion which brought vast areas of the globe under European political and military control. These areas were carved up by the European states in their imperial rivalries and very often borders were established in a quite arbitrary manner and without much reference to local political or ethnic structures.

European occupation and administration of large areas of territory in Africa and Asia meant that any indigenous and autonomous political development was halted and translated into European terms. The political and administrative organisation that was imposed in these areas was European, and even where a structure of local administration was established it was on the basis of European administrative principles. Thus in the post-Second World War era of decolonisation, when virtually all of the territories gained 'independence' in one form or another, these entities could be seen as 'fabrications' manufactured by European states and released into a world, an international system, which had been fashioned by European states and whose principles of operation derived from European history and European political philosophy.

It is worth reflecting here that the identity of a state is almost as much a manifestation of others' imagination and perceptions as of the citizens of the state itself. The comparison with individual psychology is instructive here, where individual identity is a complex amalgam of self-perception and other people's perceptions of oneself. This is particularly the case with the states formed comparatively recently from former colonial territories. For them, after all, the system into which they were born was a given; it had a structure, norms and principles of behaviour which had already been established and which they had no part in bringing about. In many senses new states have to conform to a pattern of statehood established by others. Those 'others' in this case were the European states and their derivatives (especially the United States). The European states claim a legitimacy derived from history, the organic growth of a political culture, continuity of existence and a degree of success demonstrated by a social and political coherence. Compared with these long-established 'organic' states of Europe, the new states have the characteristics of 'fabricated' entities, which explains to some extent their continued 'tenuousness' both internally in the political and cultural schisms that exist within many of their societies, and externally in their often blurred territorial definition.

Having said all that, however, acknowledgement must be made of the school of thought which holds that there is an Arab state tradition and that many of the Arab countries are not only old societies but old, and even ancient *states*.[10] Most of the Arab states can demonstrate a continuity between old and contemporary state structures; the only exceptions being the modern states of the so-called Fertile Crescent – Syria, Iraq, Transjordan, Lebanon and Palestine – where Ottoman imperial rule, followed by mandated status under the League of Nations, effectively broke the continuity of local political structures. Moreover it was in these states that the thesis that the state system as a creation of colonialism originated – a thesis which undermines the legitimacy of the very notion of the Arab state. It is perhaps ironic that in this sense contemporary western 'analysts' and Arab nationalists connive together in pursuing the thesis of the 'fabricated' Arab state.

The combination of this state of affairs and the vast economic wealth conferred on the European states by their industrial revolution of the nineteenth century, which was not allowed to spread to the colonial territories themselves, is the source of the contemporary conflict between the developed and underdeveloped world, between the 'modern' and 'pre-modern' world, which is reflected not only in terms of the disparity in economic wealth but also in terms of the domination of European value systems which determines how the world system operates.

This describes briefly the general condition in which the non-developed states of the world find themselves. We must caution against oversimplification of these issues because since the war there has grown a wide variation in the relative patterns of development. Thus blanket terms like 'the Third World', 'the underdeveloped world', 'the South' are inappropriate because they tend to mask that variation in development between states in the non-European world. However, the Middle East does not fall easily into this pattern of colonialism primarily because even in the period of nineteenth-century European imperialism the territories of the region were significant not because of their intrinsic economic value but because of their derivative value in terms of other colonial territories and in terms of the rivalries of the European powers themselves, especially Britain and France. This partly derives from the fact that much of the territory now known as the Middle East was, during the nineteenth-century period of European expansion, part of the Ottoman Empire. It was the parallel rise of the European empires and the decline of the Ottoman Empire that made the Middle East an object of rivalry among the European states themselves and between the European states and the Ottoman Empire.

It is in the final demise of the Ottoman Empire after the First World War that the states of the Middle East have their origin. The Ottomans had lost most of their North African territories during the nineteenth century to France and Britain (Algeria to France in 1830; Tunisia to France in 1881; Egypt to Britain in 1882; Sudan to Britain/Egypt in 1898). Indeed, together with Aden, acquired by Britain in 1839, these were the only Middle Eastern territories occupied by European states during their period of imperial expansion in the nineteenth century. This was due mainly to their importance in the control of the Mediterranean, the Suez Canal, access to British India and to British and French colonial interests in the rest of Africa.

The more central Middle Eastern territories only became oc-cupied by Britain or France after the First World War as territories mandated to these states for administration under the newly formed League of Nations. Lebanon and Syria were mandated to

France; Iraq, Palestine and Transjordan were mandated to Britain. Though the *de jure* transfer of sovereignty took place in 1923 on the signing of the Treaty of Lausanne, *de facto* control began in 1919 with the effective British military occupation of the territories after the First World War had ended. Thus in the case of Iraq, British control of the territory was only short-lived, but she took the opportunity to impose a degree of coherence on an incoherent situation. To find a leadership which could provide a common focus for a disparate set of regional, political, social, tribal and religious forces was a tall order indeed. But the priority for any great power in administering its colonial territories is order rather than legitimacy and that was the British objective when it took over the mandate.

Notwithstanding Saddam Hussein's insistent claims to the integrity of an Iraqi state which pre-dates the British mandate and even Ottoman suzerainty, the fact of the matter is that Iraq is a fabrication of the British and, more accurately, a small band of British colonial servants[11] who set about creating a state out of an incoherent set of conflicting forces. A national identity manifest in the idea of a nation-state is predicated on an organically developed 'political culture' which serves as the vital cement of continuity and coherence of any state. The development of a political culture itself cannot be fabricated or imposed; the only insitution that can substitute for it and produce a degree of stability which can in turn form the basis of development is a strong leadership. This was the objective of the British. They looked for a leader who would attract a wide range of support, or at least acquiescence, and who would provide a rival focus to emerging nationalist, republican and pan-Arab sentiments. Unfortunately the whole history of 'strong Iraqi leaders', from Bakr Sidqi in the 1930s to Saddam Hussein himself, is a testament not to the strength of the Iraqi state but on the contrary to the continuing tenuousness of Iraqi national identity and integrity.

British policy in Iraq during this period has been described as 'king making' rather than nation building[12] in that it imported the Hashemite family from the Hejaz, whose then current head, Faisal, had been the leader of the Arab revolt, overthrown as King of Syria in 1920 but who presented the British with perhaps the lowest common denominator among Iraq's political forces. Thus even the monarchy had to be 'fabricated' in order to rule over a 'fabricated' state. King Hussein of Jordan is the only remaining ruler of the Hashemite dynasty. It may be understandable that, as the new mandatory authority, Britain should have adopted what it regarded as the least risky strategy of imposing a traditionalist political structure on an otherwise fragmented people. However, such a strategy had the effect of frustrating the development of liberal, nationalist and middle-class political parties which might in the longer term have made the country more susceptible to western democratic influences. As it was, these forces, which perhaps might have contained the seeds of a western-style liberal democratic system, became the focus for anti-royalist, anti-imperial, Arab nationalist, anti-British and thus ultimately anti-western sentiments.

It was perhaps the example of Mustapha Kemal (Ataturk), the Turkish general, who had 'de-Ottomanised' Turkey in the aftermath of the collapse of its empire at the end of the First World War and had established a secular, modern and westernised Turkish state, that provided the model for many military leaders in the Middle East and in the former colonial world as a whole. In the face of fragmented social, ethnic, religious and political structures in these territories, the military has often performed the function of an agent of modernity and political coherence (albeit using the weapon of repression). It was 1936 when General Bakr Sidqi began what has come to be a characteristic of Iraqi politics with a military coup which overthrew the Iraqi government but left the monarchy intact. The example was followed in 1941 with a pro-Axis military coup which was put down only with the help of British forces.[13]

The Hashemite kingdom in Iraq survived – with the astute and perhaps indispensable help of Nuri al-Said, the veteran Iraqi 'political manipulator', – to become the anchor of British policy in the Middle East designed both to counter the Arab nationalism of Gamal Abdul Nasser in Egypt and to provide a bulwark against the spread of Soviet influence in the Cold War against communism, which had supplanted the hot war against Nazism. Britain's plan was that Iraq led by Faisal and Nuri al-Said would become the foundation of the Baghdad Pact (later to become the Central Treaty Organisation – CENTO) which would be the focus of both these functions. It was this role that was effectively to be the undoing both of the Hashemite Kingdom and of Nuri al-Said. Perhaps it is symbolic that they were both being entertained to dinner by the British Prime Minister, Anthony Eden, in July 1956 when the news came through of Nasser's nationalisation of the Suez Canal Company.[14] It was of course Britain's (and France's) eventual reaction to this event by invading Egypt, an adventure which ended in failure and humiliation, that was the turning-point in so many ways in post-war international politics. What it did mean was the end of British influence in the Middle East and it put in jeopardy any British allies in the region. The Hashemite family and Nuri al-Said were to survive it barely two years. In 1958 they were both overthrown and killed by a nationalist republican military coup led by Abd al-Karim Qassim.

During the inter-war period it could be said that Britain and France could still behave as imperial powers, though the substance of their global power proved to be extremely tenuous, demonstrated in their policies of irresolution in both Europe and the Far East. In the Middle East they still exercised a dominion over colonies, mandated territories and 'independent' states (Iraq and Egypt) alike. The internal politics of most of the Middle Eastern countries were a reflection of the imperial rivalry between Britain and France themselves and the playing out of rivalries between competing traditional elites and ruling families, forces of nationalism, Arabism and socialism. The imperial powers dabbled in this maelstrom of internal Middle Eastern politics to their own advantage, in general supporting the traditionalist forces over the nationalist ones but not averse to favouring oppositionist forces where it suited them to do so.[15]

After the war neither Britain nor France had the power or, in the case of Britain at least, the will to continue an imperial role. Britain saw more quickly than France the 'inappropriateness' of continued imperial pretensions.[16] The new post-war British Labour government began the process of 'retreat from Empire' with the crucial granting of independence to India and Pakistan. For Britain this set the pattern and essentially made the continued retention of the rest of the Empire rather irrelevant – its demise was relatively, though not entirely, smooth. Not so with France, where there was a greater reluctance to accept the post-war 'logic' of the end of imperialism, which resulted in two major colonial wars – in Indo-China and in Algeria. Defeat in Indo-China and eventual retreat from Algeria were traumatic events in post-war French history which had as much significance for French domestic politics as for French foreign policy. It was France's involvement in the Algerian War in the 1950s that led to her involvement in the Suez debacle, and it was Britain's (or more accurately Antony Eden's) overestimation of her power to stem the tide of Arab nationalism that led to her collusion with both the French and the Israelis in order to bring down Gamal Nasser and with him the popular appeal of Arab nationalism, under the guise of protecting the Suez Canal.

The Suez Crisis can be seen as the 'last spasm' of the imperialist strain in British political culture.[17] British decolonisation was the result not only of a decline in power, of a war-weariness and of a turn to internal preoccupations, but it was also due to a recognition of the 'inappropriateness' of empire and a recognition that the 'imperial moment' had passed. Certainly it can be said that Britain's failure at Suez perhaps saved it from something worse – the consequences of success. The re-establishment of a British military presence in the Middle East that would have followed a successful Suez operation would have been much more costly than the consequences of failure. It was of course the instrument of that failure, not Gamal Abdul Nasser but the United States of America, that stood to gain most from it. The Suez crisis, a turning-point in many other ways, was certainly the watershed between predominantly European imperial influence in the Middle East and a superpower Cold War influence.

Thus the end of European imperialism in the Middle East did not mean the end of external influence and intervention. If European imperial intervention frustrated the organic development of an internal political culture in many of the Middle Eastern countries up to the 1950s, there were two other 'distorting' factors that were subsequently to dominate Middle Eastern politics. One was the development of the Cold War antagonism between the Soviet Union and the United States; the other was the creation of the state of Israel in the mandated territory of Palestine in 1948. Middle Eastern politics have effectively been 'frozen' by these two conflicts during the whole of the post-war period. In many ways the Arab–Israeli dispute, an indigenous Middle Eastern dispute (albeit created by Europeans), has fed off the Cold War conflict. Like many other disputes in the world this dispute has been prolonged by the Cold War and translated into Cold War terms. The fostering of client states was a Cold War obsession of the superpowers so that local conflicts and disputes have been exacerbated by political, military and moral support of the opposing sides by the respective superpowers. It is undoubtedly the case that the problem of the existence of Israel and that of the Palestinian state would have received more urgent attention from the great powers had the global system not been dominated by the Cold War. The Arab–Israeli dispute has forced many Arab states into a pro-Soviet stance and given freer reign to the forces of repression and despotism in the whole region. Cold War interests (both strategic and economic) in the region have enabled Israel to hold the United States to an anti-Arab stance on the basis that Israel is America's only true ally in the region; and of course it has been the Cold War that has enabled the Jewish lobby in the United States to hold such sway over America's Middle Eastern policy ever since the creation of the Israeli state.

We have seen the more recent and dramatic evidence of the way the Cold War has stultified political change and cultural expression particularly in Eastern Europe and the former Soviet Union. Those who expound the thesis of 'the end of history'[18] have got it almost diametrically wrong. It was the Cold War that stopped history, it is the end of the Cold War that has started it again – almost where it left off. The end of the evils of the Cold War does not entail a more peaceful and stable world. It is more likely to be quite the opposite; the releasing of the constraints of the Cold War will be both creative and dangerous. One of the dangers is illustrated by the Gulf conflict itself – a conflict which was a direct manifestation of the end of the Cold War. It may be hoped that the creative forces of political development, in the Middle East especially, will now have some prospect of progress.

Chapter 2

Crisis: The provocation and the protagonists

Iraqi forces invaded Kuwait at 4.00 a.m. on 2 August 1990. Within twenty-four hours Kuwaiti military resistance had effectively ceased, the Kuwaiti government had fled to Saudi Arabia and Iraqi troops amassed on the Kuwait–Saudi border. With a rapid and effective military operation Saddam Hussein had presented the world with a *fait accompli* and the Iraqi military occupation of Kuwait lasted 210 days. It effectively ended with the cessation of military operations by the UN Coalition forces on 27 February 1991. That six-month period saw a most remarkable constellation of events – some of the most remarkable since 1945.

This chapter will examine the causes of the invasion, the motivations and interests of the various protagonists both inside and outside the region, and the factors that determined the response to Iraq's action.

EXPLAINING THE IRAQI INVASION

As has been indicated in the Introduction, an international event cannot be fully explained or understood if considered on only one level. Thus Iraq's invasion of Kuwait cannot be satisfactorily explained by considering Iraqi–Kuwaiti relations alone, nor by considering only the nature of the Iraqi political regime which engaged in such behaviour, nor only by an examination of the wider structural context within which the event took place. Relevant explanatory factors at all levels of analysis have to be considered in order to build a picture of the interaction of these factors and then make some judgement as to their relative significance in explaining the events. It is not only the motivations of those making the decision to invade that have to be considered –

that is, the incentives for taking the action they took – but also the absence, or at least the weakness, of the disincentives for taking such action. The question has to be considered not only why the action was taken but why it was taken at that time and not at another time.

Thus a distinction also has to be made between the immediate *casas belli* and the longer-term or 'permanently operating' factors, as well as between what might be called the articulated reasons and the unarticulated, background causes. To begin with, it is necessary to examine the nature of Iraq, the nature of the Iraqi regime and the state of relations between Iraq and Kuwait.

THE NATURE OF IRAQ AND ITS BA'ATHIST REGIME

Iraq came into existence as an independent state in 1932 with the ending of its 'mandated' status under the League of Nations. Britain had been the protecting power and, as a result the major external influence on Iraq, was British. The nature of the regime was determined by the British, who had established an Iraqi consti- tutional 'monarchy' which ensured that by the time the Cold War emerged in the aftermath of the Second World War, Iraq would be pro-western. This was important in two respects. Firstly it ensured western and particularly British access to Iraqi oil re- sources, and secondly it would ensure western influence, not to say domination, over an important strategic area of the Middle East. This was manifested in the formation of the Baghdad Pact in 1955, with Turkey, the United Kingdom, Iraq and Iran joining together to form a bulwark against the Soviet Union's southern flank. The association was converted more formally into a Cold War alliance in 1959 when its name changed to the Central Treaty Organis- ation (CENTO) and, with NATO and SEATO, was part of the ring of western alliances surrounding the Soviet Union. However, it was never a very effective organisation and became less so when Iraq withdrew its membership with the overthrow of the monarchy in 1958. The other function for British interests that the Iraqi mon- archy performed prior to its downfall was to resist the spread of Arab nationalism, being fomented by the Egyptian leader Gamal Abdul Nasser, which was gaining influence against western int- erests in the Middle East and developing an increasingly close relationship with the Soviet Union and China.

The humiliation of Britain and France in the Suez crisis of 1956 gave a fillip to the anti-western pressures in the region and really spelt the end of the Iraqi monarchy. There was a military *coup d'état* in July 1958, and a new revolutionary government was formed under General Abdul Karim Qassim. In 1963 Qassim himself was assassinated in a counter-coup led by Colonel Abdul Salam Aref, benefiting from an alliance between the Ba'ath Party and the armed forces. Though this alliance did not last long – after some nine months it had lost the confidence of the Iraqi military – it gave the Ba'athists their first taste of power in Iraq.

Iraq's history has been characterised by a struggle to establish an identity. More than most former colonial territories in the region it has been riven by tensions; ethnic tensions between its three regions, Mosul, Baghdad and Basra – especially the conflict between the Kurds of the north and the central administration – and also by the religious cleavage between Sunni Muslims in the centre and north and the Shi'ite Muslims of the south. The actual experience of present-day Iraq belies its meaning in the Arabic language – it is derived from an Arabic word meaning 'deep-rooted and venerable'.[1] Saddam Hussein's continual reference during the crisis to Iraq's great and long history was not the reflection of an actual reality but a continuing attempt to create a reality – that is, the reality of a coherent national identity. Indeed part of the reason for the common phenomenon of dictatorial, authoritarian, repressive regimes in former colonial territories has been the necessity to develop a coherent political culture which can both define the nation and attract the allegiance of the population. The dominant underlying characteristic of Iraq has been an incipient fragmentation. The Ba'athist succession in 1968 finally provided a mechanism to counter the centrifugal forces making for its break-up and the ever-tightening grip of the Ba'athist regime on the Iraqi political system for the last twenty-three years or so is in stark contrast to the endemic instability of successive revolutionary regimes that followed the overthrow of the monarchy in 1958. Thus Ba'athism has meant not only brutal repression within Iraq but also stability and the attempt to forge both an identity and a role in the Middle East.

THE NATURE OF BA'ATHISM

Ba'ath means rebirth or renaissance. Ba'athism is a mixture of pan-Arabism and Arab socialism. Its ideology laid down by the

Ba'ath founder, Michel Aflaq, calls on a number of potentially incompatible and conflicting ideas. It is pan-Arabist in its aspirations yet appeals to individual nationalisms. It assumes the existence of an Arab nation and calls for the establishment of a single Arab state,[2] but at the same time it is used by its leaders in Syria and Iraq as a powerful mechanism for establishing the power and legitimacy of those states. It appeals to Islamic religious principles and the traditions of Arab history whilst at the same time aspiring to create a secular modernity, which it recognises as the basis of western prosperity and power. The socialist dimension of Ba'athism is reflected in its claim to eliminate the conflict between the different ethnic groups found in Middle Eastern countries, thus denying the monopoly of power to any one group.[3] In practice, particularly under the rule of Saddam Hussein, it has on the contrary resulted in the concentration of power into the hands of a small clique, many of the members of which have family connections. From an international perspective Ba'athism's socialist aspirations entail the rejection of liberal economics based upon capitalistic principles and, at least in Cold War terms, it saw the Soviet Union as its natural major supporter in its stand against what it conceives to be western imperialist influence and intervention in the Middle East.

Ba'athism is a revolutionary philosophy whose technique has not been to foster and lead revolution from below – the very fragmentation of many Islamic societies precludes sufficient solidarity at the grass-roots to make a general uprising a viable strategy. The method is to capture power by whatever means possible and institute the revolution from above. Thus in the two countries where Ba'athism has taken hold, Syria and Iraq, it has demonstrated the characteristic strategies first for survival, then for the acquisition of power and further for the continued retention of power. A cell structure of organisation and a clandestine ethos was the mechanism of survival; the forging of a base and allies among the key sectors of society, both civilian and military, the prerequisiste for acquiring power; the brutal and ruthless exercise of violence and repression, the means of hanging on to it.[4]

Iraq's endemic political instability and its propensity for violence and fragmentation have posed particular problems for the creation of an Iraqi identity, a coherent political culture and a universal political legitimacy. Such have been the problems of Iraq that it has been characterised as the least united of the Arab states and perhaps even the least governable.[5] It is in this context that since the second Ba'athist succession in 1968 Iraq has seen an unprecedented period of 'stability' in entire contrast to the almost continuous political incoherence since the state's formation in 1932.

Ba'athism has been able to remain in power in Iraq only through the creation of a structure of coercion and control composed of a party membership of some half a million, a tight structure of party cadres and activists and a security police organisation responsible to the party rather than the state. In this respect the Ba'ath Party has aspired to become the state. Moreover, the party has penetrated all the major civilian sectors of Iraqi society – the unions, the civil service, educational institutions and professional organisations. But perhaps the key to the Ba'athist retention of power is the Iraqi military. The first Ba'athist regime in 1963 failed after only nine months predominantly because of the army's withdrawal of support. Thus the central priority of the second Ba'athist regime, and particularly of Saddam Hussein since he became leader in 1979, has been to retain the loyalty of the military. This has been done by a mixture of coercion and incentive. Bribery is one instrument – the army is given large resources both in terms of equipment and in terms of a personal standard of life. More positive incentive is provided by the opportunities for military officers to become entrepreneurs in a wide range of productive activities in both the private and public sectors.

> Army officers control economic empires and employ tens of thousands of civilians, whose pay is better than in either the civil public sector, or the private sector. They share successfully in their country's economic growth, especially by running its most technologically advanced and economically productive units[6]

Coercion is used in ruthless and periodic purges of military officers who show signs of disaffection or even demonstrate an uncertainty as to the legitimacy of the Ba'athist regime or give any cause to question their loyalty to Saddam Hussein personally. The penetration and surveillance of the military machine where Ba'ath apparatchiks or political commissars are attached to each unit, ensures adherence to the party line and provides little opportunity or incentive for disaffection.

There is little doubt that the Ba'athist regime in Iraq had, at least before the Gulf War, achieved authority and had exercised it ruthlessly not only in order to remain in power but also to keep a lid on the inherent tendency to disintegration. It is in this function of repressive regimes to ward off domestic instability and ensure the integrity of the state, that has led western governments to tolerate (not to say actively support) such regimes in conditions of incipient instability. It is more doubtful if Ba'athism has had any success in converting its authority into a legitimacy and an identity which could then replace it as the mechanism of stability and continuity in the Iraqi state and nation. The abortive attempts by both Shi-ite groups in the south and Kurds in the north to unseat Saddam Hussein and overthrow the Ba'athist regime in the aftermath of the second Gulf War signals the persistence of the forces of fragmentation and testifies to the continued ascendancy of authority over legitimacy in Iraq.

It is worth noting here that the idea of socialism (however applied) has been a source of discipline and order in Third World countries in the post-colonial period – very often as the only locally acceptable alternative to unambiguous western-style capitalism and indigenous traditionalism or fragmentation and political chaos. It has been introduced often by western educated local intellectuals or aspiring politicians. In practice it has been manifest in these countries as a European idea married to local values. Thus Ba'athism is a product of the European ideas of socialism and nationalism married to the indigenous ideas of Arabism and traditionalism. It has been secular in principle whilst accepting (and using) in practice the local power of Islam. Chapter 10 of this book examines the prospects for change in Iraq as a consequence of its military defeat in the Gulf War.

Before we leave this discussion of Ba'athism it might be appropriate to consider briefly the phenomenon of two Arab states espousing the same ruthless political ideology but finding themselves on the opposite sides of a major military conflict in the Middle East. Syria, although also ruled by a Ba'athist regime, became a member of the UN Coalition supplying military forces in the war against Iraq. The differences between Syria and Iraq are very deep and extremely antagonistic. One dimension of their antagonism is the common ideology which they both espouse. When two states follow the same ideology one of the main issues that arises between them is whose interpretation of the ideology is correct, whose is the orthodox, true ideology. This of course was one of the main factors leading to the Sino-Soviet dispute which has lasted some thirty years. So far from being a source of solidarity, a common ideology is more often than not a source of dissension.

Another factor is that though both are secular regimes the respective leaderships are derived from opposing Islamic sects in each of their countries. President Afez Assad and the Syrian Ba'athist leadership are Alawites, a Shi'a minority sub-sect, governing a predominantly Sunni Arab population; Saddam Hussein and his Ba'athist leadership in Iraq are Sunni Muslims representing only half the Iraqi population; half of those are non-Arab Kurds demanding autonomy and the rest Shi'ites in the south of Iraq. Thus Syria supported Iran against Iraq in the first Gulf War despite the fact that the Syrian Ba'athist leadership is a secular one and the Iranian government is an Islamic fundamentalist one. Again, though both are among the most 'radical' of the Middle East regimes in terms of their anti-westernism and anti-Israeli stance, they have for example supported opposing factions in the Lebanon. Thus even if Syria had not more positive reasons for joining with the UN Coalition, the most that could have been expected of them in the Gulf crisis would have been a studied neutralism. As it was, Syria had a more definite incentive in the changed circumstances of the post-Cold War world to take sides against Iraq even though she became an ally of her greatest former enemy, the United States.

SOURCES OF THE IRAQI DECISION TO INVADE KUWAIT

Chapter 5 of this book traces the history and validity of Iraqi territorial claims over Kuwait, from which it can be seen that Iraqi attitudes to Kuwait have been ambiguous at the very least. The territorial claims themselves cannot be the major reason for the invasion but have no doubt acted as a 'permanently operating factor' in Saddam Hussein's and the Ba'ath Party's foreign-policy orientation – as a 'target of opportunity'. In the event the claims served as a rationalisation for the invasion rather than a reason. The salience of the claim to Kuwait in Iraqi diplomacy has been determined by factors other than merely the desire to see a just end to a legitimate territorial dispute. The extent to which Iraq presses its claim to Kuwait has depended upon events at any one time and the degree to which pressing the claim can serve other purposes.

We can separate the sources of Iraqi antagonism to Kuwait into a number of different groups – firstly the 'cultural' differences between 'northern' Arabs and 'southern' Arabs of the Gulf; secondly, economic factors; thirdly, Iraqi strategic aspirations and anxieties; and fourthly, Iraqi regional political aspirations. It is important to recognise that the territorial claim to Kuwait was not a reason in itself for the invasion; the claim has been used merely to legitimise and justify Iraqi actions which have in fact been taken for a combination of these other factors.

What might be called a 'sub-plot' of the Gulf conflict is an underlying antagonism between the Arabs of the north (Arab al-Shimal) and the Arabs of the south, or Gulf area (Arab al-Khalij).[7] That dichotomy in the Arab body politic of the region can be further characterised in Mohammed Heikal's formulation as the most recent manifestation of the struggle between the people of the cities and the people of the desert. It was the peoples of the cities – in particular Cairo, Beirut, Damascus and Baghdad – that struggled for national independence and have since been plagued by poverty and attempts to confront western imperialism which have brought forth radical, repressive, socialist regimes and bankrupt economies. It was the peoples of the desert in the form of the Gulf states and Saudi Arabia who became fabulously wealthy through the fortuitous presence of oil beneath their territories. They were also less radical, largely because of the absence of colonial and post-colonial conflict, less populous, more pro-western and anti-secular. A paradox of the Arab Middle East is the extent to which the secular Arab regimes have on the whole been anti-western and the orthodox Islamic regimes have been pro-western. It has until recently been the accepted lot of the Gulf Arabs to fund the economies and radical politics of the Arab al-Shimal. This practice may be seen as a hypocritical attempt on the part of these wealthy regimes to enjoy a vicarious international radicalism whilst paying to keep the radicals from their own doors. One dimension of the Gulf crisis has been a growing reluctance on the part of the Gulf Arabs to maintain the obligation to the regimes of 'the north'.

This leads to the second group of sources of Iraqi antagonism towards Kuwait – the economic factors. The central immediate cause of the Iraqi invasion can be seen to have been the pressing economic straits Iraq was finding itself in as a result, among other things, of the cost of the war with Iran together with a general increasing reluctance on the part of the Gulf Arabs to continue to fund the adventures of their northern cousins. The specific manifestation of this general reluctance was the refusal on Kuwait's part to grant Iraq's request to restrict its oil production in order to keep the price high and thus maintain or increase Iraqi oil income.

Related both to the economic sources of Iraqi antagonism and to her territorial claims was the status of the Rumaila oil-field. This field straddles the Iraq–Kuwait border and has been a specific source of dispute between the two sides. In the first place Iraq claims that the whole of the field should legitimately be in Iraqi territory, but secondly, even accepting the status quo, Iraq claimed that Kuwait was extracting more than her fair share of the reserves. There may have been some justification in Iraqi claims and indeed they had received a degree of sympathetic consideration in the Gulf Cooperation Council. In the absence of an Iraqi claim to the whole of Kuwait, her claims regarding Rumaila may well have been largely conceded (see Map in Appendix III). But the issue was the subject of particular indignation by Iraq, whose plea was that not only would Kuwait not honour her obligations to an Arab brother who had saved it from the fundamentalist Shi-ite onslaught from Iran, but that by taking more than her fair share of Rumaila oil she was further undermining Iraq's own ability to finance her economic recovery.

However, there was another dimension to Iraq's economic difficulties. It was not only the effects of the war with Iran itself that were responsible for the economic crisis but the economic strategy employed to solve that crisis.[8] The strategy amounted to a massive economic liberalisation and privatisation programme in all sectors of the Iraqi economy. A process of economic liberalisation and privatisation requires a process of deregulation, decentralisation and a withdrawal of government activity in the economy. Rule by the Ba'ath Party in general and Saddam Hussein in particular rests upon repression, centralisation and a structure of political control that reaches deep down into the fabric of Iraqi society. If such a structure of political control and repression is a requirement of, or indeed a substitute for, the political legitimacy of Saddam Hussein and Ba'ath rule then there is a fundamental incompatibility between the political regime and economic liberalisation. A programme of economic liberalisation that does not recognise the need for a parallel process of political liberalisation is bound to fail. The choice faced by the Iraqi regime was thus either to pursue economic reform and accept the necessity for political reform; or find an alternative to economic reform to solve the economic troubles of the country. An alternative economic strategy had to be found because political reform was not consistent with the continued political control of Saddam Hussein and the Ba'ath. However much the country required economic liberalisation, it would not be bought at the expense of a loosening of political control by Saddam Hussein and the Ba'ath. On the other hand unless the economic crisis could be solved, political stability and continued Ba'ath power could not be guaranteed.[9]

This shows the narrowing perceived options available to the Iraqi leadership. Economic restructuring, could not be achieved without political restructuring which in turn would undermine Ba'athist power and control. Moreover, the continued failure to secure adequate external help to fund economic recovery and service Iraq's huge debt to other states seemed to leave only one option for Saddam Hussein. Thus it can be seen that the Kuwaiti invasion was carried out not only to attempt to salvage the Iraqi economy by pillaging Kuwait and annexing its oil production but also to ensure the continued survival in power of Saddam Hussein and the Iraqi Ba'ath Party. So there is a link between economic motivations and domestic political motivations. Using an external military adventure is a device often used by governments to divert popular attention from domestic political and economic problems that might undermine support for, or at least acquiescence in, the government's power. In the case of Iraq the invasion of Kuwait served to divert Iraqi public attention, publicly blame others for Iraq's economic plight and provide the financial wherewithal to solve the economic crisis and avert any potential challenge to Ba'athist control and re-establish cohesion within Iraq.

Though the immediate economic situation in Iraq and its political consequences represent the most direct causes of the Iraqi invasion, there are other factors that need to be considered. For example, perhaps the question needs to be asked whether the ideology of Ba'athism is inherently expansionist and thus whether the invasion was merely a manifestation of that natural aggressive expansionism. Here it is difficult to distinguish the role of Ba'athism from that of Saddam Hussein himself. It has already been established that Ba'athism is pan-Arabist and in this sense has an aspiration towards a greater Arab state. However, pan-Arabism has never manifested itself in terms of territorial expansion of individual states. Abdul Nasser's charter, presented at the Inaugural Session of the National Congress of the Forces of the People on 21 May 1962, states quite categorically that 'Unity cannot be, nor should it be, imposed . . . . Therefore coercion of any kind is contrary to unity'.[10] Although under Ba'athism Iraq always refers to itself as the 'Iraqi region of the Arab homeland',[11] the essentially rhetorical nature of the attachment to pan-Arabism can be noted in the following: 'While Ba'athist regimes have put themselves forward as propagators of pan-Arabism, especially through their stance on the liberation of Palestine, their ambitions emerge purely on the nation-state level, as mere Iraqi or Syrian ambitions'.[12] So the notion of pan-Arabism does not entail the expansion of one state to physically unify the Arab peoples, but the desire to provide a leader for the Arab peoples, has always been a potent aspiration for some Arab leaders. Nasser himself during the 1950s and 1960s articulated much of the philosophy of Arab unity but ultimately was never very successful in bringing it about. There is little doubt that Saddam Hussein saw himself as a successor not only to Nasser but to other more ancient leaders in Arab history and mythology such as Saladin, who led the Arabs against the Christian Crusaders. However, although this aspiration may be regarded as a 'background' factor explaining the invasion, an aspiration that would clearly be served by such action, it cannot be regarded as a direct cause of the aggression.

The last dimension of the Iraqi invasion to be considered here concerns Iraqi regional strategic requirements. Few perhaps would dispute the legitimacy of Iraq's security and strategic interest in the Persian Gulf. Iraq has always regarded access to the Gulf as a vital requirement not only for economic and trade purposes but also for security purposes: whoever controls the Gulf has a vital regional asset – hence the British policy towards the Gulf since the late nineteenth century and the more recent struggle for hegemony in the region between Iraq, Iran and Saudi Arabia. Iraq's concern in this respect was the ostensible reason for Iraq's attack on Iran in 1980 over control of the Shatt-al-Arab waterway and indeed was, notwithstanding Iraqi claims to the whole of Kuwait, the reason why Iraq has more than once considered Kuwait's offer of leasing the Islands of Warbar and Bubiyan, since they control Iraq's access to the Gulf. But again it should be seen that regional security concerns were not the direct and immediate cause of Iraqi action, but they provide what might be called a 'permanently operating' feature of Iraq's policy to Kuwait, and a successful annexation of Kuwait would have solved this strategic problem once and for all.

There is yet another dimension that would have served the grand vision of Saddam Hussein's political aspirations, and indeed was probably the major stimulus to the US military response. This was that the Iraqi annexation of Kuwait really did alter the geo-strategic stability of the region. The action demonstrated that Saddam Hussein was prepared to take such action even in the face of well-known western economic and security interests in the area, and as a matter of fact it put Iraqi troops in position to threaten Saudi Arabia. As has been pointed out in another chapter in the logic of the western response, a failure to respond to the Iraqi annexation of Kuwait would have sent a well-received signal to Saddam Hussein that Saudi Arabia would not be defended against a similar move. Since Saddam, while having carefully fashioned a formidable reputation for misjudging opportunities, is neverthe-less an opportunist, there is little doubt that he would have gone on to a conquest of Saudi Arabia. That position would have served virtually all of his purposes remote, proximate and immediate, and moreover would have given him considerable geopolitical power *vis-à-vis* the United States and other western states (Fig. 2.1).

Having considered the major incentives or 'push factors' for the Iraqi invasion, it is important to assess the status of what might be called the restraining factors or disincentives for such an action. Action by states in the international arena may be seen as the resultant of the balance of incentives and disincentives for taking it. Not only does it require the existence of positive incentives for action to take place but also a weakness of disincentives or restraining influences. The effect of one of those potential restraining influences, the Soviet Union, is discussed in the section on the impact of structural conditions. The other potential restraining influence on the decision to invade was the expected

	Cultural cause	Strategic cause	Economic cause	Political cause
Remote (background) cause	"Orientalism" Habit of imperalism / interventionism			
Proximate cause		Breakdown in balance of power in Gulf sub-region with potential for an Iraqi hegemony in whole Middle East	Impact on oil supplies / market	Safeguarding interests in Middle East Demonstration effect to other potential post-Cold War acts of aggression
Immediate cause		Threat to Saudi Arabia		

Figure 2.1 Reasons for the Iraqi invasion

Note: The distinction between remote, proximate and immediate causes of war was discussed by Bruce Russett in his *Power and Community in World Politics* (San Fransisco: W.H. Freeman, 1974), ch. 10.

response of the states with major interests in the area – notably of course the United States.

However 'irrational' Saddam Hussein's foreign-policy decision-making is (see Chapter 4), it seems improbable that a decision to invade Kuwait would have been taken by the Iraqi Ba'ath leadership without some assessment of likely American reaction. The major questions here are, firstly, was such an assessment made by the Iraqis and, secondly, did the United States send misleading 'signals' to the Iraqis in the period immediately prior to the invasion leading Saddam Hussein to expect that the United States would not be greatly exercised by such an act.

There is little direct evidence of the Ba'ath leadership's attitude to American views on their likely actions. However, the historical and biographical evidence suggests that Saddam Hussein is characteristically a pragmatist and a calculator.[13] Thus there are three possible scenarios: (1) he was concerned about American reaction and thus tried hard to conceal his intentions from them, (2) he was concerned about American reaction so he indicated to them the extreme importance the Iraqis attached to the dispute with Kuwait and its relationship to Iraq's economic situation with the implication that a statement of US sympathy for Iraq's plight would be tantamount to a declaration of American indifference to Iraq's actions, and (3) he did not really care about US reactions and was prepared, even anxious, to confront the United States since this might serve other purposes as well.[14] Most plausibly the explanation is a combination of (2) and (3) above. But a rather more detailed discussion of these issues is needed.

Intelligence failures leading to false expectations, misperceptions and miscalculations are notorious factors contributing to the outbreak of hostilities between states. Failing to send the appropriate signals regarding one's interests, expectations and intentions, or failing to receive the appropriate signals (i.e. failing to collect, recognise or interpret highly relevant information about the other party's intentions and interests) are almost endemic in crisis and pre-war situations.[15] There is a contention that Saddam Hussein had been signalling his intentions for some six months prior to his invasion and the western powers had failed to detected those signals.[16] According to this thesis the reason for this failure was the *idée fixe* that existed in the American State Department and the British Foreign Office that as a result of the experience of the Gulf War with Iran Saddam Hussein had recognised the limits of Iraqi power in the region and was now a reformed and sobered character. This apparently immovable perception of Saddam Hussein had survived a whole series of data which, it is contended, should have alerted western intelligence analysts to the regrowth of Saddam's ambitions in the region. This information included increasing anti-American rhetoric, the unambiguous announcement of Iraqi development of chemical weapons, which they would not hesitate to use on Israel, intervention in the Lebanon, increasing military expenditure and the very public challenge to western sensibilities in the hanging of the Iranian born British journalist Farzad Bazoft for spying. In addition to this were the revelations of the Iraqi attempt to buy nuclear weapons' triggers and the impounding in Britain of pipes to be used for the Iraqi construction of a 'supergun'. It is held that the western and particularly the American response to all of these 'signals' was either non-existent or not sufficiently clear and unambiguous to deter Iraqi designs on Kuwait.

But the incident that is claimed to have finally persuaded Saddam that he had a free hand in Kuwait was the now famous interview he gave to the American ambassador to Baghdad, April Glaspie, on 25 July 1990. During this interview Ambassador Glaspie assured Saddam that the United States had some sympathy for Iraq's economic plight and that Washington had 'no opinion on Arab–Arab conflicts, such as your border disagreement with Kuwait'. [17]

In assessing the contention that the United States effectively 'invited' Iraq's invasion of Kuwait by signalling its 'indifference' to such an eventuality we have to balance the incentive the Iraqis had for sending a false signal with the possible failure of the United States to receive the correct signal from Iraqi behaviour and declarations. There are two implications in such a contention. One is that the United States failed to interpret the signals, got it wrong and were thus taken by surprise when the invasion occurred. This situation would be a failure given the vast array of intelligence gathering and analysis resources deployed by the United States on a global scale. Following on from this is that if such an intelligence failure had not occurred, the Americans would have received the correct signals, interpreted them correctly and would thus have been able to prevent the invasion. Thus an intelligence failure entails some culpability in the invasion – it was, on this argument at least, partly the fault of the United States. A similar argument was heard in the aftermath of the Argentinian invasion of the Falkland Islands in 1982. In any case this assumes that even if the United States did receive the correct signals, they would have been able to dissuade Saddam Hussein from invading. This in turn assumes that he was 'dissuadable' that is that he would have been deterred by an American warning that such an action would bring a confrontation directly with the United States. If on the other hand Saddam wanted a confrontation with the United States this would not have been a deterrent.

A possible argument in favour of the 'conspiracy theory' is that a pre-invasion American warning and diplomatic confrontation with Saddam Hussein may actually have constrained a US response when the invasion did occur. Belligerent language by the Americans designed to deter an Iraqi invasion could have been used by Saddam Hussein and other Arab states to accuse the United States of interference in an Arab dispute and could have started an anti-American and anti-interventionist campaign which might not have ultimately prevented an American response to an invasion, but it might well have made the construction of a UN-based coalition much more difficult if not impossible. Such a turn of events would have had the effect of polarising the crisis into an Iraq–American confrontation which would have been to Iraq's advantage and America's disadvantage. Indeed Saddam Hussein strove unsuccessfully to do just that throughout the crisis and subsequent war.

But the other implication is that the United States is more directly and deviously culpable in that this intelligence failure was a deliberate one in order to inveigle the Iraqis to invade so that the United States would have a pretext to intervene (1) to elim-inate Saddam Hussein and the Ba'athist regime and (2) to establish an American military presence in the region. To achieve surprise requires ignorance or collusion on the part of your opponent. Whether intelligence failure constitutes ignorance or collusion is a debatable point. That the Iraqi invasion was part of an American deliberate strategy seems inconceivable. Such a conclusion would be to succumb to a monumental conspiracy theory of the Gulf conflict and would perhaps be the least plausible of explanations, because, like all conspiracy theories, it assumes a degree of control over events which those who study foreign policy recognise as being utterly unrealistic.

Before we leave it this issue must be related to that of 'strategic surprise' (see also Chapter 8), The sending of correct signals about one's intentions and the achievement of strategic surprise are of course mutually incompatible. Thus in order to achieve strategic surprise Saddam Hussein himself would have had an incentive to send misleading signals – hence here the diplomatic use of 'strategic ambiguity'. There would only have been point in him sending correct signals if he wanted to be persuaded out of his proposed action. If on the other hand he wanted to succeed in achieving surprise (a necessary prerequisite of victory – i.e. to present a *fait accompli* to the world) it would have been necessary to send the wrong signals. It is interesting in this respect to note that authoritarian leaders in non-democratic systems have most incentive and opportunity to use surprise tactics. Saddam Hussein had been used to using such tactics in his domestic struggle to acquire and maintain power and it is a characteristic of his foreign-policy behaviour.

To suggest in any case that Saddam would have demurred if Washington had directly indicated its commitment to defend Kuwait perhaps overrates even superpower influence over the behaviour of other states and moreover suggests that Saddam could have been warned off. In any case the *idée fixe*, if there was one, on the part of the United States was rather that Saddam's aspirations in respect of Kuwait were restricted to the border dispute – that is, over Rumaila and the strategic islands of Warbar and Bubiyan, the Iraqi claims to which had received a degree of sympathy from the west. Hence Ambassador Glaspie's assurance to Saddam Hussein that Washington had no opinion on Arab–Arab disputes – including the Iraq–Kuwait border issue. Whatever Saddam Hussein and US critics have said subsequently, such a statement cannot be construed as implying that the United States would accommodate the annexation and disappearance of Kuwait as a sovereign state; and, wily chap that he is, neither is it plausible that Saddam Hussein construed it as such. However, he probably did construe America's embarrassment (at least) on its revelation after the event and perhaps even made the judgement that the revelation of the interchange would somehow constrain a US military response to the annexation.

Having said all that, however, it is not unknown for Washington to have no policy, or at least a policy of insufficient clarity, in a particular area, until such an action takes place – after which clarification is rapidly forced on foreign-policy decision-makers.

There is a precedent in America's reaction to the North Korean invasion of South Korea in 1950. It has been claimed similarly that Secretary of State Dean Acheson's speech in January 1950 implying that Korea lay outside the US security perimeter encouraged the North Koreans to believe that the United States would have 'no opinion' on an attempt forcibly to incorporate the two halves of the country.[18] It is unlikely that Acheson meant any such thing but attempting to send different signals to different audiences with the same speech risks an ambiguity which can lead to misunderstanding and miscalculation.

The problem is that in retrospect such pieces of information when taken together seem incontrovertible evidence of intentions. The invasion of Kuwait seems a logical extension of Saddam Hussein's previous series of actions and declarations. But in a sense this a false logic, or it is a logic that can only be appreciated in retrospect. The Kuwaiti invasion can be seen to have been an act in keeping with the previous train of logic. However, it does not follow that such an action could necessarily have been predicted at the time on the basis of that train of behaviour. The question to ask is in what way was Saddam's behaviour different such that this time rhetoric would be converted into action – given the potential costs for Iraq and Saddam himself of such action? There was a similar 'logic' in the period leading up to the Argentinian invasion of the Falklands; and likewise such a train of behaviour and declaration had been seen before without such an outcome.

Ultimately the problem for the intelligence analyst is to distinguish between rhetoric and intention. A state or leadership or culture that habitually uses elaborate rhetoric in its declaratory diplomacy always risks being misinterpreted. At times rhetoric is used for precisely this purpose – that is, to deceive, to intimidate, to confuse – and often in this context rhetoric itself is a form of action.[19]

In the final analysis it is impossible to read ambiguous signals 'correctly' precisely because they are ambiguous – ambiguous signals reflect indeterminacy of policy. Thus if the policy-maker(s) are uncertain of their policy, it is unlikely that their intentions can be read correctly. The argument about American intelligence failure assumes that the correct signals were being sent and that Saddam Hussein long had the intention (at least since February

1990 and even earlier) of invading Kuwait. This is unlikely to have been the case given the *ad hoc* nature of Saddam's foreign policy making.

CHANGED STRUCTURAL CONDITIONS: THE ROLE OF THE SOVIET UNION AND THE END OF THE COLD WAR

The Introduction to this book discusses the importance of 'structural factors' in explaining international events. There it was suggested that structural factors can rarely if at all be considered as direct causes of events but that they do set the context within which events happen and constitute a set of propensities – that is, the structural context makes it possible or probable for certain types of events to take place. Whether they do or not depends upon contingent factors.

Though the Soviet Union did not on the face of it play a central active role in the Gulf crisis, its role was in fact pivotal in two respects. On the structural level there is a direct connection between domestic events in the Soviet Union over the past five or six years and the international system. The internal movement for reform in the Soviet Union entailed and required a radical departure in Soviet foreign policy and effectively a withdrawal from its Cold War competition with the United States. The consequences of that for many Third World states have been and will be profound. Many such states have benefited from Soviet sponsorship particularly if they pursued an anti-western radical foreign policy. That sponsorship has taken the form of diplomatic support and economic aid (though the Soviet Union could never compete with the west in these terms). But more significantly it has taken the form of military support both in terms of military equipment and military training. The fostering of client states in the Middle East has been an important foreign-policy priority for the Soviet Union since the mid-1950s. Indeed the post-Stalin foreign-policy reforms of Nikita Khrushchev were spearheaded by moves to foster a close relationship with Egypt; the granting of Soviet military aid to Nasser was one of the precursors of the Suez crisis of 1956. This was part of a more outward looking foreign policy for the Soviet Union designed to break the long-standing isolationism pursued by Stalin. But more significantly it was a recognition of the need for the Soviet Union to accommodate the rapid changes in the international system brought about by the dismantling of the European empires and the large numbers of new, potentially radical, states being created in its aftermath.

More specifically the Middle Eastern states were regarded as particularly important for the Soviet Union because it had legitimate security and economic interests in the area. The region occupied a crucial geopolitical position on the southern flank of the Soviet Union and Soviet leaders saw the need to foster clients in the region in order to counter the western attempt to forge anti-Soviet alliances all around the Asian land mass. This Soviet policy over the period since the 1950s has had varying degrees of success – but at no time has the Soviet Union had the freedom of action in the region that the western powers have enjoyed.

However, the Cold War competition in the Middle East has had two effects. First the Cold War stalemate has effectively been imposed on the Middle East. As in many other parts of the world, conflicts and disputes arising out of local relationships have been frozen by the determination of the respective superpowers to take one side or another. For the superpowers Middle Eastern policy has constituted merely part of their respective Cold War policies. Thus as has been mentioned in Chapter 1 the dispute between Israel and the Arab states on the one hand and the Palestinians on the other has got caught up in the antagonism between the United States and the Soviet Union which effectively has prevented a solution.

But the other dimension is that though the Cold War has preserved these conflicts it has also ensured that the superpowers have been very anxious to retain some degree of control over their 'clients' and to ensure that conflicts in the Middle East did not lead to direct conflict between the superpowers. Thus the clients have been kept on a reasonably tight rein, though not without risks. So the superpower competition in the region has had the effect of keeping conflicts running whilst seeing that they do not escalate out of control.

The ending of the Cold War antagonism on a global scale has clearly had desirable and positive effects in lessening tension, and in reducing the arms competition and the nuclear threat between the superpowers. Indeed it may well have paved the way for some movement in solving long-standing Middle East problems such as that of the Palestinian–Israeli conflict. In the longer term this will be seen as having been crucial. However, the corollary of all this is the negative effects of the loosening grip of the superpowers – in this context the potential destabilising of some of the regional security systems. During the Cold War the superpower 'client' states were constrained in the range of their behaviour and were deterred from taking actions which might be detrimental to the interests of their superpower ally. The loosening of the restraining influence on these states entailed greater scope for 'adventurous' behaviour. It is difficult to see that the Soviet Union would have allowed the Iraqis to invade Kuwait had their influence and interest in the region, and particularly in Iraq, not declined. Such an action in the Cold War context would have had serious consequences which the Soviet Union would have been extremely unwilling to risk. In Cold War terms the invasion of Kuwait would have been seen as a direct move against acknowledged western security and economic interests and as a Soviet move out of her own legitimate sphere of interest into that of the United States and the West. Under those circumstances then a superpower response would have been certain – and that response would not have been conducted through the United Nations. It would have been unilateral – or together with allies who have interests in the region. Thus such a move would have seriously risked a large-scale Cold War conflagration which is why the Soviet Union would have been very unlikely to have allowed it. It was in this sense that the Gulf crisis can be seen to have been a manifestation of the end of the Cold War and indeed the first post-Cold War crisis.

But if the decline of Soviet power released the constraints on Iraqi behaviour and encouraged the invasion of Kuwait, it also paradoxically laid the foundation for a united global response to it. If the decline of Soviet power was the key to Iraq's invasion, it was also the key to the construction of its defeat. The Soviet role in the crisis diplomacy of the Gulf conflict is dealt with in more detail in Chapter 4, but it should be said here that the new policy of *perestroika* laid the foundations for superpower cooperation in the UN Security Council. It was the Soviet need for economic aid from the west that provided the positive incentive for cooperation, but it was Eduard Shevardnadze, the Soviet Foreign Minister, who rapidly made Soviet foreign policy in response to the invasion pre-empting any more deliberate, and particularly Soviet Communist Party, consideration, which might have adopted a more equivocal not to say pro-Iraqi stance. Thus it was entirely fortuitous that the Soviet and American Foreign Secretaries happened to be together in the Soviet Union when the invasion took place that enabled an immediate forging of a joint and cooperative approach to it and enabled that policy of cooperation to acquire a head of steam within the Soviet Union that virtually precluded a more hardline response that might have been forthcoming from the conservatives in the CPSU.[20] Shevardnadze's initiative was so important that support for the United States may well not have emerged without it.

Indeed it was this 'capturing' of Soviet foreign policy by Shevardnadze and the *perestroika* wing of the Soviet leadership that injected more determination into the hardline conservatives in the Soviet Union to resist and turn back the reforms. The extent to which that pressure was succeeding led to Shevardnaze's resignation in December 1990, a considerable blow to Gorbachev's ability to hold fast to his Gulf policy. It was no doubt behind the Soviet attempt to get Saddam Hussein off the hook so late in the day before the ground offensive began in February 1991. Indeed one could go so far as to say that the attempted *coup d'état* against Gorbachev in August 1991 was a delayed consequence of the Iraq war. It is perhaps rather far-fetched to suggest that the Gulf War directly induced the attempted coup. It is likely that such a coup was an inevitable attempt by the Soviet communist 'old guard' to halt the reform movement and retrieve their lost ground. However, it is plausible to suggest that the Gulf War, and the Soviet role in it as a facilitator of American action, did paint a picture of a subordinate Soviet Union in a world in which its old 'allies' and 'agents of influence' in the world were effectively being thrown to the capitalist wolves, that may have swept aside any residual uncertainties that the old guard might have had that an overthrow of the reformers was essential. In retrospect Saddam Hussein's invasion of Kuwait may have been the precursor of the most profound changes that have taken place in the Soviet Union since the revolution of 1917 and the most profound changes in the international system since the defeat of Nazi Germany in 1945.

THE PRO-IRAQ STATES

Those few states which did support Iraq during the conflict can in no sense be regarded as a coherent 'Coalition'. There were few states outside of the Middle East which expressed even the mildest sympathy with Iraq. Indeed Cuba was the only state which fell into this category and was significant only because it was a non-permanent member of the UN Security Council at the time of the crisis and was motivated largely by an endemic anti-Americanism coupled with a 'western imperialism' interpretation of the UN response to the Iraqi invasion. Of those states within the Middle East which supported Iraq, Libya provided rhetorical solidarity with a fellow Arab radical regime but little else; Yemen provided perhaps the most significant 'independent' support for Iraq and worked for her interests in the Security Council (see Chapter 3); Jordan and the Palestinians (not of course a state) were essentially dependants of Iraq and could provide little in the way of material, or indeed even moral, sustenance to the Iraqi regime.

Jordan

Jordan's position in the Gulf conflict was a classic case of a state being completely at the mercy of its environment. King Hussein is temperamentally, and indeed by history and training, pro-western. He has ruled precariously and astutely in Jordan for some forty years. A large proportion of his population is Palestinian and much more radical than he. The state of Jordan is contiguous with both Israel and Iraq and the King has had the difficult task of reconciling Iraq's extreme radicalism on the Palestinian issue with a more pragmatic *modus vivendi* with Israel. But Jordan could not avoid her geopolitical situation. If Iraq attacked Israel it would use either Jordanian air space or actual territory. Hence during the actual crisis Israel warned that the presence of Iraqi troops on Jordanian territory even if on the Iraqi border would attract a pre-emptive strike from Israel. Indeed during the war phase of the crisis Jordanian air space was breached by the infamous Scud missiles on their way to Israeli cities.

Economically Iraq is a benefactor of Jordan – the source of its oil and the destination of many of its exports. Saddam Hussein was paying Iraq's war debt to Jordan in the form of cheap oil. That economic tie has also to be expressed in political terms even though the King would not want to be separated entirely from the west. Moreover, he had to heed his own population, which was radically pro-Saddam. The logic of King Hussein's stance was simple: if he made the wrong choice in backing Saddam Hussein, it was conceivable, likely even, that the west would understand his dilemma and forgive him eventually; if he made the wrong choice in backing the UN Coalition it was certain that Saddam Hussein would not forgive him and would undoubtedly unleash his wrath against the King at some future date. In these circumstances King Hussein had little choice.

But the King's commitment to the west should not be overestimated. In recent years he has become rather disillusioned with the western powers and frustrated at their apparent lack of urgency in pressing some solution to the Palestinian issue and in particular their failure to put sufficient pressure on Israel to make concessions on the occupied territories. Had King Hussein felt a pro-western stance would serve that end, he might have been inclined to be less ambiguous. But as it was there was little incentive for him on that score and there was a great deal more urgency for him to take the opposite stance. Eventually a policy of studied ambiguity emerged. However, in the longer term, para-doxical though it might sound, King Hussein's pro-Iraqi stance in the Gulf crisis was in the interests of the west. The fact was that the King did not really have the freedom to choose between the coalition and Saddam Hussein. The population, both Jordanian and Palestinian, were vehemently pro-Saddam. The Iraqi invasion of Kuwait was seen by most Jordanians and other Arabs all over the region as the beginning of the forced Arab unity[21] that would bring the wealth of the Gulf states to the service of the bankrupt and poverty stricken Arabs of the north, manifesting an increasing envy of and contempt for the wealth and profligacy of the Gulf Arabs. Expressing a rather incoherent rage against 'western im-perialism' it was in effect an expression of frustration both against the west for not bringing Israel to a solution of the Palestinian problem and to the Gulf states for their easy wealth. If the King had not gone along with his population it is very unlikely that he would have survived – so pro-western has he been that even by his own people he has been called a 'western puppet'.[22] The downfall of the King would at best ensure another radical regime – at worst a situation of chaos. Thus again King Hussein probably made the right decision even though it put his relationship with the United States and the west in general under some considerable strain.

The Palestinians

The PLO leader Yassir Arafat came out immediately and osten-tatiously in favour of Iraq and press pictures of his embrace with

Saddam Hussein shortly after the invasion were viewed with as much distaste in the west as they were with delight among much of the Arab populations of the region. Irony and paradox abound in Middle Eastern relations, and not the least irony in this context was Arafat's acquiescence and support for the pillaging of a country in which he himself made his fortune[23] and where large numbers of dispossessed Palestinians had found stability and even prosperity. Arafat's decision was partly a deliberate one. His recently developed moderation in going along with the US Middle East peace initiative had yielded nothing, and even the grass-roots inspired *intifada* in the West Bank was now acknowledged to have failed to bring any change in Israeli or western positions. But there was also an element, as with King Hussein, of being dragged into a pro-Saddam stance by the Palestinians both in his own movement and in Jordan. His leadership was unlikely to have survived a refusal to embrace the 'new Saladin' in Baghdad. The pro-Iraqi stance of both Jordan and the PLO might be regarded as the 'politics of desperation'. Certainly the Jordanian and Palestinian peoples believed they had little to lose. They had been neglected for so many years that the possibility of the pan-Arab solution to their problems that Saddam Hussein's invasion promised was too glittering a one to pass up – whatever the consequences of failure might be.

The longer-term implications of Arafat's pro-Saddam stance will be considered in the final chapter of this book, but perhaps its most significant aspect will be seen to have been Arafat's acquiescence in Saddam's offer to exchange occupation of the territory of one Arab state (i.e. that of Kuwait) for that of another Arab state (i.e. that of Jordan and the West Bank). The offer of such a deal equates one with the other and implicitly acknowledges that Saddam's action was no different to that of Israel. It might be that this dimension of Iraq's action will ultimately serve to sideline Arafat altogether and ensure his exclusion from any settlement of the Palestinian issue.

The Yemen

Yemen had few other than ideological reasons for supporting Iraq. A radical pro-communist regime, the Yemeni government was anti-pathetic to the Gulf states and Saudi Arabia, whose oil wealth it does not share and whose pro-western stance it abhors. The

Yemen however played an important role in being, together with Cuba, the only pro-Iraq voices in the Security Council at the time of the invasion. Indeed the Yemen's role as chairman of the Security Council for a number of weeks during the pre-war crisis period ensured that the pro-Iraq case was heard rather more loudly than it might otherwise have been. The Yemen's UN representative presented an impressive diplomatic demeanour and perhaps the only public 'near credible' case in favour of Iraq and pressed consistently for a moderate and non-violent response to Iraq's invasion of Kuwait.

THE ANTI-IRAQ COALITION

The problems of Coalition management

The motivations and interests of the United States as the leader of the anti-Iraq Coalition and its chief protagonist are discussed at various other points in this book (notably in Chapter 4) so will not be discussed in detail in this chapter. However, it is important to reiterate the crucial role that the United States performed in providing the focus of the global response to the invasion as well as the political and military resources to confront it. The role pointed up again the necessity for what might be called a 'galvaniser' of the international community in situations of this nature. That does not mean that the United States placed itself at the service of the international community; there is little doubt that America was serving its direct and indirect interests in the role it performed. However, the solidarity of the United Nations and the global community was a testimony to the fact that in doing so it was also serving at least some of the interests of that community – and moreover global interests that could not effectively be served in this context without the United States. By definition of course such a dual role is bound to produce conflicts of interest – in the last analysis they are incompatible. But short of the last analysis there was mutual benefit. The *quid pro quo* was that on the one hand American action was constrained by the need to serve the international political constituency (as well as its own domestic constituency) and on the other the international community had to accept American leadership (and the risk that it was being manipulated) in return for high-profile United Nations involvement. For the United States UN involvement conferred legitimacy for its action, for the United Nations American leadership conferred a degree of involvement and political saliency in the crisis it would not otherwise have enjoyed. There was not an 'equality' of benefit but there was at least some exchange of benefit. It is doubtful if the response to the crisis could have been anywhere near as effective had it fallen to a 'coalition of equals' to take the initiative. Indeed it is one of the lessons for the future that any 'collective security' system does and will need to be led by a powerful individual state.

The UN Coalition brought together in the Gulf crisis was an example of a single-issue coalition – a coalition of states brought together by a common interest in a particular issue at a particular time and not one based upon broader and longer-standing commonalities of ideological or geographical security interest. The United States has had long experience in 'managing' the western Cold War Coalition represented by NATO and no doubt that experience stood her in good stead in her tasks of the management of the UN Coalition in the Gulf crisis. A single-issue coalition, however, does produce a range of rather different problems and also perhaps a rather more limited range of plausible solutions. A characteristic feature of the UN Coalition (like that of NATO) was the asymmetry of power among the states in it – most notably of course that between the 'core' power, the United States, and the other states in the Coalition. Such disparity in power among members has both advantages and disadvantages. One of the disadvantages is that there is an implicit, forever present 'suspicion' of the core power held by the other members – a suspicion for example that the core power is working to a covert agenda that is different from the apparently agreed one; that it has its own interests and objectives which it is merely using the Coalition to achieve and often at the expense of the interests of the other members.

A state's membership of a coalition must be the reflection of a combination of genuine self-interest and perhaps a degree of coercion (or persuasion) by other members or the 'core' power. It is in this balance between the state's perceived self-interest in its membership of the Coalition and the degree to which its commitment has to be coerced or 'bought' that determines the necessity for 'management'. There are two intimately related aspects of the task of management – one concerns the political and diplomatic necessities of keeping the members committed to the Coalition; the other concerns the problems associated with organising and implementing the means to achieve the desired objective(s) of the Coalition.

For the United States, Coalition 'management' consisted firstly (and primarily) of securing the sustained support, and active cooperation, of the major anti-Iraq Arab states; and secondly of treading a delicate path through the diplomacy of the United Nations Security Council; and thirdly of trying to ensure that its western allies were playing a supporting role.

The role of the major non-Arab members of the Coalition, as well as that of the Soviet Union and China, are discussed at other points in this book, so what follows in this section is a general statement about their signficance in the Gulf conflict. It is possible that the United States could have taken the action it took in the Gulf crisis without the active support it received; it is very unlikely it could have taken such action in the face of active opposition from its major allies. Indeed one could go as far as to say that the crucial determinant of a successful political (and eventually military) response to Iraq's invasion was the formation of a coalition of states composed of the most significant states in the 'western' camp, other important Arab states and, at least the acquiescence of, 'active semi-detached' states such as the Soviet Union and 'passive semi-detached' states such as China.

Thus it can be seen that there were three major axes of the coalition management task for the United States:

1 US–Arab axis.
2 US–Security Council axis.
3 US–'western camp' axis.

The Security Council dimension is discussed in more detail in Chapter 3. However, it is clear that without the acquiescence of China in the Security Council the action could not have assumed the imprimatur of the United Nations. In the face of active opposition of the Soviet Union the task would have been immeasurably more difficult both in terms of the politics of fashioning an anti-Iraq coalition and in achieving the military defeat of an Iraq that could rely on Soviet material support. The absence of a European component to the Coalition would have deprived the United States of military support which it could have accommodated without much difficulty. But more importantly it would have deprived the United States of the political and moral support for its action in the Middle East, which would have been less sustainable. The fact that two of the major European states had interests and motivations of their own in confronting the Iraqi invasion ensured a welcome solidarity with the United States but also made bearable the rather more reticent stance of other members of the European community – notably of course Germany.

Both the United Kingdom and France contributed substantial military forces to the coalition and both played signficant roles in the military operations. The closest collaboration took place between the Americans and the British both in Security Council diplomacy and also in the military operations during the war phase. There is little doubt that the United States could have achieved military success without British military support but the absence of British collaboration would have made the political task immeasurably more difficult for the Americans if not actually impossible. Similarly the fact that France was prepared in the final analysis to contribute significantly to the ground military operations, even whilst maintaining a 'distance' from the Americans and British, was a demonstration of a reluctant solidarity with 'the west' in the face of Iraqi aggression. Nevertheless France's policy of keeping her options open until the very last minute caused irritation to the United States and United Kingdom and was a continuing indication that France regards itself as having interests in the Third World which are often not consonant with those of the United States or the United Kingdom.

The semblance of a unified European response was manifest in the fact that many of the European states (apart from the United Kingdom and France) contributed support mainly in limited naval forces under the aegis of the Western European Union (WEU). But in the case of many of the European states this can be seen as a device to offer symbolic support whilst minimising their military contribution. (Those states contributing forces under the WEU can be seen in Appendix V.) However it was Germany which came under a great deal of moral pressure over its stance on the crisis and which gave rise to the beginnings of a debate about the status and role of German military power which will become increasingly urgent both in Germany's domestic context and also in the international domain. For the first time since the end of the Second World War Germany was expected to participate in a military conflict outside of Europe. Such military activity is prohibited in the German constitution, which was set down by the victorious Allies in the immediate post-Nazi period. But the Gulf crisis revealed a conflict between these constitutional provisions and her contemporary status as one of the world's top three economic powers. The question arose as to whether it was defensible for an economically powerful state to refrain from helping to maintain the order of a system from which it derives a great deal of economic wealth. Though the German dilemma was not resolved on this occasion, a mechanism was arrived at by which she would meet a large proportion of the financial costs of the operation. This device no doubt solved a short-term problem but clearly cannot be a satisfactory basis for future German participation in such operations.

One of the US tasks in managing both formal and informal members of the coalition was to restrain their independent diplomatic activity in the crisis lest such action crossed wires with the Americans' own coercive diplomacy. There was, for example, always a danger that the Arab members of the Coalition would succumb to the argument that the whole issue should be dealt with by and within the Arab world and that outsiders should withdraw. Some concession by the Iraqis could have made it difficult for the coalition Arabs to resist such a call. In the event Saddam Hussein's intransigence demonstrated that there would not be much hope of resolution within an Arab context.

The only member the United States could rely on in this respect perhaps was the United Kingdom with whom the United States has had a strong diplomatic and military relationship. On the other hand France posed considerable potential for disrupting American crisis diplomacy through their traditional anxiety to exert their political autonomy in international matters – especially vis-à-vis the 'Anglo-Saxons' – and who had their own political associations and objectives in the Middle East.

There was also a danger that Soviet independent diplomacy could derail America's programme both in the crisis phase of the conflict and war phase. The Soviet Union's legitimate interest in the region and the general lack of certainty as to what extent Soviet external behaviour in the crisis would be subject to the effects of the radical internal changes that were taking place within the country, led to some anxiety about continued Soviet commitment to cooperation with the United States in the Security Council. This became particularly tense in the period before the ground war began when the obvious internal pressures on the Soviet leadership from the military and the communist hard line, which had already caused the departure of Eduard Shevardnadze, might have led it to break ranks and attempt to prevent the launch of the ground offensive.

The Arab members of the Coalition

One of the chief constraining forces on American ability to forge and maintain a coalition with the major Arab states was the clash between her relationships with the Arabs and her relationship with Israel. The balancing of those two axes of American interest has been a fundamental focus of US Middle Eastern policy. The US–Israeli affinity always injects a degree of ambivalence to say the least into America's relationship with even the pro-western Arab states. The corollary of this of course is that the pro-western Arab states themselves have to tread the delicate path of maintaining relationshps with western countries (for both national and dynastic interests) whilst showing no compromise in their hostility against Israel. It was in order to help the Arab members of the coalition to avoid having to make a choice between these two basic interests that it was a very high priority US task of coalition management to keep Israel out of the conflict.

Israel might with some accuracy be termed the 'sleeping partner' or the 'dormant member' of the Coalition. This image should not be overstated, but there was a sense in which the US needed as much cooperation from Israel as from the Arab members of the Coalition. If the major Arab countries had to be provided with incentives (especially Egypt and Syria) to join the Coalition, then Israel had to have incentives not to! – at least in any active sense. This is clearly too glib as a complete description of the respective relationships – it does however convey the sometimes paradoxical relationships, that events often force upon states. Though Israel was not a formal member of the coalition for obvious reasons, she had to respond to US pressure as if she were.

Saudi Arabia

Any substantial response to Iraq's invasion – politically, economically or militarily – required the leadership of the United States. That was unpalatable to many people inside and outside the Middle East but is a fact of contemporary international life. It was a necessary condition of successful action against Iraq, but it was not a sufficient one. Perhaps the most important prerequisite of any 'western' action in the Middle East in the contemporary international system is the support of major Arab states in the region. The general Arab sensitivity about external, particularly western, intervention in the Middle East meant that any western action against Iraq independently of Arab states would be regarded as another manifestation of 'western imperialism' and was thus out of the question. The key Arab state in this respect was not Kuwait, which early after the invasion called on the United States and other western states to support them, but Saudi Arabia. Saudi Arabia is the 'senior' southern Arab state, and indeed it was from Saudi Arabia that any military response to Iraq would have to be mounted. Moreover, of course, apart from Kuwait, Saudi Arabia had the greatest incentive to call on US support, since the conquest of Kuwait posed a direct security threat to Saudi territory and oil resources.

Even in these circumstances there was a reluctance on the part of Saudi Arabia to call on external help immediately. Over recent years Saudi Arabian foreign policy in the region has been characterised by a degree of caution motivated by a recognition of the tightrope the Saudi regime walks between its 'brotherly obligation' in keeping the economies of radical Arab governments afloat and its role as a western-sponsored guarantor of security in the Gulf. The Saudi government maintains a strict Islamic orthodoxy whilst at the same time running a western-oriented oil economy. The ruling Saudi royal family is vulnerable domestically on two counts: first to the spread of popular Arab radicalism exacerbated by the disparities in wealth within Saudi Arabia and increasing resentment of the ever-extending privileged circle of the 'House of Saud'; and second to the threat of Islamic fundamentalism. Thus Saudi reaction to the Iraqi invasion of Kuwait had to be sensitive to the risk of inflaming both these potential sources of internal dissension. In some respects of course these opposition forces cancel each other out because as well as being opposed to the Saudis they are also opposed to each other.

Thus it was that initially Saudi Arabia favoured an Arab solution to the crisis, as of course did many Arab states. It was not until it became clear that this was unlikely to be achieved with the Iraqi annexation of Kuwait on 8 August 1990 that Saudi Arabia, as well as Egypt and Syria recognised that an external intervention to solve the problem would be necessary. At the first Arab League meeting after the invasion, seven out of twenty-one members voted against Iraqi withdrawal – these were Iraq, Jordan, Sudan, Libya, Yemen, Mauritania and the PLO. At the next meeting in Cairo on 10 August only three Arab states voted to oppose UN economic sanctions, to oppose an invitation to US troops and to oppose the sending of an Arab defence force – these were Iraq, Libya and the PLO.[24] In addition to this it was likely that the Americans themselves 'firmed up' Saudi resolve prior to the Saudi invitation to the United States to send troops. Dick Cheney, the American Secretary of Defence, travelled to the Middle East on 6 August primarily on a coalition-building mission. The invitation had to come from the Saudis but the Americans themselves were instrumental in ensuring that the invitation was sent.

Egypt

Perhaps of equal significance for the Coalition was Egypt. Even with Saudi membership of the Coalition, its credibility would have been perhaps fatally undermined by the the absence of Egypt. Long the most powerful and the most populous of the Arab states and straddling the Suez Canal, a vital geostrategic asset, Egypt was the focus of the Middle Eastern diplomacy of both superpowers during the whole of the Cold War. The origin of the most successful period of Arab nationalism led by Gamal Abdul Nasser in the 1950s and 1960s, its invasion by British and French forces in the Suez crisis of 1956 has become the symbol in Arab political culture of post-war western imperialism and has operated an astute policy of playing one superpower against the other. However, among radical and nationalist Arabs, Egypt – and particularly Anwar Sadat – has never been forgiven for concluding a separate peace with Israel in the Camp David Agreements of 1978 and 1979. Since then, and since its estrangement from the Soviet Union, Egypt has benefited from western, and particularly American, military and economic aid, being seen by the west as a bulwark against both Soviet influence in the Middle East and the spread of Islamic fundamentalism. There is little doubt Egypt's fundamental interests lay in supporting the coalition, particularly in the light of the demise of Soviet power and more pertinently in the light of the necessity for western support of its economy.

Specifically, the *quid pro quo* for Egyptian participation in the Coalition force was the American agreement to write off $3 billion worth of debt.

If it was clear that membership of the Coalition was in the interests of the Saudi and Egyptian governments, this was not the same as having the support of their respective populations. It was a major strategy of the Iraqis to attempt to separate the Arab peoples from their governments by appealing to them directly as brother Arabs with an obligation to mount a *jihad* in order to defend Islam's holy places in Mecca from foreign forces. In order to counter this appeal both the Saudi and Egyptian governments were very careful to ensure that the sending of Arab forces to join the Coalition received the sanction of the highest religious authorities in their respective countries.[25]

Syria

It seemed that the most that could have been expected from Syria in the face of the Iraqi invasion of Kuwait was perhaps a studied indifference. The Syrian Ba'athist government is an implacable enemy of the Iraqi Ba'athists; but also the radical, traditionally pro-Soviet Syrian government had no love for the Kuwaiti regime. Perhaps to sit back and watch the discomfiture of both the Iraqis and the Kuwaitis might have been the preferred strategy of the Syrians. Syria's decision to go along with the Cairo Summit of Arab leaders in sending a pan-Arab force to Saudi Arabia to supplement the United States-led military build-up was one of the most startling features of the crisis – a seeming reversal of all Syria's previous stances on Middle Eastern issues. Vehemently anti-western, the leader of the radical states of the region, opposed root and branch to Egypt's rapprochment with Israel, it had long been a haven for anti-western terrorist groups and probably even a sponsor itself of anti-western terrorism. Hafez al-Assad had in the face of much Arab radical dismay and criticism both internally and externally decided to support and aid a foreign military action against a fellow Arab state. Three factors explain this apparently anomalous behaviour.

One was simply the opportunity to secure the downfall of his major Arab enemy Saddam Hussein; the second was the recognition by Assad of the changed and still-changing political and security environment. The decline in superpower antagonism and the apparent end of the Cold War had profound implications for the Middle East and particularly for the historically pro-Soviet Arab states. Assad could see his Soviet benefactor decline and along with it the approaching end of its economic and military sponsorship of Syria. That, together with the increasing economic and political disadvantages of the antagonistic relationship with the United States and other western states, required a radical revision of its relations with the west – a need to come in from the diplomatic and economic cold that had for years characterised Syria's relations with the west.

The third factor explaining Syria's stance in the Gulf conflict was Assad's aspirations in the Lebanon. The Kuwait crisis had deflected Iraq's attention from the Lebanon and weakened Iraqi support for the Christian Maronite militia led by General Aouon, thereby allowing Syrian troops to push home their advantage and break the political and military log-jam in the Lebanon. Indeed the US preoccupation with events in the Gulf meant that Syrian action in Lebanon would not attract the western resistance that it might otherwise have done. There might even have been a tacit deal in which Syria was allowed a 'free hand ' in the Lebanon in return for a pro-western stance on the Gulf issue and a commitment to make a genuine and strenuous effort to secure the release of western hostages in the Lebanon once Syrian dominance had been secured. A further factor consequent upon the decline of Soviet political influence in the region was the need to develop a much more positive attitude to the Gulf states and thus a need to play down Syria's traditional radicalism. Syria would clearly need a benefactor to fill the gap created by the effective retreat of the Soviet Union from the region – the only source of such resources were the Gulf states. Thus there would be a *quid pro quo* for supporting Kuwait which no doubt Syria would cash in at a later date.

Inevitably Syria's association with the United States in the Coalition was an ambivalent one. Though Assad was an implacable opponent of Saddam Hussein, he did not want Iraq's status as the major confrontational state against Israel to be compromised. Assad also had an interest in maintaining Syria's position as the major Middle Eastern antagonist of both Israel and the United States. So whilst accepting the Saudi promise of $1,000 million over the year in return for its collaboration,[26] he was both despatching military support to Saudi Arabia and maintaining the anti- American rhetoric. Perhaps the cynicism of such a stance was acceptable to the Americans since one crucial consequence of Syria's participation in the UN Coalition was that it spiked any effective Arab opposition to the American-led military reversal of Iraqi action.

This chapter has identified the nature and sources of the provocation of the crisis and has established the various interests and constraints of the respective pro- and anti-Iraq protagonists. The following chapter examines the United Nations context of the conflict.

Chapter 3

The United Nations and the Gulf conflict

The Gulf conflict was regarded as a 'make or break' issue for the United Nations. Certainly the United Nations figured prominently in the crisis; ostensibly one side of the crisis was being conducted by the United Nations, or was it being conducted by the United States on behalf of the United Nations – or even, as some think, was the United Nations simply being manipulated by the United States to serve its own interests? Was the United Nations a party to the crisis or was it merely a forum within which the diplomacy of the crisis was conducted? The role of the United Nations was a complex one and there is a degree of misperception or misunderstanding regarding the nature of the United Nations, its purposes and functions, what it can and cannot do; and perhaps there are unrealistic popular expectations about what the United Nations can achieve.

The intention of this chapter will be to make clear some of these issues in relation to the Gulf crisis. In particular the source of much misunderstanding is the ambiguity of the role of the United Nations on the one hand as an actor in international politics and on the other as a forum for the conduct of diplomacy between states. Of course this ambiguity (and potential conflict) is not only a per- ception but a reality and its significance will be explained in the context of the Gulf crisis.

THE UNITED NATIONS AND MILITARY CONFLICT: A BRIEF HISTORY

The central features of the UN Charter are firstly its provisions regarding the peaceful settlement of disputes – that is, for the resolution of disputes between member states before they reach the stage of overt military conflict (Chapter VI of the UN Charter) – and secondly its provisions regarding the notion of collective security – that is, the collective commitment to go to the aid of a member state which is subject to aggression whether by a member or a non-member (Chapter VII of the UN Charter). A third feature which has become an important part of the actual activity of the United Nations has been the mechanisms it has developed for the termination of conflicts and the policing of conditions of cease-fire pending the longer-term solution of disputes involving armed conflict. This latter feature has arguably been the most successful feature of United Nations activities throughout its existence. But it is a feature for which there is no formal provision in the Charter and the mechanisms for the initiation and management of peacekeeping operations have been developed, essentially by the General Assembly, on an *ad hoc* basis.

However, the history of the United Nations in achieving the resolution of disputes by peaceful means has been very unhappy. This is primarily because a state will only refer its disputes with other states, or agree to its disputes with other states being referred to the United Nations, if it believes that it is in its interests to do so. If states judge that their objectives will not be achieved by allowing the United Nations to intervene in their disputes with other states, then they are unlikely to refer to the United Nations. Involvement of the United Nations in such disputes under Chapter VI of the Charter can only be with the consent of the respective parties to a dispute; the United Nations has no power or right to intervene otherwise.

It is because of the high public expectations of the United Nations's ability to resolve disputes and the high incidence of military conflict in the world consequent upon its failure to do so that there has been widespread disillusionment about the effectiveness of the United Nations and scepticism about whether it has any role at all to play in the contemporary international system. There have been only two occasions in its history where United Nations forces have been involved in military conflict as a belligerent. The first was the Korean War in 1950–3 and the second was the Congo in 1960. Neither of these cases was 'typical' nor was either of them unambiguously provided for in the Charter. The incident which provoked the former was the North Korean invasion of South Korea in July 1950. The matter was referred to the Security Council of the United Nations, which passed a resolution demanding the cessation of hostilities and the withdrawal of North Korean troops and asking member states to assist in the execution of the resolution.[1] The United States sent forces in response to the provision in the resolution of the Security Council, which then passed another United States resolution requesting members to assist in repelling the invasion of South Korea. Britain and her former dominions responded immediately (and later sixteen other states joined in). A resolution was then passed putting all contributing troops under a unified command under the United States, who then appointed General MacArthur as Supreme Commander.

But this apparently smooth and united action was not the result of unanimity among members of the Security Council. The fact that these resolutions passed through the Security Council was due to the fact that the Soviet delegate had been withdrawn from the Council in protest over the fact that the Formosa (Taiwan) government occupied the seat for China in the United Nations rather than the communist government of mainland China. The fact is that the Korean War was a 'cold war' war conducted predominantly by the United States under the flag of the United Nations – a situation brought about by a quite fortuitous circumstance which was unlikely to recur.

The other case where the United Nations has acted as a belligerent in a military conflict, the Congo in 1960, was equally controversial and is equally significant in determining the limited role it has been able to play ever since. United Nations forces became embroiled in military conflict in a chaotic and confused post-colonial struggle for power. Belgium had left its territory in an unstable condition and, when the new government of the Congo came under extreme pressure from internal political instability, attempted to return in force to maintain order. The return and presence of Belgian troops was unacceptable to the government of the Congo, which then requested a United Nations force to help the government maintain order, which would then obviate the need for Belgian troops. In the event the operation was to last nearly four years and was controversial for two main reasons.

Firstly the operation led troops serving under a United Nations flag to become entangled in an internal struggle for power within a sovereign state. Secondly the operation was effectively initiated and conducted by the Secretary-General of the United Nations, who secured authority for his action from the Security Council. Thus it was the Secretary-General who was instrumental in bringing the United Nations action about and who played a very prominent role in the activities of United Nations forces during the early stages of the operation. In doing so the Secretary-General, Dag Hammerskjold, made himself very unpopular among some member states, who felt that he was exceeding his mandate as Secretary-General of the United Nations. In effect the United Nations force in helping to keep the new Congo government *in situ* was opposing revolutionary forces, supported by the Soviet Union, and preventing them from coming to power in the Congo. Thus the Soviet Union was a very prominent critic of Hammerskjold and as a result of the Congo operation the Soviet government, led by Nikita Khrushchev, pressed hard for the abolition of the post of Secretary-General in favour of what came to be known as the *Troika*, that is, three individuals representing respectively the west, the Communist countries and the non-aligned countries. This attempt did not succeed but the controversy over Hammerskjold's role in the Congo operation has ensured that since then the post of Secretary-General has been occupied by essentially weak, undemonstrative characters who would be unlikely to take initiatives that might be contrary to the interests of the more prominent members of the Security Council. The death of Dag Hammerskjold in a plane crash in the Congo in 1961 is still largely unexplained.

Thus the history of United Nations inaction in circumstances of conflict between its members has been a manifestation of the total lack of consensus in the Security Council due essentially to Cold War antagonisms between the superpowers; and also by the fact that successive Secretaries-General (with the exception of Dag Hammerskjold) have not been strong enough personalities to attempt to pursue autonomous United Nations action. These factors are crucial to an understanding of the role of the United Nations in the Gulf crisis and perhaps in making a judgement about how significant a role it might play in the future, in the light of the Gulf conflict, in the field of the peaceful resolution of disputes and in carrying out action under the provisions of collective security.

THE UNITED NATIONS AND THE GULF CRISIS

As implied above, the United Nations suffers from the conflict between on the one hand its two major functions – peaceful settlement of disputes and collective security – and on the other its two major roles as mediator between conflicting parties and as participant in conflict between two of its members. These problems also reveal the 'schizophrenic' nature of its existence: is the body an organisation which can act 'independently' rather like a nation-state or is it merely a manifestation and reflection of the states' system itself with all the limitations that that implies? The ability of the United Nations to act in any dispute and the effectiveness with which it can do so is, not surprisingly, a product of its own structure, the personalities involved at any one time and the particular environment and circumstances that it has to deal with. Historically it can be seen that the United Nations has only been able to take action when the circumstances allow. This essentially has meant only when political relations between the major powers have found it useful for the United Nations to perform a role or when there is such confusion and ambiguity in the international system that the United Nations acts almost by default or where there is a circumstance that allows the United Nations to be used in the interests of one party against those of another.

It has been shown above that in the case of Korea the United States was able to take military action 'on behalf' of the United Nations primarily owing to a diplomatic blunder by the Soviet Union. In the case of the Congo the United Nations was able to take a direct military role as a result of the combination of a very confused post colonial internal political situation in the country in which the major powers were in many ways unable clearly to discern precisely what action was in their interests together with the presence of a dynamic United Nations Secretary-General who had a particular agenda of objectives he wanted to achieve. This demonstrated that a forceful and resourceful Secretary-General can create scope for quasi-independent action in a confused political environment. However, in situations where the major powers have a clear set of interests at stake in an issue, the United Nations, however resourceful the Secretary-General, is unlikely to be able to find an independent role unless it is in the interests of those powers for him to do so. The Gulf conflict was a case in point where the Secretary-General, Perez de Cuellar, did not play a major role because essentially the major United Nations actor was a member of the Security Council. Thus it was the United States that was taking the leading role in the crisis, leaving little room for the Secretary-General to play a part.

United Nations Security Council resolutions

The United Nations Security Council consists of fifteen members, of which five are permanent – Soviet Union, France, China, the United Kingdom and the United States – and ten are non-permanent, and these are elected by the General Assembly to serve for two years. At the time of the Iraqi invasion the non-permanent members were Canada, Colombia, Côte d'Ivoire, Cuba, Ethiopia, Finland, Malaysia, Romania, Yemen and Zaire.

During the crisis the Security Council passed twelve resolutions beginning with Resolution 660 in the early hours of 2 August 1990, which condemned the Iraqi invasion and ending with Resolution 678 on 29 November 1990, which authorised 'all necessary means' to ensure the implementation of Resolution 660 if it had not been complied with by 15 January 1991. The purpose of the first resolution (660) was essentially to define the invasion as a breach of international peace and security under Article 39[2] of the Charter and to place on record the demand of the Security Council that Iraq should withdraw from Kuwait and that the two parties should begin immediate attempts to resolve their dispute preferably within the context of the Arab League. This first resolution was a sort of holding operation which established the concern of the Security Council and signalled its intention to take some action. It had the effect of placing the issue on to the international agenda immediately without having to await agreement on what should be done about it, which was bound to take a little more time. In the event it was some four days before the second Security Council resolution (661) was passed, which imposed mandatory sanctions on Iraq and Kuwait covering all items except medical supplies and foodstuffs 'in humanitarian circumstances'.

The 'ethos' of the United Nations is for 'peaceful settlement' of disputes and for the peaceful implementation of its resolutions. The idea that the imposition of sanctions is inherently a peaceful solution to the problem of aggression belies the fact that sanctions are unlikely to be effective unless there is some mechanism to enforce compliance. This ultimately entails a willingness and an ability forcibly to prevent goods and materials from reaching and leaving the aggressor state. This implicit ethos of the United Nations very often puts the organisation in the position of willing the ends without providing the means for the achievement of their policies.

It is one thing to argue that sanctions can be an effective instrument of coercion and will achieve the desired objective of changing a state's behaviour. It is quite unrealistic, however, to expect a sanctions policy that is not effectively enforced to achieve that objective. Thus the question arose as to whether Resolution 661 imposing mandatory sanctions was anything more than an exhortation upon members to refrain from trading with Iraq and Kuwait or whether yet another specific resolution authorising the use of force to effectively blockade Iraq was necessary. The United States and Britain at least took the view throughout that in fact Article 51 of the Charter (the inherent right of individual and collective self-defence) (see Appendix IV) conferred their right to furnish Kuwait with whatever assistance they jointly decided was appropriate independently of specific and further Security Council authorisation. Indeed paragraph 9 of Resolution 661 declares that its provisions do not 'prohibit assistance to the legitimate government of Kuwait'; and it was on this basis that one or two naval interceptions had taken place by United States ships and even some shots fired to deter sanctions breaking. Nevertheless the United States for political reasons took the issue back to the Security Council after having to modify its previous reference to 'minimum force' to enforce sanctions to 'measures commensurate to the specific circumstances' (Resolution 665, 25 August). The sanctions provision was further strengthened on 25 September with the passing of Resolution 670 which extended the provisions of Resolution 661 to include all means of transport including aircraft.

Up to 29 November, when Resolution 678 was passed by the Security Council, the policy of the United Nations towards Iraq was one of condemning its behaviour and attempting to change that behaviour with the use of economic sanctions. But that was not the only source of coercion against Iraq. Parallel to the United Nations policy towards Iraq was the policy of the United States whose military preparations were being conducted within the provisions of the United Nations Charter but without the specific authorisation of the Security Council. Article 51 of the Charter allows the 'inherent right of individual and collective self-defence' which then takes place outside of the auspices of the United Nations. It was Resolution 678 which converted the United States policy of military coercion against Iraq under Article 51 into a United Nations policy of military coercion under Article 42, which allows 'such action. . . as may be necessary to maintain or restore international peace and security'(see Appendix IV). However, such a 'United Nations operation' under Article 42 would not have been possible had not the United States already taken action under article 51. This really points up the implausibility of the United Nations itself being able to exert effective military coercion if left to the playing out of its own ethos and its own timescale. If the military dimension of the response to the Iraqi invasion had not been brought into the picture until the end of November 1990, military action would effectively have been precluded and the Iraqis would have achieved their objective.

It could be said that the one act which brought Iraq and the United Nations into inevitable conflict was not so much the invasion itself but Iraq's annexation of Kuwait on 8 August 1990. This act entailed the elimination of Kuwait as a sovereign state and its incorporation as an integral part of Iraq. The implication for the United Nations if it acquiesced in that act was that it would no longer have a role in bringing about the peaceful settlement of a dispute between two sovereign members of the body. Any conflict going on there would be reinterpreted as being the internal affairs of Iraq and thus of no interest to the international body. Since this act was contrary to the fundamental principle of the acceptance of the sovereign independence of each member of the United Nations, an immediate response from the Security Council was imperative. The implication was that if one member's sovereign independence could be snuffed out without response, so could that of any other member. Thus the resolution (662) condemning the annexation and declaring it illegal was passed unanimously on 9 August, attracting the support of even the pro-Iraqi states.

Iraq's response was to begin the task of assimilating Kuwait 'from the inside' so to speak by changing the demographic composition of the Kuwaiti territory by moving Kuwaitis out of, and Iraqis into, the territory and to attempt to destroy all the civil records of the former population in order to bring about the *de facto* elimination of Kuwait. Security Council Resolution 674 of 29 October condemned this activity and affirmed Iraqi responsibility and liability for loss and injury to Kuwaitis and third-state nationals. Resolution 677 of 28 November followed this up by mandating the Secretary-General to accept for safekeeping a copy of the population register of Kuwait. The implication of this was that documentary records existed against which any future disappearances could be checked and Iraqi liability established.

Resolutions 664 (18 August) and 667 (16 September) related to the Iraqi treatment of third-state nationals, diplomatic personnel and diplomatic premises all of which was contrary to the Charter of the United Nations and to the Vienna Conventions on diplomatic immunity.

Voting on Security Council resolutions

Voting on non-procedural matters in the Security Council is by nine affirmative votes, including the concurring votes of the five permanent members. Here the term 'concurring' means an affirmative vote or an abstention; a non-concurring vote by a permanent member is a veto. Of the twelve resolutions five were passed by unanimous vote; one resolution (660) was passed 14–0 with the Yemen not participating in the vote; three were each passed 13–0 with two abstentions; one was passed 13–2; one was passed 14–1; and one was passed 12–2 with one abstention. The only two members to vote against any of the resolutions were Cuba and Yemen, who also accounted for all the abstentions except one. All the permanent members voted affirmatively on all the resolutions save one – that was Resolution 678 in which China abstained. Such a record of voting in the Security Council on a major security issue was unprecedented.

Of the five resolutions passed by unanimous vote, three related to Iraq's breaches of international law – specifically the annexation of Kuwait, the treatment of third-country nationals and the treatment of diplomatic personnel and property; one related to assistance to members suffering hardship as a result of imposing sanctions on Iraq; and one related to the Iraqi attempt to alter the demographic composition of the population of Kuwait. Of the three resolutions attracting the abstention of Cuba and Yemen, two related to the imposition and implementation of sanctions against Iraq, and one related to the treatment of third-country nationals, collection of information on Iraqi breaches of international law regarding those persons and the Iraqi liability for loss and injury as a result of such breaches. Two of the three resolutions attracting negative votes related respectively to the determination of 'humanitarian circumstances' that might warrant exceptions to the resolution on economic sanctions against Iraq, and the authorisation for the use of 'all necessary means' to restore peace and security to the area. The one resolution in which a negative vote by Cuba was not accompanied by a Yemeni one was 670, extending sanctions, to aircraft as well as sea and land transport. Though Yemen had abstained in the resolution imposing sanctions, she had by that time declared her intention to abide by the Security Council resolution.

THE INTERESTS OF THE MAJOR ACTORS IN THE SECURITY COUNCIL

The major actors of the crisis as far as the United Nations Security Council was concerned were firstly the five permanent members, without whose collaboration or acquiescence the United Nations could have taken very little action at all, and secondly two of the non-permanent members of the Security Council at the time, Yemen and Cuba, who were the chief proponents of a non-military solution to the problem. In this section American interests and actions will not be directly discussed since they form a large part of the discussion at many other points in this book. This section will discuss the interests of the other four permanent members, the Soviet Union, China, France and the United Kingdom, and the two pro-Iraqi non-permanent members Yemen and Cuba.

The Yemen and Cuba

Though Cuba and Yemen were the most persistent obstacles to unanimity in the Security Council, their stances were dictated by different motivations. Yemen found itself in a difficult situation being the only Arab member of the Security Council at the time and an ally of Iraq. Yemen had to tread the delicate path of maintaining its generally pro-Iraq stance without appearing to condone clear Iraqi contraventions of international law. Its main approach was to condemn the presence of western, and part-icularly American, forces in the region and advocate an Arab solution to the crisis; this of course despite the failure of Arab forums to prevent the Iraq–Kuwait dispute from spilling over into war in the first place. Yemen's failure to vote in the first resolution (660) condemning the Iraqi invasion was apparently a result of its representative not receiving instructions from the Yemeni government and was probably a measure of the difficult position it found itself in. But it is significant that even Iraq's staunchest supporter in the Security Council recorded only two negative votes – one (666) requiring a clear demonstration of any declared need of humanitarian exceptions to sanctions, and the other (678) 'authorising all necessary means' to ensure Iraqi compliance with Security Council resolutions. Yemen's ambassador to the United Nations was perhaps the most articulate advocate of a more moderate approach to the problem, but even he found it difficult to justify the more blatant of Iraq's contravention of international law.

Cuba on the other hand was more likely to have been motivated by a crude anti-Americanism and a definition of the crisis as a manifestation of western imperialism against a Third World state. The Cuban stance was perhaps the best guide to what a Soviet 'Brehznevite' stance might have been to the crisis. (Though of course it is unlikely that the invasion would have occurred at all in the Brehznev era.)

The Soviet Union

The most remarkable phenomenon was the near total unanimity of the permanent members of the Security Council. The key to this was the attitude of the Soviet Union. As has been argued elsewere in this book, it is likely that the changes in the Soviet Union since 1986 made the Iraqi invasion of Kuwait possible; but it also made possible the solidarity of the international response. What would have been a much more serious eventuality would have been if the changes in the Soviet Union had been sufficient to weaken Soviet restraint on Iraq but not sufficient to have allowed an American–Soviet collaboration in the United Nations Security Council to counter the invasion. Such a situation would have risked a serious east–west crisis and may well have provided the basis for an earlier and more successful coup against Gorbachev and the reform movement in the Soviet Union. It may be that the fortuitous presence together in the Soviet Union of

James Baker, the American Secretary of State, and Eduard Shevardnadze, the Soviet Foreign Minister, at the time of the invasion, pre-empted that situation. The uniformity of their reaction to the invasion enabled an initial common position which in retrospect can be seen to have gained a momentum (see Chapter 2). The Soviet Union was unequivocal in its condemnation of the Iraqi invasion and joined with the United States in calling for a world-wide ban on arms supplies for Iraq. However there is some evidence of a difference of view between Shevardnadze and other members of the Soviet government which was indicated by a subsequent distancing of the Soviet position from that of the United States.

There was a clear incentive and even desire for the Soviet leadership to cooperate with the United States in its United Nations diplomacy in the crisis. The process of reform that had been proceeding fitfully in the Soviet Union since Gorbachev came to power in 1986 required the support and understanding of the west in general and the United States in particular. The Soviet need for large-scale western aid to help to facilitate economic restructuring would encourage the abandonment of her old Cold War allies in favour of closer ties with the United States. However, a combination of the sheer difficulty of changing habits and the continued internal strength of the communist old guard injected a residual element of diffidence into Soviet crisis diplomacy. A genuine fear of a large-scale war close to her own southern borders and the necessity to placate to some extent internal opposition, particularly among the Soviet military, acted as a restraint (albeit in the event only marginal) on complete and unequivocal support for the United States. In addition it must be remembered that the region of Iraq and the Gulf is an area of legitimate Soviet security, economic and diplomatic interest – and that would be the case even outside of the context of the Cold War.

As a result of these factors the Soviet Union laid much more stress on sanctions as the means to effect an Iraqi withdrawal, and where the use of force was contemplated it was placed by the Soviet Union firmly within a United Nations context. A willingness to contemplate a military solution was indicated by Shevardnadze on 17 August when he made reference to the Security Council Military Staff Committee as the mechanism by which the United Nations could assume a military role.[3] There was clearly a Soviet fear that the United States might be tempted to take military action outside of the United Nations context, which it would not be able to condone.

Soviet diffidence about 'seeing the task through' was demonstrated by their frantic diplomacy (together with Iran) in the hiatus between the end of the deep air interdiction campaign and the opening of the ground war. The Soviet Union was motivated by a number of factors. One was no doubt a genuine desire to prevent a ground war which might prove to be very bloody and costly in lives and which moreover they would have been reluctant to have been associated with. Secondly it was an attempt to inject their influence, which had essentially been absent for the five weeks of the air campaign, back into the conflict – this time to be seen as a moderating influence. During this period they had had to defer to the United States (and her allies) and leave them to carry out the task entrusted to them by the Security Council. Thirdly the Soviet Union was anxious to limit the damage to its own legitimate influence in the region which was now in prospect of disappearing virtually completely in the face of an American military triumph in the region. If the Soviet Union could persuade the Iraqis to comply with United Nations resolutions even at this late stage, they could retain some influence in the region and prevent a situation where the United States would effectively have a free hand after a comprehensive defeat of Iraqi troops.

The potential consequences of an American victory and the downfall of Iraqi Ba'athism were of serious concern to the Soviet Union. Even during the Cold War Soviet and American interests were at one in wanting to prevent the spread of Islamic fundamentalism from Iran to other parts of the Middle East and to the Soviet republics of Central Asia. Both superpowers had seen Saddam Hussein, however obnoxious a regime he led, as a bulwark against Islamic fundamentalism. The uncertainty caused by the possibility of a political and military vacuum in Iraq following military defeat raised again, for the Soviet Union, the vulnerability of her own Muslims to fundamentalist influence and the potential for Muslim disaffection within the Soviet Union. President Gorbachev would have been particularly sensitive to this possibility given the problems he was then experiencing of holding both the Soviet Union and the communist political system together in the pre-Soviet coup period in early 1991. Even Gorbachev would no doubt have preferred the survival of Saddam Hussein to the possibility of Islamic fundamentalism in Baghdad. Indeed the Gulf crisis and the Gorbachev/Shevardnadze approach to it stimulated an attempt by the old guard of the KGB and the Soviet military to reassert their influence. The Soviet attempt to get Saddam Hussein off the hook before the ground war started can be seen in part to have been the response to demands by the Soviet communist old guard that Soviet interests in the region be protected against American power.

But in the conditions prevailing at that time the Soviet leadership had to walk the delicate path between rescuing both Saddam Hussein and the Soviet position in the Middle East on the one hand and on the other future relations with the United States upon which the very survival of an integrated Soviet Union depended. Ultimately Gorbachev was forced by his need for United States aid to compromise Soviet influence in the region, and refrain from presenting further obstacles to the pursuit of the ground war by the United States and the coalition forces. Had Saddam Hussein been more accommodating to the Soviet Union at this stage he could have enhanced Soviet weight in the United Nations diplomacy and indeed could have made it difficult for the Americans to launch the ground war. As has been suggested elsewhere in this book, it is likely that Gorbachev's role in the Gulf War was seen as a failure by the communist old guard in the Soviet Union and may be seen as the 'last straw' argument in favour of the attempted coup in August 1991.

China

If the cooperation (and even collaboration) between the United States and the Soviet Union was an important and distinctive feature of the Gulf conflict, an equally important requirement for America's Security Council diplomacy was the acquiesence, if not cooperation, of China. It would have been an irony indeed if the long-desired Soviet–American collaboration in the Security Council in the post-Cold War world had been stymied by a Chinese veto. In the event China voted affirmatively on every Resolution in the crisis except one – and that was the last, Resolution 678, authorising 'all necessary means'. Again this was a remarkable record given the history of antagonism between China and the United States and is explicable in terms of its position in a rapidly changing world.

The rapid economic and political changes together with the

incipient collapse of communism in the Soviet Union by 1990 had left China somewhat isolated. Not of course that there was any love lost between China and the Soviet Union since the dispute between them came to a head in 1962. Even if they disagreed profoundly on many issues – both ideological and practical – at least they were both 'anti-capitalist imperialist' and found a minimum degree of security in that situation. The changes brought about by Gorbachev, in particular his opting out of the Cold War and the de-escalation in Soviet–United States military confrontation, were interpreted by the Chinese as a sell out to capitalism. Ironically the Chinese had already embarked on economic reform some years earlier – indeed with some success. However, what the Chinese leadership could not tolerate was the political consequences of those economic reforms. The crucial relationship between economic freedom – represented by the market – and political freedom is something that the Chinese communist old guard found very hard to accept. This led to the very public demonstration of the Chinese communist leadership's refusal to countenance political reform seen in the Tiananmen Square massacre of 1989. This event damaged China's relations with the west, and her cooperation with the United States in the Security Council Gulf conflict resolutions was a manifestation of China's desire not to rekindle memories of Tiananmen and not to halt the improvement in relations with the west that had gradually taken place since that event.

Another factor encouraging the Chinese to adopt a low profile during the Gulf crisis was the ambiguity in her traditional dual claim to be on the one hand a great power (if not a superpower) and on the other the leader of the Third World. Though Iraq itself is seen as a Third World state, so is Kuwait, and it would have been difficult for China to be seen to be supporting Iraq against a fellow Third World Arab state, particularly when the majority of the Third World governments opposed Iraq's actions – some even sending troops to join the United Nations coalition force (see Appendices I and V). To have exercised a veto in the Security Council resolutions would have placed China at the centre of events and would have focused criticism against her as the major obstacle to a United Nations response to the crisis. She would have derived very little benefit from such a stance and would have alienated those western powers with whom she wanted to improve both economic and political relations. Even one or two direct attempts by China to bring about some diplomatic resolution met with an intransigent Iraq.

France

France has a long-standing interest in the Middle East based, like Britain's, upon her colonial association with the region. Moreover, President Mitterand claimed a 'long standing' friendship with Iraq, which had been manifestly demonstrated in France's support for Iraq in its war with Iran. It was upon that basis that it reserved the right to criticise Iraq for its invasion and annexation of Kuwait. Traditionally suspicious of an Anglo-Saxon alliance, France was careful to distance herself from the Anglo-American collaboration and pursued what might be called a 'semi-detached' policy of being involved with the United Nations Coalition but nevertheless not necessarily constrained from conducting its own independent diplomacy. This with a view not only, perhaps quite legitimately, in claiming a degree of influence in Baghdad that the Americans could not claim but also undoubtedly with a view to hedging its bets and putting itself in a position to resume friendly, and economically beneficial, relations just as soon as conditions permitted.

Indeed France came in for some criticism for keeping her aircraft carrier *Clemenceau* in the Red Sea beyond the range where her aircraft could actually reach Iraqi targets. Such a policy is to some extent explicable in terms of its possible diplomatic benefits; the very presence of an aircraft carrier in the region was symbolic of her condemnation of Iraqi behaviour but its lack of military credibility a signal to Iraq that France believed that a non-military solution to the crisis was preferable. It was conceivable that France was the only possible plausible candidate for a last-minute diplomatic effort during the last twenty-four to forty-eight hours before the launch of the air offensive. Once hostilities had commenced, however, the French took an effective (though perhaps still slightly ambivalent) role in the military operations and indeed played a significant part in the great western flanking movement which encircled Iraqi troops when the land war began.

Britain

Britain also has close historical associations and interests in the Middle East as a whole and in the Gulf region in particular. Britain's role in the history of both Iraq and Kuwait is discussed in more detail in Chapters 1 and 5. Having been previously involved in ensuring the integrity of Kuwait against Iraq and having close relations with Saudi Arabia and the Gulf states, Britain had a clear interest in Iraq's invasion and annexation. Notwithstanding Mrs Thatcher's role in shoring up a 'wobbly' President Bush in the initial stages of the crisis, Britain's stand with the United States was probably more important politically for the United States than militarily. Though the British military commitment was an overt demonstration of that political support, it should be said that the British performed important military tasks at sea, in the air and on land.

Britain had clear political and economic interests in the crisis which determined her response. Nevertheless there is little doubt that the United Kingdom is a 'natural' ally of the United States. It is not necessary to invest too much sentiment in the idea of the 'special relationship', but on pragmatic grounds for both parties the relationship is always signficant – whether or not it is symmetrical or equally important for both parties, and even though it might fluctuate in intensity. The two countries often see the world through similar lenses because they share a common language and to some extent a common political culture – or at least a common subscription to basic political values. Moreover, in a real and deliberate sense the United States has taken over the British global role – the role was virtually 'bequeathed' to the United States by the United Kingdom in the 1920s,[4] though she was not prepared to accept that role until after the Second World War; and now there is little that she can do to avoid it. To some extent Britain's close adherence to American foreign policy can be seen as a means of still maintaining a more prominent international role than might otherwise be the case.

However that does not mean that Britain will support the United States willy nilly. For example, the United Kingdom refused support for America in the Vietnam War and neither did she support the United States invasion of Grenada and was critical of her activities in Central America. Moreover, though Britain tends to support America's stance on major security issues, there may be much less common ground over economic issues and matters of free trade where Britain's interests lie more across the Channel than across the Atlantic. Nevertheless in British solidarity with the United States in the Gulf conflict there was no doubt an element of repayment for important (even critical) American help to Britain in the Falklands War of 1982. This is not to say that British support for the United States over the Gulf crisis would have materialised merely as a debt to the United States (as some have alleged) if there had not been genuine British interests at stake in the Gulf. As a member of the United Nations Security Council the United Kingdom had similar interests in confronting this breach of international law as the United States herself.

THE MILITARY STAFF COMMITTEE

The Military Staff Committee, composed of the Chiefs of Staff of the five permanent members, is one of the formal organs of the Security Council designed to give effect to the provisions of Article 43 of the Charter regarding the maintenance of international peace and security. The body was conceived as a mechanism for giving the United Nations its own military force. However, it has lain dormant since 1946 owing to the failure to agree the arrangements for the commitment of troops to such a body and how they would be deployed and controlled.

Though the suspicion and antagonism between the Soviet Union and the United States no doubt seriously contributed to this failure to agree, the central problem for the idea of the United Nations having its own military force to carry out the resolutions of the Security Council is precisely the reluctance of members to commit their own troops to a force commanded perhaps by the nationals of another country, and in circumstances over which they might have little control. That reluctance is not only a manifestation of the Cold War, it is inherent in the idea itself. States are content to contribute troops to peacekeeping forces whose function is to act as a buffer between forces who have already agreed to stop fighting. However, few states would be willing to commit large scale military equipment and their own nationals to fight a war in a force over which they may have little control, and where there may not be complete confidence in the military competence of some commanders. Thus there is no reason to believe that the Military Staff Committee will be less dormant after the Cold War than it was during it. It is extremely unlikely that a military operation on the scale of the Gulf War could ever be mounted under the auspices of the Military Staff Committee.

WAS THE UNITED STATES USING THE UNITED NATIONS FOR ITS OWN PURPOSES?

This was the central reason why, if there had to be resort to a military solution, it had to be conducted and led essentially by one powerful member of the Security Council under its general 'authorisation', albeit with the active support of some of its members. This situation inevitably led to the questioning of the role of the United States in the conduct both of the crisis diplomacy and of the military action when it came. Was the operation to be defined as a United Nations operation with the United States acting as its agent, or was it essentially a unilateral American operation using the United Nations to legitimate its actions so to speak? The problem is a real one and would be the same whatever state was in a position of leadership. The issue points up a fundamental problem of whether the United Nations can ever be 'autonomous'. The United Nations is essentially a reflection of the political forces in the international community and, most centrally, of the mutual accommodation or lack of it between the major powers in the system. Thus independent military action on the part of the United Nations is unlikely ever to be a possibility, since it has no unique territory or population to fight for. It has only become an issue now, forty-six years after its formation, because the Cold War has kept the possibility of United Nations action under Article 43 (the maintenance and restoration of peace and security) firmly off the agenda. But the prospect of agreement and collaboration among the permanent members of the Security Council has paradoxically revealed the intrinsic limitations of such a concept.

So whatever the motivations of the United States its emergence as the only state with sufficient military power to effect a military solution meant that its role was bound to be an ambiguous one. Thus the answer to the question as to who was using whom must be that it was a bit of both. There was little doubt that the United States had its own agenda and interests independent of the United Nations. There was also little doubt that its interests and those of the principles of the United Nations overlapped such that serving one would serve the other. On the other hand the pursuit of American interests through the United Nations was not an act of altruism on the part of the United States. Careful United Nations diplomacy was a precondition of American action, and in that sense the need for the United States to work through the Security Council acted to some extent as a constraint. There was some clear indication of a degree of conflict between the United States and the United Nations Secretary-General, Perez de Cuellar, in the latter's persistent emphasis on peaceful resolution and the United States pursuit of a coercive strategy against Iraq which involved the possibility of military action.

An example of this was, during August 1990, Perez de Cuellar's repeated dissociation of the United Nations from the United States view that Resolution 661 gave legal authority to impose sanctions by force if necessary. Similar caution with regard to the use of force to impose sanctions was expressed by the Soviet Union, France and China. Indeed the United States was forced to modify its reference to 'minimum use of force' and replace it by 'measures commensurate to the specific circumstances' in Resolution 665, which was passed on 25 August. However, once having obtained United Nations backing, its position was immeasurably strengthened. Though it can be strongly argued that there was sufficient authority under Article 51 to take military action to force an Iraqi withdrawal and that specific Security Council authorisation was not necessary, nevertheless the United States could plainly see that such authorisation was politically necessary if not legally required. In the event the securing of Security Council authorisation (in Resolution 678) formed the final plank in the American coercive strategy against Iraq. The United States could then be seen to be implementing specific Security Council resolutions using means that had received specific Security Council authorisation.

The United Nations on the other hand could not take action without the United States. If the United States had not taken on the leadership role both in United Nations diplomacy and in the use of its own military resources then it is doubtful if the United Nations could have succeeded in bringing effective action to bear against Iraq at all. The relationship was one of mutual dependence from which both benefited. The extent to which that benefit was an equal one is a subject that will be discussed in the final chapter of this book, but it is likely that the United States got more out of it than the United Nations as an institution. It is conceivable that the United States could have served its own interests in the crisis without the United Nations – albeit at considerable political cost. It is much less conceivable that the United Nations could have served its interests in the matter without the action and leadership of the United States.

WAS THE CONCLUSION OF THE GULF WAR A "VICTORY FOR THE UNITED NATIONS?"

This is an important question because the future status of the United Nations is at stake and many expectations will be invested in it. From that point of view it may be important that it is regarded as a victory for the United Nations but whether that actually exaggerates its role or misrepresents what actually happened is perhaps a matter for investigation and debate. The most plausible conclusion is that it really is victory for United States diplomacy in the United Nations and a victory for United States military power and efficiency which was put at the disposal, not of the United Nations but of the resolutions that it passed.

Insofar as the United Nations acted in this crisis it acted as a result of the mobilisation of diplomatic activity and pressure by the United States in the United Nations and backed it up with its military power. Without the leadership of the United States in this respect it is highly unlikely that there would have been such firm United Nations action. The United Nations as a body is not independent nor does it have an independent interest or capacity to act. Thus it is of course unrealistic to expect action by the United Nations but rather action through the United Nations. The natural tendency of the United Nations is for indecision, prevarication, and action in accordance with the lowest common denominator. The fact that the Gulf crisis prompted uncharacteristic qualities of action, determination and clear sightedness was due to a particular constellation of forces at the time.

A number of factors contributed to the conditions or setting, in which the United Nations could take successful action. One was the clarity of the issue in hand (i.e. an unamibguous act of aggression), the resolution and skill of United States diplomacy and power, the tangible support that the United States managed to get together (especially Britain, Egypt, Saudi Arabia and Syria), the crucial support of the Soviet Union in the Security Council – particularly in the diplomatic phase when Shevardnadze was still Soviet Foreign Minister, the fact that, again crucially, China had something to gain in its own terms and especially in its relations with the United States and the west, which determined its acquiescence in the Security Council. But it must be said that even with these very powerful factors in its favour there were times when the United Nations coalition looked somewhat rocky – particularly with the apparent change of attitude of the Soviet Union after the resignation of Eduard Shevard-nadze in December 1990 and some wobbling in Europe (Germany, Italy and Spain all at one stage or another during the crisis showed a reluctance to contemplate the use of force to resolve it).

The point to be made very strongly here is that despite the fact that it was dealing with the most unambiguous act of brutal ag-gression since 1945, it was still very difficult to manage the United Nations system in order to get a challenging response and to maintain and escalate that response. Moreover, it took the most powerful nation in the world to lead the United Nations diplomacy and carry out the military mandate of the United Nations. Less clear-cut cases, or cases in which the major powers have more clearly conflicting interests, may not produce such results. The point is that the responsibility for maintaining international security cannot just 'be given over to the United Nations'. The role for the United Nations, as ever, is as the forum within which the diplomacy for the settlement and resolution of disputes can take place, and through which more overt political, economic and even military action can take place. Even in the 'new world order' it is very unlikely that the United Nations will itself have an independent military capability which it can use to serve its collective purposes, primarily because it rarely has collective purposes. It will still require powerful independ-ent states to take such action on its behalf. The Gulf military operation is an example, *par excellence*, of an extremely well co-ordinated military coalition composed, not of military equals, but under the professional military leadership of the most powerful state in the world, which contributed the overwhelming proportion of military personnel and equipment. It is likely that any such operation in the future will have to be conducted in a similar way. But it may well be that such a constellation of coincident interests will rarely occur again. It may be vesting too much hope and expectation in the United Nations if it is thought that the Gulf operation is a precedent for the future.

Chapter 4

The diplomacy of crisis

Crisis is the term used to describe a particular type of international interaction between states. It constitutes an identifiable pattern of interaction with particular characteristics such that all crises between states will show the same structure, similar processes and behaviours. The implication is that it is a category of inter-state behaviour and that though each crisis is unique in the ultimate sense, in that each will occur within its own historical and structural context, all crises show sufficiently similar characteristics to be recognised as belonging to a distinct type of phenomenon.

There are two important implications of these claims. One is that since in many respects all crises demonstrate the same features it should be possible to predict, within limits, the playing out of any particular crisis. The other is that the conduct of or involvement in one crisis should give pointers to the successful conduct of subsequent crises. So the understanding of the structure and dynamics of crisis situations will lead to prescriptive 'lessons' as to how to deal with future situations of the same nature.

Thus the crisis literature is not only concerned with understanding the nature of crises but with understanding how they are managed by the protagonists; and moreover it is claimed that prescriptive rules have been developed that will enable more successful 'crisis management'. By what criteria success is to be judged is an important issue here and one which will be dealt with later in the context of the Gulf crisis.

THE CHARACTERISITCS OF CRISIS

Interaction between states is said[1] to be characterised by the following:

1 Highly intense bargaining which may be explicit or implicit. In other words such bargaining may not involve diplomatic negotiation but may consist of declaratory, symbolic or rhetorical interaction conducted 'at a distance'. Indeed diplomacy itself may be conducted through 'actions' rather than words. The type of interaction may vary from phase to phase of the crisis and indeed face-to-face negotiation may constitute a very short period of the crisis often just before 'crisis termination'.

2 An explicit time-frame. In other words, the crisis has a 'beginning' caused by an identifiable event, and it is anticipated that it will have an end. That is not to say it will be short or that the 'end' of the crisis can be specified. However, an important feature is that the necessity for an end to the crisis may be a crucial dimension of the nature of the crisis interaction. For example, the time factor might be more important to one party than the other and in this case the timing of the diplomacy and attempts to alter the time-frame of the crisis will constitute important crisis 'instruments'. As will be seen later, this was a particular feature of the Gulf crisis.

3 Perceived high values at stake. Both sides in a crisis will be motivated in their behaviour by their respective beliefs that very highly valued interests are threatened. It may be that in the process of the playing out of crisis diplomacy one side has to be persuaded (implicitly or explicitly) to redefine those perceived interests and perhaps forced to demote them from the level at which they have to be defended by going to war. It may be that those values have been overestimated at the beginning and the crisis serves as a mechanism for revaluing interests.

4 A situation of high risk and danger. Parties to a crisis will typically be negotiating their way between the risks and dangers of war and the risks and dangers of losing highly valued interests. Elimination of risk and avoidance of danger are thus high-priority objectives of the parties.

5 One of those dangers (to one side at least) is that crisis usually occurs where there is a potential for radical change either to the status and interests of the participant(s) or to the environment in which they exist or both. Thus a potential change in the balance of power in any region will be a potent source of crisis.

6 Thus a high probability or possibility of war is a typical charac-

teristic of crisis (whether it is a necessary characteristic is open to disagreement).

7 Following on from all the above characteristics, crisis is a situation in which the 'natural' conditions of the international environment, that is uncertainty and complexity are substantially increased. Indeed as Schelling points out 'the essence of crisis is unpredictability'.[2] The higher the degree of unpredictability and complexity, the higher the degree of risk and danger.

GOALS AND OBJECTIVES IN CRISIS

Clearly the sort of goals and objectives the participants in a crisis have will determine the way they conduct their crisis diplomacy. The two broad objectives of both sides in a crisis are to protect or further their respective vital interests at stake in the conflict and to avoid war. But of course the condition that makes a crisis in the first place means that these two objectives are incompatible. Thus, 'Each party faces the uncomfortable choice between preserving its politico-strategic interests by standing firm at the risk of war, or ensuring peace by sacrificing important interests'.[3] The outcome of crisis is a manifestation of the calculation made by each side of their respective incentives for compromising perceived interests on the one hand and of the strength of the disincentives to war on the other. Because much of the crisis literature has developed in the context of the Cold War confrontation between the superpowers, there has been a disporportionate emphasis on the avoidance of war as the prime objective of crisis diplomacy. So overwhelming was the disincentive to war in superpower crises that the expectation was that interests would have to be compromised and that mechanisms such as 'face saving' formulas would be needed to facilitate compromise. This is because much of the literature is essentially a description of just one superpower crisis, the Cuban missile crisis, which has become something of an archetype. This has proved to be a rather distorted guide to the conduct and development of the Gulf conflict, as it was of the Falklands conflict before it. If war is to be avoided, at least one of the parties has to be persuaded that his 'perceived interests' are not worth a war. If on the other hand the priority of both sides is the furtherance and protection of their self-defined interests then war is almost inevitable.

It is also because of the superpower context of the crisis

literature that there has been such an emphasis on crisis management. This is a reflection of the view of the Cold War as a sort of 'adversarial collaboration' in which an implicit principle was that the competition must be conducted within limits – that is, short of war. Thus there was a sense in which crises had to be a sort of implicit cooperation between the superpowers where their joint objective was to 'manage' their interaction in order to avoid war. However, the two major crises/conflicts that have arisen most recently outside the superpower context – the Falklands conflict and the Gulf conflict – have shown that in the absence of the nuclear dimension, and in situations where there are no implicit common conventions regarding crisis diplomacy, the restraints on escalation and war are much less effective. The characteristic feature of both of these crises has not been crisis management but a more overt and less restrained 'coercive diplomacy'.

Given the conditions of crisis described above, the chief characteristic of crisis diplomacy is coercion – that is, the threat of violence to compel the other party to act, or refrain from acting, in a certain way. This raises the problem of control in crisis. One of the objectives of the conduct of crisis is to avoid uncontrolled escalation of tension and action towards war. The objective is not to avoid escalation altogether – indeed deliberate but controlled escalation of tension and pace in crisis interaction is one of the mechanisms of coercion.

THE PRECIPITATION OF CRISES

It is important to recognise that the act that precipitates a crisis is not the initial act but the resistance or reaction to that act.[4] An act of 'conflict behaviour'[5] will not entail a crisis unless another state resists it in some way. Thus it was not the Iraqi invasion that created the crisis (though it may have caused it) but the US reaction to it. Thus it is the reactive state that effectively defines the crisis. The initial element of surprise has the effect of putting the reactive state on the diplomatic defensive from the beginning. This will be further referred to in the discussion of who sets the diplomatic pace of a crisis and the fact that the Americans were fighting a rearguard diplomatic action for most of the crisis phase.

Another feature of the Gulf crisis which helps to explain to some extent the dynamics of the interaction was its asymmetry. This was seen not only in the asymmetry of power between the two sides – the sheer size and power of America versus the 'weakness' of a Third World, underdeveloped state. An asymmetry was established right from the beginning in that the precipitating act of the Iraqis was an act of aggression – that is, the actual use of military force (as opposed to the threat of its use) was the initial act. The significance of this in crisis terms is that in a sense the war threshold had already been breached. The peaceful resolution of crisis requires that there is a certain initial 'equality' or symmetry between the two sides and the implicit assumption is that the perceived asymmetry that has arisen as a result of the initial act can be regularised by a non-violent 'adjustment' of some kind. Thus whatever the initial act, it is assumed that it does not require military action to resist it. Indeed with this sort of crisis it requires a specific act to start a war. However, an initial act of aggression requires a military response unless something happens to prevent it. In this sort of crisis there is an inbuilt imperative to war which can only be avoided if both sides recognise it and take specific avoiding action. A crisis in which the initial act is an act of aggression requires a specific act to stop a war. This is another structural feature of the Gulf crisis which helps to explain its dynamics and the apparent inexorability of the trend towards war.

Indeed it could be further held that the Gulf 'conflict' did not constitute a 'crisis' at all but may be described as a war from the initial act of aggression to the cessation of hostilities. The Gulf conflict is similar to the Falklands conflict in this respect. In both cases the period of apparent 'crisis' was merely that period between the initial act of aggression and the military response to it. The gap was dictated by two factors: – one was the sheer logistic inability of responding with military force immediately; the other was the need of the 'responding powers' to fashion an international and domestic political climate in which a military response could be seen to be appropriate. These 'crises' contained an inherent dynamic towards war which few people recognised (least of all apparently the leaders of the respective initiatory states.)

THE INITIAL ACT OF AGGRESSION

The two major questions to pose about the initial Iraqi act of aggression are:

1 To what extent did the Iraqis perceive the United States as an 'enemy' or at least a potential enemy? (It is commonly held that crises occur typically between governments which identify each other as enemies or at least potential enemies.)[6]
2 To what extent did the Iraqi leadership itself recognise that the act would be perceived by the United States as one to which it had to respond thus converting it into a crisis?

With regard to point 1 above it might be said that crises between mutually identified enemies are perhaps less dangerous than those that break out between states whose relations might be described as 'ambiguous'. States who share a mutual perception of each other as an enemy also share a mutual caution in their dealings with each other for fear of precipitating a crisis. By no means could Saddam Hussein's regime in Baghdad be described as a friend of the United States; but neither could the two states be regarded as enemies. There was clearly no moral or ideological affinity between the two. The US attitude towards Iraq has been dictated by *realpolitik* related to their perceived interests in the area *vis-à-vis* the Arab–Israeli dispute, their more clearly identified enemy, Iran and their previous Cold War conflict with the Soviet Union. The Iraqi attitude was no less pragmatic in playing off the interests of the respective external powers against each other whilst pursuing a number of regional interests which would not necessarily be to the liking of any of them.

But it is that very ambiguity in the status of Iraqi–US relations which might have given rise to misperception and miscalculation. It is difficult to determine if Saddam Hussein's invasion of Kuwait resulted from calculation or miscalculation. In the light of subsequent evidence it seems clear that Saddam identified the United States as an interested party in the matter of Kuwait; it is less clear whether both sides recognised that Iraqi action would of necessity entail an American response. So the question arises as to whether the crisis was brought about by negligence – by the failure of both sides to define sufficiently clearly the extent to which their respective behaviours had importance for the other.

There are only two possibilities: either Saddam miscalculated and underrated America's response; or he calculated correctly and a direct American response was part of those calculations together with an assessment that such a response could be coped with. It has been argued elsewere in this book that a miscalculation is not a plausible explanation, despite the well-known saga of the Glaspie interview. Saddam Husssein could not have expected the United States to stand by and watch without demur the elimination of a sovereign member of the United Nations. Moreover, his sub-sequent behaviour in the crisis when the US reaction was known gives absolutely no indication whatever that the Iraqis believed they had made a mistake. Indeed they moved very rapidly to consolidate their gains. It is more likely that the calculation was that the risk could be taken and that the Americans would be constrained in the extent of their response by domestic and international political circumstances. What the Iraqis probably did not calculate was the solidarity of the global opposition to their invasion and annexation of Kuwait. More particularly the Iraqis underestimated the extent of Arab opposition to the invasion.

Having said that, there are precedents for America's failure to make explicit its interests and being forced to do so only when specific action is taken by another state. The North Korean invasion of South Korea in 1950 is a case in point (see Chapter 3). The question is not whether the Gulf War was avoidable – the thesis of this book is that once the invasion had taken place it probably was not. The more important question is to what extent Iraq's invasion of Kuwait was preventable – that is, could or should it have been predicted and if so could anything have been done to deter Saddam Hussein from taking such action? This issue is discussed in more detail in Chapters 2 and 8 but here a number of clarifying statements can be made. Firstly, it is likely that inform-ation was available at the time that with hindsight can be said to have indicated Saddam Hussein's intentions. Secondly, similar information and indications had been present on previous occasions without being followed by an invasion. Thirdly, Am-bassador Glaspie's apparent declaration of US 'indifference' to the dispute with Kuwait cannot be construed as a 'invitation' to annex Kuwait; rather Glaspie's point was to convey America's 'neutrality' in Iraq's border dispute with Kuwait (after all there was *some* justice in it). Fourthly, for signals to be accurately received they have to be accurately sent. Fifthly, the Iraq–American relationship was sufficiently ambiguous as to make accurate interpretation of signals from both sides almost impossible.

FACTORS THAT DETERMINED THE US RESPONSE TO THE IRAQI INVASION

What does have to be explained is why America found herself assuming the initiative in responding to the Iraqi invasion given the fact that the two countries could not be regarded as 'enemies' in the usual sense (such as, for example the United States and the Soviet Union were during the Cold War), and that there were few if any issues over which they were in direct contention (unlike the United Kingdom and Argentina over the Falkland Islands). Perhaps the first thing that needs to be said is that given her immense independent power the United States was the only country that could respond. If America had decided not to respond it is almost certain that there would have been no response – at least no response that was likely to effect an Iraqi withdrawal.

However, having said that, the factors determining America's response were indirect rather than direct, related as much to her status and 'responsibilities' as a global power as to the threat to her vital and direct national interests. Perhaps the main determinant of US response was the implication of not responding. As has been argued elsewhere in this book, very often states are motivated in their actions by the necessity to avoid the consequences of inaction rather than because there is a 'positive' reason for taking action. Oil was certainly a factor but was only one among others and even then its importance lay not so much in the American demand for energy as in the oil-dependence of the world economy as a whole. But especially important was the dependence of Europe and Japan on Middle Eastern oil. Another oil crisis for Europe and Japan would eventually affect the US economy itself. So the American interest in the 'oil factor' was as much to do with its macro-economic significance as to the amount of American corporate money directly invested in the Kuwaiti oil-fields.

The two other major reasons related more directly to America's political and strategic interests in the region and to the potential American role in the future world security order in the aftermath of the Cold War. The Iraqi invasion and annexation of Kuwait represented a change in the balance of power in the Gulf region and hence in the Middle East as a whole. Certainly as a major adversary of Israel any Iraqi expansionist moves would expect an American interest. But even in the absence of the Israeli factor

America would have a clear interest in ensuring the integrity of the western-oriented Arab states in the Gulf region, including Kuwait and Saudi Arabia. It was the implied Iraqi threat to Saudi Arabia that made an American response inevitable – notwithstanding the British prime minister's alleged chiding of the American president that it was not a time for 'wobbling'.[7] An enduring American self-interest is a more likely explanation of America's response to the Iraqi invasion than the chivvying of a British prime minister.

The longer-term 'global' context would also have been an important dimension of America's perception of Iraqi actions. What might be termed the 'loneliness of the single global policeman' syndrome will no doubt have been a consideration in the analysis and planning of the American crisis decision-makers. The breakdown in the post-war global balance of power between the 'east' and 'west' entails the relaxation of the superpower restraints on Third World client states and a potential for more violent and coercive behaviour by a number of regimes in this category. American inaction in response to Iraq's invasion would have risked the message being received (even if it had not intentionally been sent) by many of these regimes that similar action by them in the future would not bring forth an American reaction. So the principle of *pour decourager les autres* would have been an important reason for the United States to be seen to be taking action even though she ensured it was in the context of the United Nations. It was in this context also that an American 'victory' was inevitable. A future world security order based upon a *pax americana* would require a clear demonstration in the first post-Cold War crisis of the American ability and willingness to take action. An American 'defeat' in the Gulf crisis would have had far more serious consequences than the American 'defeat' in Vietnam (both for the United States and for the future system of international order), which to some extent explains the American determin- ation to pursue its objectives in the crisis to a conclusion. (Fig 4.1 summarises the reasons for the US response in diagrammatic form.)

THE STRUCTURE OF THE GULF CRISIS

Most international crises demonstrate a similar 'structure' or pattern of phases. A convenient way of conceptualising this general pattern is shown in Figure 4.2.[8] Time is shown on the

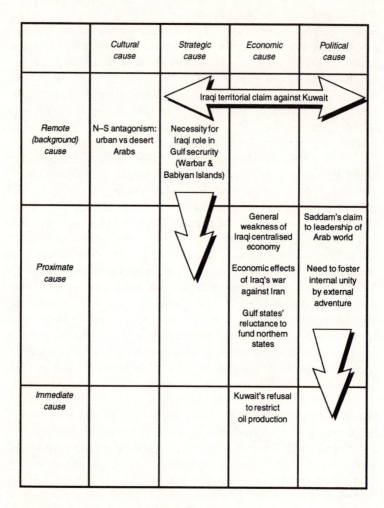

	Cultural cause	Strategic cause	Economic cause	Political cause
Remote (background) cause	N–S antagonism: urban vs desert Arabs	Necessity for Iraqi role in Gulf security (Warbar & Babiyan Islands)		
Proximate cause			General weakness of Iraqi centralised economy Economic effects of Iraq's war against Iran Gulf states' reluctance to fund northern states	Saddam's claim to leadership of Arab world Need to foster internal unity by external adventure
Immediate cause			Kuwait's refusal to restrict oil production	

Figure 4.1 Reasons for the US response

horizontal axis and degree of tension on the vertical axis; the dotted line shows the level of tension which might be regarded as the crisis threshold. Activity below the crisis threshold shows normal pre-crisis behaviour and diplomatic interaction. The rising of tension to breach the 'crisis threshold' requires not only the initial action by one party but a resistant response by the other party. It is the response to the initial action that creates the crisis;

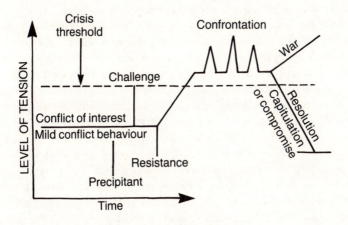

Figure 4.2 The structure of international crises
Source: G. H. Snyder and P. Diesing, *Conflict among Nations*,
(Princeton, NJ: Princeton University Press, 1977).

in this respect it is the 'responder' that defines the crisis – the
initial action is defined by the responder as one which challenges
or threatens some aspect of its range of vital interests. Whether the
initial action is intended to elicit such a response or whether it is
recognised by the initiator that such an action will require a
response from the other party, is not clear. In the discussion above
it is suggested that it is not necessary for the parties to be
acknowledged 'enemies' for a crisis to occur; an ambiguous relationship where there is uncertainty as to the respective interests
and intentions is just as likely to lead to crisis and indeed one in
which constraints on action are weaker and thus where the
dangers of uncontrolled escalation are greater.

Interaction above the crisis threshold is characterised by
fluctuating tension as actions are taken or declarations made
which appear to further escalate or de-escalate the trend towards
violent conflict. The 'point of no return' is reached where there is
a turning-point (in the medical sense it will be the crisis point in
the development of an illness which will determine either the
recovery of the patient or his demise) in which the crisis either
further escalates into war or de-escalates into resolution, either in
the capitulation of one side or in mutual compromise.

Figure 4.3 shows an application of this general model to the
Gulf crisis, indicating the breach of the crisis threshold as a result
of the American resistance to Iraq's invasion demonstrated by the
sending of the initial contingent of troops to Saudi Arabia on 7
August. The period up to that point may be regarded as the
'post-invasion pre-crisis' phase. This was the brief period of three
or four days in which the Iraqis quickly consolidated their military
position in Kuwait whilst the initial formal and symbolic responses
from the international community began to take place. During
this pre-crisis phase the United States had emerged as a coord-
inator of a global response to the invasion with President Bush
encouraging a number of major countries to freeze Iraqi and
Kuwait assets and ban oil imports from Iraq and Kuwait, and
instituted mandatory sanctions against Iraq in Security Council
Resolution 661. The escalation of tension to breach the crisis
threshold was sustained by further Iraqi actions in the first few
days after the invasion – for example, the moving of Iraqi troops to

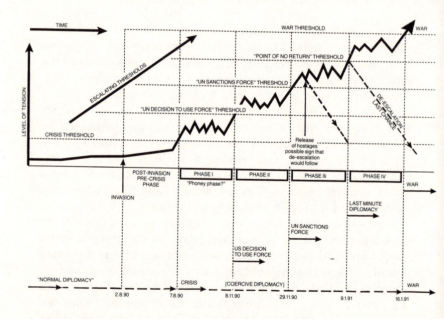

Figure 4.3 The structure of the Gulf crisis

the Kuwait–Saudi Arabian border on 3 August, the seizure of thirty-five British servicemen in Kuwait, the setting up of a new Kuwaiti government composed of Iraqis rather than Kuwaitis and the announcement of the annexation of Kuwait on 8 August.

But perhaps the most significant indication of the eventual outcome that occurred in this pre-crisis phase was the almost immediate joint US–Soviet statement calling for an Iraqi withdrawal. It was this unfamiliar US–Soviet 'solidarity' that just about survived the exigencies of the six-month crisis and war that really determined the eventual Iraqi defeat.

A blow by blow account of the development of the crisis is not possible here but it is important to give an impression of the overall structure of the crisis. It is possible to determine a number of intermediate thresholds between the crisis threshold and the outbreak of war itself. Within the general fluctuation of tension as the crisis progressed, three major points can be distinguished, each of which made it progressively more difficult to de-escalate the trend towards a violent resolution. These intermediate thresholds can be seen to delimit four phases of the crisis up to the beginning of the air war on 16 January 1991.

Given the discussion earlier that suggested that the crisis began not with the Iraqi invasion but with the United States response to it, it is contended here that the crisis threshold was crossed not with the 'generalised' responses to the invasion described above but with the ordering of American ground troops and combat aircraft to Saudi Arabia on 7 August. The committing of American troops to Saudi Arabia and the Iraqi annexation of Kuwait can be seen as the two actions taken by the respective parties which served to commit them to mutually incompatible values and interests and thus identified them as the principle opposing actors in the crisis.

The first phase of the crisis can in some ways be regarded as the 'phoney phase'. It was essentially the phase during which the Iraqis took actions which served to communicate their determination to stay in Kuwait and in which the Americans and her close ally the United Kingdom had to consolidate international opinion against that action. It was a period during which Allied coercive pressure on Iraq lacked credibility because it lacked a time-scale and it had not specified the consequences of the failure of the Iraqis to withdraw from Kuwait. This was partly because the American administration was not certain how far it was prepared to go in getting the Iraqis out of Kuwait and it was not certain how far politically it was possible to go in terms both of its domestic constituency and in terms of the international community. The continuation of such a lack of clarity and credibility of its intentions risked a diplomatic defeat for the Americans.

The 'low pressure' strategy adopted by the Americans during this phase was thus partly making a virtue of necessity and partly the required ground-laying of a more offensive coercive strategy in the next phase of the crisis. The major element of coercion in this low-pressure strategy was the imposition of sanctions. In terms of the structure of the crisis sanctions served a number of purposes. Firstly they a served symbolic function – at least something was being done to exert pressure on Iraq. Secondly, and perhaps more cynically, the imposition of sanctions, whether effective or not, served to ease the collective conscience of the United Nations and in any case, from the point of view of the leaders of the opposition to Iraq, were a necessary political precursor to make acceptable more intense pressure later on. It might be going too far to suggest that sanctions were essentially a cosmetic, but it was clear from the beginning, despite views to the contrary by some quite prominent foreign-affairs observers, that economic sanctions would not be enough to pressure Saddam Hussein to withdraw his forces from Kuwait. (An elaboration of this argument can be seen in Chapter 8.)

The major practical functions of the reliance on sanctions as a coercive instrument during this 'phoney phase' were firstly that time was required to assemble a credible military force for use if necessary, and secondly, time was required to achieve the political consensus in the United Nations to authorise the use of force if necessary. By early November some ten Security Council resolutions had been passed condemning Iraq, which indicated a considerable degree of consensus in the international community; the United States had succeeded in achieving an unlikely coalition among the major Arab states, Saudi Arabia, Egypt and Syria, and the American mid-term Congressional elections had been completed. It was now necessary for the Americans to convert what had hitherto essentially been a less than credible threat against Iraq into a more active coercive strategy.

The requirements of what Thomas Schelling has called a strategy of 'compellence'[9] are that you must make it clear what you want your opponent to do, within what time-scale he should do it and what consequences will follow if he fails to comply. The credibility of the coercive threat depends upon firstly specifying these elements clearly, secondly communicating them unambiguously to your opponent and, thirdly, clearly demonstrating your will and capability to deliver the consequences threatened. The latter depends not only on the possession of the military power to do so but on the construction of the necessary political climate internationally and domestically that would make it possible.

The next phase of the crisis was signalled by the crossing of the first intermediate threshold – 'the US decision to use force threshold'. The American assessment that force would have to be used to eject the Iraqi military from Kuwait may have been made earlier, but it was not clearly signalled until the announcement on 8 November of a massive reinforcement of American military forces in the region. This decision converted the American force in Saudi Arabia from merely a defensive one to an offensive capability necessary to force an Iraqi withdrawal from Kuwait rather than merely deterring an Iraqi attack on Saudi Arabia. The rest of this second phase, much shorter than the previous phase, was devoted by the Americans to firming up their coercive credibility firstly by continuing the military build-up and secondly by ensuring a United Nations sanction for the ultimate use of force. The crucial factor determining the latter was agreement by the Soviet Union. It was announced on 27 November that Mr Gorbachev agreed to the ultimate use of force. Security Council Resolution 678 of 28 November authorised 'all necessary means' to effect Iraqi compliance with UN resolutions and stipulated a deadline, 15 January 1992, by which that compliance had to be completed.

Thus the crucial elements of America's strategy of compellence against Iraq were essentially in place and the passing of Resolution 678 represented the next intermediate threshold which began the third phase of the crisis. It was America's capability and willingness to use force, together with the agreement of the international community through the United Nations that it would sanction such a course, that was the major 'watershed' of the crisis – the point after which war seemed the most likely outcome. It was from that point that maximum coercive pressure was applied to Iraq.

The third phase saw the continued build-up of Coalition military capability in the region in order to further strengthen the credibility of the threat to Iraq whilst at the same time allowing the significance of that pressure to seep through to the Iraqi leadership in the hope that it would be persuaded to comply with UN resolutions. This was the phase that saw most pressure for some face-to-face negotiation at which the effect of this coercion could be made manifest by some agreement that would resolve the matter short of actual war. A significant feature of this phase was the argumentation over direct negotiations. For both sides direct negotiations were necessary not only to explore areas of possible compromise but, perhaps more importantly, to be seen to be willing to give their respective opponents the benefit of the doubt and not appear to go to war without having exhausted every possibility of avoiding it. In fact the talks themselves became one of the instruments of coercion and that is why their timing assumed such importance. This issue is explored in more detail in the section on the instruments of coercion in this chapter but suffice it to say here that it was in Iraq's interest to engage in talks as late as possible and then to engage the Americans in lengthy diplomatic wrangling that would proceed beyond the UN deadline in order to disrupt the American and coalition timetable for compliance with the UN resolutions. For the Americans on the other hand it was important not to get into a long drawn out diplomatic wrangle in which they might well lose a propaganda war which would then make an actual war untenable. Talks for them were important firstly to be seen to be going through the motions, and secondly to make sure directly that the Iraqi leadership and specifically Saddam Hussein accurately understood the determination of the United States and her allies and clearly understood the certainty of the consequences of persisting in their occupation of Kuwait. For the Americans the talks were the last necessary precursor to the actual resort to force once the UN deadline had passed.

It was in this sense that the talks, when they did occur, can be regarded as the 'point of no return' threshold. The failure of the talks in Geneva between Tariq Aziz, the Foreign Minister of Iraq, and James Baker, the US Secretary of State, on 9 January 1991 represented the last chance for a negotiated settlement and a de-escalation of the crisis. It was at that point that Iraq needed to indicate clearly its willingness to withdraw if war was to be averted. The unambiguous intransigence of the Iraqis at that meeting conveyed the unmistakable message that they were prepared for war. The last and fourth phase of the crisis was the short period remaining before the UN deadline during which frantic last-minute, but essentially doomed, diplomacy by the French and the UN Secretary-General Perez de Cuellar took place and failed.

The crisis ended with the crossing of the final threshold – the war threshold – and the beginning of the air bombardment of Iraq on 16 January 1992 some twenty-six hours after the expiry of the UN deadline.

CRISIS MANAGEMENT AND THE INSTRUMENTS OF COERCION

In the crisis literature there is some disagreement as to what 'crisis management' is and what its objectives are. It is not the place here to get into a theoretical discussion about these issues but the differences of opinion among academics do give some indication of the problems faced by practitioners and decision-makers in having to deal with crises. Crisis management and coercive diplomacy can be seen as alternative means of dealing with crisis – the former is the means adopted if the emphasis is on the avoidance of war as the major objective, the later is the means adopted if the major objective is the protection or furtherance of vital national interests. It is not that coercive diplomacy is absent in crisis management, it is that the latter consists more of a mixed pattern of threat and the offering of incentives to your opponent for compromise or even for backing down. Coercive diplomacy relies essentially on threat – both direct and indirect – in order to persuade your opponent to back down. In this sense crisis management can relate merely to the extent to which your behaviour leads to the achievement of your objectives. In this case 'success' is judged not by whether war is the outcome of the crisis but whether you have protected or furthered the vital interests that had been threatened. The explanation of much of the difference of view that emerged among both the public and the commentators outside the decision-making circles during the Gulf crisis was that for some people the priority was to avoid war and for others it was to see the playing field levelled before issues of 'justice' were considered – that is, that the precondition for the international consideration of Iraq's claims was a re-establishment of the *status quo ante* and that entailed the withdrawal of Iraqi troops from Kuwait.

There were two conditions that made war a likely outcome of the Gulf crisis from the beginning. First was the absence of the nuclear dimension. In Cold War crises the possibility of a nuclear conflagration between the superpowers acted as an ultimate restraint on their conduct. It meant that the avoidance of direct war was the priority objective and that the pursuit of interests was conducted only within that ultimate limit. Although there was a nuclear dimension to the Gulf crisis in the anxiety and uncertainty over the extent of Iraq's capability, there was little serious consideration that nuclear weapons would be used and certainly there was no risk that there could be a massive nuclear exchange. The point being made here is that the absence of the nuclear dimension had the effect of lowering the war threshold compared with that in the superpower relationship. The second condition that made war a likely outcome of the crisis was the fact that it had been provoked itself by an act of war, by military aggression. One way of looking at the crisis is that it was the breaching of the war threshold that caused the crisis, and in order to avoid a military response to that act of aggression there had to be de-escalation from that point, not further escalation. Unless there was de-escalation in the form of a reversal of the act of aggression or some act of contrition then war was really the only plausible outcome.

The instruments of coercion

It has already been established that one element of the 'asymmetry' of the crisis was the fact that one side had already used military force and the other side had not. Another manifestation of asymmetry in the crisis was in the respective coercive stances they had to adopt. Both sides were operating a system of deterrence but the Iraqis adopted a 'passive' deterrence and the American-led Coalition an 'active' deterrence. This was built into the structure of the crisis – the Iraqis had to defend their newly-established position, the Americans had to attack it, either diplomatically or with the use of various forms of sanction. The essence of the difference between the two stances is that passive deterrence uses a threat to deter an opponent from doing something he intends, or might be tempted, to do and is formulated as follows: 'If you commit act A, then consequence X will follow'. Active deterrence on the other hand is the use of a threat to persuade an opponent to do something he would otherwise not be inclined to do and is formulated as follows: 'If you do *not* do *B*, then consequence *Y* will follow'. This more active form of deterrence has been termed 'compellence' as previously referred to. [10]

Having already committed an act of aggression the Iraqi stance was one of passive deterrence; it was saying to the Americans, 'If you make any attempt to remove Iraqi troops from Kuwait the following consequences will ensue'. The Americans on the other hand adopted a 'compellence' stance and were saying to the Iraqis 'If you do not withdraw your troops from Kuwait then the following consequences will ensue'.

The essence of successful deterrence or coercion is the credibility of your threat. In other words you must convince your opponent that you have the capability and the willingness to carry out your threats, that to do so will be in your interests and cause unacceptable damage to the interests of your opponent. This requires a firm and clear communication of your resolve and also fine calculation of the potential effectiveness of your threat on your opponent's beliefs. In other words, what is important in determining the behaviour of your opponent is not necessarily what is the case but his perception of what the case is. Moreover, you have to have an accurate picture of what your opponent perceives his interests and values are and to recognise that they may not conform to what you might regard as the rational.

In many ways the Americans had the simpler but more difficult task. Though the coercive threat was a simple one, it required a great deal of effort and time to make credible – this was essentially because it entailed the reversal of a *fait accompli* and that required positive action. The Iraqis on the other hand had to manipulate a more complex threat in order to achieve the simpler objective of merely staying put in Kuwait. This is why for most of the crisis period the initiative for action rested with the Americans. That of course is the far more difficult role to play – and the crucial factor here was time.

It is in this context that the first phase of the crisis can be regarded as a 'phoney' phase. This phase was one in which the nature of the coercive threat had to be defined and consolidated. It was characterised essentially by a 'low-pressure' strategy of sanctions imposed by the UN Security Council. The weakness of sanctions as a coercive threat against Iraq rested not on their credibility. Indeed there was a chance that in the short term at least sanctions could have been the most effective example of economic pressure in terms of compliance that there had ever been, so universal was the opposition to Iraq. Rather, that weakness lay in the intrinsic inability of sanctions to change the behaviour of the Iraqi leadership because, as has been argued elsewhere in this book, they had effectively isolated themselves from such pressure by large stockpiles of foodstocks and military capability. Whether or not such stockpiles would have sustained the leadership is less important than its belief that it would have done. For it is the belief that will change behaviour not necessarily the actuality.

In addition to this intrinsic lack of effectiveness of sanctions was the absence of a time-scale. The essential element necessary for the exertion of a coercive threat in crisis diplomacy and one that is missing from the formulation outlined above is that of a deadline. So the full formulation of a coercive threat in compellance is: 'If you do not do action B by time t then consequence Y will follow'. In the phoney phase the deadline was merely a generalised one of the form that military action would be taken 'when sanctions are seen to have failed' or 'when diplomatic means have been exhausted'. Such unspecific deadlines are not sufficient for compellence to work; and even then during this first phase the military consequence was less than credible given insufficient military means in the area at that time and the doubts in this period as to whether the international community would actually go along with a military solution. The open-ended time-scale of such a policy of course made it impossible to conduct since in the long term the international solidarity against Iraq would gradually have softened and there would have been progressively less incentive to maintain sanctions as time went on and as the issue of the Iraqi occupation of Kuwait lost its salience on the international agenda.

So if sanctions were to be the main measure of pressure against Iraq together with a vague, unspecified and untimed resort to military means 'if they failed', then a coercive threat against Iraq could not be sustained. In this situation a high priority for the Americans was to impose an explicit time-frame on the crisis. For political as well as logistical reasons the United States had to start drawing boundaries round the crisis and begin depicting its conclusion. To this end it had to begin to exert more credible pressure on the Iraqis and focus the collective mind of the Iraqi leadership by imposing a deadline. The next two phases of the crisis were devoted to making explicit the three major elements of the coercive threat – that is, the action that was required of the Iraqis (withdrawal from Kuwait), the date by which that action had to be effected and the consequence that would follow failure to comply (a massive military onslaught). The second phase (see Fig. 4.3) began with the United States decision for a massive military build-up that would make credible its military threat in terms of capability, and also its international diplomacy that would ensure that any military action taken essentially by the United States would constitute a UN action taken on behalf of the international community as a whole and not merely a unilateral American action. The third phase began with the UN permission for 'all necessary means', which included military means and crucially included a specific deadline beyond which those means would be used against Iraq.

It can be seen then that the American objective during these later phases of the crisis was to impose clarity on the situation – to impose clear definitions, clear requirements, clarify consequences and specify time-scales which would entail the closure of the crisis. The Iraqis on the other hand had quite other objectives. Their objective was obfuscation rather than clarity, to cloud issues rather than define them, to maintain an open-ended nature of the crisis – all of which would allow them to consolidate their *fait accompli* and to make it increasingly difficult for their opponents to take any positive action against them. Hence the differences in their respective attitudes to 'negotiations' or 'talks'. It was not only whether and when such contacts would take place between the two sides but even how they should be defined that became an important issue in the 'implicit' crisis bargaining. For the Americans the purpose of any such contacts was simple and straightforward. Since for the Americans (on behalf of the United Nations) there were no 'issues' to be negotiated, short at least of an Iraqi withdrawal, the purpose of any contact with the Iraqis was to ensure that their message was getting across to them. In order to fulfil one of the prime requirements of coercive diplomacy, the Americans wanted to make sure that their coercive message was simple, unambiguous and that it was being received and clearly understood by the Iraqi leadership. Short of direct contact between the two leaders – never likely, not least because Saddam Hussein would not have felt (or perhaps been) safe outside Iraqi territory – the surest way of achieving that objective was a contact between the repective leaders and the opposing Foreign Secretaries. The Americans were very keen to regard any such meeting as merely 'contact' or 'communication' and in no sense should it be regarded as 'talks' or 'negotiations'.

If clarity of communication was the major American purpose in any direct contact, another purpose would have been the 'public relations' or 'political' one of being seen by the international community to have pushed the diplomatic option as far as it would go before resorting to force. Thus the Americans wanted a short, sharp contact resulting in either an Iraqi agreement to withdraw from Kuwait or in a direct and unambiguous refusal. A clear refusal would have signalled the failure of coercive diplomacy – the way would then be politically clear for the use of force after the UN deadline.

The Iraqi purpose was the direct opposite of this picture. They had a number of purposes for wanting rather more extended contact with the Americans. For them any direct contact with the Americans would be defined, quite reasonably and plausibly, as 'diplomatic negotiations', which would imply the possibility of mutual concession which in turn would in a sense 'legitimise' their invasion of Kuwait by making it subject to 'negotiation'. Such negotiation would also signal their apparent 'reasonableness' to the international community. But perhaps most importantly the Iraqis were clearly aware that to lock the Americans into a complicated and long drawn out process of diplomatic negotiation which could be spun out beyond the UN deadline would effectively preclude the military option and muddy the waters of the clear diplomatic principle that states should not be seen to benefit from unprovoked military aggression.

Hence the 'conditions' set by the Iraqis under which they would be prepared to withdraw from Kuwait: firstly that Iraqi withdrawal should be part of a grand solution to the central problem of the Middle East, the Arab–Israeli conflict, and secondly that the UN Coalition forces should withdraw from the region to allow an Iraqi withdrawal from Kuwait to be negotiated and supervised by Arab countries alone. The first would have locked the Iraqi occupation of Kuwait into the long term and intractable problems of the Middle East – especially the problem of a Palestinian homeland – and would thus have enabled Iraq to remain in Kuwait for the foreseeable future. The second would have eliminated the possibility of a military solution to the Iraqi occupation and thus have removed the coercive threat to Iraq. Clearly from the American point of view (and that of the UN) the Iraqis should not be allowed the opportunity of establishing those formal bargaining positions in diplomatic negotiations. The American strategy was to compress the time-scale and keep the issues and communications clear and unambiguous. The Iraqi strategy on the other hand was to expand the time-frame and de-escalate the trend towards military action on the principle that the longer they could spin out the diplomatic process, the longer they would be able to hold on to their gains, and the less likely in the long term that they would have to withdraw.

The importance of the deadline is fundamental. It is impossible to apply a military threat in an open-ended time-frame – such a threat possesses no coercive power, neither is it logistically plausible. Hence the Iraqi desire to breach the deadline and the American determination to adhere to it. The deadline could not even plausibly have been delayed, once set, because a second deadline is effectively no deadline at all. Allowing a deadline to lapse without action fatally undermines the credibility of any subsequent deadline. Both military and political factors determined the American commitment to the 15 January deadline once it had been set by Security Council Resolution 678. Firstly delay much beyond that time would have pushed military action into the 'hot season' in the region and have made fighting a war in such conditions more difficult for both men and equipment – though it may be that this factor was exaggerated precisely in order to strengthen the credibility of the deadline. Secondly the longer the vast Coalition military force remained in the desert without action, the lower the morale of troops would become and the less efficient as a fighting force and the more expensive their maintenance in the field, the greater the incidence of equipment failure, and so on. Thirdly the longer the military force remained there without action, the more difficult it would have been to maintain UN solidarity as well as popular support in both the United States and Europe.

THE IRAQI THREATS OF COERCION AND DETERRENCE

Having established the difference between the respective crisis strategies of the two sides as that between active and passive deterrence, and having discussed implicitly at least the nature of the active coercive threat to the Iraqis applied by the Americans, it is necessary to discuss briefly the 'counter-threat' that the Iraqis used to deter UN military action – that is, what consequences were the Iraqis threatening if the UN Coalition attempted to force them to withdraw and how credible were the threats?

There were five main threats. Firstly military action would result, either as a result of war or more deliberately in a scorched-earth strategy, in the destruction of the Kuwaiti oil-wells, which would have both severe global economic effects and serious environmental effects. The credibility of this threat rested not only on the Iraqis' ability to carry it out but on the strategic purpose it would serve and what actual effect it would have. Environmentally it was a potent threat not so much in the actual damage such a measure would cause, since this in itself was uncertain, but in the public perceptions in the west of such an eventuality given the high political profile of environmentalism in Europe and the United States. Economically the threat was less potent given the adjustment the world had already made to the 1973 oil crisis and given anyway the prospect that the world market would be deprived of both Iraqi and Kuwaiti oil production if sanctions were allowed to continue in the long term. Strategically from Iraq's point of view destruction of the Kuwait oil-wells would be a pointless action, carried out for retributive purposes rather than for any strategic value. Even if such an action did raise the price of oil (and in the event it was only marginally) it would not be in circumstances in which Iraq could benefit. (The Iraqi action in destroying Kuwaiti oil-wells is discussed in the context of the laws of war in Chapter 6.)

The second major threat posed by the Iraqis was that if a UN Coalition invasion of targets in Kuwait and Iraq took place then western hostages held by Iraq would be killed either directly by Iraqi forces or by placing them at strategic sites to be killed by Allied bombing. The hostage issue played a very important role in the Gulf crisis. The issue showed Iraqi political ineptness on two scores – first in the taking of western hostages and second in releasing them. The taking of hostages that has become such a feature of Middle Eastern international politics over the past two decades is probably the one form of behaviour that in western perceptions demonstrates the ultimate barabarism of Islamic and Arab politics and culture. Whether those perceptions are accurate or not is less important perhaps than the fact that the practice has served as the major barrier between Islam and the modern European mind in contemporary world politics. The use of the practice by the Iraqis in the Gulf crisis thus served to demonstrate to the world the essential injustice and barbarism of the Iraqi regime, and if there was one issue that demonstrated to western public opinion that Saddam Hussein had to be defeated it was probably this. Saddam's political insensitivity and even ignorance on this issue was totally at variance with the common perception that he was politically very astute and might well out-manoeuvre his western opponents in the crisis. This insensitivity was demonstrated by his appearance on television with the hostages which proved a major public relations error. Moreover, the taking of hostages directly undermined the factor that he regarded as his major asset in the crisis – that is, his belief that western public opinion, and especially American public opinion, would not tolerate a war in the Middle East. That may well have been a more plausible judgement had he not taken every opportunity to demonstrate to western opinion that he was a public danger who had to be dealt with.

But having taken the hostages it really was another major strategic error to release them unless he did not intend to push the crisis to war. Where he probably was right was his judgement that placing western civilian hostages at key strategic sites would have posed a serious political problem for the Coalition conduct of the air war. The fact is that although the hostages were a political liability to the Iraqis, they were a strategic asset. Having already committed the political blunder of taking and using them for crisis bargaining, their only use for them after that was as a strategic deterrent. The value of the hostages was in the threat to their lives not in the carrying out of that threat. Their release eliminated their value as a 'human shield' deterrent and on the basis of this logic the most plausible interpretation of their release was that Saddam Hussein and his regime were not prepared to fight a war with the UN Coalition and that it was a gesture to improve the political climate for gaining some diplomatic concession in de-escalating the crisis. If on the other hand he still intended to go to war rather than withdraw then he clearly and mistakenly believed that releasing the hostages could re-establish the restraint represented by western public opinion on the ability of the United States and her allies to pursue a war with Iraq. So the credibility of the use of hostages as a deterrent threat was at best ambiguous; their release eliminated the threat altogether.

The third element of the Iraqi deterrent was the threat of large-scale coalition casualties and a long drawn out war if the Americans did launch an attempt to remove Iraqi troops from Kuwait. There were three elements to this threat. One was that a war with Iraq would produce many Allied deaths, and second, that the so-called 'body-bag' factor would politically undermine the ability of the western members of the Coalition to continue a war with such high cost. This was potentially at least quite a potent deterrent to the American use of force to resolve the crisis. In fact the effect of the prospect of large-scale casualties was not to weaken the resolve of the United States but to strengthen their caution and determination that a military onslaught would be overwhelming in general and that a land campaign would only be commenced once superiority (or even in the event supremacy) had been achieved in the air and the morale of the Iraqi will to resist had been all but totally undermined. So in effect the repeated claims of Saddam Hussein only served to increase the resolve of the United States to engineer the comprehensive military defeat of the Iraqis should war be necessary.

But in itself the apparent Iraqi belief that the fact that their major opponents were democracies acted as a constraint on their ability to go to war and to pursue such a war to a conclusion was misjudged. That democracy is a source of weakness rather than strength is a particular misconception of demagogues. What democracy does on the whole is to ensure that wars are not entered into frivolously by governments subject to legitimate challenge by opposition forces, but once entered into are supported. However, there are two conditions to such support: – one is that the cause has to be seen to be a just one and the other is that the war is conducted in a 'humane' and reasonably efficient manner. The false deduction from the American experience in Vietnam made by the Iraqis was that it was the scale of casualties that led to the withdrawal of public support. In fact the scale of casualties were significant but only in the face of a lack of clear and justifiable reason for being in Vietnam in the first place and secondly in their apparent inability to draw the war to a successful conclusion. This was one of the contexts in which the Americans were determined that a Gulf War would not be 'another Vietnam'.

However, what was much less credible as a deterrent threat was the claimed ability of the Iraqis to hold down the Coalition forces in a long drawn out war (*à la* Vietnam) which would go on for months if not years. There was never any prospect of that happening primarily because Iraq was so completely isolated. Ultimately the reason the North Vietnamese could hold out virtually indefinitely against the Americans was their continuous resupply from outside – from the Soviet Union. In a war with the US–led Coalition force Iraq would not be able to call on external sources of the massive military and economic support that would be required to sustain a long campaign. Neither was it realistic to expect that there existed within Iraq the military will and capacity nor the economic depth necessary for such a campaign.

A more serious deterrent directly posed by the Iraqi regime was Saddam's consistently declared threat that an attack on Iraq would bring forth a retaliatory attack on Israel. It was not the attack on Israel itself that constituted the deterrent threat but the assumed consequences of such an attack. The logic behind Saddam's strategy was that Israel would not be able to restrain itself from a direct military response to an attack on its territory from Iraq and that such a response would convert the Gulf conflict over the occupation of Kuwait into a large-scale Middle East conflict which few states in the region would be able to ignore. The implication here was that no Arab state could be seen to be fighting on the same side as Israel against brother Arab states. This would entail the defection of the Arab members of the UN Coalition force and essentially the breakdown of the whole anti-Iraq coalition. Such a Middle East-wide conflagration might also lead to general popular uprisings and the overthrow of moderate, pro-western Arab regimes such as Egypt and Saudi Arabia. This would be a truly nightmare scenario both for western interests and for stability in the region.

The key link in the chain of argument leading to this prognostication of course was the Israeli response. The credibility of the Iraqi threat to Israel was clear; less certain was the inevitability of the consequences of an actual attack. In the event this was the link to which most American attention was devoted in order to prevent such an Israeli response. Ultimately the weakness of this deterrent threat was that the carrying out of the threat was not in the hands of the Iraqis. They could and did attack Israel; they could not however determine the Israeli response. That particular element of the Iraqi deterrent rested with the Americans and Israelis and thus was beyond Iraqi control.

WHY THE CRISIS ENDED IN WAR

As a conclusion and review of this chapter it is appropriate to deal with the question as to why the crisis ended in war, why crisis management did not succeed in averting the final resort to force. We have already discussed the difference between explanations of events that emphasise broad structural factors and those on the other hand that emphasise contingent factors (see the Introduction). That is a useful distinction that helps to focus on the crucial determinants of the outcome of the Gulf crisis.

It is important to reinforce here the point already made that the crisis was special in the respect that it was caused by an act of aggression. This factor meant that there was an in-built propensity for a military resolution of the crisis – that there was a dynamic to war which had to be positively disrupted if that war was to be avoided. Clearly some caution is necessary in using the word 'inevitable', but the point to be made is that there was a strong structural propensity for war in the absence of a positive mechanism for avoiding it. If that point is accepted (and it is a crucial one for the understanding of the crisis) then the focus of the explanation for the war turns on the reasons why the mechanism for positive de-escalation was not found (or perhaps even looked for).

It is here that the importance of contingent and, in particular, idiosyncratic factors is seen. There is not space here for an exhaustive consideration of the effects of ideological, cultural and personality factors on the outcome but at least the beginnings of such an analysis can be attempted. It is common in the popular media to depict an international crisis as a conflict, a duel even, between the two opposing individual leaders. While this sort of treatment grossly oversimplifies the nature of state interaction and avoids the structural and historical complexities which lie behind most crises, there is in fact a whole body of international-relations literature which deals with the psychological and individual dimensions of crisis decision-making.[11] This type of analysis is very important so long as it is placed within the context of the broader structural picture. Clearly this sort of factor will be more relevant in the explanation of events the more a single individual dominates decision-making in any particular case. In general terms this is less likely to be the case in 'democratic' systems than in 'authoritarian' systems. Having said that crises are situations in which even in democratic systems decision-making bodies are reduced in size so that only a few individuals are responsible for taking decisions and guiding policy. In these circumstances not only are democratic procedures short-circuited and the democratic-constraint diluted to some extent but strong individual leaders are able to exert a disproportionate impact on decisions. In these circumstances personality and structures of perception and belief are likely to offer plausible dimensions of explanation of what happens.

In the case of the Gulf crisis it is fruitful to consider the impact of the two leading personalities, President Bush and Saddam Hussein, and what factors might have determined their respective attitudes to the crisis. It is first of all important to recognise that the American president is locked into a democratic system which entails that his 'freedom of action' is limited by his ability to convince the American electorate of his competence and judgement. The constraints operating on an American president at any one time are a function not only of the system itself but of a whole myriad of contingent factors, including the relevant personalities involved, the constellation of domestic political and economic forces operating at the time and so on. Both democratic and authoritarian leaders have the task of balancing the domestic and international political forces within which they operate in order to give them the greatest freedom of action. The major difference between them is the mechanisms which are available in order to determine that balance. The instruments of coercion, intimidation and violence that many authoritarian leaders avail themselves of in their domestic politics ensure the maximisation of their freedom of action. The democratic leader has to deploy a range of more subtle political skills in order to make his own room for manoeuvre.

Three main factors can be isolated that might have been influential in determining President Bush's attitude to the crisis. The first was the 'second term' factor. Any American president, in modern times at least, automatically thinks of a second term of office and begins doing so almost immediately he is elected for the first. A 'successful' outcome to the crisis was clearly a necessity if Bush was to expect to be re-elected in 1992. How a successful outcome for the United States was to be defined is less clear. The idea that a military resolution to the crisis was dictated by Bush's future electoral ambitions is not easy to substantiate given the ambiguous state of American public and Congressional opinion certainly during September and October 1990.[12] It is significant that Bush waited until after the mid-term Congressional elections in early November 1990 before making the decision for massive military reinforcements in Saudi Arabia. Indeed the persistent 'luke-warm' attitude of Congress would not itself have encouraged a military resolution of the crisis. In electoral terms, thus, a military solution might be regarded as a high-risk strategy for President Bush and thus the second-term factor cannot necessarily be regarded as a strong determinant of American crisis policy – at least not one which explains the American willingness to resort to war.

The second factor that was held by some to be a significant determinant of American policy was the so-called 'wimp factor'. The theory was that Bush had gained a reputation as vice-president, and indeed during the presidential campaign, for being somewhat less than robust in policy terms and that the Gulf crisis was a heaven-sent opportunity for him to demonstrate his 'machismo'. In fact this might be regarded as a 'permanently operating' feature of American politics. All American presidents have to demonstrate a certain 'machismo' in foreign affairs. This is partly a product of American public expectations of their leaders in the conduct of relations with other states and partly the perceived necessity after the Second World War for presidents to adopt robust stances in the context of the Cold War competition with the Soviet Union. A well-known case is that of President Truman, whose uncompromising approach to the Soviet Union on coming to office in 1945 was dictated, it is held, by the need to demonstrate to domestic public opinion and to the international community (especially the Soviet Union) that he was no 'push over', after having spent such a long time as vice-president in the shadow of Roosevelt. Moreover, some have gone so far as to suggest that this was one of the major 'causes' of the breakdown in the wartime coalition between the United States and the Soviet Union into the antagonistic condition of Cold War.

Certainly Bush had spent a long time in the 'shadow' of President Reagan, but where his case differs markedly from that of Truman is that Bush had spent a good deal of his public political life in the foreign-policy arena, notably as Ambassador to Beijing and as Director of the CIA. Certainly Bush has perhaps a justified reputation as a rather weak and somewhat indecisive character. It is plausible to suggest that he might have 'locked on' to a major foreign-policy issue on which he might have felt on surer ground to demonstrate his capacity for action and 'tough' decision-making. However, parallel to this is an equally plausible contention that his foreign-policy expertise would have conferred on him the sort of understanding of the international system and America's place in it that neither Reagan nor Truman themselves initially possessed. This suggests that he personally could see the wider significance of the Iraqi invasion in the post-Cold War international system and the role that the United States might play in the future world order. There was a strong logic in the idea that if future calls on US action were to be limited then firm action was required in the Gulf crisis. So once again, if the idiosyncratic factor did play a part in American crisis policies it was as a reinforcement of the structural propensities of the crisis. On the other hand it must be said in contradiction to this that 'experience' in foreign affairs is not always a guarantee of good decision-making in crises. Anthony Eden in the Suez crisis is a case in point, where historical analogy based upon long personal experience led to disastrous consequences; and there is some theoretical underpinning for the idea that long experience can actually lead to inappropriate decisions especially in novel situations.[13]

The third factor that played a strong part in American attitudes to the crisis was the 'Vietnam factor'. Again this factor would have been important to any post-Vietnam president since the 'ghost' of Vietnam lurks deep in the contemporary American psyche. Any president who could exorcise this ghost would clearly put his name down in American history, and that might have been an overt factor in Bush's thinking. However, once again it is important to determine how that factor operated rather than merely to assume that it militated in favour of a military solution that would not otherwise have been warranted. Indeed there is every reason to believe that the Vietnam factor acted as a cautionary or restraining factor on American crisis policy rather than one making for reckless risk-taking. It encouraged very deep reflection on the consequences and implications for the United States of again taking massive military action far from its own shores. It is likely that the decision for military action was taken on its own merits; the most likely influence of the Vietnam factor was on the way that action in broad terms was to be executed. Hence the rapid build-up to a capability for overwhelming military force, hence the careful coalition-building and hence the American determination to work through the United Nations. On all these fronts the United States was very careful not to be out on a limb, not to be isolated politically or of course militarily. The Vietnam factor was thus likely to have been a moderating influence on American policy rather than one that encouraged extremes.

In the case of the Iraqi leader, Saddam Hussein, the impact of idiosyncratic factors are rather more clear-cut. There is little doubt that Saddam dominated Iraqi decision-making to the extent that it is likely that no decision was ever made, however trivial, without his imprimatur.[14] Indeed this is another dimension of the asymmetry between the two sides – the democratic-constraint factor which operated on the American side was absent on the Iraqi side. It is a common misperception, and one clearly subscribed to by Saddam Hussein and his government, that the democratic factor would act as a constraint on the western-led Coalition. Of course in many ways it did – both domestically and internationally. What this perception fails to understand is that the need to satisfy a democratic constituency means that policies are subject to much greater critical scrutiny. The implication is that if those policies survive democratic critical appraisal then they are more likely to be sound and to receive popular support to boot. Clearly this point must not be overstated; it is not to say that decision-making by democratic governments is bound to be right. But the democratic dimension does not only serve inherent political values held highly in western political systems, it also provides a valuable measure of quality control in policy-making. The absence of the democratic-constraint factor on the Iraqi side no doubt made it easier for Saddam Hussein to take policy decisions but it also precluded the quality-control element of policy-making which a democratic constituency provides. The only constituencies he had to satisfy were his sycophantic government ministers and himself – neither of which were likely to be very critical.

The issue here is that the absence of a critical policy environment in Iraq allowed Saddam Hussein to pursue policies that bordered on the irrational and which served very little purpose other than his own self-delusion and his unreflective, untutored view of the world. He had only visited the west once and was essentially ignorant of how western societies and political systems worked.[15] The characteristic feature of Saddam's decision-making milieu was its closed nature. It showed all the classic cognitive features making for what have been called 'decision-making pathologies' which lead to misperception and miscalculation. Three of the most important of these pathologies[16] are particularly helpful in explaining Saddam's crisis behaviour. They all relate to the problem of interpreting the world and to the tendency we all have to a greater or lesser degree of seeing what we expect to see and seeing what we want to see. It is when these tendencies reach pathological proportions that serious problems are likely to result; when a serious gap emerges between perception and reality.

The first of these pathologies clearly discernible in Saddam Hussein is the overvaluation of past success. Certainly the idea that the eight-year-long Iran–Iraq war was a 'success' for Saddam was etched in his psyche and no doubt played an important part in the persistence with which he pursued a disaster course towards a war with the United States. The fact that the Iran–Iraq war was an unmitigated failure made it fatal to base upon it any prediction of future success or to use it to demonstrate his ability as a strategist. Even had Iraq achieved success in its war with Iran not many lessons could have been learnt from it that would have provided a reliable guide in a war with the United States; moreover, such a success would have been achieved despite Saddam's leadership not because of it.

Saddam Hussein's self-image is clearly important here. He saw himself as treading in the footsteps of Nasser as a great Arab leader with an ambition to bring about the final unification of the Arab peoples. The ideology of Arab unity is one of the destabilising forces of the Middle East the persistence of which makes it a necessary instrument, in rhetoric at least, for any Arab leader with ambitions for personal and national aggrandisement. In his claims to spiritual if not direct personal descent from such great historical figures as Saladin and Nebuchadnezzar it is difficult for the observer to distinguish rhetoric from reality; and there is at least the suspicion that Saddam himself experienced the same difficulty. Rhetoric is a legitimate diplomatic instrument which can serve an important purpose in relation both to the international community and to the domestic constituency. When rhetoric becomes self-delusion the consequences can be disastrous, particularly in circumstances of international crisis.

Here a very important question relates to the Iraqi assessment of the objectives, interests, intentions and capabilities of the United States and other major western states. Most of this assessment was couched, in public at least, in the simple, crude rhetoric which attributes the explanation of all US actions to 'western imperialism'. It is difficult to detect any more realistic assessment or any systematic policy study by the Iraqis of their potential opponents. It looks at least likely that Saddam's own false images and perceptions of the Americans led to his disastrous policies and actions. One of the most common features of bad crisis decision-making is the underestimation of one's opponents. It is likely that Saddam did miscalculate in underestimating the US response to his invasion of Kuwait and that once having done so he lacked the cognitive resources to 'undo' that miscalculation. His closed mind and self-image entailed that he had to persist with that policy and make a virtue of necessity, pretending that it was a strategy when of course it was nothing of the kind. Such 'cognitive rigidity'[17] enhances the propensity for reliance on past experience, the propensity for relying on stereotypical images of your opponent, and the filtering out of information not consonant with these fixed images.

Any attempt to analyse the logic of Saddam's crisis decision-making finds it difficult to avoid resorting to the term 'irrational' at some stage. Clearly one must be senstitive to the familiar charge of ethnocentrism (or rather more baldly, racism), where cultural differences are interpreted as examples of irrationality. Here we must acknowledge the distinction between an 'absolute' rationality and a 'contextual' rationality; in the case of Saddam Hussein we must make a distinction between the contextual rationality of a policy directed to the interests of the people and state of Iraq and that of a policy directed to the interests of Saddam Hussein as an individual. It is in assessing the crisis policies pursued and the risks taken by Saddam Hussein in relation to the national interests of the Iraqi people that one is forced to resort to the notion of irrationalism.

This relates to the second of the decision-making pathologies portrayed by Saddam Hussein – that of irrational overconfidence in his crisis policies. His apparent belief in his ability to engage the Coalition in 'the mother of all battles', to be able to litter the Arabian desert with tens of thousands of Coalition dead, to tie down American military power in a war that would last for years, were – if anything more than rhetoric directed to his own constituencies – sheer delusion. This became even more so in the event of the war when he voluntarily conceded air supremacy to the Coalition by withdrawing his own air capability. There is a limit to the extent to which one can keep searching for the 'hidden and inscrutable logic' in such behaviour. The most obvious and probably most accurate conclusion is that the man is either irrational or absurdly incompetent or both.

The third decision-making pathology that Saddam Hussein demonstrated himself a victim to was that of an insensitivity to warnings. Cognitive rigidity gives rise to overconfidence which itself increases the resistance to information critical of the perceptions or policies being pursued.[18] Even the starkest of information which shows the inappropriateness of a particular course of action is likely to be ignored or even utterly mis-interpreted in order to maintain the internal coherence of a set of beliefs. Wishful thinking is the main determinant of the way discrepant information is dealt with rather than a radical reassessment of policy. An example of this we have already mentioned was the interpretation of 'democracy' as an element of weakness or constraint rather than as a source of strength and determination. A perhaps less important but nevertheless indic-ative example was the Iraqi misreading of the Conservative Party overthrow of Margaret Thatcher as leader, and thus as British prime minister, as an indication that the 'British people' did not agree with the government's policy which might entail war with Iraq.

This brief survey has indicated that idiosyncratic factors are more likely to explain Iraqi crisis decision-making than that of the United States. A single statement explanation as to why the crisis resulted in war rather than de-escalation and a non-violent res-olution might be as follows: the Americans were locked into a set of structural imperatives which entailed an Iraqi withdrawal from Kuwait in the short term; the Iraqis were locked into a set of cognitive imperatives which operated to preserve the belief system of Saddam Hussein and which precluded a withdrawal short of actual war.

Chapter 5

The Gulf conflict and international law

INTERNATIONAL LAW AND THE BEHAVIOUR OF STATES

There is a common popular cynicism about the effectiveness of
international law; there is even a scepticism among academics and
lawyers as to the actual existence of international law. The common view seems to be that international law is honoured more in
its breach than in its observance and that since it seems to be
broken so much and almost at will it can hardly be said to exist at
all. Moreover, it is argued that there is little evidence that international law restrains states from pursuing their interests in the
international system. Such extreme scepticism is on the whole
misplaced.

The fact of the matter is that the vast body of international law
is complied with most of the time and that states are pretty
reluctant to break international law and whatever they do they are
anxious to portray their behaviour as in accordance with international law. But apart from a common misperception as to the
frequency of the breaking of international law the major source of
the sceptical attitude towards international law lies in the
supposed differences between it and domestic or national law
within states. From a legal perspective it is held that the major
distinction between the national system and the international
system is that in the case of the latter there is no overarching
authority equivalent to a national government, that there is no
formal legislative body that brings law into being (like Parliament,
which passes Acts and statutes), there is no mechanism to force
states to take their disputes to court and there is no enforcement
mechanism to ensure either that the law is complied with or that
law breakers are brought to justice.[1]

It is true that there is no overarching authority such as a world government. In other words the international system is not a centralised system but a decentralised one where there is no sovereign authority above that of the state. No state looks to a superior legal authority for permission to do what it does. This absence of an overarching authority akin to a national government which can impose order has been regarded as a central characteristic of the international system; that is, that a condition of anarchy exists where the major principle is one of 'self help' – in which states have to take action on their own behalf in the event of disputes with other states. In this sense then there is an element of 'anarchy' in the international system, a sort of centrifugal force persistently making for the disintegration of the international community as each state takes autonomous action to look after its own interests in the system. However the system is held in balance by what might be regarded as an opposing 'centripetal' force of interdependence in the system which tends to prevent disintegration into anarchy and chaos. There is a sort of balanced tension between anarchy and interdependence.[2] It is a condition, like that of domestic societies, where the individual members cannot exist on their own and thus have a vested interest in sticking together. Part of the manifestation of this interdependence in the international system is the web of rules and customs that have developed both formally and organically to govern their interactions.

It is also true that there is no single body like Parliament or Congress that makes the law. That does not mean, however, that there is no law-making mechanism. In fact there are a number of ways in which international laws come into existence. One is akin to the formal legislative procedure of domestic states – that is, where institutions like the United Nations, agree charters and resolutions which then have the force of international law with regard to their members. In the case of the United Nations since every state in the international system is a member those provisions apply universally. Another mechanism for the creation of law is the conclusion of treaties, either bilaterally or mulilaterally, the provisions of which have the force of international law. Lastly there is the custom and practice of states in their interaction with each other which has developed over time and through habit has gained the force of law.

Another important feature that is often held to distinguish

international law from domestic law and which is held to disqualify the former from the status of 'law' is its consensual nature – that is, states in the international system are only bound by the law if they consent to be so bound. Thus states cannot be compelled to submit to the arbitration or peaceful settlement of disputes between them by a third party. States in breach of international law cannot be compelled to submit their case to the international court. This is of course unlike the domestic system of law, where those in breach of the law, if and when apprended, are compelled to stand trial and to accept the sentence if found guilty.

However, it is here contended that this is not an ultimate distinction from domestic law since in the final analysis even domestic law requires the consent of those to whom it applies. The feature common to both systems is that whether or not an individual in the national system or a state in the international system consents to be bound by the law, there are costs entailed in the breach of the law. It is the costs that result from the breach of law that in the final analysis ensures that the law is observed in both systems. If states breach international law it is because they have judged that the objectives are worth the costs that will be incurred as a result of that breach. Thus it is the cost entailed in breaching it that ensures overwhelming compliance with international law.

INTERNATIONAL LAW AND THE GULF CRISIS

Much of the Gulf crisis was about the breaking of international law and the ability of the rules of international law to govern and restrain the behaviour of states and even its ability to bring individuals to justice for international crimes. It was not only the fact of the violation of international law by the Iraqis that assumed such an important role in the crisis but the apparent blatant contempt for international law that the Iraqi leadership displayed in its justification for its actions and in the conduct of its crisis diplomacy. The importance of international law was demonstrated on the one hand by the fact that it was this very contempt that increasingly consolidated the anti-Iraqi sentiments in the United Nations and the world over and demonstrated the imperative of opposing Saddam Hussein and his regime; and on the other by the care and patience with which the United Nations Coalition was put together by the major Security Council members – the US,

Britain and France – and the meticulous regard for the United Nations and international law in each step that was taken by the Coalition in confronting Iraq. It was clearly regarded as politically expedient on the part of the United States to be seen to be conducting its diplomacy with close association to international law.

This was done primarily of course through the United Nations. It is a moot legal point whether it was the United Nations pursuing its diplomacy using the United States as its instrument and agent or on the other hand whether it was the United States pursuing its own interests using the United Nations as its instrument. The political dimension of this nice distinction is discussed in Chapter 3, but the legal implications of this type of action on the part of or on behalf of the United Nations will be an important issue for consideration when discussing the future role of the United Nations in the post-Cold War and post-Gulf crisis world.

Thus it was the status and principles of international law that were claimed to be being upheld, that were determining the actions and behaviour of the United Nations Coalition, and it was the rules of international law that were framing and restraining that behaviour. If nothing else the crisis demonstrated that states justify and explain their actions in terms of international law. However, there is often a tension between law and interest, and where there is a conflict between the two it is a matter of fact that interest often predominates. However, it is also mainly a matter of interest that law is obeyed; the deterrent to law-breaking is the resulting cost – which may be anything from minor diplomatic inconvenience to major military conflict.

The following sections will consider firstly the international law relating to Iraqi claims against Kuwait, secondly the role of international law and the United Nations in the conduct of the Gulf crisis and thirdly the international law of economic sanctions.

THE INTERNATIONAL LAW RELATING TO IRAQI CLAIMS AGAINST KUWAIT

Territorial disputes have been common in the history of relations between states. Many of the disputes over territory in the contemporary era derive from the consequences of the European empires and their disintegration in the post-war period. International law permits territorial claims of one state over another but a distinction must be made between a situation where a state claims sovereignty over part of the territory of another state and a situation where that state claims sovereignty over all of the territory of another state. The Charter of the United Nations, parts of which have the status of international law and are binding on members, recognises that there might be legitimate territorial claims of one state over another.

Chapter VI exhorts members to settle such claims peacefully and submit them for mediation and arbitration to the United Nations. Chapter VI, however, is not binding – in other words there is no power to compel states to submit their disputes for arbitration or mediation by the United Nations. Nevertheless there is a body of international law which governs territorial disputes derived essentially from customary practice over long periods of time.

However, the post-war existence of the United Nations has provided a mechanism for establishing the legitimacy of states. This has been an important function in the post-war world, where membership of the international community has more than doubled with the creation of many new states on the granting of independence to the vast majority of the former European colonial territories. Membership of the United Nations has come to be regarded as an international recognition of the existence and legitimacy of states. There is a distinction between recognition of the existence of a sovereign and autonomous *state* and recognition of a *government* or *regime* as the legitimate exerciser of sovereign power and control within the territory of that state. Recognition of a government is a technical matter and subject to relatively frequent change according to the internal politics of the state concerned. In general different states have different criteria which they apply in deciding whether to grant or withhold recognition of a new government. In normal circumstances this is not a problem where governments change as a result of normal constitutional procedures. It becomes a problem where there is internal strife or civil war, where governments come to power as a result of military coups or other unconstititutional methods. But the recognition of governments is a practical matter and the criteria for recognition usually relate to the ability of the new government to control the majority of the territory of the state and whether it can exercise administrative competence over its population. Thus it is not uncommon that a state accepts the existence of another state but does not accept a particular government as the legitimate government of that state. For example, for a number of years after the war the United States, whilst it recognised the state of China, refused to recognise the communist government in Beijing as the legitimate government of China.

It is important to draw attention to this distinction at this time firstly to clarify the issue but also to demonstrate the legal difficulty of withdrawing recognition of the existence of a state in the present international system where legitimacy of existence is conferred almost formally by acceptance of membership of the United Nations. It would thus be difficult for the United Nations to countenance a contested claim to the whole of a territory of a member; that would be to accept a legal basis for the demise of one of its own members. Since the legality of a state's claim to sovereign independence is one of the criteria applied by the Security Council in considering its application for membership of the United Nations, it is unlikely to undo its own legal judgment. Moreover, once a state has been accepted as a member and accepted as having sovereign existence that situation acquires a momentum that is very difficult to stop (short of a unanimous and constitutional decision by the state to incorporate itself into another state). Indeed during its existence no member of the United Nations has ceased to exist as a sovereign state. The last time something of this nature did happen was the Soviet annexation of the Baltic states in 1941 during the Second World War and during the hiatus between the operation of the League of Nations and the formation of the United Nations. The status of the Baltic states as part of the Soviet Union has never been recognised by many states, including Britain and the United States. There were clearly political constraints on the western response to that annexation both during the war and whilst the Cold War between the superpowers existed. It is a measure of the persistence of statehood in the modern era, however, that the sovereign independence of the Baltic states has now been re-established and their reincorporation into the international community has been formalised by their acceptance as members of the United Nations.

The relevance of this discussion to the dispute between Iraq

and Kuwait is that whilst an Iraqi claim to part of the territory of
Kuwait would be the subject of legitimate consideration on legal
grounds, its validity being judged by applying the recognised
conventions and customs that have been developed over such
issues, a contested claim to the whole territory is unlikely to be
considered legitimate.

CRITERIA FOR JUDGEMENT OF TERRITORIAL CLAIMS

A territorial claim is judged according to three main criteria. The
first is the documented history of the sovereignty exercised over
the territory in question; the second is the behaviour of the claimant state with regard to the state whose territory is claimed; and
the third relates to the established behaviour of other states and
the international community as a whole.

Documented history criterion

The validity of the claim based upon documented history is a
matter for judgement of the circumstances in each individual case.

The Iraqi claim[3]

The Iraqi claim to Kuwait is based firstly upon its interpretation of
the status of Kuwait as part of the Ottoman Empire – that is, as
part of the Ottoman province of Basrah; secondly upon the fact
that the state of Iraq was constructed out of the unification of the
Ottoman provinces of Mosul, Baghdad and Basrah after the First
World War, and since Kuwait was part of Basrah it should also be
part of Iraq. Thirdly, it is implicit in the Iraqi case that had Turkey
been able to oversee the succession to its empire, Kuwait would
have been made part of Iraq.

Thus any judgement as to the validity of the Iraqi claim must
rest upon three considerations:

1 An examination of Iraq's contention regarding the status of
  Kuwait as part of the Ottoman Empire.
2 Whether there was any 'natural' continuity in the status of the
  provinces that became Iraq from pre-Ottoman times upon
  which a post-Ottoman structure could be based; in other words,
  is there a pre-Ottoman logic making for the state of 'Iraq' and

could Kuwait be said to be part of it?

3 Some judgement as to the validity of the succession to the Ottoman Empire in the absence of Turkey as a key player.

It might be useful to deal first with the second item above. The three Ottoman provinces of Mosul, Baghdad and Basrah were collectively known as Mesopotamia; in many of the documents, treaties and conferences in the immediate post-war period the term 'Mesopotamia' is commonly used to refer to the three provinces.[4] However, its existence as a legal entity – in the sense of being a coherent state – cannot be established. Indeed taking the claim further back and suggesting that there is some superior cohesion in the term 'Mesopotamia' which would substantiate Iraq's claim to an organic statehood only serves further to cloud the issue. Even those who claim to trace the Arab state system back to the pre-Ottoman period make an exception in the cases of Syria, Jordan, Palestine and Iraq where the state-system itself is recognised as being a creation of colonial powers.[5] Kuwait's relationship to a pre-Ottoman Mesopotamia (even if such an entity could be said to have existed) must be regarded as even more tenuous than its relationship to the Ottoman provinces.

The status of Kuwait in history

Ever since the eighteenth century the status of Koweit (as it was then referred to) had been an ambiguous one, being on the periphery of the Ottoman Empire; on the one hand it was considered as being inside it because it flew the Ottoman flag, but on the other being sufficiently autonomous and even 'wild' as not to be within the military control of the Ottoman Empire. Indeed it is a measure of its ambiguous status that in January 1899 Britain felt both the freedom and the need to conclude a secret agreement[6] with the Sheikh of Koweit in which the latter pledged not to receive the representative of any power nor to cede land or grant occupation to any power without the sanction of the British government. Indeed later, in September 1901, in the so-called Status Quo Agreement[7] the Turkish government agreed not to send Turkish troops to Koweit and to maintain the status quo on condition that the British did not occupy it or establish a protectorate over it.[8]

Such was the beginning of the process of imposing some form

of clarity on the ambiguous status of Koweit at the end of the nineteenth century. The motivation of the desire for this clarification was the probability that the Koweit area was to be the terminus on the Persian Gulf of the proposed Baghdad railway. Britain could clearly see the potential of such a project in both commercial and strategic terms, and moreover there was some suspicion that Germany and even Russia might have designs other than merely the establishment of a railway terminus.[9] The fact that Turkey also at this time began to assert its claims over Koweit attests to the fact that up to that time Koweit was by no means unambiguously within the Turkish Empire.

It seems that Britain may at one time have conceded, at least privately, Turkish 'influence' over the Koweit area but not power to effect control.[10] In any case there was never any doubt that Britain regarded herself as the major power in the Persian Gulf and was in a position of bringing that power to bear on land (as she did on a number of occasions) if she saw her interests being threatened. So long as Koweit's uncertain status continued Britain was prepared to stand back to some extent; however, as soon as it seemed that others might be attempting to change the status quo, and that Britain might thereby suffer some disadvantage, then she felt she had to exert her power and clarify the status of Koweit in her favour.

The acceptance by the Sheikh Mubarakh of Koweit of the status of 'Kaimakam' (provincial governor) from the Ottoman Sultan was the subject of disagreement even among British officials – one regarding it as merely an honorary appointment (the Sheikh refrained from using the title 'Pasha' – the equivalent Turkish term) and another suggesting that such acceptance effectively precluded recognition of the Sheikh's independence.[11]

Both Britain and Turkey appeared to want to avoid any direct confrontation over the status of Koweit. Several times British forces in the area were authorised to step in on the side of the Sheikh against the Turks should it be necessary. But the British were reluctant to declare Protectorate status for Koweit in the absence of a direct attempt by the Turks to take military action against Koweit which would end in Turkish military occupation. On their side the Turks appeared reluctant to give the British a pretext for taking such action. Thus it was that the condition of ambiguity continued; the anxiety of both sides to ensure that the situation did not change to their disadvantage led to the Status

Quo Agreement of 1901. But even then, as the Marquess of Landesdowne, Secretary of State at the Foreign Office, admitted in 1902, it was doubtful if any one really knew what that status quo actually was.[12]

A key document in the process of clarification of the status of Koweit which was a manifestation both of the declining power of the Ottoman Empire and of the increasing British interest in potential oil reserves in Koweit, was the Convention[13] signed between the British government and the Ottoman imperial government in July 1913. This is a key document because it seems to establish in large measure the independent status of Koweit – again not without some ambiguity – but the status of the document itself is uncertain because it was not ratified owing to the outbreak of the First World War.

Though this agreement was not ratified, its contents do give an indication of the perception that the Turks had of Koweit's status in relation to Ottoman power in the area. The agreement recognises Koweit as an 'autonomous *kaza*' of the Ottoman Empire but also stipulates that the

> Imperial Ottoman Government shall abstain from interference in the affairs of Koweit, including the question of the succession, and from any administrative act or occupation, and from any military act, in the territories forming part thereof.[14]

It defines the autonomous Koweit territory (an area around the present Kuwait City) and an outer area whose tribes shall come under the administration of the Sheikh (see Map 1 in Appendix III). Even in this outer area the Ottoman Government would not exercise any administrative function without permission of the Sheikh of Koweit and neither could they 'take any military step there whatsoever without having previously come to an understanding with His Britannic Majesty's Government'.

Of course the amibiguity in this Convention concerns the extent to which a territory can be said to be part of an empire if the imperial power has no jurisdiction, administrative function nor the right or power to take military action within it. The only symbols of Koweit's association with the Ottoman Empire contained in the agreement was the designation of Koweit as a *kaza* of the empire, that it should fly the Ottoman flag (but was allowed to have the word 'Koweit' in the corner of the flag) and perhaps more substantially – but no less ambiguously – Article 9, which stipulates that full proprietary rights must be exercised by the Sheikh 'in accordance with Ottoman law'. However, the British government interpreted the Convention as giving the Sheikh complete sovereignty over Kuwait's resources.[15] At the very least the relationship of such a territory to the imperial centre must be regarded as tenuous. Indeed it is that very tenuousness that both enabled and required intervention by the British government.

It was on the outbreak of war, and with the prospect that the Convention of July 1913 would now not be ratified, that in return for action against the Ottoman Empire, including the occupation of Umm Qasr, Safwan and Bubiyan and an attempt to take Basra, Britain would extend formal protection to the Sheikh of Koweit and declare his Sheikhdom an independent government under British protection. It is really from this act that Kuwait's status as a self-governing territory under British protection dates and persisted until its formal independence in 1961 and later its membership of the United Nations was approved by the Security Council in 1963.

The fact is that both politically and legally the Iraqi case is weak. It is centrally based upon the supposed status of Kuwait as part of the Ottoman Empire and subsequently on a 'would have been' situation. In other words, the case assumes that had the Ottoman Empire still existed at the time of the succession to the colonial regimes after the First World War, then Kuwait would have been made part of Iraq. But of course the historical fact of the matter is that the former colonial power was not still in existence at the time to oversee the succession. It was the British that took over that responsibility. Indeed Kuwait was given independent protectorate status by the British before the demise of the Ottoman Empire; the Ottoman Empire had ceased to exist when the Territory of Iraq was mandated by the League of Nations to the United Kingdom. It was thus the political reality of the post-Ottoman situation that determined the succession to the former Ottoman territories.

There is clearly a political legitimacy that derives from a colonial territory which revolts and throws off the power of the metropolitan country; there is also a political legitimacy in a colonial power arranging the independence on terms that it works out with the people of the territory. If the colonial power no longer has the power to effect these arrangements then of course they go by default and no subsequent claim can be based upon what the arrangement would or might have been. The fact is that Iraq itself is as much a 'fabrication' of what did happen, of the actual arrangements that were made, as Kuwait is. So those grounds could equally be the basis for the questioning of the legal and political legitimacy of Iraq itself.

Behaviour criterion

Behaviour of Iraq

First we need to consider how the behaviour of the claimant state can weaken or effectively preclude its claim – the technical legal term is *estoppel*. A state may effectively estop itself from territorial claims against another state (1) if it has formally recognised that state, (2) if it has entered into normal diplomatic, political, economic and legal relations with it, and (3) if it has not, or not consistently, taken opportunities to establish its claim or restate its claim over time.

Clearly a formal recognition of one state by another, or a failure to qualify that recognition in terms of the claim, precludes a legitimate claim over the whole of its territory. Iraqi behaviour with regard to Kuwait has been inconsistent. Iraq has reiterated its claim to Kuwait on a number of occasions and at particularly significant times – for example, when Kuwait was declared independent in 1961 and when its case for membership of the United Nations was considered by the Security Council in 1963. However, at the same time Iraq has more or less treated Kuwait both implicitly and explicitly as a sovereign and independent country. For example, Iraq suggested the exchange of consular representatives as a prelude to establishing formal diplomatic relations which can only exist between sovereign states. Iraq itself has supported Kuwaiti membership of international organisations – including agencies of the United Nations – which itself would constitute an implicit recognition of Kuwait's independence. Commercial and trading relations have been established between Iraq and Kuwait. Both Iraq and Kuwait have been members of the Gulf Cooperation Council; and moreover, Iraq has more recently been the beneficiary of Kuwaiti financial and economic assistance both during and subsequent to the Iran–Iraq war. All of such behaviour, which is typical of normal relations that other sovereign independent states have with each other, would tend to estop Iraq from successfully pursuing such a claim to the whole of Kuwaiti territory and indeed preclude it from challenging the very existence of Kuwait as a sovereign state.

For long Kuwait had already possessed many of the pre-requisites of a state – currency, laws, courts, postage stamps – and had been recognised as such by many states even during its 'protected' status from 1914 to 1961. That recognition was granted even by other Arab states – in particular after formal independence in 1961 the Arab League accepted Kuwait as a member against Iraq's opposition. Indeed Iraq itself has formally recognised the independence of Kuwait on two separate occasions. One was in July 1932, when the Iraqi prime minister, Nuri Pasha, agreed the existing frontier between Iraq and Kuwait;[16] the second was in October 1963, when the new Iraqi government that had succeeded Colonel Qassim recognised the independence of Kuwait with the boundaries specified in the agreement of 1932.[17] In outlining their case during the crisis the Iraqis claimed that neither of these acts of recognition have validity because neither was ratified by the Iraqi legislative authorities. However, the Vienna Convention on the Law of Treaties (1969) Article 46 states:

1. A state may not invoke the fact that its consent to be bound by a treaty has been expressed in violation of a provision of its internal law regarding competence to conclude treaties as invalidating its consent unless that violation was manifest[18]

In addition to this, Iraq has on a number of occasions actually suggested leasing part of the land in question from Kuwait – for example, the island of Bubiyan – an act which of course implicitly recognises it as belonging to Kuwait.

On the other hand, Iraq has, notably in 1961, given notice of its preparedness to bypass international law and use military force to intimidate Kuwait and threaten a forcible takeover. This again might be regarded as demonstrating a lack of confidence that such a claim would find any favour among the international legal community.

Behaviour of other states and the international community

We have already referred to membership of the United Nations as a mechanism for conferring the sovereign existence of a state.

Iraq, being already independent in 1945, was one of the original members of the United Nations. Kuwait became a member of the United Nations on 14 May 1963, the Security Council rejecting Iraqi claims to the whole of Kuwait. The Soviet Union voted in favour of Iraq's case but this is likely to have been motivated by political and Cold War considerations rather than any strict adherence to international law.

But the vast majority of the international community have dealt with Kuwait as if she were a normal independent sovereign state. Moreover, the Arab states themselves have clearly not paid a great deal of heed to Iraq's claim.

INTERNATIONAL LAW, THE UNITED NATIONS AND THE GULF CRISIS

Territorial disputes and questions of sovereignty are common causes of international conflict. The most recent case imprinted on the consciousness of British people – the Falklands conflict – is a case in point and an indication that such disputes are still regarded by states as a *casus belli.*

A legal claim to territory is always undermined by the use of force to acquire it. An unsuccessful act of force to resolve a territorial dispute has the effect of taking the claim off the international political agenda for the foreseeable future. Such has been the case with the Falkland Islands; such will now be the case with Iraq's claim over Kuwaiti territory.

Article 6 of the United Nations Charter provides for the peaceful settlement of disputes. The unprovoked aggression of Iraq against Kuwait on 2 August 1990 was a breach of the United Nations Charter. Article 2, paragraph 4 states that 'all members shall refrain in their international relations from the threat or use of force against the territorial integrity or political independence of other states'. The use of force is not outlawed absolutely. Article 51 allows for an inherent and legitimate right of self-defence in the face of such aggression. Thus Kuwait had the right of resistance to Iraqi aggression. However, given the size of its territory and the comparative size of its armed forces it was unlikely that Kuwait's resistance would last very long. Within less than twenty-four hours Iraqi troops effectively controlled Kuwait and had penetrated to Kuwait's southern border with Saudi Arabia.

The question arises as to how long resistance is allowed. The right of 'individual or collective self-defence' under Article 51 is qualified by the phrase 'until the Security Council has taken the measures necessary to maintain international peace and security'. During the Cold War when there was an ideological stalemate in the Security Council such measures were very often a long time coming – indeed not at all in the military sense (except in the only two cases of Korea and the Congo). It seems unlikely that the United Nations could expect a member state to suffer military disadvantage whilst waiting for a Security Council action to counter an act of aggression. Thus a state would have the right to immediate self-defence and continued resistance until the Security Council could provide collective military support or non-military measures which would lead to the restoration of 'international peace and security'. The question then arises as to whether the imposition of economic sanctions constituted those non-military measures and whether upon their imposition Kuwait was precluded from further military resistance. It is unlikely that anyone could reasonably hold that the existence of economic sanctions debarred further Kuwaiti military or armed resistance against the Iraqi occupation inside Kuwait; and if such internal resistance is not debarred, neither would be the use of external military support to effect the same objective – that is, the ending of the Iraqi occupation of Kuwait. Thus there does not in this case seem to be a time limitation on the right of a collective military response to the Iraqi invasion.

This relates to an issue raised at several other points in this book – that is, the difference between aggression and war. It is only resistance to aggression that creates war. Thus it was Kuwaiti resistance to Iraqi aggression that entailed war. It can be contended that so long as Kuwaiti resistance continued, the war continued, and that the Coalition military action was part of that war, representing a counter-offensive against the Iraqi invasion notwithstanding Iraq's persistent description of a Coalition military counter action as 'aggression'. On this point it is worth pointing out that Iraq's own treaty obligations estops it from such a claim. Article 5 of the Treaty of Brotherhood and Alliance between Iraq and Transjordan 14 April 1947 (came into force 10 June 1947) contains a list of acts which were deemed acts of aggression but paragraph (c) of this article states:

The following shall not be deemed acts of aggression:

1 the exercise of the right of legitimate defence, that is, resisting any act of aggression as defined above.
2 actions taken to implement the provisions of the Charter of the United Nations.[19]

Though this treaty itself was not concluded with Kuwait, those general principles regarding the definition of acts of aggression could reasonably be used to suggest that on both counts Iraq estops itself from categorising the Coalition military response to its invasion of Kuwait as aggression.

This argumentation of course relates to the contention that before an Coalition military response took place a further Security Council resolution would be required specifying the use of force if necessary. We have established that the United Nations Charter and international law did not actually require such specific authorisation. The fact that the United States and the other Coalition members sought such authorisation was due to political rather than legal necessity. A specific authorisation put all the political and legal authority of the Security Council (including the permanent members) behind the action. A reliance on Article 51 to take such action would have risked detaching the Coalition leaders – notably the United States and the United Kingdom – from the rest of the Security Council and the rest of the international community. This is another demonstration of the importance of international law in the behaviour of states.

The question also arises as to what extent third parties might legitimately become involved in supporting the victim state outside of the United Nations framework or prior to the Security Council taking action. Article 51 provides for the inherent right of both individual and collective self-defence which would enable the victim state to call on third parties to assist it – whether those third parties were fulfilling a formal treaty obligation or merely responding to an *ad hoc* request.

So clearly Kuwait had the right to call on the United States and the United Kingdom to go to her aid both diplomatically and militarily. Of course the United States and United Kingdom were free to respond as they thought fit; when they did so they were doing so as 'allies' of Kuwait and Saudi Arabia not as agents of the United Nations. They were later able to perform the function given them by the Security Council (Resolution 678) because they had already responded under Article 51.

But of course the actual order of events was that United States and United Kingdom troops were sent out to Saudi Arabia at the request of the Saudi government in order to deter an Iraqi invasion of Saudi Arabia. Iraqi troops were building up on the Kuwaiti–Saudi border. Indeed the initiative for the sending of United States troops may have come from the Americans themselves. There was a good deal of Arab hesitation in responding to the Iraqi action and no doubt the Americans prompted the Saudis. But the Saudis did issue the invitation after which the Coalition troop build-up ensued. But again this relates to an issue discussed in Chapter 3 – the extent to which the response to Iraq was a United Nations response working principally through the United States or on the other hand a United States response using the United Nations for its own objectives. Even if it is judged to be the latter it is clear that all concerned on the Allied side were very careful to be conforming to the principles of international law.

It is not clear at what stage, if at all, Kuwait actually asked the United States for military aid in ejecting the Iraqis from Kuwait. It is clear that President Bush's decision to do so took place sometime after the Congressional elections in early November 1990. But again the United States was careful, if that was a unilateral decision, to give effect to it through United Nations channels. The two requirements for that were a Security Council resolution authorising 'all necessary means' and a specific ultimatum date. These two conditions were provided for in Resolution 678 on 29 November 1990. So the military action which the United States Coalition began on 16 January 1991 was legitimised by Article 51 of the United Nations Charter and by specific Security Council resolution – the first time such action had been taken with the unanimity of the permanent members in the history of the organisation.

But it is worth noting that had the United States and the United Kingdom not taken action independently of the United Nations in sending troops to Saudi Arabia initially, they would not have been in a position to carry out the Security Council's mandate when the time came. Though the United States began their response under Article 51 (self-defence) that response was legitimised by Security Council Resolution 678 as an action in furtherance of a Security

Council objective – that is, the response was converted into a United Nations enforcement action under Article 47. That objective went further than might have been strictly possible under Article 51 since it provided for the restoration of 'peace and security' in the area. Thus it was the Security Council resolution that enabled the Coalition to take a level of military action and to pursue aims much wider than that merely of the ejection of Iraqi troops from Kuwait.[20] It enabled, for example, the objective of the destruction of Iraqi military capability and even the undermining through military action (in the event, air bombardment) of the ability of the Ba'athist regime and Saddam Hussein to maintain political and administrative power since these were the two major forces in Iraq which constituted the continuing threat to peace and security in the region.

This is further substantiated by Article 2, paragraph, 7 which says:

> Nothing contained in the present Charter shall authorise the United Nations to intervene in matters which are essentially within the domestic jurisdiction of any state; *but this principle shall not prejudice the application of enforcement measures under Chapter VII.* (emphasis added)[21]

The point here is that 'non-interference' is not absolute. The Charter allows such interference when dealing with breaches of the peace and acts of aggression under Article 7 and might thus be interpreted as allowing the Coalition to pursue Saddam Hussein if that was considered in furtherance of dealing with the aggression and restoring peace and security. The reason that in the event they did not pursue him was political rather than legal and is discussed in Chapter 8.

What is surprising regarding the use of international law in the crisis was the attitude of the Iraqis. It was their contempt even for a superficial acknowledgement of international law that alienated them from virtually the whole international community. Their references to it were so crude and inconsistent as to be outrageous, such that even those states which might have some ideological affinity to the Iraqi regime, were careful not to be associated with such behaviour.

The Iraqis made a number of justifications for the invasion of Kuwait:

1 Kuwait is part of Iraq.
2 Part of Kuwait is part of Iraq.
3 Iraq was invited in by revolutionary democratic forces who wanted to overthrow the Kuwaiti government.
4 Kuwait was undermining the economic well-being of Iraq by refusing to limit oil production and thus helping to keep the price of oil low.
5 Iraq's contention that the 'Kuwait problem' could be considered in the same context as the Palestinian problem with the implication that Iraq would withdraw from Kuwait at the same time as Israel withdrew from the occupied territories. The implication of that is, that Iraq invaded Kuwait in order to solve the Palestinian problem.

It has already been established that Iraq's territorial claim is a very weak claim and moreover is undermined by claiming at one time the whole of Kuwait and at another only part of it. Point (3) above was merely a device and not persisted in for more than a couple of days, after which the annexation of Kuwait was announced. In any case even if true it would not be a valid reason for invasion. Similar pretexts have been used by other states, notably the Soviet Union in its invasion of Hungary 1956, Czechoslovakia 1968 and Afghanistan 1979. But in these cases, however contrived the pretext, at least the state taking aggressive military action ensured that it was the constituted authorities in these countries that invited in the foreign troops. The Iraqi government could not even claim that and apparently did not even attempt a pre-invasion coup in Kuwait that could provide even a flimsy pretext. Point (4) may or may not have been valid but does not constitute a legal reason for the use of military force. Point (5) is incompatible with all the other four points and of course undermines the validity of all of them.

THE INTERNATIONAL LAW OF ECONOMIC SANCTIONS

The use of economic sanctions as a coercive measure against states has on the whole not had a very successful history. There is a certain amount of disagreement among academics and commentators as to the efficacy of such measures. It is likely that the most that can be said in their favour is that sanctions may have an impact in the long term and even then that is only the case if the international community as a whole complies and the opportunities for bypassing them are rigorously kept to a minimum.

Notorious cases of multilateral sanctions that have not worked – such as those against Italy after the invasion of Abyssinia in 1935, against Southern Rhodesia after its unilateral declaration of independence in 1965 – are usually due to the inability to impose strict enough controls. In 1935 the League of Nations policy of sanctions against Italy was made almost totally ineffective by the exclusion of many strategic commodities, notably oil; and in the case of Southern Rhodesia the use of friendly South Africa to route its trade, both in and out, ensured that most goods could bypass the British blockade at Beira in Mozambique – indeed Rhodesia carried on an almost normal trade throughout virtually the whole of the sanctions period. [22]

There were a number of reasons why the economic sanctions imposed on Iraq by the United Nations might have been regarded as an exception to the general pattern of non-adherence. Firstly Iraq's behaviour was regarded almost universally as so unacceptable that it was likely that most states would agree to be bound by the sanctions resolution. Secondly there were on this occasion no large friendly contiguous states which could or would act as a benefactor to Iraq and facilitate the evasion of sanctions. Thirdly the major Coalition allies, the United States and Britain, were prepared to blockade all sea routes to Iraq as well as air routes if there was seen to be a need. Of the states contiguous with Iraq, Syria had long been an implacable enemy; Turkey was a member of NATO and thus a firm member of the Coalition; Iran, though having declared itself neutral, had not long finished a long bloody war with Iraq and moreover had ambitions to improve relations with the western powers and did not want to alientate them by sustaining the Iraqi regime. The Soviet Union, which would have been an obvious benefactor in the past, was otherwise preoccupied and no longer had an ideological incentive to support Iraq (in any case, as has been said elsewhere, it is most unlikely that Iraq would have invaded Kuwait had it still been a client state of the Soviet Union).

Articles 41 and 42 of Chapter VII of the United Nations Charter provides for active measures to support Security Council decisions in the face of acts of aggression. Article 41 provides for the isolation of the aggressor state in economic, diplomatic and political terms and if such measures prove inadequate Article 42 provides for the possibility of military action to give effect to Security Council decisions.

Following the failure of Iraq to respond to Resolution 660 of 2 August 1990 calling for Iraqi withdrawal and Iraq–Kuwait talks to resolve their differences, the Security Council adopted Resolution 661 on 6 August 1990 imposing sanctions on Iraq and Kuwait. The only possible exception was humanitarian material and Resolution 666 of 13 September 1990 was to decide that the Security Council would determine whether such exception was warranted and if so that such material would be channelled through the United Nations. This resolution did not provide for the enforcement of sanctions and so the imposition by the United States and the United Kingdom of a maritime blockade of Iraq in the Persian Gulf and the Red Sea in support of resolution 661 was of questionable legality. In declaring the blockade the United Sates and Britain claimed two authorities: one was the request of Kuwait and the other was the right of collective self-defence under Article 51. The tying together of rights under Article 51 and the specific Security Council Resolution 661 does seem questionable – it is essentially using a right to action outside the United Nations framework to justify enforcing a Security Council resolution which the Security Council had not provided for itself. However, this might be a fine legal point to make; it might have had more significance had the Security Council not itself provided for enforcing action later. In fact the blockade was brought into legal existence by Resolution 665 of 25 August, which called upon 'those states with martime forces in the area to use such measures commensurate to the specific circumstances' to ensure compliance with Resolution 661. The use of the term 'commensurate measures' clearly allowed for the use of force if necessary and indeed shots were fired on a number of occasions to intercept vessels which were reluctant to allow verification of their cargoes and destinations.

Enforcement of sanctions via land access had of course to rely on those states contiguous with Iraq. We have already mentioned the disincentive for Iran breaking sanctions. It became apparent that Iran was playing an astute diplomatic game during the crisis with the objective of re-establishing her diplomatic credibility with the western powers and maintaining her right and capability to play a role in the post-crisis security structure. She was unlikely to jeopardise these objectives by sustaining her old enemy in

Baghdad even though she was vehemently opposed to the western military presence in the region. However, there were fears that there might be a lot of local smuggling across the border which would effectively evade the sanctions order. Not much could be done about this, but neither was such activity likely to be a major breach of sanctions.

Jordan, however, was recognised as having been in a difficult political position. Her own port in Aqaba at the head of the Red Sea was blockaded, but she had adopted an ambivalent position with regard to sanctions and certainly came out in political support of Iraq. Insofar as she did so she might be regarded as being in contravention of international law. Article 2, paragraph 5, states that 'all members shall give the United Nations every assistance in any action it takes in accordance with the present Charter, and shall refrain from giving assistance to any state against which the United Nations is taking preventive or enforcement action'. This was clearly an area where sanctions enforcement was difficult. The blockade of Aqaba was to ensure that material for Iraq was denied access via Jordan; on the other hand Jordan itself could not but suffer economically from such action. Her later declaration of compliance no doubt precluded any charge of non-compliance with United Nations resolutions under Article 2, paragraph 5.

A perhaps more difficult area was preventing air access to Iraq. Resolution 670 of 25 September 1990 prohibited overflying of aircraft bound for Iraq or Kuwait. Enforcement action in the air would present more delicate problems, but there was little doubt an air-blockade was as legitimate as the maritime blockade. No incidents of air blockade running were reported.

The obvious question arises as to why, if sanctions against Iraq were likely to have been the most comprehensive and most effective example of the use of such coercive means, they were not used as the sole means to pursuade Iraq to withdraw from Kuwait. This is discussed in more detail elsewhere, but the fundamental reason concerns the judgement of the effectiveness of achieving the objectives of the Allies. It is not enough for United Nations resolutions on sanctions to be complied with by the whole international community, nor only that Iraq should have been effectively isolated from that international community. That isolation in moral and economic terms has to be translated into compliant action by the target government for sanctions to be successful. The ultimate objective was the withdrawal of Iraqi forces from Kuwait and it was doubts as to whether sanctions could effect this objective that pushed the use of force up the agenda. The fact was that the most optimistic assessments of when this was likely to begin to happen was one year – other assessments put it much later. When considering such a time-scale all sorts of other political and military factors would begin to obtrude and begin to undermine the unity and resolve of the international community to effect Iraq's withdrawal from Kuwait.

Sanctions were an essential first step designed both to signal to Iraq the seriousness with which the invasion was viewed and secondly to forge an international solidarity against Iraq. From the beginning it was unlikely that sanctions could achieve an Iraqi withdrawal. Once the major members of the United Nations Coalition had come to that conclusion then the use of force was an inevitable consequence of Iraq's refusal to withdraw its forces from Kuwait.

The logic of sanctions is that they will cause economic, commercial, diplomatic, political and moral isolation that will (1) make it difficult for the government to continue to function as an international entity and (2) cause such internal hardship and dislocation as to pressure the government to comply. For this sort of pressure to be effective the government in question has to be concerned for the welfare and support of the population and has to depend on them. The Ba'ath regime in Iraq had effectively insulated itself from the population as a whole. It depended upon the military and some 400,000 secret police and party activists. Its only task to ensure survival was to look after the welfare of these sectors. No doubt Saddam Hussein and his government had sufficient resources, food and so on stockpiled to keep these groups happy and dependent for a long time. Sanctions would not have undermined his ability to continue in office with his power intact, nor arguably would it have undermined his ability or willingness to risk a war at a later date.

Chapter 6

The laws of war and the Gulf conflict

Violent conflict has inbuilt limiting factors,[1] but formal conventions have grown in order to ensure 'fair play' and to try to impose a degree of moderation in warfare. Those who express scepticism about the existence of international law *per se* no doubt express even more scepticism about whether there can be laws of war. In fact war has historically been one of the most formal, almost ritualistic, forms of human interaction with complex customs and rules determining how it should be conducted. The Christian doctrine of the just war, for example, includes not only those principles which should govern resort to war (*jus ad bellum*) (see Chapter 7), but also those rules and moral tenets which should govern the conduct of war (*jus in bello*). The growth of 'laws' of war has emanated from the gradual development of these customary conventions. It was the developments in military technology consequent upon the industrial revolution in the nineteenth century that induced attempts to outlaw certain types of weapon. But it was the Hague Conventions of 1899 and 1907 that began the codification of the rules and conventions governing the conduct of war. A number of key agreements subsequent to these constitute the essential laws of war which govern the conduct of all international war and even internal war.

The first Geneva Convention, in 1864, dealt with the treatment of wounded in times of war and this has been supplemented and expanded by successive Geneva Conventions in 1925 and 1949, providing for rules governing land, naval and air warfare, outlawing of gas warfare, the trying of war criminals, the rights of civilians which in turn have been reinforced by general conferences and conventions reaffirming commitments to the limitations and prohibitions contained in these conventions.[2]

A book of this nature cannot deal comprehensively with the laws of war; it is most relevant to deal with the issues of law that were raised by the Gulf War and then trace their legal provenance as required.

SELF-DEFENCE UNDER ARTICLE 51 VERSUS ENFORCEMENT ACTION UNDER ARTICLE 47

We have already seen that the action of the United states and the United Kingdom in seeking specific Security Council endorsement for the use of force converted their response from one of self-defence under Article 51 to one of a UN enforcement action under Article 47 via a specific Security Council resolution. This had important implications. First of all it was done for political rather than legal reasons – there is little doubt that the United States and the United Kingdom would have been perfectly entitled to take military action under the provisions of Article 51. But there were also potentially quite serious political and military costs of such a move in that formally the control of military action would now lie in the Security Council rather than with the Coalition leaders themselves – and this gave rise to the possibility of conflict over both the control of military operations and their objectives – both military and political.

In one sense the Security Council Resolution 678 actually widened the potential military conflict by allowing for the 'peace and security' criterion to be the ultimate limitation of war aims; whereas action under Article 51 would in theory have allowed only those measures that could be characterised as self-defence. In practice it is likely that they would have been interpreted in the same way, so taking the matter back to the UN risked getting the issues tied up in Security Council wrangling but the pay-off for the Coalition leaders was a wider mandate. The United States no doubt made the decision to refer back to the Security Council on a judgement that it was likely to get what it required to take the sort of military action it thought necessary.

The question of control however remained. This raised the general issue of the relationship between the United Nations and the military coalition which was actually conducting the military operations. This was similar to the Korean War, where an ostensible UN action was in effect conducted and controlled from Washington. Since the Military Staff Committee, provided for in the UN Charter but which has never been operational (see Chapter 3), was not functioning, the Security Council had no technical means of controlling actual operations. Effectively the relationship was that the Security Council gave the Coalition, led by the United States, the mandate to carry out its objectives within the terms of its resolutions. It was left entirely to the Coalition leadership to conduct such operations according to its own military judgement.

Still at least potentially there was always the danger that actions taken by the Coalition would be regarded or interpreted by some as beyond the remit of Resolution 678. This was reflected in speculation as to whether (1) entry into Iraqi territory would be necessary or allowable and (2) whether occupation of Iraq and overthrow of the regime could be regarded as a legitimate objective under the resolution.

The solidarity of the international community and its manifestation in a Security Council Resolution under Article 47 (virtually for the first time) raises the interesting and potentially awkward question as to the status of the Gulf conflict as a war. It is a fact that of the 150 or so conflicts since 1945 very few, if indeed any, have involved a formal declaration of war. The reason for this is that military conflict has become a much more 'informal' mode of interaction; a state of affairs that 'emerges' rather than begins at a stated time. Also the nature of the international system is such that most of the conflicts have not been like the pre-Second World War international system where great powers engaged in war as a formal mode of behaviour. Many post-war conflicts have been internal wars with external interventions; many have been guerrilla wars; some have been 'end-of-empire' wars.

To reflect these changes in the system the custom of international law has now changed such that the laws of war apply in a conflict whether or not war has been formally declared. The failure of Iraq to respond to the Security Council ultimatum entailed a state of war even in the absence of a declaration of war. Bearing in mind that the United Nations now became one of the belligerents – not its usual third-party/mediatory role – it no longer had the power to arbitrate; though perhaps the behaviour of the Secretary-General, Perez de Cuellar, suggested that he did not always comprehend that change of role.

But reflecting on the notion of a declaration of war in the context of a United Nations collective security military operation it is pertinent to raise the question as to whether the United Nations can actually declare war on, or even be at war, with one of its own members. Georg Schwarzenberger agrees that on the face of it there may be some substance in the view that collective action taken by the United Nations under Chapter VII of the Charter does not amount to war – and thus that the application of *jus in bello* does not arise.[3] However, as he later concludes, such formal interpretation could hardly be justified – so that few are likely to claim that UN forces are not bound by the rules govering the conduct of war. Specifically the Geneva Red Cross Conventions of 1949 are intended to be applied in all circumstances.[4] This is clearly a case in which the norms governing the behaviour of states must keep pace with the changing nature of the international system. The military action was none the less real and devastating despite the fact that war had not been formally declared.

HOSTAGES, 'GUESTS' AND INTERNATIONAL LAW

The Iraqi policy which perhaps attracted most odium among the world community was the detention of foreign civilians all of whom had quite legitimate reasons for being in Iraq or Kuwait before the invasion. This was clearly the Iraqi strategy during the post-invasion crisis period designed to put coercive pressure on the major Coalition actors (see Chapter 4). The rules governing the treatment of civilian populations in time of war are covered by the Geneva Convention IV 1949 (acceded to by Iraq 14 February 1956),[5] and Article 42 states that 'the internment or placing in assigned residence of protected persons may be ordered only if the security of the Detaining Power makes it absolutely necessary'.[6] Article 35 states that all protected persons may if they wish leave the territory of a party to a conflict at any time 'unless their departure is contrary to the national interests of the State'.[7] It would be difficult to make the claim that the third-party nationals detained in either Kuwait or Iraq were detained as a legitimate security precaution. So the actual detention of these people was contrary to international law.

The manner of their treatment as detainees was also contrary to law. Under Article 28 of the Geneva Convention protected persons 'may not be used to render certain points or areas immune from military operations'. (Article 83 also prohibits the setting up of places of internment in areas particularly exposed to the dangers of war.) The Iraqis contravened this provision by locating many of the foreign detainees at military, nuclear and chemical production sites with the express purpose of deterring air bombardment of such targets. Moreover, the transfer of third-state nationals from Kuwait to Iraq was contrary to Article 49, which states that 'forcible transfers or deportations of protected persons from occupied territories to the territory of the Occupying Power . . . are prohibited'.

Clearly these people had been detained by the Iraqis as hostages, as bargaining counters, to exert some deterrent pressure on those states whose nationals they had detained. This contravenes Article 34 of the 1949 Geneva Convention IV, which states quite baldly that 'The taking of hostages is prohibited'.[8]

Section I of Part III of the Convention may also be regarded as offering the same prohibition on the use of detainees for public display as on such use of prisoners of war. The display on video tape of third-state detainees by the Iraqis may be regarded with particular opprobrium. The use of hostages to affect British public opinion to bring pressure to bear on the British government was a crude propaganda device. In particular it demonstrated the hypocrisy of a leader who was anxious to portray himself as a 'family man' on television with the hostages whilst at the same time preparing to use them as a human shield to protect his military installations. Moreover, the grotesque image of Saddam Hussein fondling a 9-year old British boy beamed into the homes of virtually the whole of a British population in the grip of an obsessive anxiety about child abuse was perhaps the crassest of a number of Iraqi propaganda blunders during the crisis.

Having said all this, however, there might in the event be a legal loophole in the definition of a protected person under the Fourth Geneva Convention 1949 since Article 4 states that

Nationals of a neutral State who find themselves in the territory of a belligerent State, *and nationals of a co-belligerent State*, shall not be regarded as protected persons while the State of which they are nationals has normal diplomatic representation in the State in whose hands they are. (emphasis added)[9]

Britain's ambassador did not leave Baghdad until 10 January 1991, when all the British people who might have been regarded as protected persons had left. It is unlikely to be tested in an international court but it could plausibly be argued that the Iraqis could have been expected to treat those nationals as if they were protected persons under the Convention since there was no reason to treat them otherwise. This raises another question regarding the perceptions of the Iraqis themselves, for it could be said that Saddam Hussein's detention of foreign nationals indicates his assumption of a state of war between Iraq and the countries of origin of those nationals. Indeed one could even ask whether the internment of these persons could itself be regarded as an act of war.

But the civilian hostage issue arose during the crisis phase of the conflict and during which the relationship between Iraq and the major Coalition states was an ambiguous one. For some purposes, as is suggested at other points in this book, the Coalition states can be regarded as having been in a state of war with Iraq as soon as they agreed to go to the aid of Kuwait under Article 51 of the UN Charter. For others that state of war did not exist until the Coalition powers launched the air attack on Iraq on 17 January 1991. The beginning of that attack ended the state of ambiguity in their relationship and whether or not a war had actually been declared between the belligerents, a state of war existed and thus the laws relating to the conduct of war can be held to have applied until the war ended.

In relation to the date of the existence of a state of war between Iraq and the Coalition allies it is significant that the International Committee of the Red Cross issued notices to Iraq and Kuwait regarding their obligations under the Geneva Convention on 2 August 1990; but such notices were not issued to other parties until 17 January 1991, when Coalition air hostilities began.[10] However, it is unlikely that any of the parties would have been freed of such obligations outside of those dates merely as a result of the actions of the Red Cross. For example, though no actual hostilities took place between Iraqi and British forces before 17 January, they could have done in consequence of enforcement of the economic blockade on Iraq. Under those circumstances the Geneva Conventions would have been expected to apply.

PRISONERS OF WAR

The rules governing the treatment of prisoners of war are contained in a series of conventions which include the Hague Conventions and Declarations of 1899 and 1907, the Convention on the

Treatment of Prisoners of War 1929 and the Geneva Convention III Relative to the Treatment of Prisoners of War 1949. The latter replaces previous conventions on the subject between parties to those agreements. The Iraqis contravened these rules in three main ways: in their mistreatment of Coalition prisoners, in their use of some of these prisoners for propaganda purposes and in their use of prisoners as human shields to deter attacks on military and other targets.

The appearance on television of captured British and American airmen shot down in the early stages of the Coalition air campaign was a breach of Article 13, which states that prisoners should not be held up to public display for ridicule or for propaganda purposes. The actual appearance itself was a breach of law since it was designed to arouse public anxiety for the safety of these people; but so was the fact that the Iraqis forced the airmen to read out statements condemning the actions of their own governments. It was speculated at the time that these prisoners had been ill-treated, but some caution was expressed since their visible injuries were consistent with what might have been the result of ejection from their aircraft. However, subsequently the individuals themselves have testified that they were subject to varying degrees of mistreatment varying from undernourishment to physical assault and neglecting to provide medical attention to injuries. Article 13 states the general requirement that prisoners of war must be treated in a humane way.[11]

ENVIRONMENTAL DAMAGE

The use by the Iraqis of 'scorched earth' strategy on leaving Kuwait by opening oil valves that allowed oil to flow unchecked over land and sea and the setting fire to oil-wells both had predictably dire environmental effects. There is some doubt as to whether such actions would fall under the UN Convention on the Prohibition of Environmental Modification Techniques since Article 2 defines these techniques as those used through 'the deliberate manipulation of natural processes'.[12] It may be doubtful if Saddam Hussein's actions in this respect can be held to fall under this definition. However, the 1977 Geneva Protocol I on International Armed Conflicts does make provision for the protection of the natural environment. Article 55(2) says that 'attacks against the natural environment by way of reprisals are prohibited'. However, though the United States and the United Kingdom are signatories (but with reservations), their accession to the Convention has not been ratified; moreover, Iraq is not a signatory. The question then arises as to whether Iraq could be held to be bound by a convention to which she was not a party. It may be thought that such action would be better dealt with under provisions against reprisals and retribution.[13] The other question would be whether such action had a legitimate military rationale. To the extent that these actions might have marginally impeded Coalition air operations over Kuwait or sea-borne operations in the upper Gulf they might fall under that category. But then the question of proportionality would apply, that is, proportionality between the action and its military effect, and here there is a clear disproportion between the massive environmental effects of the action and its marginal military effect.

Article 56 of that same Convention prohibits attacks on 'works and installations containing dangerous forces. . . if such attack may cause the release of dangerous forces and consequent severe losses among the civilian population'.[14] This prohibition is extended to 'military objectives located at or in the vicinity of these works'. The question arises as to whether the Allied bombardment of the Iraqi chemical and biological warfare (CBW) sites and the sites housing Iraq's nuclear weapons programme would have been prohibited under this convention. These were acknowledged and declared prime targets of the Coalition powers. Paragraph 2 of Article 56 says that such a prohibition ceases if the installations in question are 'used in regular, significant and direct support of military operations'.

Clearly the Iraqi installations relating to nuclear weapons and CBW weapons were not at the time used in regular, significant and direct support of their military operations. They were targets of Coalition attack precisely to prevent these means from assuming such status. It has indeed been claimed that these attacks did release nuclear radiation and toxic chemical clouds which were potential hazards to civilian populations. However, it is likely that even if it could be established that Article 56 of the 1977 Geneva Protocol I did apply in this case (doubtful, apart from its actual provisions, because Iraq itself is not a signatory), the Coalition allies could claim *kriegsraison* (military necessity) to justify a legitimate breach of international law.

KRIEGSRAISON

It is said that 'the rules of warfare are the result of a continuous tug-of-war between two formative agencies: the standard of civilisation and the necessities of war'.[15] The concept of military necessity is difficult to apply since it is difficult to determine who should decide what is and what is not militarily necessary and whether the term is being used to disguise mere military convenience.[16] It is plausible that *kriegsraison* cannot legitimately be applied to Iraq's scorched earth strategy but on the other hand can legitimately be applied in the case of Coalition attacks on Iraqi CBW production sites and nuclear weapons research facilities.

A 'scorched-earth' strategy by a retreating army is allowed under Article 54 of the 1977 Protocol I in order to 'safeguard themselves';[17] that is, if leaving resources would strengthen the enemy and allow him to pursue the retreating army more effectively. But it is unlikely that this could be claimed as the 'military necessity' to allow Iraqi retreat from Kuwait. The Protocol even allows the destruction of foodstuffs and agricultural areas in order to defend one's own national territory from attack. Indeed Saladin, whom Saddam Hussein claimed to be emulating, used a scorched-earth 'strategy of hunger' in the twelfth century to prevent the Crusaders advancing on Jerusalem.[18] Here there was a clear strategic rationale in attempting to achieve military objectives by the use of least costly means – if by denying the enemy the capacity to sustain himself in the field he can be defeated without even going to battle then clearly that is a legitimate, and even desirable, strategy. However, Iraqi scorched-earth actions were carried out for purely vindictive purposes and did not, and would not, have deterred the Coalition forces one iota. Thus there was no military rationale for the policy that Iraq could refer to and thus could not justify a breach of international law. Moreover, there is a general prohibition against reprisals against civilian property or retribution in warfare which could reasonably describe Iraq's actions in Kuwait.

On the other hand reference to military necessity by the Coalition to justify attacks on sites where the manufacture of obnoxious weapons was taking place is rather more plausible since the bringing into operational use of such weapons represented a serious threat to Coalition forces and indeed to civilian populations within range of Iraqi missiles.

An interesting case where derogation from the rules of war might be justified is the claimed destruction of holy places and cultural sites by the Coalition air forces – none of which incidentally has been substantiated. The Hague Convention on the Protection of Cultural Property and the 1977 Protocol I provide some protection for cutural sites and holy places. The first question arises as to whether any damage to religious or cultural places that can be substantiated was the result of deliberate attack or was merely 'collateral'. If the former then derogation may apply if it could be shown that substantial military resources were hidden or thought to be hidden in them. There were stories that tanks, aircraft and personnel were housed at such sites in order to avoid Allied bombardment. For example, it was found that the Iraqis had hidden military aircraft near the Ziggurat at Ur, one of the great archaeological treasures of the world.[19] If that was the case then that in itself was a breach of law. In such a case all that would be required to justify a breach of the law by the Coalition would be not only the evidence of damage but the evidence of matériel being hidden in such places. Damage to such places as an unintended consequence of attacks on nearby legitimate military targets would not in itself be contrary to the laws of war.

Similarly with civilian sites, there was substantial evidence that the Iraqis hid aircraft among civilian dwellings when they discovered that their hardened aircraft shelters were being breached by Coalition weapons. The concealing of military equipment and personnel in otherwise 'protected' areas would be considered an act of perfidy (see below) and would have the effect of suspending protection under the humanitarian rules of war. Thus such acts would deprive both civilians and cultural property of protection from attack at such sites. However, there is no evidence that the Allies succumbed to the temptation to attack these locations even though there may well have been due cause to claim 'military necessity'.

It is worth pointing out that there would have been a severe political disincentive to the Coalition deliberately targeting such sites and would hardly have been risked particularly given the other major military advantages they had. It may also be noted that the very fact that the Iraqis employed such a tactic demonstrates their belief that the Coalition would be constrained by their need to be seen to be conforming to the laws of war – an indication that the notion of law and humanity does have an impact on the conduct of war.

CIVILIAN POPULATIONS

One of the major distinctions drawn in the laws of war is that between combatants and non-combatants – the latter covers civilians not taking part in hostilities and those combatants who for one reason or another are *hors de combat*. References to the exclusion of civilians as targets in military operations can be found in the Hague Convention of 1907, but the main and specific provisions regarding the protection of civilians in times of war are contained in the 1949 Geneva Convention IV and the 1977 Protocols I and II.[20] These provisions however do not specifically cover air warfare, and the only documentary source of rules governing the status of civilians in relation to air bombardment is contained in the 1923 Hague Draft Rules of Aerial Warfare which, as the title suggests, are not binding.[21] However, the provisions of the 1977 Protocols, though not specifying air warfare, are sufficiently broad in their use of the term 'attack' as to include air bombardment.

The three main circumstances in which the issue of the treatment of civilians arose in the Gulf conflict concerned (1) the behaviour of Iraqi military forces towards civilian populations during their invasion and occupation of Kuwait, (2) the air war conducted by the Coalition forces against targets in Kuwait and Iraq, and (3) that conducted by the Iraqis with the use of missiles against Israel and Saudi Arabia.

There were many reports from Kuwait (and indeed Iraq) of contraventions of many of the specific provisions of the Geneva Conventions and the 1977 Protocols. The provisions outlaw murder, physical and mental torture, corporal punishment, mutilation, 'outrages upon personal dignity ... degrading treatment ... any form of indecent assault', hostage-taking and acts of terrorism. Reports of brutality, summary execution, public execution, torture, rape, arbitrary detention, transporting of Kuwaitis to Iraq, and so on, are numerous and are subject to continuing investigation. But there is little doubt that the Iraqi regime and individual Iraqi military personnel would have serious charges to answer under international law if the UN Coalition were ever in a position to take legal action. (The issue of war crimes is discussed below.)

There have been few if any reports of contravention of these provisions by Coalition land forces and in any case these forces never really came into contact with Iraqi civilian populations except briefly in some towns in southern Iraq at the end of hostilities.

As to air warfare, the 1923 Hague Draft Rules state that 'aerial bombardment for the purpose of terrorizing the civilian population, of destroying or damaging private property not of military character or injuring non-combatants is prohibited'. (Article 22).[22] These rules were drafted in the early years of the development of aircraft for the purposes of warfare and there has been a reluctance to make the rules binding partly because of the uncertainty of their effect on the use of this powerful new technology. The use for the first time of air bombardment on a large scale by Italy in Abyssinia, by Germany in the Spanish civil war and by Japan in China, all in the 1930s, made plain the need for the basic principles governing air warfare which were set down by Neville Chamberlain in 1938 and later incorporated into the League of Nations.[23]

These principles were simply stated:

1 Direct attack against the civilian population is unlawful.
2 Targets for air bombardment must be legitimate, identifiable military objectives.
3 Reasonable care must be taken in attacking military objectives to avoid bombardment of a civilian population in the neighbourhood.

The strategic bombing campaigns of both sides during the Second World War called into question the commitment or even possibility of abiding by these rules. Nevertheless their import has been incorporated into the 1977 Geneva Protocols I and II. (It is worth noting here that the United States's signature – though not ratification – of the Protocols was subject to the reservation that the Protocols were 'not intended to have any effect on and do not regulate or prohibit the use of nuclear weapons').[24]

The area of ambiguity upon which the difficulties of applying these rules centres is that related to the unintended consequences of aerial bombardment as it affects non-military personnel or property. Chamberlain's principles urge that 'reasonable care' be taken to avoid such consequences. Article 57(1) of the 1977 Geneva Protocol I talks of 'constant care to spare the civilian population'. It is perhaps worth quoting the whole of Article 57(2):

2. With respect to attacks, the following precautions shall be taken:
  (a) those who plan or decide upon an attack shall:
    (i) do everything feasible to verify that the objectives to be attacked are neither civilians nor civilian objects...;
    (ii) take all feasible precautions in the choice of means and methods of attack with a view to avoiding, and in any event to minimizing, incidental loss of civilian life, injury to civilians and damage to civilian objects;
    (iii) refrain from deciding to launch any attack which may be expected to cause incidental loss of civilian life, injury to civilians, damage to civilian objects, or a combination thereof, which would be excessive in relation to the concrete and direct military advantage anticipated;
  (b) an attack shall be cancelled or suspended if it becomes apparent that the objective is not a military one or is subject to special protection or that the attack may be expected to cause incidental loss of civilian life, injury to civilians, damage to civilian objects, or a combination thereof, which would be excessive in relation to the concrete and direct military advantage anticipated;
  (c) effective advance warning shall be given of attacks which may affect the civilian population, unless circumstances do not permit.[25]

It is in the vagueness and uncertainty of such phrases as 'do everything feasible', 'take all feasible precautions', 'may be expected to cause', 'damage. . . which would be excessive', 'unless circumstances do not permit' that difficulties arise. These phrases are of course designed to limit the use of force without inhibiting the legitimate pursuit of military objectives. Ultimately there is no precise formula which would ensure behaviour strictly in accordance with the rules. The provisos which in effect acknowledge the principle of 'military necessity' are all subject to interpretation and judgement in the light of particular circum-stances prevailing at any one time.

A number of issues arise in the context of the Iraqi Scud missile attacks on Israel and Saudi Arabia. Firstly the attacks on Israel were unprovoked, and since Israel was not a member of the Coali-tion forces they could be regarded as a fresh act of aggression, which by definition was a breach of international law. But more specifically the questions arise as to (1) the intention of the attacks and (2) whether the missiles were accurate enough to be able to discriminate between civilian and military targets. In the event the vast majority of missiles either fell on centres of population or in open territory. There was only one report of a military hit and that was on the American army base at Dhahran in Saudi Arabia. There is every reason to believe that the intention of the Iraqis was indeed to target civilian populations in Israel in order to provoke Israeli entry into the conflict. But even if the intention had been to attack only military targets, the accuracy of such weapons was such that near centres of population they would not have been able to discriminate between the two with sufficient precision. Thus both on grounds of intention and on grounds of the 'appropriateness' of the weapons used the Iraqi Scud attacks were clearly contrary to international law.

The controversey over Coalition activity in the air war mainly concerned the number of civilian casualties as a result of air raids on Baghdad. Much scepticism has been expressed regarding the 'surgical' or 'precision' nature of the air bombardment of Baghdad. It may well be that more non-precision guided munitions were used than guided ones, but in general it is clear that precision-guided weapons were used in situations where legitimate military targets were located in populated areas, and where they were necessary for military purposes; and in general non-precision weapons were used to attack broad targets or desert targets where precise locations were uncertain – more particularly Iraqi troop and equipment emplacements in Kuwait and southern Iraq.

In the absence of the availability of detailed battle damage assessments it is not possible to be certain but it does seem probable that on the whole the use of precision-guided weapons against military targets in built-up areas was successful in minimising civilian casualties. Eye-witness accounts of damage to target buildings in Baghdad report very little, if any, damage to surrounding property.[26] Though it must be said that judgements about what is an 'acceptable' or 'justifiable' level of civilian casualties are always subject to disagreement. Given that the general figures of civilian casualties are within broad bounds of expectation 'in the circumstances' (e.g. the number of civilian casualties compared to the tonnage of explosive used in the air bombardment) it is likely that any application of the laws of war to the Allied air campaign would centre on the question as to whether 'all feasible precautions' were taken (1) to ensure that all military targets were accurately identified as such, (2) to ensure the choice of means that would minimise civilian casualties, and (3) that there was a proportionality between the importance of the military target, the means used and the risk of civilian casualties (1977 Geneva Protocol I, Article 57).

The military benefit of very sophisticated and accurate guidance technology lies in the high degree of efficiency in destroying targets in terms of the explosive capacity of weapons, the 'specificity' of the target–weapons relationship and the number of weapons that have to be used to destroy any particular target. Set in these terms and in the context of centres of population, military efficiency entails the minimising of civilian casualties and enhances the possibility of achieving 'proportionality' in the use of military force. So the very use of these weapons complies with points (2) and (3) above, perhaps to a degree never before possible.

The major controversey concerned point (1) – that is, the accuracy of intelligence in identifying military targets, with particular reference to the attack on the Amiriya Bunker in Baghdad which resulted in 300 civilians killed. It is still unclear what the status of this bunker was but it seems that the attack was the result of an intelligence failure on the part of the United States military.[27] The bunker had been used as a military operations centre but this was apparently 'old intelligence'; it had since been converted into a civilian air-raid shelter. It is likely that any legal question would centre on whether the incident could be regarded as merely the result of 'the exigencies of war' or whether there was some culpable negligence in the targeting of the bunker.

There are two other possibilities regarding the attack on Amiriya. One is the possibility that the Iraqis deliberately housed civilians in the bunker knowing that it would be a target of the

Americans with a view to causing political damage to the American military effort. The other is the story that the Americans deliberately targeted a civilian air-raid shelter because it contained the families of many of the Iraqi leadership elite with the intention of undermining their will to continue or to encourage a coup against Saddam Hussein. Each of these cases would be a serious breach of the international laws of war.

USE OF OBNOXIOUS WEAPONS

The shadow lurking in the background of the whole conflict was the possibility that chemical weapons, and perhaps worse, would be used. The use by Iraq of chemical weapons in the war with Iran and even against defenceless Kurdish civilians was a clear indication that Saddam Hussein and the Ba'athist regime had little inhibition about using any strategy or device that they thought would serve their purpose regardless of its consequences or moral implication. It was thought that the Iraqis would use such weapons either on the Israeli population in the event that merely high explosive Scud missiles did not provoke them or as a last resort on the battlefield in order to attempt to prevent a rout of Iraqi troops. In the event they were not used and it can only be speculated as to the reasons. But the most likely reason was the uncertainty of their effectiveness against an enemy which was prepared for them and which was highly trained to continue military operations even during chemical attack. But perhaps the major deterrent was the ambiguity surrounding any Coalition response to the Iraqi use of chemical weapons. There is no doubt that the first use of chemical weapons in a conflict would be a contravention of the Geneva Protocol of 1925. However, many signatories of that convention have stipulated the reservation that they are only bound by it so long as the enemy does not use such weapons first. Thus these states reserve the right to use such weapons in retaliation to a first use by their opponent. Certainly these are the terms by which Britain, France and the United States adhere to the protocol – as incidentally does Iraq. Thus had the Coalition forces used chemical weapons in retaliation against an Iraqi first use they would not have been in breach of international law.

The other possibility was that the United States and her allies might have regarded the Iraqi contravention of the Geneva Protocol in this respect as sufficient reason to retaliate with nuclear weapons; this may well have been another fear on the part of the Iraqis since the United States signature to the 1977 Geneva Protocol I Relating to the Protection of Victims of International Armed Conflicts is qualified by the reservation that it does not preclude the use of nuclear weapons. In fact such a response would have been highly unlikely given the political and other consequences of doing so and given the vast superiority that they had over the Iraqis in terms of conventional weaponry. But perhaps a more plausible deterrent against the Iraqi use of chemical weapons on Israel was the arguably higher probability of an Israeli nuclear response.

There was also some controversy over the use of 'fuel air explosives' in the Coalition attacks on dug-in Iraqi troops. The effect of such weapons is to create a fire ball which effectively consumes all the oxygen in the air over a considerable area thereby asphyxiating whoever happens to be there. Such weapons were the subject of concern at the conference which concluded the 1981 UN Convention on Prohibitions or Restrictions on the Use of Certain Convention Weapons, but no agreement could be reached and they were not outlawed.[28]

ACTS OF PERFIDY

As has been indicated at various other points in this book, the behaviour of the state in both peace and war is very often directed to determining or altering the perceptions of other actors so that they see the world and behave in a way which serves its purposes. In warfare the use of deception is a legitimate device designed to achieve this objective. The elaborate use by the Coalition commanders of troop movements, emplacements, training, and communications traffic patterns to encourage the Iraqis to believe that there would be a combined amphibious assault on Kuwait and a frontal northward thrust, was a classic use of deception on a strategic scale. At the tactical level an almost equally significant use of deception was the use of fake scud missile launchers and tank emplacements by the Iraqis to deceive Allied air attacks.

However, military deception (or 'ruses of war' as it is termed in the 1977 Geneva Protocol I) must be distinguished from 'perfidy'. The latter involves:

Acts inviting the confidence of an adversary to lead him to believe that he is entitled to, or is obliged to, accord protection under the rules of international law applicable in armed conflict, with intent to betray that confidence

(1977 Geneva Protocol I, Article 37)[29]

The reported use of reversed gun turrets on Iraqi tanks in order to facilitate their advance on the town of Khafji on 29 January 1991[30] would, if true, have been a clear contravention of this rule and would be considered an act of perfidy since such behaviour is a conventional signal of the desire and intention to surrender. A person clearly expressing an intention to surrender is regarded as *hors de combat* under Article 41 of that Protocol and is entitled to protected status.[31] The feigning of such status with the objective of deceiving the enemy into extending protection is a breach of international law.

MUTLA RIDGE

One of the most controversial operations of the war was the attack on the Iraqi forces withdrawing from Kuwait on the highway at Mutla Ridge. So controversial indeed that its predicted impact on western public opinion was perhaps the major influence in the American decision to stop hostilities when it did – at a time when there were sound military reasons for continuing. The incident has come to be termed a 'massacre' or a 'turkey shoot', the implication being that defenceless retreating troops were needlessly slaughtered.

In terms of international law there is no doubt that the Allied troops were quite within their rights. A retreating army is regarded as still within the bounds of war operations and as such is a legitimate target. There is no indication that these retreating troops had either laid down their arms or had attempted to surrender and the Allies were entitled to continue their attack until there were clear signs to this effect. It is not clear whether the decision to withdraw from Kuwait was a decision of the Iraqi high command (i.e. Saddam Hussein) or the decision of a local commander. The fact is that if the Iraqis had wished to surrender they could have communicated that fact to the Allied forces either locally or to the overall commander, General Schwartzkopf. It may be regarded as just another example of the Iraqi refusal to abide by the 'rules of war' and in this case at the expense of the lives of many of their own troops.

Having said this, however, the rationale for the Allied attack is far from clear. The Iraqi troops seemed to be retreating in disarray together with their 'loot' and 'bounty' plundered from Kuwait City. In this condition it is difficult to assess the extent to which they represented a potential threat to Coalition forces advancing from the west and north-west. But in the absence of a clear surrender the Coalition forces were entitled to make a worst-case analysis; and in any event there was a case for denying the Iraqi military the opportunity to retreat back into Iraq in good order together with their arms and military equipment to fight another day.

However, there are reports that American commanders regarded the attack as a form of retribution,[32] a form of execution in return for the Iraqi rape and plunder of Kuwait. If this turned out to be the reason for the attack rather than merely a *post hoc* moral justification then that would only constitute a breach of international law if 'disproportionate force' could be demonstrated. Reprisal is an accepted principle in warfare but it must be in proportion to the initial violation.[33] What is not a principle of warfare is 'vengeance'; but determining the difference between reprisal and vengeance may be a very difficult task in practice. In the case of Mutla Ridge the legitimate military rationale would no doubt save the attack from the charge of vengeance.

WAR CRIMES

It is often said that war crimes are defined by the victor. It is only the victorious state after a war that is in the political and administrative position to be able to investigate and prosecute breaches of the laws of war. This fact may justify some scepticism about war crimes prosecution but it does not justify outright cynicism. If there is clearly some asymmetry as to the application of the law, it does not follow that there was symmetry in the breach of the law. In other words just because there is little incentive for the victor to search for breaches of law on its own side does not mean either that it should not investigate breaches on the other nor that there must have been equality in the scale and seriousness of breaches. Moreover, if the very idea that there should be rules, conventions and laws governing the conduct of war is desirable then there clearly should be some mechanism for bringing those who break such laws to justice. The fact that the mechanism itself may be flawed[34] and perhaps less than comprehensive in operation does not invalidate the notion of war crimes or of war crimes trials.

The contemporary approach to war crimes derives from the principles established by the International Military Tribunal at Nuremberg in 1945 which were affirmed by the General Assembly of the United Nations (Resolution 1(95)) on 11 December 1946.[35] State and individual responsibility for crimes is established as follows:

(a) Crimes against peace: namely, planning, preparation, initiation or waging of a war of aggression, or a war in violation of international treaties, agreements or assurances, or participation in a common plan or conspiracy for the accomplishment of any of the foregoing.

(b) War crimes: namely, violations of the laws or customs of war. Such violations shall include, but not be limited to, murder, ill-treatment or deportation to slave labour or for any other purpose of civilian population of or in occupied territory, murder or ill-treatment of prisoners of war or persons on the seas, killing of hostages, plunder of public property, wanton destruction of cities, towns or villages or devastation not justified by military necessity.

(c) Crimes against humanity: namely murder, extermination, enslavement, deportation and other inhumane acts committed against any civilian population, before or during the war, or persecutions on political, racial or religious grounds in execution of or in connection with any crime within the jurisdiction of the Tribunal, whether or not in violation of the domestic law of the country where perpetrated.

(Article 6)

There is little doubt that the Iraqis at almost every level of command could be prosecuted under any or all of these categories. However, despite the declarations of both Prime Minister Margaret Thatcher and President Bush, the limited nature of the war aims of the Coalition allies left them in a position after the war of not effectively being able to bring alleged war criminals to trial. There are two aspects of this inability. One was that stopping the war short of unconditional surrender and occupation of Iraq meant that they were unable physically to apprehend suspected individuals from Saddam Hussein himself downwards. Secondly there was in any case – in conditions of Allied occupation or otherwise – a political disincentive to press war crimes charges.

There is built in to the very notion of war crimes trials an element of vindictiveness. The Nuremberg War Crimes Trials of Nazi leaders were in many senses, despite the validity of the charges, 'show trials' in that they served to designate the Nazi regime, ideology and war as officially beyond the moral pale – a sort of symbolic sealing of the end of the Nazi era. Such connotations attributed to a post-Gulf War war crimes trial would not have been tolerated by the Arab nations since they would have had much wider implications and may have appeared to take on the nature of an anti-Arab or anti-Islamic witch-hunt. Thus it can be seen that a war crimes trial would not have been in the interests of a post-war peace structure. There is ample prerequisite for such charges and indeed there is legal provision for bringing alleged criminals to trial in any of the belligerent countries or even by international tribunal under UN auspices. The main deterrent to such a procedure was political.

Chapter 7

Morality and the Gulf conflict

MORALITY, INTERNATIONAL RELATIONS AND WAR

It is clear that moral principles are developed in human society within particular cultural contexts. This means that different cultures will have developed different systems of ethics which may well dictate different moral principles to govern similar situations. So not only is some scepticism warranted when addressing the issue of the ethics of political behaviour within states there are particular difficulties when it comes to investigating the role of morality in relations between states.

It is a common perception that war is the very antithesis of morality, that the condition of war is the ghastly manifestation of the absence of morality. In absolute terms that may be the case but there are serious consequences that result from considering any form of human behaviour as beyond the moral pale. There is not space in the context of this book for an exhaustive enquiry into the ethics of inter-state behaviour. The stance taken here is that no category of human activity can or should be regarded as beyond the reach of moral judgement. To claim, for example, that war is a manifestation of the absence of law or of the breakdown of moral principles and that therefore law or morality cannot be applied to it leaves the way open for the justification of any behaviour during war on the grounds that such a category of activity in some way falls outside of the moral system. Moreover the Hobbesian view that 'there is neither morality nor law outside the state'[1] is not appropriate in an international system which has specifically attempted to establish and codify acceptable norms of international behaviour (through such institutions as the United Nations, the European Court of Human Rights, conventions on the laws of war, etc.). Neither is the Hegelian notion of the state as 'the realized ethical ideal'[2] appropriate, at least with regard to liberal western states, where it is not the state that is judged but the individuals who act on its behalf.

The question is not really *whether* moral criteria are appropriate in judging the international behaviour of states (or rather decision-makers who act on their behalf) but *what* moral criteria are appropriate, in what circumstances they are applied and what consequences follow from their application. There are two modes of enquiry: the first sets down and justifies criteria of ethics and morality and then judges international behaviour in any particular case against them; this is an exercise in applied ethics. The second is an empirical enquiry which investigates the extent to which moral principles do in practice act as determinants of, or constraints upon, that behaviour. We cannot engage in that empirical enquiry in this book since it would require a detailed investigation into the decision-making in the crisis for which the sources are not yet available. The concern of this chapter is to discuss some of the issues of morality that arose in the Gulf conflict (for example the issue of 'double standards', the moral implications of weapons technology, the notion of jihad, the morality of sanctions) and perhaps more centrally to examine some of the argumention related to the application of 'just war' principles to the war.

MORALITY AND RAISON D'ETAT

It is important to reiterate the point made above that as individuals we all live in a moral system – that is, all our behaviour has a moral context and that we are all either implicitly or explicitly guided in our actions by general moral principles. Few of us apply a system of explicit moral imperatives explicitly in our everyday lives. We all do however occasionally confront situations which require a rather more explicit and conscious consideration of the moral consequences of our behaviour. So it is with international relations. The everyday routine behaviour of states in the international system does not require the explicit application of explicit moral principles. However, certain situations such as war do require rather more attention being given to the moral context of state action. That is not to say that ethical principles should or do wholly determine behaviour in these situations. The moral dimension will be more explicit first because of the context itself –

the possibility of death and destruction as a result of a policy decision will of itself force moral issues on to the decision-makers' agenda. But secondly these issues have become more salient in recent decades, particularly in western countries, partly because of the experiences of the Second World War but also because of the increasing 'public' dimension of external affairs. In other words it is perceived at least that public opinion concerning a state's behaviour overseas provides a degree of constraint and ensures that governments pay more attention to balancing 'moral' and 'interest' dimensions of their policies and actions. For the Americans at least the searing experience of the Vietnam war is still very relevant. In Vietnam the United States found itself in a political, military and moral quagmire and one of the reasons for this was that a common American perception of the Cold War was that of a confrontation between two great 'moral systems'. The perception of the Cold War as a moral crusade (characterised by John Foster Dulles at the beginning of the Cold War and Ronald Reagan at the end) led to such questionable military behaviour in the field that eventually the morality of the American presence in Vietnam became an issue which helped to undermine domestic support for the war.

A distinction can be made between what might be called 'reactive' moral behaviour and 'initiatory' moral action. That is, on the one hand a state behaving within certain moral limits in pursuing its relationships with other states, and on the other a state which makes 'morality' one of its foreign-policy objectives. It is the latter initiatory moral action that converts foreign policy into a moral crusade. That inhumanity can result from a belief in moral superiority is the main reason why it is not desirable that moral principle should be the major determinant of action. Indeed it might be a plausible maxim that 'secular pragmatism' as a guide to action in foreign policy is more likely to lead to moderate behaviour than 'morality'.

If the moral context of war as a mode of behaviour between states is blurred then we ought to be as clear as we can be about what war is. War occurs not as a result of aggression but as a result of resistance to aggression. As Clausewitz so perceptively points out, 'The aggressor is always peace-loving (as Bonaparte always claimed to be); he would prefer to take over our country unopposed. To prevent his doing so one must be willing to make war'.[3] This makes clear that it is not war *per se* that should attract moral opprobrium since war only occurs as a result of defence against aggression. However 'peace-loving' the aggressor, it is he that is, through his aggression, morally culpable. So quite clearly the crime is not war but aggression. Thus war can only be a crime if resistance to aggression is construed as a crime. In opposing war pacifists in effect sanction aggression and place a prohibition on resistance to it. Iraq committed aggression in its invasion and occupation of Kuwait. Kuwaiti resistance converted that aggression into war. It is a moot point as to what situation obtained in the period between the Iraqi conquest and the start of the UN Coalition air bombardment. You could say that the Iraq–Kuwait war had been concluded and Kuwait lost. In this circumstance Allied action against Iraqi forces in Kuwait could have been regarded as a fresh act of aggression. This was the interpretation (1) of the Iraqis – for obvious reasons and (2) of many of those in the west who opposed a military solution *per se*.[4]

The other interpretation of that period was that the overwhelming of the Kuwaiti resistance and subsequent retreat of its government was only the first phase of the war and that the mobilisation of her allies and a subsequent counter-attack was the second phase. This would seem to be a rather more sensible as well as a more just interpretation. Of course it did put the onus on the Allies for continuing the war in order to restore the *status quo ante* but the responsibility for the crime of aggression remains with the Iraqis.

THE ISSUE OF 'DOUBLE STANDARDS'

One line of argument states that America was in no position to resist Iraq's invasion of a small neighbouring country since she herself has perpetrated a number of such invasions in the past; Panama, Grenada, Nicaragua, Vietnam and so on are quoted as examples. Certainly, one can agree that American action in these cases was questionable at the very least. But surely past breaches of any moral code should not preclude current conformity to that code. America's past behaviour in this respect neither logically nor morally precludes her military response to Iraq's invasion of Kuwait. Moreover it is difficult to understand why past 'misdemeanours' on the part of the United States (even if one agrees to regard them as such) should preclude Kuwait and Saudi Arabia from calling on its aid to resist Iraqi aggression.

The issue of 'double standards' which figured prominently in much comment during the crisis is at root one of 'consistency' rather than morality. Absolute consistency is perhaps a luxury reserved for the all-powerful and the all-knowing. The reason why states appear to demonstrate inconsistent responses to apparently similar situations is the fact of differing interests. What primarily determines a state's behaviour in the international system is self-interest. There is nothing reprehensible about this; indeed it is difficult to see how states could or should have any other motive. Altruism in both states and individuals is rare; and where it is apparently found then it is suspect. A much more open and plausible principle for action is the pursuit of legitimate self-interest with due regard to the self-interest of others. The issues that give rise to conflict between states arise not over the principle of self-interest but over the definition of self-interest in any particular case, the manner in which that self-interest is pursued and to what extent it contravenes the self-interest of others. It is right and proper that these issues should be subject to debate and negotiation both between states and within states. Indeed these issues are the very stuff of diplomacy and politics. On this basis it is appropriate that the United States should be challenged on its international behaviour; but to repeat the point, America's invasion of Grenada, for example, does not justify Iraq's invasion of Kuwait nor does it preclude America's intervention on Kuwait's behalf.

The charge of 'double standards' arises from arguing on one level only – that is, on the moral level of argument. The assumption here is that action is determined by moral principle and thus should be consistent; in other words the principle should be applied in all circumstances regardless of the context or the consequences. What this line of argument ignores is that behaviour both of states and of individuals is determined by a complex of factors and insofar as morality plays any part it will do so only in conjunction with these other factors. In the case of states the major determining factor is self-interest. It is indeed the principle of legitimate self-interest which ensures the non-arbitrary behaviour of states. It may well be that there is an inherent conflict between interest and morality, or at the very least there will be many cases in which the two criteria for action are contradictory. The task of the foreign- or security-policy maker is to attempt to balance the two. Moral principle will rarely be an explicit or overt criterion for action; however, we can only hope that action taken for reasons of self-interest is tempered by moral principle. Though it must be conceded that often self-interest masquerades as moral principle.

The explanation for what appears to be double standards in the behaviour of states lies in the different contexts of action and the different sets of interests that may or may not be involved in different cases. The explanation for the apparent inconsistent American responses, say, to (1) the Soviet invasion of Hungary of 1956 during which the United States refrained from intervention and (2) the Iraqi invasion of Kuwait of 1990, is a combination of perceived self-interest, the likely cost of response and the likely prospect of a successful intervention. In the context and conventions of the Cold War US legitimate interest in Hungary was low whereas in the Middle East in 1990 that interest was high. It was not only America's self-interest that was being served in the Gulf conflict (though it was being served – we should not doubt that) but also that of the international community as a whole. It is in all our interests that the aggressive acts of military dictators are challenged; whether they always are in practice is a different matter. The fact that not all dictators or acts of aggression are challenged should not entail that none are.

As to the likely cost and the prospect of success, in the case of Hungary in 1956 the cost of response would have been very high indeed and the prospect of victory low or at least extremely problematical. In the case of Iraq the cost (in all its terms) of response was judged as 'tolerable' whilst the prospects of victory must have been judged at the least as reasonable. The latter is a technical issue as far as military strategy is concerned; however, how 'victory' is defined has considerably wider connotations. A short-term military victory over Iraq (however that is defined) might not be so clear-cut from a political or economic point of view in the longer term. The calculation of costs and consequences is particularly fraught. They will be manifest in the domestic politics of many of the participants, in the Gulf and Middle East regional politics as well as in the wider international community. Many issues rested on the outcome of the Iraqi crisis. (The problems of the calculations for war are discussed in Chapter 9.)

'JUST WAR' PRINCIPLES APPLIED TO THE GULF CONFLICT

The notion of a 'just war' is a Christian theological doctrine dating from St Augustine which sets down the conditions that must be met before a war can 'justly' be entered into (*jus ad bellum*) as well as a guide to acceptable behaviour in war (*jus in bello*). Clearly the social and political conditions for which the principles were established are now very different. However, they do provide a valuable guide and starting-point for a general set of rules for the declaration and conduct of war in the contemporary world. Appeal to 'just war' theory often results either from a search for a justification for not engaging in war at all or on the other hand from a desire to seek some sort of absolution from the moral doubt about actually engaging in war. Neither objective is likely to be satisfied. To look for moral absolutes, especially in politics or in times of war, is a fruitless search. But that does not mean that discussion of 'just war' theory is fruitless. It is absolutely essential if war is to remain within the moral/ethical domain of human behaviour. That sounds a contradiction, particularly to those who automatically believe that war is beyond the ethical pale, that war stems from the breakdown or absence of morality and law. If war as a human activity is beyond the moral pale then morality/ethics can have nothing to say about it and can exert no restraint in the decision to go to war or the way it is conducted. That is a dangerous position and one to be avoided. To pose the alternatives as between absolute moral restraint and no moral restraint at all is both unnecessary and unrealistic.

The principles of *jus in bello* (i.e. the rules of conduct within war) have been codified and expanded into the formal international laws of war and these are discussed in Chapter 6. In this section the principles of *jus ad bellum* (the circumstances under which entering into war can be regarded as just) will be discussed in relation to the Gulf conflict.

There are by common consent six criteria by which a war may be judged as 'just' and each of them will be discussed in turn.[5]

Criterion 1: war can be just if it results from a resistance to aggression either by the invaded state or by a third state going to its aid. On that score there seems little doubt that intervention by the United States and the UN allies was 'just'.

Criterion 2: war should be legally declared by legal authorities. There is every reason to believe that the governments of the Allied powers were the proper legal authorities of those states. However, the legal declaration of war is more problematical. It is the case that of something like 145 wars since 1945 very few if any have actually been declared – in the traditional sense in which, for example, Britain declared war on Germany in 1939. In fact the Gulf War was no exception to this general trend. (See also Chapter 5 for the legal consequences of the absence of a declaration.) However, although there was no actual declaration of war an ultimatum was declared by Security Council Resolution 678 which authorised 'all necessary means' and which constituted part of the pressure mounted against Iraq during the diplomatic phase. The ultimatum was that if a withdrawal or specific plans for a withdrawal had not been effected by 15 January 1991 all necessary means, including the use of force, would be exerted to bring about an Iraqi withdrawal. The reason for this was that there should be no possible doubt that Iraq had been made aware of the consequences of failure to withdraw. This for international purposes would have satisfied this particular 'just war' criterion.

However, the legal declaration of war was a potential problem domestically for some of the Allied powers. The American president, for example, under the War Powers Act of 1973, can commit troops only for a period of sixty days after which specific Congressional approval must be sought. In any case Congress has to approve a formal declaration of war, which is one of the reasons why contemporary American presidents prefer to avoid it. But American presidents often nevertheless find their freedom of action constrained if they have to seek Congressional approval to pursue action or to finance military operations, particularly in circumstances where public enthusiasm for the operation is waning. In the Iraq crisis President Bush might have confronted greater problems had the early public, and even Congressional, scepticism about American military involvement in the Gulf crisis been maintained. In the event, as the crisis progressed the increasingly outrageous behaviour of Saddam Hussein, at least in the eyes of the American public, hardened domestic opinion against him and undermined the very factor that seemed to be a large part of his strategy – that is, to detach the American public and Congress from the administration pursuing the anti-Iraq policy. In fact even in the face of Iraqi intransigence when finally President Bush did seek Congressional support for his actions he secured only a marginal majority of three. It was a demonstration of the American administration's lack of certainty of gaining Congressional approval for military action in the Gulf that they left it right to the last minute, just before the expiry of the 15 January deadline, before putting the issue before Congress. Indeed the administration had built up an international consensus in favour of military action before putting the issue formally to Congress, which may well have secured its approval. The consequences of a situation in which the American government had lined up the UN Security Council and virtually the whole international community in favour of action only to be rejected by the United States's own Congress would have been a severe embarrassment to say the least.

Criterion 3: response to the aggression should be confined to repelling the invader's forces and establishing a just peace. There were severe problems satisfying this criterion. The first problem and one which is inherent in this particular principle is that there might in any war be an incompatibility between these two requirements. It may not be possible to establish a just peace by confining military action to the objective merely of repelling the invader. This would be the case for example if repelling the invader did nothing to inhibit the possibility of his future aggression. The persistence of a condition of extreme insecurity on the part of the invaded state could hardly be regarded as establishing a just peace.

Indeed, one of the many dilemmas that faced the Americans and their allies was whether their war aims should be confined to the liberation of Kuwait or whether they should proceed further and divest Iraq of the capability of once more invading her neighbour. This latter option does not on the face of it strictly conform with the 'just war' principles but may well be regarded as serving the 'just peace' criterion if in the longer term it could be seen to be preventing a repetition of these events at a 'later stage' when the scale of activity may very well be much larger and the consequences much more serious. This would be particularly the case if by that 'later stage' the Iraqis had acquired a nuclear capability. The justice of a peace which included an Iraq with a nuclear capability may be regarded as less important than the potential disorder represented by that fact. A case perhaps where there was a conflict between a condition of short-term justice at the expense of a long-term disorder and a short-term injustice in the interests of a longer-term order. This argument would have equal weight even in the absence of the nuclear dimension. Repelling Iraq's invasion without curtailing its capability or incentive to mount a future aggression might serve the short-term justice of the 'just war' criterion but only at the expense of the longer-term order and thus the longer-term justice.

The second major problem is the very definition of a 'just peace'. This issue goes to the very heart of the nature of the international system and the apparent mutual incompatibility of 'order' and 'justice' among states. In other words, to strive for order entails some, and possibly a great deal of, injustice; to strive for justice entails disorder because of the very subjective nature of 'justice' – that is, a condition that may be just for one will appear unjust for another. There is a utopian idea firstly that it is a contradiction to suggest that justice can be imposed once a structured order has been achieved and secondly that it is possible to construct an international system in which order is predicated upon justice. Those who put order before justice believe that the greatest degree of injustice in the world derives from a condition of disorder and that any degree of justice is predicated upon order. Those who put justice before order believe that ultimately order depends upon the establishment of justice; a just system would remove the seeds of disorder and thus produce an ordered world.

The pragmatist on the other hand accepts the given condition of the international system and regards it as the task of the decision-maker to balance order and justice. This entails a recognition that in most relations between states there has to be a measure of compromise between the two and that conducting relations with other states entails a judgement as to what position on that spectrum between order and justice the compromise must be made in any one case.

In the case of the Gulf different parties in the region will have different conceptions of a 'just peace'. Kuwait will want to feel secure, Iraq will want her legitimate concerns dealt with; a peace that entailed the continued presence of non-Arab forces would not be considered just by many Arabs in the region, neither would it be tolerable to Iran. On the other hand a peace without a non-Arab guarantee might very well not be a peace at all. Would a just peace in the Gulf include the wider issues that Iraq claimed to want to bring into the equation, namely the Palestine/Israel question? If it does, a just peace in the Gulf might be a very long time coming. The interconnectedness of the international system means that many of the intractable problems between one set of states are related in some way or another to problems between other sets of states. To suggest that one set of problems cannot be addressed until all the other problems are addressed is ultimately to accept complete stalemate and to accept that no problems should be addressed. Of course the Iraqis appreciated this very point and thus knew that linking the Gulf issue with the Israeli issue would ensure that they would not have to forgo their gains at least in the short to medium term.

Another useful perspective is gained by posing the question not, what would be the moral consequences of going to war, but what would be the moral consequences of not going to war. For example, if no military action were taken by the Coalition and Iraq had been left in possession of Kuwait, would the 'just peace' criterion have been satisfied then? This issue is discussed more fully under Criterion 6.

Criterion 4: the resister and its allies should have a reasonable hope of military success. This in fact was a major preoccupation of the United States and her allies during the diplomatic phase of the crisis. There were two major issues. The first was that it was a requirement of American crisis diplomacy that if Iraq was to be persuaded to withdraw from Kuwait she had to be convinced of the consequences of not doing so – that is, comprehensive military defeat. The second was that it would have been irresponsible in the extreme to take or contemplate taking military action against Iraqi forces in Kuwait unless sufficient force had been assembled to make victory a reasonable prospect. There is a moral dimension to both of these issues. Arguably it might have been morally preferable for coercive pressure to have achieved the goal of Iraqi withdrawal short of further military action. Thus, paradoxical though it may seem, the military build-up can be seen as a necessary mechanism for avoiding military action. It was for political as well as moral reasons that the magnitude of the Coalition military machine had to be such as to make victory as certain as could reasonably be done and as rapid as could reasonably be achieved. This was for two reasons: first to minimise casualties on the Allied side, and secondly to minimise the 'war duration' factor. A long drawn out and inconclusive slogging match would eventually, perhaps quickly, have produced an international reaction against military action. All these factors induced the Americans to engineer rather more than 'a reasonable hope' of success; for political, coercive and moral reasons there had to be 'a reasonable certainty' of success.

Having said that, however, the validity of this criterion may be questioned since it suggests that any weak state faced by over-whelming aggression should not resist and raises the issue as to whether Kuwait's request for assistance was in accordance with 'just war' principles.

Criterion 5: the ejection of the aggressor and the establishment of a just peace cannot be achieved without resorting to war; that is, that all alternatives have been tried and that war is the last resort. In many ways this criterion can never be achieved to universal satisfaction because it is virtually impossible to get universal agreement that all resort short of war has been attempted – either energetically enough or for long enough. For many people – particularly those of a pacifistic tendency – if a peaceful resolution has not been achieved it is by definition because you have not tried hard enough or for long enough. For such people the diplomatic op-tion can never be exhausted. Even for those who do not occupy this pacifist position there still might not be agreement about what constitutes a last resort.

Part of the problem is a misconception about the relationship between the diplomatic instrument and the military instrument in the conduct of crises. They are not alternatives in the sense that the one only comes into use when the other one stops. The military factor is always present in diplomacy whether it appears as active coercion or merely passive deterrence in the mere posses-sion of a military capability. The crucial criterion for judging 'last resort' is not whether there is some other diplomatic avenue that can be explored but that the pursuit of a diplomatic solution must not be allowed to continue to the point where the state will be at a military disadvantage should hostilities take place. The judge-ment as to when that point has been reached is exceedingly difficult and is bound to attract the charge from some people that military action is premature – whenever it takes place. Moreover, if the state's military power is compromised by the undue pursuit of a diplomatic solution then one of the other criteria for a 'just war' is undermined – that is, that there must be a reasonable prospect of success.

It was held by many that the United States and her close allies showed 'indecent haste' in their apparent rush to military action to solve the Iraqi problem. Moreover many thought that there was scope for more diplomacy, that more time could have been given for sanctions to work and persuade Iraq to withdraw without the necessity for military action. The options for the United States are discussed in more detail in Chapter 4, but put simply the Americans had an incentive to bring a solution to the problem sooner rather than later. This was not out of an eagerness to use military force. It was because if there were to be an Iraqi withdrawal it had to be achieved in a relatively short time-scale or not at all. Allowing the Iraqi occupation to continue long enough for sanctions 'to work' would undoubtedly have entailed waiting for many months if not for years and even then there would be no guarantee of an Iraqi withdrawal. In any case the longer sanctions continued the greater the likelihood of international solidarity breaking down. There was also the problem that if military action were to be taken it had to be taken reasonably quickly in order to take advantage of the best climatic conditions. Delaying for months or even weeks would have reduced the chance of military success.

For the pacifist of course the pursuit of diplomacy to the point where military coercion would be untenable is a desirable objective; as it was of course for Saddam Hussein and incidentally as it was for General Galtieri in 1982. The upshot of that eventuality was that there would have been little incentive for Saddam to leave Kuwait, the world in the longer term would have acclimatised to his occupation of Kuwait; he would essentially have achieved his objective and would have tested to destruction the embryonic 'new international order'.

Given that in these circumstances the diplomatic phase could become infinitely elastic, the task for those resisting aggression is to work for a resolution within a reasonably short time-frame and in a fashion that does not give the aggressor the opportunity to compound or consolidate his aggression. There must reasonably be a time limit on this. The difficult judgement is exactly where that limit is to be established. This will be determined not by doggedly pursuing an infinitely elastic diplomacy but by setting reasonable conditions for the aggressor to fulfil within a reasonable time-frame. Thus the necessity of converting the notion of 'last resort' into a practical guide to the transition between diplomacy and war.

Criterion 6: this relates to the question of proportionality – that the good done by going to war outweighs (or is reasonably expected to outweigh) the evil of war itself. Political alternatives are rarely if ever between good and evil – but between evils. There were three broad options in response to Iraq's act of aggression: (1) do nothing, (2) a non-military reponse and (3) a military response. An important point to understand is that to do nothing is to do something. A second and equally important point is that, especially for prominent member states of the international community, it is very difficult to remain indifferent to any event in the international system. Thus, if the United States had ignored the invasion, she would have been effectively making all sorts of implicit declarations about her interests and intentions in the system. The imperative to do something is the need to have some sort of control over what messages are sent to other states. Thus for great powers at least it is almost impossible to have a 'non-response' to any event in the international system. So effectively the broad choice was between a non-military and a military response. The deciding factor in general terms between these two options will be a judgement as to whether the objectives can be achieved in a reasonable time-frame without the use of military force. The time-frame is important (see Chapter 4 for more detailed discussion of this issue). There is not unlimited time available and if a reasonably short-term peaceful solution is not possible then military force is a likely outcome.

What 'good' was being done by the Allied use of the military instrument? At the time of the crisis the issue of 'proportionality' was often portrayed as one of extreme 'disproportionality' – of a massive military superpower crushing a small Third World state for no other reason than rabid imperialism. If that had been an accurate interpretation it is extremely doubtful whether such a degree of global consensus on the issue could have been achieved. In the first analysis the sovereignty of Kuwait was to be restored and the principle that the aggressor should not reap the benefits of his aggression upheld. Quantifying the price of upholding such principles is very difficult if not impossible. The question arises that since Kuwait is such a small country with a small population governed by an undemocratic if paternalistic regime, how much should we be prepared to pay to protect its sovereignty? The 'far away country' syndrome is still present among some people. Nevertheless these are vitally important issues in the international system. Despite all the analogies that have been made to justify the charge of 'double standards', it is a fact that Iraq's invasion of Kuwait was a very special circumstance entailing the conquest and annexation of a member of the United Nations; and in this respect it was unprecedented.

But there were not only principles at stake – there were also interests; not only interests of individual states but also the interests of the system and the future stability of the system. So like most state action the major allies in the UN Coalition were motivated in their intervention by a mixture of principle and self-interest. Moreover in many respects 'principles' become established as a result of 'systemic interest'. For example, a stable international system requires as one of its conventions the principle of respect for sovereign independence. So a systemic requirement becomes a 'moral' principle.

It was in the coincidence of a number of factors – both interest and principle – that the criterion of proportionality can be seen to have applied. Certainly the direct interests of the western powers were at stake – the impact of an Iraqi domination of a large proportion of the world's oil supplies. More indirect, but none the less real, geopolitical interests were also at stake – the balance of power in the Middle East and the undesirability (both to the west and to most of the Arab states) of an Iraqi hegemony in the Gulf and beyond. It is after all still a strategically important area even in the post-Cold War world. The principle of sovereign territoriality had been blatantly contravened and the right of resistance to its infringement had to be established. There was undoubtedly an element on the part of the United States at least, if not its close allies, of establishing a precedent *pour decourager les autres* in the post-Cold War international system where the major powers, led by the United States, would be the only states powerful enough to be able to confront aggressive dictators freed of the constraints of the Cold War system.

One of the crucial features distinguishing Iraq's annexation of Kuwait from many of the other examples of invasion or apparent aggression was that in these latter cases total annexation of the territory was not involved – for example, Turkish invasion of Cyprus, Syrian and Israeli incursions into the Lebanon. Moreover in these cases there were genuine and complex security or ethnic problems where the issues were not clear-cut. Also in some of the cases claimed to be analogous (e.g. the Indonesian invasion of East Timor or the Chinese annexation of Tibet) the status of the invaded territory was in some way ambiguous or had not been defined and in any case did not constitute a sovereign independent state as a member of the United Nations. This clearly does not justify their invasion or annexation but it does to some extent explain the response, or lack of it, of the international community in these cases.

Making judgements about the moral validity of state actions will never produce unambiguous or uncontentious answers. It is in the nature of such enquiry that the issues are 'essentially contested'. This analysis has revealed the difficulty of making decisions that are absolutely free from moral taint. Clearly 'just war' theory will not provide a moral *carte blanche* for military action, but its criteria can provide a framework of restraint and require that action is measured against such principles. Despite its origins in Christian Europe of the Middle Ages the principles that the theory sets down can provide a valuable checklist for investigations into the actual behaviour of states such as this study. They could also constitute the source of what might be called a 'principled pragmatism' as a basis for collective action in the new international order.

JIHAD

Some mention of the notion of jihad in the context of morality is appropriate since it became an issue at various points during the crisis. Saddam Hussein himself called on all Arabs to wage a jihad against all his opponents during the conflict. We must be careful not to assume that jihad is the Islamic equivalent of 'just war'. In fact the two concepts differ in scope and also in the functions they respectively perform.

The first and major distinction is that 'just war' is a Christian moral formula for application in wars between Christians. When established the 'just war' principles specifically did not apply to wars against 'barbarians' and unbelievers – indeed in such wars no moral restraint was deemed warranted. On the other hand jihad is an Islamic doctrine with considerably less precision and, where it applies to overt war, it can only be waged against non-believers –

jihad is forbidden against fellow Muslims. Thus the Iraqis had no theological backing for calling for a jihad against the UN Coalition forces since those forces contained substantial numbers of Muslims, both Arab and non-Arab.

But jihad has considerably wider connotations than the notion of the just war. There are two major meanings of jihad – one internal and one external. The internal jihad is the Greater Jihad and refers to an inner spiritual struggle to overcome one's animal tendencies; the jihad is directed to bringing those animal passions under control and achieving spiritual purification of one's own heart by 'doing battle with the devil'. 'Man has a tendency to overestimate himself and to underestimate his spiritual potential. He has a tendency to control and exploit his environment and other human beings. Jihad is essentially against such tendencies'.[6] This quotation rather appropriately contains both a diagnosis of Saddam Hussein and a prescription to remedy himself of such a condition. Rather than calling a jihad against the Coalition forces he could perhaps more appropriately have been declaring a jihad against himself.

But this is the spiritual path to fulfil jihad – that by the heart. There are three others ways – by the tongue, by the hand and by the sword. Jihad by tongue and hand refers to the propagation of the Islamic faith by 'evangelism', where persuasion is the major instrument. Jihad by the sword refers to physical war against the enemies of Islam. Historically military jihad has been used to produce the conditions in which unbelievers might be more 'receptive' to Islamic persuasion.[7] In modern times, however, jihad by the sword is justified only if the faith is in danger. Indeed engaging in wars of conquest not related to religion or faith is a consequence of a failure to engage in the Greater Jihad. Iraq's invasion of Kuwait contravened the Koran, which urges Muslims to 'fight for the sake of Allah those that fight against you, but do not attack them first. Allah does not love the aggressors'.[8]

Arguably the more insidious threat to the Islamic world is the ubiquity of western culture. The Islamic world like all traditional cultures is increasingly vulnerable to what is seen as western 'cultural aggression'. It is the Greater Jihad that is the more appropriate weapon of resistance to this threat than 'jihad by the sword' but is the one most difficult to put into practice. It is this that is the source of the revival of Islamic orthodoxy and fundamentalism in the Middle East.

THE MORALITY OF SANCTIONS

It is worth drawing some attention to the moral context of the policy of sanctions as a means of coercion. Sanctions are almost universally and perhaps unthinkingly regarded as morally superior to the use of force. Even in situations where aggression has taken place there is usually great pressure from some sections of opinion for the use of sanctions as a means of coercing the aggressor to withdraw or as a means of punishment for the aggression. The assumption, usually unquestioned, is that on all occasions a non-military solution is better than, and morally preferable to, a military one. The logic of sanctions is that economic, political, military and moral isolation is used to make it impossible for the aggressor to continue his aggression by undermining the ability or the will to continue. The action of such coercion is two-fold: firstly to deny the leadership the direct military and economic resources necessary to continue; secondly to detach domestic public support from the leadership and its act of aggression.

It is in the use of the aggressor state's civilian population as an intermediate target of sanctions that such a policy raises moral issues. Part of the logic of sanctions is that conditions are made so uncomfortable or even intolerable for the population that they withdraw support from their own government and actually force it to reverse the aggression. This of course makes the assumption that the leadership is vulnerable to public pressure, that it is in some way dependent upon public support and that withdrawal of support would make it politically impossible for it to continue. In other words the assumption is that the political system is a reasonably democratic one. But, of course, the Iraqi leadership, like many of the governments that commit acts of aggression, did not rely on its population in this direct way. Saddam Hussein and his Ba'athist government maintain power through coercion and repression and public support is more accurately described as passive acquiescence rather than active enthusiasm. Moreover in the case of Iraq civilian suffering was likely to be the major consequence of a policy of sanctions since the leadership had built a colossal economic and military stockpile reserved both for the elite which maintained the regime's internal structures of coercion and control and for the military in order to sustain the military operation in Kuwait.

But aside from the efficacy of such a strategy in achieving the declared objective of stopping or reversing the aggression, there are moral consequences that follow from the way it is achieved. The moral issue is that it is a direct intention of the policy of sanctions to create hardship, suffering and even death among civilian populations as a means of exerting coercive pressure on the aggressor leadership. Those conditions of suffering are likely to include starvation and arguably there is little difference between death by starvation and death by military attack. The moral issue can be stated quite baldly: what is the moral distinction between an unintended civilian death caused by military 'collateral' damage and an intended civilian death caused by a policy of sanctions? All other things being equal it is the question of intention that is crucial. Thus it can be clearly seen that sanctions is not a policy without moral consequences and is certainly not the morally cost-free option that is often assumed by those who pose it as an option obviously more desirable than military force in resisting aggression.

MORALITY AND THE TECHNOLOGY OF THE GULF WAR

'Technology cannot make men bad, but it may surely give rise to circumstances in which it is increasingly difficult to be good'.[9] The history of the technology of war since the industrial revolution is a demonstration of the validity of this insight. Indeed it was the consequences for war of the increasing sophistication of military technology that prompted the construction of rules and conventions for the conduct of war in order to constrain the use of the more obnoxious weapons.

The idea that technology is itself morally neutral but that it is the use to which it is put that may be immoral is a common perception. There is some validity in this contention insofar as it is true that the moral dimension only becomes apparent when the technology is put into a social or political context. However, the extent to which the technology itself can determine the use to which it is put in society will be a measure of its inherent 'political' or 'moral' nature. Nuclear weapons are a case in point. The massive destructive power of nuclear weapons entailed a move from the use of technology in war to the threat of its use in order to prevent war rather than to actually wage war. But the arcane theorising of nuclear deterrence required that opposing sides made themselves vulnerable to a massive second strike which would effectively entail their destruction as viable states; and the requirement for this was that each side directly targeted the mass populations of their opponents. It was in this condition that lay the deterrence; each side was deterred from starting war for fear that their civilian populations would be all but completely destroyed. Thus the technology determined the strategy and moreover it entailed the potential breach of a fundamental principle of the 'civilised' conduct of war – that is that non-combatants should not be directly targeted.

So insofar as nuclear deterrence prevented a superpower war it did so by a policy of mutual vulnerability and a deliberate and purposeful threat of breaching a fundamental moral principle in the conduct of war. Such was the paradox of the 'security' maintained by the Cold War rivalry. It is necessary to refer to the nature and strategic effects of nuclear weapons because they illustrate the problem of what it is in military technology that raises moral issues. In fact there are two major issues: first is the problem of the scale of human destruction and secondly the problem of the manner in which that destruction takes place. Nuclear weapons seemed to add a new moral dimension to war. Those who emphasised this moral dimension assumed that a 'moral line' could be drawn between conventional war and nuclear war. The problem of scale in itself could not be the justification for this stance since surely there can be no moral distinction between the death of a hundred human beings and the death of a hundred thousand brutal as that may sound. On the other hand a more plausible moral case can possibly be made from the indiscriminate nature of the effects of nuclear weapons. Lack of discrimination breaches the proportionality criterion of 'just war' and also of course breaches the moral distinction between combatants and non-combatants as legitimate targets in war.

It was the moral dimension of discrimination and proportionality in warfare that assumed significance in the context of the use of so-called 'smart weapons' by the UN Coalition in the Gulf War. Given the remarks above on discrimination it follows that the more discriminate a weapon is in its targeting and effects the more morally acceptable it becomes, all other things being equal. Weapons that find their target with a very high degree of accuracy and which cause a very low degree of 'collateral' damage, in principle at least, are highly desirable given the context of war. The post-nuclear technology of Stealth, Cruise missiles, laser-guided bombs, and so on, seems to represent a major move away from the indiscriminate nature of nuclear weapons and makes it possible to reintroduce the elements of discrimination and proportionality in weaponry. This was reflected in the idea discussed during the Gulf conflict of the possibility of a morally 'clean' war. There are differences of view as to whether the effects of such weaponry in Iraq would justify such a description. Some cite the relatively few destroyed and damaged buildings in Baghdad with very little surrounding damage as an indication of the success of this weaponry;[10] others suggest that there was in fact considerable 'collateral' damage and at least 10,000 Iraqi civilian deaths.[11]

But moral issues also arise from the manner of the death and injury caused by military technology. It is this factor that has made the issue of chemical and biological weapons so sensitive in the moral and legal dimensions of war. The use of chemical weapons by the Iraqis in the war with Iran, and more particularly against unarmed Kurdish villagers, has attracted a great deal of moral opprobrium to the Iraqis. The expected use of such weapons by the Iraqis against the Coalition forces added further world-wide moral condemnation of Iraqi behaviour. This dimension may have been one of the reasons why in the event chemical weapons were not used (though it must be conceded that the major reasons were likely to have been strategic and political rather than moral).

Chapter 8

The economic dimension of the Gulf conflict

The purpose of this chapter is to examine the economic dimension of the Gulf conflict, concentrating on three major aspects. Firstly the political economy of oil will be considered and its significance in explaining both the initial Iraqi invasion and the western response. Secondly the problems of costing war will be discussed. Thirdly the impact of the conflict on the domestic economies of the major actors and the global economy as a whole.

It is often held that the Gulf War of 1991 was the first of a new species of 'resource wars' that will become more and more common as ecological and environmental pressures build up and affect the international political economy. The implication is in this contention that oil was the real reason why the war was fought. A further, moral, implication was that it is somehow less justifiable to fight a war for resources than it is for some principle or other.

The first response to these propositions is that it is not obvious that despite increasing global environmental problems resource issues are any more common in disputes between states than they ever have been. That is not to say that they will not in the future but that there is little evidence that they are now. Secondly it is probably true to say that most wars to a greater or lesser degree have been resource wars – that is, wars about territory and what exists or lives under, on or above it, including human beings which constitute both a resource and a consumer of resources. It is not a startling insight to perceive that issues of principle between states are very often reducible to issues of interest when the fog of diplomacy has cleared.

So to characterise the Gulf conflict 1990–1 as a 'resource war' is not really providing any great insight into its nature, causes or significance. Indeed, as the other chapters in this book reveal, it would be a gross oversimplification to conclude that the Gulf War was 'simply about oil'. Neither is there a great deal of reason to suggest that oil will become the object of increasing conflict in the future. It may be possible to go even further and suggest that for the Arabs, as a political and economic agent of influence, or even *raison de guerre*, oil is a declining asset.[1]

We have seen that there were a number of issues at stake – political issues, economic issues, strategic issues as well as even issues of principle and law. The absence of any one of them from the picture would have affected the significance of the others and may well thus have affected the justification for going to war or the willingness of the participants to do so. Perhaps it is important to engage in the sort of 'mind game' that speculates whether the war would have occurred if it had not been for the 'oil dimension'; or to hold that issues of principle could not have been very important in the Gulf War because similar principles have not been de-fended in other parts of the world and in other political contexts. However, we have stated elsewhere that 'single cause' explanations of events are always to be treated with suspicion and that interna-tional politics involve such complex processes that the explanation of events requires the investigation of many different factors. What makes the Middle East an area of such political complexity and an area which has been the focus of much international politics in the period since the Second World War is precisely that it is a region in which many of these 'single factors' come together in a complex web of interaction. That is not to say that all the different forces and interests are all of equal importance for explaining conflict; indeed the different factors will have different relative signficance at different times and in different situations.

Having said all that it is probably the case that the three major consequences of the Iraqi invasion that entailed an American response were firstly an adverse change in the balance of power in the region, secondly the threat to one of the United States's agents of influence in the region, and thirdly the threat to the future security of oil supplies from the Middle East. An Iraqi take-over of Saudi Arabia would have put Saddam Hussein in control of 50 per cent of the world's oil reserves and would have enabled him to dominate OPEC and effectively run it to serve Iraq's interests, no doubt at the expense, potentially at least, of the interests of the economies of the developed and less-developed world alike.

THE POLITICAL ECONOMY OF OIL

It is not an exaggeration to say that oil is the very heart of the global economy and the foundation of the economies of the 'western' developed world. The two factors that tie the western powers inexorably to the Middle East are its geostrategic position and its vast reserves of oil. The geostrategic dimension of the west's interest in the Middle East pre-dates the oil factor. Britain's concern for the region was originally derivative of its Indian empire. During the twentieth century that concern has been inherited by the United States and reinforced by the discovery of oil and its crucial role in the development of the western in-dustrialised economies, by the necessity to protect trade routes between Europe and the Far East, and more recently by the strategic significance of the region in the Cold War competition.

The role of oil has assumed an increasing international political dimension in the period after the Second World War due to the combination of two factors – firstly the importance of oil in the post-war success of the western economies, and secondly the fact that control of oil production has passed from the large western oil companies (known as the 'seven sisters') to the governments of the producer countries themselves. In the period up to 1970 the major oil companies were acting essentially within the strategic regimes operated firstly by the United Kingdom and then by the United States which ensured market stability, security of supplies, low prices (the real price of oil has declined in the post-war period) and high profits.[2]

The disruption to this regime of stability and security was brought about firstly by the flexing of the political muscle of the producer country governments in the wave of nationalisation of foreign-owned oil-producer companies and secondly by the mili-tary conflicts in the region in which oil was used as a political weapon against western states. The need and desire for producer governments to have control over their own resource reserves was built into the 'logic of decolonisation'. But there was also an economic necessity as far as the producer governments were con-cerned because the real price of oil was actually falling, and thus so were their revenues, whilst the price of those manufactured goods they were importing from the west were actually rising.[3] There was initial resistance to nationalisation by the western powers when in 1951 the Iranian leader, Muhammed Mossadegh, nationalised the Anglo-Iranian Oil Company (AIOC). The British were able to stop Iran from selling its oil thus leading to his overthrow.[4] Again in 1961, when Iraq attempted to expropriate IPC's concession areas inside Iraq, the company so cut back production and exports as to make the Iraqis back down.

In 1960 the governments of the oil-producing countries attempted to bolster their solidarity and their bargaining power *vis-à-vis* the oil companies by forming the Organisation of Petroleum Exporting Countries (OPEC) composed of both Middle East and non-Middle East producer governments. Even so the producers had little effect on the consumer countries and failed to exert any restraining pressure on the United States during the 1967 Arab–Israeli war. This was because the United States at that time did not import enough Middle Eastern oil to make it vulnerable to such pressure. Moreover the oil states were hardly in a financial position to sustain a long-term oil embargo which would deprive themselves of oil revenues.

By the time of the Arab–Israeli war in 1973 the oil producers were in a better position to be able to support an oil embargo and the oil weapon was used by the Arabs in a rather more subtle and selective way aimed at splitting the United States from its European allies, especially Britain and France. The objective was to progressively restrict oil production by 5 per cent per month until Israel withdrew from those territories occupied during the war.

The consequence of this was the so-called 'oil shock' and a price rise from a fluctuating range between $1 and $3 per barrel in the period up to 1973 to $11.50 in 1974; this represented something like a 500 per cent increase in the price of oil virtually overnight. The non-Arab members of OPEC were content to cooperate with the production cut-backs because of course they benefited from the dramatic price increases even though they had no political axe to grind with the consumer countries.

Though this represented a rather more successful use of the 'oil weapon', it was facilitated by particular market circumstances. There had been a period of increasing demand for petroleum before the 1973 war together with accelerating inflation which had reduced the real price of oil.[5] The major factor on the supply side was that the United States had progressively run down its excess oil capacity to zero by 1973[6] so that it could not supplement the shortfall from the OPEC producers and thus negate the price rise

induced by this artificial shortage. This had come about by a
'drain America first' policy in which the American oil corporations
can demand import quotas in order to keep American domestic
oil prices high and insulate them from the cheaper world market
price. A more rational policy in the American national strategic
interest would have been to use cheaper imported oil whilst con-
serving a proportion of domestic production capacity which could
then be brought into operation in times of emergency such as the
1973 crisis.[7]

But the Organisation of Arab Petroleum Exporting Countries
(OAPEC) soon came up against the ultimate limitations of the oil
weapon. The use of economic means of coercion eventually and
inevitably have feedback consequences for the economies of the
coercing powers. Persistent use of the oil embargo would eventually have a drastic effect on the industrialised economies, induce
recession and lead to a reduction in demand for oil which would
affect the revenues of the producer countries. In addition to this,
although OPEC was formed in order to consolidate and co-
ordinate the economic power of the member states in the form of
an international cartel, they have in effect found it very difficult to
achieve those objectives.

The reasons for the failure of OPEC effectively to operate as a
cartel relate partly to conditions of supply and partly to conditions
of demand. On the supply side the major problem has been the
difficulty of maintaining sufficient solidarity and discipline among
OPEC members in order to follow a consistent policy on production and pricing. This is primarily because many of the members
have conflicting interests and are susceptible in varying degrees to
domestic and international pressures that inhibit their ability to
conform with OPEC cartel policy. Indeed Iraq itself refused to
engage in the use of the oil weapon in 1973 because it was not
discriminating enough.[8]

On the demand side OPEC had little control over the ability of
consumer countries to become more energy efficient, or over the
development of oil-substituting technologies and strategies. The
consuming countries would have greater incentives to pursue such
strategies in the face of higher oil prices, and moreover such a
policy would bring substitute energy technologies within the
bounds of economic viability. Additionally the slower growth and
even recession in the developed consumer economies, as a result
partly of the economic cycle and partly of the high price of oil

itself, would lead to a reduction in demand for oil. It is of considerable long-term significance to OPEC (and other oil producers) that between 1973 and 1987 the amount of oil needed to produce one dollar's worth of GDP fell by 35 per cent in the United States, by 40 per cent in Europe and by 50 per cent in Japan.[9] So lack of control over the market particularly in the medium and long term means that OPEC has only limited ability to operate as a cartel and thus its ability to exert political pressure over the consumers of its product is restricted at least in the long term.

However, that is not to say that in the short term concerted operation of a cartel by OPEC cannot have a seriously disruptive effect on the oil market, which might spill over into the medium term and induce uncertainty about such consequences on the global economy in general. This relates partly to psychological factors where fear of drastic effects on the oil market to some extent acts as a self-fulfilling prophecy but also partly to the parallel difficulty that OECD countries find in acting with sufficient solidarity or cohesion to counteract the attempts of the producers to act as a monopoly.

For example, consumer countries such as Japan, Italy and Denmark have few energy sources of any kind and are dependent on OPEC sources of oil. France, Germany and the Benelux countries have large domestic solid fuel resources but are dependent on external supplies of oil. All of these countries want low oil prices. The United States and Canada on the other hand are essentially self-sufficient in all energy sources and are thus independent of the world market. The independent oil producers in these countries want high oil prices. The United Kingdom and Norway are now oil exporters and have an interest in high oil prices.[10] However, even within the OECD oil producer countries there is a conflict of interest between the oil producers and governments on the one hand who want high prices and the revenues deriving from them and consumers on the other who want low prices. Indeed most governments will have a natural ambivalence towards oil prices, having to draw some sort of balance between the impact on domestic economic activity of higher oil prices with the increased revenue they will derive from higher oil tax revenues. By far the largest slice of the price of a barrel of oil goes to the governments of consumer countries in the form of oil taxes (Table 8.1). The one sure consequence of the oil shock of 1973 and the subsequent shock of 1979 with the withdrawal of Iranian oil production after the Islamic revolution, was the vast increase in OPEC oil revenues. From a total of $11,023 million in 1971 to a total of $264,025 million in 1980. Saudi Arabia dominates OPEC with over 30 per cent of its exports and 30 per cent of its oil reserves, and its revenues are by far the largest: rising from $1,886 million in 1971 to $102,212 million in 1980[11] – well over 500 per cent increase in a decade.

Table 8.1 Breakdown of oil price per barrel, 1973

In April 1973 the price of oil in Europe was $16 per barrel, of which:

Production costs	1.8%
Producers' revenues	9.6%
Companies' costs/profits	33.3%
Consumer govt taxes	55.3%

Source: Peter Mansfield, *The Arabs* (Harmondsworth: Penguin Books, 1985), p. 489.

Among the main factors preventing OPEC solidarity are the disparities in oil revenues between the members and the disparities in the respective populations that those revenues have to serve. Algeria and Iraq have large populations to service whereas Kuwait, Bahrain, Qatar and the United Arab Emirates have very small populations. There have also been disparities regarding the purposes to which those revenues have been put which have caused enmities within OPEC. For example, in Saudi Arabia and the Gulf States there has been some internal development but very little industrialisation other than refining and petrochemical installations. Most of their oil revenues have been invested in foreign countries, thus providing even more revenues, allowing a large proportion of their indigenous populations to live easily and rely on immigrant peoples to do the less savoury work. It has been said that the Kuwaiti economy before the invasion effectively existed outside its own territorial borders except for some refineries, petrochemical plants and desalination plants; and that since 1986 Kuwait has earned more from its investments overseas (particularly in Europe and the United States) than it has directly from oil.[12]

Iraq on the other hand, with a population some eight or nine times that of Kuwait, has attempted to invest in internal industrialisation and development as well as spending a large proportion of its revenues on military equipment both from the west and from the former Soviet Union. In addition to this, for eight years from 1981 Iraq engaged in a war with Iran which consumed much of its revenues and put drastic strain on its economy. Given this situation it is clear that Iraq would be much more sensitive to price and revenue fluctuations than Kuwait or the other Gulf states.

Table 8.2 demonstrates the crucial importance of oil to the global economy; Tables 8.3 and 8.4 show the significance of Middle Eastern oil in the world oil market, and within OAPEC the relative significance of Iraq, Kuwait and Saudi Arabia. The basic conflict within OPEC is between those producer countries who want high production at lower prices in order to increase revenue and those who want to fix higher prices to compensate for their inability to raise output for production reasons or their unwillingness to raise output because they want to conserve more of their reserves. Thus much of the politics within OPEC concerns the balance between output and price; whether to fix the output in order to control the price or to fix the price and manipulate output to ensure it is held. Fixing the price has been found to be very difficult so much of the bargaining within OPEC is concerned with fixing production quotas and determining who is allowed to produce how much. If any member exceeds the quotas once agreed in order to raise local revenues the effect is a price reduction on the world market and a reduction in total revenues for those who stick to the quotas.

Table 8.2 Percentage composition of world energy consumption, 1979–84

	Oil	Natural gas	Coal	Hydro	Nuclear	Total
1979	45.0	18.4	28.5	5.9	2.2	100
1981	42.4	19.3	29.2	6.2	2.9	100
1983	40.3	19.2	30.3	6.8	3.4	100
1984*	39.3	19.7	30.3	6.8	3.9	100

* Estimated.
Source: Stephen Gill and David Law, *The Global Economy: Perspectives, Problems and Policies* (Hemel Hempstead: Harvester/Wheatsheaf, 1988).

Table 8.3 Top twenty producers of crude oil, 1988

	000s barrels/day
USSR	11,679
United States	8,140
Saudi Arabia*†	5,288
China	2,728
Iraq*†	2,646
Mexico	2,512
Iran*	2,259
United Kingdom	2,232
Venezuela*	1,903
Canada	1,610
UAE*†	1,606
Kuwait*†	1,492
Nigeria*	1,450
Indonesia*	1,328
Norway	1,158
Libya*†	1,055
Algeria*†	1,040
Egypt	848
India	635
Oman	617

* OPEC member.
† OAPEC member.
Source: The Economist Book of Vital World Statistics (London:
Hutchinson, 1990).

Iraq and Kuwait have about the same quantity of oil reserves, roughly 9 per cent of total world reserves; Kuwait exports approximately 77.8 million tonnes (coal equivalent) and Iraq exports 151 million tonnes. But a measure of the relative prosperity of the two countries is indicated by the fact that for Kuwait energy consumption per head of population is 9,191 kg. coal equivalent (US = 9542; UK = 5107; W. Germany = 5624), whereas the figure for Iraq is 735.[13] With a population of some 17 million compared with 1.9 million in Kuwait (of which only 600,000 are in fact Kuwaiti citizens) it is plain that Iraq would be rather less

Table 8.4 Top twenty exporters of crude oil, 1988

	000s barrels/day
Saudi Arabia*†	2,325
United Kingdom	1,734
Mexico	1,204
Nigeria*	1,073
Iraq*†	988
USSR	951
Norway	944
Iran*	911
Libya*†	867
UAE*†	836
Venezuela*	639
Indonesia*	636
Algeria*†	502
Kuwait*†	454
China	357
Angola	322
Oman	284
Egypt	247
Qatar*†	181
Malaysia	115

* OPEC member.
† OAPEC member.
Source: The Economist Book of Vital World Statistics (London: Hutchinson, 1990).

relaxed about total oil revenues than Kuwait. Not only are there vast disparities in the size of their respective populations for which revenues are needed but by 1990 the Iraqi economy had been devasted by its war with Iran, it had run up huge debts to its fellow Gulf neighbours (including Kuwait) and unlike Kuwait, whose overseas investment revenues exceed its oil revenues, had no other sources of income. Thus the failure of OPEC (and of the Gulf Cooperation Council) to resolve the differences between them, and Kuwait's exceeding of its production quotas, presented a serious problem for Iraq. In the early part of 1990 overproduction by Kuwait (and the United Arab Emirates) led to a reduction in the price of oil by nearly 50 per cent (from a peak of $22 in January to $13 by the spring).[14] In the context of fixed oil output this represented a very serious reduction in revenue for Iraq in the face of severe economic difficulties and a heavy debt burden.

Though there was no doubt a long-standing contingency in Iraqi strategy for an invasion of Kuwait to satisfy both territorial claims and regional power-political objectives of Saddam Hussein and the Ba'ath Party, it was probably the anger, frustration and sheer desperation on the part of the Iraqis in the face of drastically reducing oil revenues that is the most likely immediate explanation for Iraq's invasion of Kuwait.

Oil and the western response to the Iraqi invasion

We have noted elsewhere that it is difficult to isolate the oil factor as a determinant of the western response to Iraq's invasion of Kuwait primarily because it is difficult to separate the economic and the politico-strategic dimensions of the Middle East. So, although it cannot be regarded as the only reason for that response, there is little doubt that oil assumed a significant role. Given the points made above about the difficulty of either producers or consumers exerting control over the world oil market, it is not immediately obvious why an Iraqi invasion of Kuwait should invoke a response from the west purely on the basis of its concern for the supply and price of oil.

The invasion itself put Iraq in control of some 20 per cent of the world's known reserves. This is presumably an eventuality that in itself would not unduly affect the oil interests of the western powers. Indeed in the event the absence of both Iraqi and Kuwaiti production had very little impact on the market. The more significant factor was the threat to Saudi Arabia and the prospect that Saddam Hussein might find himself in control of nearly 50 per cent of the world's oil reserves. That would be a substantial portion of the world's supply and, together with the coercion he would then be able to exert within OPEC, would be sufficient to put Iraq effectively in the position of a monopoly supplier in the oil market. However, it must be questioned whether even such a concentration of production capability would in the longer term confer any greater ability to control the market since many of the obstacles to the operation of a cartel mentioned above, particularly on the demand side, would remain. The oil shocks of both 1973 and 1979 resulted in a rapid price 'hike' and were followed fairly steadily by a fall in price.

But in order to substantiate the oil factor as the chief determinant of the US response to the invasion, we have to establish the interests of the United States in the oil supply/price balance. If the logic was that the chief danger of Saddam's hanging on to Kuwait was his ability to keep the price of oil high then it is not absolutely clear that such an outcome would be contrary to US interests. Low oil prices, while good for consumers, are not good for domestic producers. Indeed the effect of overall declining oil prices since the Second World War has been to undermine American high-cost domestic producers and increase US dependence on imported oil – more than half of US oil requirements are now imported. Thus on the basis of this logic alone a recommended US response would be far from obvious and there certainly would not be a clear-cut and inexorable case for removing Saddam from Kuwait. So much for the argument that America was merely 'acting to protect cheap oil'.

This is not to say that Iraqi control of Saudi Arabian oil resources was not a (or even the) relevant factor in determining the western response. Though it was not necessarily the oil factor itself that determined the response, it was the Iraqi potential to convert oil revenue into political and military power that represented the threat to the balance of power in the region and the possibility that Iraq under Saddam Hussein would become an aggressive 'Third World superpower' which in the light of the breakdown of the Soviet–American duopoly would have been impossible to control.

The oil market and the Gulf conflict

However, 'logic' is not necessarily the determining factor of oil (or other) market movements. Whether the price is high or low, it is market stability that perhaps is the highest priority; and it is what people believe that determines the stability of the market. It might sound paradoxical but it is the market makers' beliefs and fears about future market stability that determines current market stability. That of course is circular because if the market makers fear that the future market will be unstable, that will make the current market unstable, which will in turn ensure that the future market is unstable – a self-fulfilling prophecy. So the 'irrationality' of Saddam Hussein was not the only irrationality that had an impact on the Gulf crisis. The condition enhancing the impact of this 'irrationality' was the increasing domination of world oil trading in recent years of the futures market in oil.[15] Thus it was not the actual safety of the Saudi oil-fields that contributed to market jitters but the market's belief about the safety of those fields, and also the assumed consequences for the oil market of an Iraqi take-over in Saudi Arabia. It was in order to stabilise the psychology of the market that Saudi Arabia undertook to increase its production to compensate for the absence of Iraqi and Kuwaiti production after the imposition of sanctions by Security Council Resolution 661 and the continually expressed willingness of the International Energy Agency (IEA) to release reserves to dampen down the market price.

Market prices are determined by beliefs and not by the inexorable logic of supply and demand in the market-place. Beliefs will be determined by the market makers' understanding not only of the relationship between the supply of and demand for the commodity in question but an understanding of the factors that determine movements and changes in supply and demand – economic, social and political. War very often has a profound impact upon markets not because of the direct impact upon supply and demand for commodities but because of the uncertainties that war injects into the world economy. On top of this there is the automatic expectation that war or large-scale international crisis is bound to have an adverse effect on markets. Of course the oil crises of 1973 and 1979 had instilled in market psychology the 'truth' that political crisis in the Middle East gives rise to oil crisis. Hence the rise in the oil price from $18 per barrel to over $40 per barrel in the period after the Iraqi invasion was to some extent a 'knee jerk' reaction by the market. Prices reached a peak in early October 1990 after which there was a gradual general trend downwards with short-term 'blips' within the general trend caused by the ups and downs of crisis diplomacy. The relatively rapid downward trend was firstly a reflection of the initial over-reaction of the markets to the Iraqi invasion and secondly a manifestation of a gradual return of confidence to the market as it became increasingly clear that the United States was prepared and preparing to defend Saudi Arabia (and hence her oil reserves and production) against a threat from Iraq.

But a refocusing of the markets on the current relationship of supply and demand for oil also served to inject a greater sense of reality into the psychology of the market. It became increasingly clear that the market was not drastically affected by the absence of Iraqi and Kuwaiti production. Moreover the depression in demand for oil as a result of recession in OECD countries combined with high OECD oil stocks, and the storing by Saudi Arabia and Iran of large quantities of oil in tankers at sea close to major consumer countries, had turned fear of shortage into fear of glut.[16] These factors were also enhanced by predictions about the likely effect of the war on politics within OPEC and the likelihood that there might be a price war and that in any case the power of Saudi Arabia within the organisation would be enhanced as a result of the war. Furthermore, there would after the war be an added incentive for Saudi Arabia to keep production high (and thus the price low) in order to foot the heavy bills being submitted by the major Coalition allies to pay for the war. Even when the war began on 16 January 1991 the blip in price up to nearly $30 per barrel was within hours down by something like $8 per barrel when it was rapidly realised that Coalition air supremacy meant that Saudi oil installations were essentially immune from Iraqi air attack. Thus oil, over which many claimed the war was being fought, had become irrelevant to it within hours of its beginning.[17]

THE ECONOMIC COSTS AND CONSEQUENCES OF THE GULF WAR

Two broad areas will be considered in this section. Firstly the direct quantifiable costs and secondly the general effects of the war on the global economy and on individual economies of some of the major or significant participants in the conflict.

Direct quantifiable costs

The calculation of direct monetary costs of wars is a complex task and this is not the place to confront that complexity head on. What can be done here is to give some idea of the nature of the task and the sort of considerations that need to be taken account of if some realistic estimate of cost is to be arrived at. That there already exists a range of estimates from different authorities as to the overall cost and the cost to individual economies is a testament to the difficulty of the task and lack of agreement as to what has to be included.

However, there are three categories of cost that need to be calculated:[18] the cost of mobilisation for the war, the daily recurring cost of the military action once the war has begun and the capital costs incurred in fighting the war. The first two may be regarded as 'budgetary costs' – that is, those costs incurred out of the current budget – and the third, 'resources costs' – i.e. the destruction of those resources already acquired in terms of military equipment, weapons, ammunition and so on. (see below).[19]

The cost of mobilisation includes the cost of the transport of troops and equipment, and the necessary modification of equipment and the training of troops for the particular environment in which they will have to operate – for example, in this case camouflage paint, anti-sand precautions, desert training for troops. These costs are in effect the cost involved in mobilising for this particular war as opposed to a general readiness for confronting a potential enemy. In the case of the major western allies much of the military machine was in various states of readiness both in Germany and elsewhere to fight a war in Europe against the Soviet Union. The costs of maintaining this capability throughout the Cold War may be regarded as a fixed cost; so the mobilisation costs of the Gulf War would be those costs over and above the costs already being incurred to keep those military resources at the state of readiness required by NATO.

The daily cost of the military action entails not only the cost of the actual presence and maintenance of troops in their Middle Eastern locations but also the cost of activities such as naval patrols, aircraft reconnaissance and training. This has to be calculated as the actual cost of all that on-going activity less the cost of those activities that would have been proceeding anyway if the Gulf crisis had not errupted. In all these calculations it is important to arrive at a net figure which is the total cost less that cost that would have been incurred by all this equipment and military personnel in the absence of a Gulf crisis.

For example, the wages bill of both regular and reserve forces would have to be included, but the wages bill for those troops had the crisis not happened would have to be deducted. Most of these costs relating to regular troops are fixed costs. Those reserves called up who would not have been called up in the absence of the war constitute costs in two senses: firstly their wages while in military service and secondly in the loss of production that they would otherwise have produced in their civilian employment – the so-called opportunity cost of their involvement in the war.

The evaluation of loss of life in financial terms of course is very difficult, but one source has suggested that the calculation of such costs could be based upon court awards made in the cases in civilian life of those killed by acts of negligence.[20] That is not to say that families of military personnel killed in action receive the same level of compensation. Attempting to put a monetary cost on human life is always a tasteless exercise but nevertheless has to be attempted if an accurate estimate of the cost of military action is to be made. In the case of the Gulf War, and in terms of Allied casualties only, this cost was relatively light and not nearly as high as was feared it might be.

The capital costs of military action include the value of equipment lost, damaged and destroyed in action. But from this total cost again has to be deducted the cost of damage and loss that might have taken place in the normal course of events in equipment breakdown, crash and accident and so on.

The question of how lost equipment should be valued is not an easy one to answer. If a particular piece of equipment needs to be replaced then the net cost is the replacement cost less depreciation of the lost equipment during its lifetime. However, if lost military equipment is replaced it is likely to be at a higher technical specification given the development of military technology. So as well as being more expensive than the equipment it replaced it also has a higher performance specification the value of which has to be discounted from the replacement cost in order to arrive at the net cost of the loss. However, some of the equipment will have been obsolescent and due to be scrapped anyway partly as a result of the change in security environment and the end of the Cold War. In such cases the cost could be little more than the scrap value of the particular piece.

So it is not easy to calculate the direct quantifiable economic costs of the war such that there are bound to be discrepancies between different methods of computation. Moreover an estimate of the costs of a policy of sanctions to achieve an Iraqi withdrawal from Kuwait would be necessary to get some idea of what the net cost of the war was likely to be.

GENERAL ECONOMIC EFFECTS ON INDIVIDUAL ECONOMIES AND THE GLOBAL ECONOMY

For the American economy in particular and the global economy in general war may have been a better solution than a coercive policy of economic sanctions alone. This may not have been for economic reasons only – merely that an early and clear resolution of the conflict was economically more beneficial, even if that resolution entailed war, than a long drawn out 'crisis' or period of political and therefore economic uncertainty or ambiguity. Often a situation of neither one thing nor the other is economically more damaging than a clear resolution one way or the other. The point has been made before, in relation both to the oil market and to the conduct of foreign policy, that what people believe or think about a situation is more important than its actuality since it is what people believe that determines their actions and behaviour. In economics and markets, people's behaviour is determined by their 'confidence' and that confidence is damaged more by uncertainty and lack of knowledge than by certainty and knowledge – almost regardless of what that knowledge is. Thus if war imposes clarity and resolves ambiguity and uncertainty, whatever other effects it has, it may have a less damaging effect on economic activity than may at first seem likely.

So when the war did start the release of the tension, after the long period of uncertainty during the crisis phase,[21] would itself have been economically beneficial, and that was demonstrated by the surge in world markets on 17 January 1991 when firstly the uncertainty of the crisis period was ended by the beginning of the air campaign and secondly when the devastating impact of that first onslaught made it appear likely that a quick victory was in sight. The only eventuality worse than the uncertainty of a long period of crisis irresolution and economic sanctions would have been the prospect of a long drawn out war going badly for the Coalition. Once the military disparity between the two sides became apparent the world markets reacted almost with jubilation[22] and then settled down as if the war was not happening. On 17 January the New York Stock Exchange rose 112.13 points, the second largest gain in its history;[23] this was the measure of relief felt on the launch of the Coalition counter-offensive and also perhaps an indication of a rather more tasteless jingoism.

The world's major economies were already in recession before

Iraq's invasion of Kuwait (despite some persistent denials of any such thing for months both before and long after the Gulf War). The Gulf War and its immediate effects on the world financial and equity markets may actually have served as a diversion from the underlying weaknesses of the global economy and the major economies within it. Indeed, rather than exacerbating its problems, the war actually tended to temper these longer-term and deeper economic problems. The initiation of the air war pushed the markets up to a level higher than they might have been had there been no war. This was clearly a temporary phenomenon caused by euphoria, a mere blip on the underlying pattern of global economic activity.

In the case of the United States a major factor determining the economic costs of the war was the fact that unlike the Second World War, the Korean War and the Vietnam War, the war in resource terms did not have to be serviced from current production. These previous wars were such long-lasting wars that the economy to a greater or lesser degree had to go onto a 'war footing' – in the case of the Second World War this was not only to support America's own war effort but those of her major allies, the United Kingdom and the Soviet Union. The Gulf War did not fall into this category at all – though it should be said that the amount of equipment involved and the number of personnel mobilised rivalled both Korea and Vietnam. Two factors determined that the current productive economy was barely affected by the Gulf War – one was the fact that it lasted such a short time and involved only very minor loss of equipment and secondly the equipment used was drawn from a vast military over-capacity left both by the remilitarisation policy during the Reagan administration and the demise of the 'enemy' against which it was designed to be used. Thus in that sense it was what has been called a 'pre-paid' war.[24]

The United States received pledges of financial contributions from its allies – Germany, Japan, Saudi Arabia and Kuwait – for some $53.5 billion. The US budget authorities claimed that the actual cost would exceed the total amount of pledges. However, other calculations suggest a rather lower figure.[25] The Congressional Budget Project came to a figure of $40–5 billion, whereas the House Appropriations Committee arrived at a figure of $42.6 billion. Thus there is the prospect of the United States making a profit of something like $10 billion. Such calculations are embarrassing for both the United States and its allies for the outcome may look like a direct financial transaction – 'we'll fight your war for you, you pay us $10 billion'.

The Gulf War and its implications highlighted the interesting incongruities and disparities within the leading 'western' powers – in particular on the subject of the relationship between economic power and politico-military influence and participation. For example, there is a great disparity between Britain's economic power (in terms of the western industrialised world the United Kingdom has one of the weaker economies) and her political influence in foreign policy terms; and if she does not have military power in quantitative terms on a par with the superpowers, or even with some of the militarily top-heavy Third World countries, the effectiveness of her military action and participation may be regarded as disproportionate to her economic underpinning. Thus though her economic status would not have warranted her position as a major actor in the Gulf War and crisis, her political status and military effectiveness made her the major partner of the Coalition leader, the United States. Indeed one might go so far as to say that, in political terms at least, America's task would have been very much more difficult to fulfil had the United Kingdom not assumed such a role. On the other hand the two economic superpowers on a par with the United States, Germany and Japan, have neither the political influence nor at least the overt, military power, commensurate with their economic status. That is an analytical fact on which there is much to say, though there is not much space to discuss it here. But the manifestation of these disparities that was most embarrassingly displayed in the Gulf conflict was the reluctance, not to say direct refusal, of these powers actively to participate in the war.

This reluctance was born partly of the constitutional constraints on their use of military power, imposed both by the post-war victorious powers and by the successor regimes themselves as an earnest of their new democratic virtues, but partly also of their 'fear and trembling' in the face of the prospect of their having soon to become a state as other states are – that is, where military power can legitimately be used to protect legitimate self-interest against illegitimate use of military aggression. Clearly such a transformation of both constitutional provision and foreign-policy habituation could not be completed overnight, and as a token of their recognition of their common interest with the active

Coalition partners and of their recognition that their role and status in matters relating to international military security would have to change, they agreed to contribute a large proportion of the financial costs of the war.

Germany and Japan, which provided a financial subvention to those major western allies who actually fought the war, incurred no resource costs because they contributed little in the field. In fact Germany maintained some naval forces in the eastern Mediterranean and did contribute some troops to Turkey to support Turkish troops in the event of invasion from Iraq.[26] Thus in a sense they could have been at an economic disadvantage in that they incurred financial costs without the boost to economic activity provided by the replacement of destroyed physical assets which would certainly have benefited the US economy to the extent that those assets were replaced. In Germany the coincidence of the costs of the the Gulf War and costs of reunification meant that taxes had to be raised.[27] But it is likely that that would have been necessary even in the absence of the Gulf War. Reunification has had a much more profound effect on the German economy than the Gulf War – though in the longer term both the war and unification will be seen to have had a major impact on whether and in what way Germany re-emerges as a world power in political and security terms.

There is a sense in which, because of Japan's low political and military profile in world affairs, its economy is able to operate reasonably normally during external disturbances. There seems to be a paradox in the fact that although it is locked firmly and centrally into the global capitalist economy it does not attract the same opprobrium for its 'economic imperialism', particularly from the Third World, as the United States, the central pillar of that global economy and whose economic power Japan is beginning to challenge. Indeed part of the irritation felt by the Japanese at the expectation of the major western powers – notably the United States and the United Kingdom – that they should participate in the Coalition action in the Gulf was that such participation would have the effect of associating Japan more closely in political and military terms with US action.

This factor is one reason why the Japanese economy has in the past been able to remain fairly aloof from external disruptions in the political firmament. Another factor of course is the sheer strength of the Japanese economy, which tends to make it invulnerable to all but the most severe external disruptions. Its perennial 'Achilles heel' is its total dependence on external oil supplies. Given the fact that the Gulf conflict caused only short-term rises in the price of oil, and in the longer term may have resulted actually in lower prices, the effect of the war on the Japanese economy is difficult to isolate from the effects of decisions and actions taken within the Japanese economy itself, notably the slowdown in growth during early 1991 caused by high interest rates.[28]

In general terms it is difficult to identify and extract the influence both on the global economy and on individual economies of particular events in the international system. In local terms, and also as what might be called a 'public event', the Gulf War was a violent, bloody and disruptive phenomenon. In global terms and in the longer term and in its significance for peoples' lives around the world, its impact is likely to be very marginal indeed. There are of course in any case potentially conflicting indicators – both positive and negative – and it is very difficult to assess their net effect. We have seen that uncertainty is the major factor determining economic activity and, to the extent that while the war was continuing, uncertainty continued, it would have had the effect of undermining confidence and therefore had an over-all adverse effect on the world economy. But the key factors that determined the longer-term economic impact of the war were the scale and duration of the war phase and the clarity of its outcome. In other words, if it turned out to be a short war that did not escalate in geographical and military terms, and resulted in a clear Coalition military victory then the economic effects on the major economies and the world economy as a whole were likely to be small and short-lived. One commentator places the war economically in proper context when he says that in the short run at least and as far as the American economy is concerned, 'Mr Alan Greenspan, the Chairman of the US Federal Reserve, may prove economically more potent than President Saddam Hussein'.[29]

Even in the context of weaker economies, like that of the United Kingdom, the 'Gulf War factor' could not really be blamed for economically poor performance, despite the attempt to do so. The effects of the recession in the UK economy during 1990–1 were so profound 'that even a war in the Gulf is unlikely to make them worse'.[30] There are even some who suggest that Britain may even have made a profit from the war. The estimated cost of $2 billion to the United Kingdom[31] is likely to have been almost covered by financial contributions from other countries – notably Germany and Kuwait – a quarter of which will be to replace lost equipment sometime in the future; and there was an additional gain of $1 billion in higher than expected tax revenues as a result of higher oil prices in 1990.

In fact contrary to what has been predicted by some commentators,[32] the deflationary effects of the war on the major western economies have been virtually non-existent, even where they can be detected at all. Indeed, in the case of the United Kingdom for example, it is likely that the government's own policies had such profound recessionary consequences (as opposed to merely deflationary ones) that they swamped the specific effects of the war and made them negligible and virtually undetectable. It has also proved difficult to isolate the macro-economic impact of the war. The Financial Times Survey of the World Economy published on 14 October 1991, some nine months after the war, warranted only one mention of the Gulf War when it said that 'little of last year's economic slowdown can be ascribed to the Gulf War'.[33]

It is possible, however, to identify some 'winners' and 'losers' among individual industries as a result of the war. The major losers were those related to travel and tourism, especially tour operators, airlines and hotels catering for the Middle East. Perhaps it is not surprising that the vast majority of the 'winners' in business terms were from outside of the region. Among these were arms manufacturers, cigarette manufacturers, makers of razors, but also other toiletries such as talc, male perfume, shampoo; stationery products, confectionary products, soft drinks and manufacturers of military rations. Since the area is not only a *sand* desert perhaps the most unexpected beneficiary of the war in the Middle East were condom manufacturers, whose product was found to be ideal for keeping sand out of the barrel of a gun.[34]

The significance of Egypt's participation in the Coalition's action is demonstrated by the fact that possibly alone of all the countries involved, both inside and outside the Middle East, she actually benefited economically from the war. There were losses – for example in the loss of remittances from Egyptian workers in Iraq and Kuwait, not of course alone among Middle Eastern countries in that, and in the loss of revenues from tourism, which suffered a decline as a result of the conflict, and from the reduction in dues from the Suez Canal, whose traffic was reduced – but the gains far exceeded them. She gained from the temporary rise in oil prices, but mainly (1) from compensation paid to it by Saudi Arabia and Kuwait, and (2) from her world creditors waiving large parts of its foreign debt totalling some $14 billion. But there was a price for such financial benefits in its agreement to impose IMF reforms on the Egyptian economy, which risked domestic discontent.[35]

Clearly the most drastic economic impact of the war was on Iraq and Kuwait – an estimated $100 billion for the cost of reconstruction in Kuwait alone. The economic consequences of the war on Iraq have been very profound since one of the objectives of the Coalition allies was to destroy the economic infrastructure of the country in order to undermine its capacity to prosecute the war for any length of time. Transport and communications facilities, power-generation capacity and oil-refining capacity were perhaps the most important of the losses to the Iraqi economy. It would be a gigantic task to regenerate those facilities under normal circumstances; under conditions of continuing United Nations sanctions it would be thought to be all but impossible. However, there are reports that the rebuilding of the vast majority of infrastructure and oil-refining capacity has been virtually completed within eighteen months of the end of the war. This is a measure of the vast quantities of materials and spare parts that the Iraqi regime must have stockpiled in order to survive siege conditions; and also a measure of the extent to which the regime has been able to bypass UN sanctions since the end of the war.[36]

The reconstruction of Kuwait is a task that is likely to provide opportunities for new economic activity that might help to drag the global economy out of recession. However, the unseemly vulture-like squabbling over the reconstruction spoils of Kuwait broke out between companies from Europe, Japan and the United States after the war. It is likely to lead to most contracts going to US firms as the most appropriate 'thank you' for its liberation. There is little doubt that Kuwaiti resources may be sufficient to meet both its financial subvention to the major Coalition allies and the costs of economic reconstruction. However, surprising though it might seem, Saudi Arabia is likely to experience more difficulty in coping with the economic consequences of the war. During 1991 the Saudi government twice had to seek overseas loans totalling some $7 billion in the face of the drain on its foreign currency reserves as a result of financing the war.[37]

Apart from the direct original participants, Iraq and Kuwait, if Egypt was the chief beneficiary in economic terms of the war then it is likely that Jordan was the chief victim. Her own economy before the war had been tied very closely to that of Iraq and this was one of the reasons Jordan found its room for manoeuvre constrained in the post-invasion 'shake-out' of Iraq's allies and enemies. Jordan was dependent on Iraqi oil, which was supplied at below market rates to off-set Iraqi debts to Jordan. After the war these supplies obviously ceased and Jordan has had to resort to the open market at an extra cost of something like $400 million.[38] Considerable income was previously generated by Jordan from transit trade to Iraq from the Red Sea port of Aqaba. While UN sanctions remain in force this is lost revenue. Not only this but while its former Arab trading partners Kuwait and Saudi Arabia continue to feel aggrieved about Jordan's support for Iraq during the crisis it is likely that the half-billion dollars worth of Jordanian exports to these countries will not be restored. Further economic damage has been done, as in the case of Egypt, by the elimination of expatriot remittances of Jordanian and Palestinian workers in Kuwait. But in addition to that, most of the workers who formerly provided those remittances have now had to return to Jordan to join the increasing army of unemployed, which constitutes both an economic and a political burden. There are more recent signs that the tourist trade, formerly worth some $500 million, is beginning to return, and promises of aid may offset the costs of the war to Jordan. Nevertheless there is little doubt that there have been severe short-term economic consquences of the war for Jordan, which in turn might well have longer-term political implications.

Chapter 9

War, strategy and the Gulf conflict

WAR AND DECISION

It is a conventional wisdom that war never solves problems. That is not entirely true. It may be that war does not always solve the problem it is meant to solve; but more often than not it solves some problems – and inevitably creates others. Even if it were true that war did not 'solve' anything, it does not mean that war is necessarily avoidable. The fact that war 'creates problems' does not demonstrate that war is pointless. All human action creates 'problems' in one form or another. Even if war does cause problems it very often prevents other, perhaps more serious, problems from arising. The problems that war prevents can only be speculated about – they can never be proved. There is a school of thought which suggests that Britain did not have to declare war on Germany when she did. There were indications that Hitler did not really want to take on Britain and Britain certainly did not declare war because she was under direct military threat. The ultimate reason that Britain declared war on Germany when she did was not because of an immediate threat but to forestall a future threat; a situation in which Germany had conquered Europe leaving Britain looking across the channel to a continent which was dominated by a single power against whom she would be very vulnerable. In this case the best form of pre-empting such a situation was to become involved in war sooner rather than later.

Even if war is avoidable that does not mean that it should always be avoided. In any case to say that war is always avoidable is to suggest that there is always complete freedom to take any action in a situation; that proposition ignores the fact that action always takes place in a context and that context actually limits freedom of action. Wars occur because somebody (either one person or a group of people) makes a decision to go to war (or to use force, or to respond militarily to the use of force). The notion of a 'decision for war' implies some form of 'rational calculus' that involves consideration of (1) what it is hoped is to be achieved by the war, (2) what resources are available for conducting it and (3) what the prospect is of achieving the objective. So some form of cost–benefit analysis is assumed to take place. There are costs and benefits attaching to all human actions. In the case of war the emphasis is usually placed on the costs of going to war or using military force. A cost–benefit analysis of going to war contains within it an implicit cost–benefit analysis of not going to war. It is very often the perceived costs of not going to war that determine a decision for war. It is not what will be gained from going to war but what might be lost in not going to war.

This is part of a common, if not often acknowledged, phenomenon. Decisions in many different situations, both public and private, are determined essentially by a balance of costs – that is, the costs of doing something against the costs of not doing it. Very often 'benefits' hardly come into the picture at all. This is a sort of negative decision-making, the 'making a virtue of necessity' type of decision-making and is common in politics and international relations. It is of course analogous to the notion of 'negative utility' (the idea of acting so as to minimise suffering as opposed to the maximising of happiness) and the moral problems of choosing between evils as opposed to choosing between 'good' and 'evil'.

It really arises out of the structural situation – when structural propensities (see the Introduction) progressively become structural imperatives. The fact is that any individual's freedom of action is constrained by the action of others; but also decisions taken by an individual in the past constrain his own freedom of action in the present; and decisions taken in the present constrain freedom of action in the future. They alter the agenda, they impose a structure which is beyond the power of the actor to alter. In crisis situations that structure gets tighter and, as the freedom of action becomes more constrained, so the emphasis of any rational calculation will transfer from balancing costs and benefits, to balancing costs and costs.

The reason that once mobilisation starts there grows a dynamic towards war is that progressively the costs of not taking military action outweigh the costs of using it. In addition to that is the problem of quantifying costs and of balancing or comparing essentially incommensurable components of interest. It is very difficult (both for the analyst and for the decision-maker) to calculate, and come to 'rational' decisions, using trade-offs between incommensurate factors. Costs (or at least potential costs) may be relatively easy to calculate in terms of tangible resources in manpower, weapons, aircraft, ships, tanks and all the vast range of matériel used for warfare. But it may be very difficult to balance such costs (especially in terms of human lives) against intangible benefits such as 'avoiding a potential future state of affairs', maintaining the official ideology, protecting the sovereignty and independence of an ally, maintaining the political and military stability in the region or even in global terms, or deterring other leaders from pursuing aggressive military policies. Such judgements are not subject to quantitative calculation – no precise answers can be expected. That does not mean that the 'calculation' of trade-offs cannot be done, or is not done, or is pointless. Indeed such calculations, in an increasingly complex and uncertain international system, is the very stuff of foreign-policy and security-policy decisions.

These calculations, then, have to be done, and they *are* done in decisions for war – if not explicitly then implicitly. Coping with an essentially uncertain world and having to trade off tangible and quantifiable costs and benefits against intangible and essentially unquantifiable ones is one of the most difficult aspects of the task of making foreign-policy decisions and military decisions. It is a task that has be to faced not least in times of war. This is the crucial matter – it is not whether calculations are made but rather the accuracy of the premises upon which such reasoning is based and the 'logic' of the process of deductions from those premises. It is said of Saddam Hussein not that he does not calculate but that he consistently miscalculates. Either his premises are wrong, the process of logical argument is faulty or he has poor judgement in assessing the qualitative value of the intangible or non-material factors.

In the western democracies that calculation is made even more difficult because it has to be seen to be a reasonably accurate and plausible one and therefore broadly acceptable to domestic constituencies. The calculation only becomes unnecessary if you take the initial position that whatever the outcome of the calculation war is never justified – that is, the pacifist position. If you are not a pacifist then the calculation is necessary and appropriate. The non-pacifist position is, put simply, 'there are conceivable situations in which it may be justifiable to go to war'. What determines whether you go to war at any one time is your calculation of the costs and the benefits. It is over the calculation of the costs and benefits that most disagreement over war takes place. Disagreements occur only over what factors are to be taken into account, the values to be attached to the various factors and the result of weighing the perceived costs and the perceived benefits.

CALCULATION FOR WAR: PERCEPTIONS AND RATIONALITY

There is a great deal of literature on the importance of perceptions in international relations. This arises from the simple proposition that our behaviour is not determined by the way the world is but by the way we think it is – and this goes particularly for the makers of foreign and security policy. So our general picture of the world will determine our general strategies for dealing with it; and our particular perceptions will determine how we behave in particular situations like crisis or conflict. It is because perceptions are so important in explaining the way foreign-policy decision-makers act that there is so much information and discussion about the determinants of perceptions, in human beings in general and in foreign-policy decision-makers in particular, and how perceptions are translated into actual behaviour. Hence the importance given in the literature to the problem of understanding how the human mind constructs reality, or constructs a model of reality, which then becomes the basis for its interaction with the world. The implication is that the narrower the gap between perception and reality, the more rational will be a decision, and the wider the gap the less rational.

This is relevant to the task of explaining the apparently irrational willingness of a small underdeveloped Third World country to risk, and ultimately to engage in, war with a world-wide coalition which included the most powerful states in the world. Such a confrontation would on the face of it have dictated a cautious and astute diplomacy calculated to get the best possible terms short of actual war. The question of Saddam Hussein's rationality was always a matter of speculation based either upon the possibility that he might be personally irrational or psychologically unstable, or upon the apparent 'messianic' set of values that he appeared to invoke to justify and explain his behaviour to the world. This is related to what has been coined as 'the rational use of the irrational' – in other words, of feigning irrationality as part of a rational strategy. This notion is usually discussed in terms of strategic nuclear deterrence,[1] but it is a strategy applicable in many bargaining situations not only in military and diplomatic affairs but in everyday life.

The objective of this strategy is to pass responsibility for avoiding conflict to your opponent. This is achieved by convincing your opponent that for one reason or another you have lost the power to take avoiding action so that it is only by your opponent taking avoiding action that conflict can be averted. Feigning irrationality, so the theory goes, is one way of persuading your opponent that it is only he who can make sensible decisions, so it is only he who can save the confrontation from lurching into war.[2]

In the case of the Gulf crisis it was difficult to determine whether Saddam Hussein's apparent irrationality (his messianic rhetoric and preposterous claims) was a reflection of a genuinely held picture of the world or merely a clever way of appearing irrational, suggesting that such a rationality would not allow him to back down and so if conflict were to be averted it had better be the Americans who took avoiding action. This is in accordance with the psychology of crisis bargaining – the uncertainty caused by the difficulty of distinguishing between actual irrationality and the rational use of irrational behaviour is designed to inject caution into your opponent's deliberations and destabilise his diplomacy. The problem of defining the condition of your opponent is important since in some respects there is little difference between resolve and irrationality – the objective of both is the same; the only operational difference is that resolve can be broken down (in theory at least) whereas irrationality cannot.

There is every evidence that Saddam Hussein is not an irrational individual. Most assessments of his personality and his political performance[3] suggest that he is a ruthless, brutal individual who brooks no challenge or disagreement but that he is politically quite astute in the internal politics of both Iraq as a whole and the Ba'ath Party in Iraq, which he has come to dominate. On the other hand there are signs of a megalomania which would induce him to believe that he has a competence if not expertise in any field (rather like Stalin who wrote on music, biology, philology, etc.); there is of course no natural limit to the claim to infallibility. Certainly Saddam Hussein's self-perception led him to believe that he was a great military strategist, though evidence to substantiate that belief is scanty or non-existent.

He is said to be a 'rational calculator' – it is just that his calculations are more often than not wrong.[4] However, in judging calculations to be right or wrong it is important that we have a clear idea of what the objectives are to which the calculation is directed. Clearly a military victory was a first-order objective for the Iraqis. But if a 'military defeat' is regarded as merely a second-order objective rather than a zero-sum type loss, out of which does come some benefit for Saddam Hussein and the Ba'athist regime, then that puts rather a different gloss on Iraqi behaviour. If in Saddam's 'model of reality' war with the United States was not the disaster that it would be in a western model of reality then there would be less incentive or less urgency for him to avoid it. In this case it can be seen that (unlike the model of western pacifists) war is not necessarily the 'worst' option or the worst outcome to be avoided at all costs. For Saddam in this post-invasion situation, war did not represent a zero-sum game. In other words, military defeat did not come at the bottom of his priority list of objectives in the crisis (Table 9.1, Fig. 9.1).

Thus if military defeat appeared higher on his list of possible outcomes than a non-violent withdrawal from Kuwait then war was not necessarily an unmitigated disaster. He could drop from the image of all-conquering hero with the fourth largest military

Table 9.1 Iraqi outcome priorities for the Gulf crisis[*]

Best outcome:	Military victory; remain in Kuwait (aa_1)
Worst best outcome:	No war: remain in Kuwait (presumably under a regime of UN sanctions) (a_1b)
Best worst outcome:	War: military defeat: ejection from Kuwait by force (ab_1)
Worst outcome:	Non-violent Iraqi withdrawal from Kuwait (b_1b)

[*] See Figure 9.1

machine in the world to that of a small, weak, underdeveloped Third World country valiantly confronting a rapacious superpower even though the odds were stacked against it. That could be portrayed as a victory of sorts.

It is worth pointing out here that a non-violent withdrawal from Kuwait (b_1b) is only the worst-case outcome for the Iraqi side on the premise that losing face, humiliation, avoiding the battle are outcomes that are not tolerable in the 'macho' Islamic/Arab culture or at least in Saddam Hussein's set of values. It was because it was more difficult to present Iraqi withdrawal as a victory for Saddam Hussein that he was forced by his own logic to remain in Kuwait – even though in effect it would have been precisely that – that is, a victory.

If this outcome (b_1b) is looked at from the Allied perspective then it can be seen as the worst plausible outcome and one over which Saddam Hussein actually had control. In the Coalition outcome matrix it can be seen that military defeat with all that that entails would have been the worst, but also the least plausible, outcome (Fig. 9.1). The so-called 'nightmare scenario' for the United States and the United Nations would have been a strict compliance with Security Council Resolution 660 and a withdrawal of Iraqi troops to their position as at 1 August 1990 – that is, just across the border in Iraq. Saddam's military might would have remained intact and essentially invulnerable to Coalition attack; and his presence there could have held the United States and the Coalition in a state of suspended confrontation almost indefinitely. For the Coalition this would have been politically and militarily unsustainable.

It was the inability, imposed by Saddam Hussein's own hierarchy of values, to set the costs to himself of such an outcome against the costs to the Coalition, that really entailed his own defeat. It was a sort of 'fatal attraction' of the self-image of fearless warrior over that of wily politician that in the final analysis brought his defeat – and indeed may well bring his final downfall and even demise.

Thus it is not that cost–benefit calculation does not take place prior to war but that very often the criteria by which costs and benefits are judged are not necessarily obvious and not themselves necessarily susceptible to 'rational' analysis. Additionally it is found that the assumptions and perceptions of the situation upon which such calculation is based is not necessarily accurate and

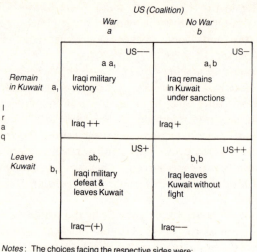

Figure 9.1 Matrix of possible outcomes in the Gulf conflict

US (Coalition)

War
a

No War
b

Remain in Kuwait a_1

US−−
$a\,a_1$
Iraqi military victory

Iraq ++

US−
$a_1\,b$
Iraq remains in Kuwait under sanctions

Iraq +

Leave Kuwait b_1

US+
ab_1
Iraqi military defeat & leaves Kuwait

Iraq−(+)

US++
$b_1\,b$
Iraq leaves Kuwait without fight

Iraq−−

Iraq (down left side)

Notes: The choices facing the respective sides were:

Iraq: a_1 – to stay in Kuwait
b_1 – to leave Kuwait

US (UN Coalition):

a – to use force
b – not to use force

aa_1
a_1b all ostensibly zero sum outcomes
b_1b

ab_1 The actual outcome was non zero sum in that the Iraqi 'loss' did not equate with US 'gain' because there was an Iraqi political 'gain' to be set alongside this military loss in the short to medium term at least, or a political or psychological gain for Saddam.

indeed may be subject to distortion due to psychological, ideo-logical, cultural and idiosyncratic factors, and so on.

So investigating the nature of the assumptions and perceptions upon which decisions for war are taken can be a very complex process. It is not clear whether Saddam Hussein made a positive decision to go to war with the Coalition forces or whether he merely failed to make the decision not to. It is more likely to have been the latter than the former. There is a good deal of evidence to suggest a degree of confusion, indecision, lack of clarity and inconsistency on the Iraqi side. It is at this distance difficult to determine the nature of the Iraqi decision-making structure during the crisis. Much of the information that is available suggests that the process was entirely autocratic, which implies presumably not only the bypassing of bureaucratic structures of foreign-policy making – the Foreign Ministry and Defence Ministry – but also the total intimidation of the inner ruling group by Saddam Hussein. Clearly the more power and freedom of action an individual has in the decision-making structure the more that idiosyncratic factors such as personality, psychology, intelligence, personal history and so on will have an impact on policies pursued and decisions taken.

The personality of Saddam Hussein is discussed in relation to crisis decision-making in Chapter 4; suffice it to say here that the decision for war was probably his and that it is a plausible proposition that rather than make a positive decision for war with the UN Coalition, he merely refrained from doing anything strenuously to avoid it, in the belief that whatever happened he and his ruling group would survive and that the United States would not have the political will to pursue the matter to a military conclusion, or that they would get enmeshed in a quagmire which would redound to the benefit of Saddam himself. In other words for Saddam Hussein (as argued above) war was not the worst outcome in his calculation of costs and benefits.

It is, however, necessary to make a distinction between the Iraqi state as a player and Saddam Hussein himself as a player. Thus for Iraq the consequences of defeat were very great – indeed devastating. But for Saddam Hussein the consequences of defeat could be better than the consequences of leaving Kuwait without a fight – for him a military defeat that could be presented as a brave and honourable one was better that the humiliation of withdrawal. But it can be seen once again that it is the balance of costs that determines the option chosen rather than the reconciliation of costs and benefits.

The hierarchy of preferred outcomes that on the face of it might be expected for the United States/UN Coalition is shown in Table 9.2. This assumes that the best outcome was an Iraqi withdrawal short of war. On this pattern of outcomes the Coalition achieved the worst of the best outcomes (as opposed to Saddam Hussein's best of the worst outcomes; – see Table 9.1). This can be explained by the asymmetry of the relationship. For the Coalition the consequences of defeat were truly enormous but could be risked because of its very small likelihood. In fact, however, as has been discussed above, an Iraqi withdrawal short of war would really have been the nightmare outcome for the Coalition. For Saddam Hussein the personal costs of a humiliating withdrawal

Table 9.2 US/Coalition outcome-priorities for the Gulf crisis[*]

Best outcome:	No war; Iraq leaves Kuwait (b_1b)
Worst best outcome:	War; Iraq leaves Kuwait (ab_1)
Best worst outcome:	No war; Iraq stays in Kuwait (albeit under sanctions) (a_1b)
Worst outcome	War; Iraq wins and stays in Kuwait (a_1a)

[*] See Figure 9.1

short of war were greater than the costs of a defeat in a war against a vastly more powerful enemy. To put it more succinctly, for the United States Coalition the certain costs of not going to war were far greater than the remote possibility of incurring the costs of defeat. Thus the use of force was the choice of the United States Coalition and the outcome was its preferred outcome.

ESCALATION AND THE MOMENTUM OF MILITARY FORCE

There is a 'logic' of war, a logic that becomes more and more insistent and difficult to resist as time proceeds in a crisis. It is one of the tasks of crisis management to control that logic and at best to break its train, to halt its apparent inevitability. In order to do this it is vital that the structure of crisis is understood. It is in the nature of military mobilisation in the technological age that once begun it is very difficult to stop short of war. The key determinant of the dynamic towards war in the process of mobilisation is the necessity not to be put at a military disadvantage if hostilities occur (see Chapter 7 of this book for a discussion of this in relation to 'just war' principles). This fear or anxiety is at the root of the increasing escalation to war in crisis. Moreover in a crisis which is caused by an act of military aggression the logic is for a military response (i.e. war) unless something is done specifically to avoid it. It has already been established in the discussion on the nature of crisis in Chapter 4 that what determines the character of the diplomatic interaction will be the objective on the part of the aggressor to so use his diplomatic instrument as to make a military response by his opponent untenable, either politically or militarily or both. The objective of the other party will be to so conduct his diplomacy so as not to be faced with a choice between diplomatic defeat and fighting a war at a military disadvantage.

This simple logic is that it is better to fight earlier, even when diplomacy might still be held to have some mileage left in it, rather than later, when both military and political conditions may have changed to your detriment. This logic does not necessarily arise out of anyone's malevolence or from military commanders being anxious to get into battle. It is an inexorable feature of crisis situations. If war is to be avoided in a crisis it is important that both sides understand the structure of plausible options within which they operate. Military mobilisation has the effect of closing down options in crisis situations. But the act that closes down options most effectively is the aggressive use of force in the first place. It is not so much for the aggressor that it closes down options, but for his opponent. In this situation it is not the aggressor who requires a 'golden bridge' of retreat but his opponent, since it is he who requires a specific pretext not to respond to military aggression with reciprocal military force. Effective crisis management requires the maintenance of a sort of symmetry, an equality of moral stance. Such symmetry is shattered by the initial act of aggression. So in the Gulf crisis, as with the Falklands conflict of 1982, there was an in-built imperative to war.

In the Gulf crisis the critics of military mobilisation were correct in their assertion that if you mobilise a massive force there is an imperative to use it, but this is not because it is directed by war mongers (it is a truism that the military, for obvious reasons, are often the least anxious to go to war) but because it is not a pretext for war that is required – that already exists. What is required is a pretext *not* to go to war. That pretext is in the hands of the aggressor. The mistake that may have been made by the Iraqis, and by many people in the west, was their belief that from a structural point of view it was the Coalition that had the room for manoeuvre and the scope for compromise and that it was the Iraqis who were 'out on a limb' and required a bridge for a face-saving retreat.

The actual situation was quite the reverse. Once the decision had been made that Saudi Arabia would have to be defended against a potential Iraqi invasion, war was almost inevitable in the absence of an Iraqi withdrawal. For the Coalition allies had to operate within a very constrained time-frame if they were to avoid the situation, referred to above, of having to fight a military operation at a disadvantage or when conditions had passed the optimum.

The situation facing the United States can be put quite simply. The defence of Saudi Arabia from a potential Iraqi incursion from Kuwait required American troops – either as a deterrent or as a force powerful enough to repulse the fourth largest army in the world. The installation of a US force sufficient merely to deter the Iraqis would have the effect of 'stalemating' the situation – that is, the Iraqis would have incentive neither to withdraw from Kuwait nor to attack Saudi Arabia. Moreover, so long as the Iraqis remained in Kuwait the US force would have to stay in Saudi Arabia – despite protestations by Saddam Hussein that he would not attack Saudi Arabia. (He had after all given a similar assurance to President Mubarak of Egypt that he would not invade Kuwait.) In the long term this would have been a politically unsustainable situation. Firstly from the point of view of the Saudis who would have become increasingly vulnerable to criticism, from within their own country and from the Arab/Islamic world externally, for using the 'Great Satan' to defend the holy places and to defend a conservative regime. The Saudi family would thus have come under increasing internal political pressure from both 'secular radicals' in Saudi Arabia and from Islamic fundamentalists (though it might be that that very incongruous combination is the factor most likely to keep the Saudi royal family in power). That may have been a train of force that neither the Saudi regime nor the Americans would have been able to resist. In that respect it is even possible to say that the war actually split the Arab and Islamic world and thus relieved such political pressure on the Saudi family.

Secondly of course an indefinite US military presence in Saudi Arabia would have been difficult to justify to the American domestic constituency, whose reaction would have been – 'either do something or come home'. In addition, the sending of a clearly designated defensive force to Saudi Arabia was an implicit (even explicit) signal that the Americans (and therefore the rest of the world) would ultimately acquiesce to the Iraqi invasion and annexation of Kuwait. Thus merely a commitment to defend Saudi Arabia would have put the United States at a diplomatic disadvantage and reduce their leverage on Iraq, making it increasingly less likely that they could escape the situation using purely diplomatic instruments.

So given that US withdrawal, once a force had been sent, was out of the question, since that would have signalled not only US acquiescence to the annexation of Kuwait but also her indifference to an Iraqi invasion of Saudi Arabia, the only way out of the stalemate was to adopt a policy of ejecting Iraq from Kuwait, either diplomatically or militarily. The requirement of that policy was that the US military presence in Saudi Arabia had to be substantially enhanced and converted into an offensive force – a force capable of driving the Iraqi military out of Kuwait should the diplomatic strategy fail.

There was in fact a similar imperative, once the Coalition military offensive had begun, to a defeat of the Iraqi military in the field and not merely a push to eject them out of Kuwait back into Iraq. Thus there would inevitably be a tendency to exceed the UN Resolution 678 (of 29 November 1990) which authorised the use of 'all necessary means' to relocate the Iraqi forces to the positions they occupied on 1 August 1990. Militarily an Iraqi defeat was required, not merely a relocation into Iraqi territory.

The crucial complementarity of the diplomatic and the military instruments of foreign-policy have been discussed in Chapter 4. International crises are characterised by a diplomatico-military interaction. In crises the military factor is always present, if not in the form of actual military force then in the form of coercive threat – explicit or implicit. It is the transition from predominantly diplomatic 'persuasive' means to predominantly threatening 'coercive' means that sees the increasing escalation of crisis towards war.

Two major thresholds can be noted in this trend to increasing coercive pressure (see Chapter 4 and Fig. 4.3 on crisis phases and thresholds). One was the change in US policy from one of defence to one of offence with the decision massively to enhance the US military force in the Gulf region; as noted above this signalled the transition from a policy of defending Saudi Arabia to one of liberating Kuwait. The other was the UN resolution authorising all necessary means and the setting of the 15 January deadline. This put war 'formally' on the agenda, as it were (Table 9.3).

COALITION MILITARY STRATEGY

The authority of Security Council Resolution 678 provided for the implementation of the provisions of Resolution 660 of 2 August 1990 – that is, to secure the withdrawal of Iraqi forces 'to positions in which they were located on 1 August 1990' – and 'all

Table 9.3 Key stages in the Gulf conflict 1990–1

Date	Key stage	Event
2 August 1990	Act of aggression	Iraqi invasion
	Beginning of war	Kuwaiti resistance and retreat
7 August 1990	Regrouping	Mobilisation of UN Coalition force
8 November 1990		Change of Coalition policy from one of defending Saudi Arabia to one of liberating Kuwait
29 November 1990		UN resolution sanctioning all means to achieve Iraqi withdrawal
9 January 1991		Failure of Geneva talks
15 January 1991		UN ultimatum expires
17 January 1991	Counter-attack	Launch of Coalition air offensive
		Hiatus after air offensive during which some diplomatic flurrying
24 February 1991	Beginning of end	Launch of land offensive
28 February 1991	Defeat of aggressor and end of war	Rout of Iraqi army

Note: Structurally the war can be seen as a whole – from the initial Iraqi invasion of Kuwait, through the brief Kuwaiti resistance, the retreat of the Kuwait army, the long period of diplomatic activity and UN military mobilisation characterised by the breaching of successive 'thresholds' (see Chapter 4), to the Coalition offensive and Iraqi defeat.

subsequent relevant resolutions and to restore international peace and security in the area'.

These provisions were essentially incompatible with each other and one of the questions that arose in translating the legal authority into military terms was to what extent the provisions of restoring 'the sovereignty, independence and territorial integrity of Kuwait' and of 'restoring international peace and security in the area' could reasonably be said to have been achieved by merely securing the withdrawal of Iraqi forces 'to positions in which they were located on 1 August 1990'. Merely relocating a half million Iraqis a few kilometres to the north of the Iraq–Kuwait border would neither secure the future integrity of Kuwait (if they could simply move back south again when conditions were propitious for them) nor, while this military capability remained, re-establish peace and security in the region. So the image of a military operation limited to a northward thrust by Coalition troops from Saudi Arabia into Kuwait pushing the Iraqi occupation troops to retreat back into southern Iraq was never a realistic picture of what would be necessary to implement the UN resolutions. Firstly the restoration of peace and security in the region could be taken to entail a substantial diminution of Iraq's military ability to constitute a threat to any of its neighbours; and secondly even a mere relocation of Iraqi troops would require a military operation much more extensive than the one envisaged by this sort of picture.

Thus the central military objective of the UN Coalition forces led by the United States was the comprehensive defeat of the Iraqi forces in the air, on land and at sea. The fact that this had to be accomplished within a reasonably short matter of weeks entailed the destruction of Iraq's capacity to sustain a long drawn out campaign.

In operational terms the comprehensive military defeat of Iraq entailed a twin assault on its two centres of gravity:

1 The strategic centre of gravity: that is, the strategic and administrative high command in Baghdad and its ability to maintain command and control of Iraqi forces in the field.
2 The theatre or operational centre of gravity: that is, the Republican Guard located to the rear of the Iraqi front line in Kuwait and southern Iraq.

All this demonstrates what might be called the 'expanding logic' of warfare. The military logic of confronting the relatively parochial problem of the occupation of Kuwait led inexorably to the necessity for the comprehensive defeat of Iraq. The liberation of Kuwait required a land offensive but the three prerequisites of such an offensive was superiority in the air over the theatre of operations, command of sea access to its territory (i.e. the northern Gulf region) and the disruption of logistic support and command communication between the strategic centre of gravity and the theatre centre of gravity.

As we suggest below the defensive strategy of the Iraqis was dictated by their objective, which was perhaps not so much victory over the Coalition allies, since in his most optimistic moments even Saddam Hussein could not have believed that possible, but rather not to lose. The essentially negative objective of not losing could on the face of it be achieved by a defensive strategy. The Coalition allies on the other hand had to achieve an unambiguous military victory and that required an aggressive offensive strategy. Whereas Saddam Hussein's only hope of retrieving anything at all from a direct military confrontation with the Allies was to convert the war into one of attrition, the major Coalition allies had seen from the First World War that a war of attrition is costly in terms of time, resources and lives – all the elements of which the Coalition had least to spare. The vast amount of resources in personnel and equipment that had been assembled in the Saudi desert had to be applied massively, quickly and effectively if victory was to be achieved. Thus it was a prime objective of the Allies to avoid that very war of attrition that Saddam wanted in Kuwait. The experience of the First World War had ensured that both American and British military philosophy emphasised the central importance of mobility and manoeuvre.

In fact the Coalition powers had to adapt a strategy and military machine designed to fight a defensive war against a mobile and rapidly advancing enemy across a broad front on the northern planes of Europe to a strategy of offence against an essentially static, well dug-in enemy with a more mobile but still dug-in reinforcement capability. Mobility was the major ground asset of the Allied forces and Major-General Schwarzkopf was to make the most of it. Indeed it turned out to be the most spectacular feature of the ground campaign, becoming manifest in the great western flanking movement that cut off the retreat of the Iraqi Republican Guard.

Thus there were three phases of the Allied strategy:

1 To destroy the command, control and air defence facilities of the Iraqi military and administrative machine – this would involve deep air interdiction of Iraqi territory; a secondary objective of this interdiction was the destruction of the Iraqi

chemical, biological and nuclear storage and production facilities.

2 To control the air space above the battlefield and to subject the Iraqi army in place in the Kuwaiti theatre of operations to a massive air bombardment designed to destroy as much of it as possible in terms of men and matériel and to undermine the morale and will to resist of the Iraqi troops.

3 To incapacitate and defeat the Iraqi army in the Kuwaiti theatre of operations and liberate Kuwait from Iraqi occupation.

THE AIR CAMPAIGN

There were a number of major objectives of the Coalition air campaign. Firstly to achieve superiority of air space above the theatre of operations. This would give freedom of action in bombarding the Iraqi front-line troops prior to a ground offensive and would ensure that once the ground offensive began there would be unhindered air support to the Coalition forces. Secondly by deep air interdiction to attack and destroy command and control targets – that is, to deny to the Iraqi high command the ability to communicate with its own forces and to control their deployment and operation. Thirdly to attack economic and industrial infrastructure targets, power stations, oil refineries and so on. Fourthly to destroy facilities for the manufacture of chemical, biological and nuclear weapons. Fifthly to attack and destroy the ability of the Iraqis to supply and reinforce their troops in Kuwait – bridges, roads and so on. Sixthly to bombard Iraqi forces in place, both in the Kuwaiti theatre and in the follow-up area of southern Iraq where a number of divisions of Republican Guard were positioned (see map 4 in Appendix III, for an indication of the targets).

The beginning of the air war on the night of 16/17 January 1991 was an immediate confirmation that the ejection of Iraqi forces from Kuwait entailed a comprehensive defeat of the Iraqi war-fighting capability. The attack on targets in the Baghdad area was an immediate answer to the pre-war question about whether there would be Coalition incursions into Iraqi territory. It was a clear illustration that in such a situation the battle in the war zone itself cannot be kept isolated from the enemy's capacity to maintain his forces in the war zone. Another illustration was the ground strategy of a massive western flanking operation south of the Euphrates river to cut off the retreat of the Iraqi army. It is another demonstration of the 'expanding logic of war'. The objective may appear to be a very limited one – that is, the liberation of Kuwait from Iraqi occupation – but the achievement of that objective actually requires an escalation in terms of the scale of military activity and of geograpical area.

The issue of whether air capability can win a war without the use of ground troops was again raised in this conflict. It has been a frequently revived contention, expectation and hope that air power can be sufficient to fight and win a war. Ever since the beginning of air strategy there has been an exaggerated expectation of what air power can achieve in warfare. The early belief that 'the bomber will always get through' was supplemented during the Second World War by rather unrealistic expectations of the accuracy of air bombardment and its effects in undermining both the military/economic capability and the psychological willingness of the enemy to continue prosecuting the war. J.K. Galbraith, a member of the United States Strategic Bombing Survey in 1945, attests to the then inaccuracy of Allied bombing when he says that 'to find a target was not necessarily to hit it. Nothing in World War II air operations was subject to such assault as open agricultural land'[5].

Two features of the air war in the Gulf conflict which did not obtain in the Second World War were firstly of course that there was little or no air-combat to hinder the Coalition bomber getting through; moreover the sophisticated radar-spoiling devices together with such technology as the 'Stealth' aircraft and Cruise missiles ensured that the Coalition had almost complete freedom of the skies. The second feature was the possession by the United States and her allies of very sophisticated target-finding and guidance technology. Thus in the Gulf conflict the loss rate of aircraft was exceedingly small compared with the number of sorties actually flown (in total something over 100,000 sorties), and with laser-guided weapons and other types of technology the accuracy of the weapons was of a standard never before achieved. Because of these factors air capability played a particularly important part in the conflict.

The major reason that an air campaign cannot be sufficient by itself to win a war is that primarily war involves territory – and territory cannot be occupied by aircraft. The capture and occupation of territory can only be achieved by troops fighting on the ground. Thus an air campaign cannot be sufficient but it can be decisive. In this case it was probably *the* decisive factor: it could even be said that effectively the war was won on the first night of 16/17 January when it became apparent that, for whatever reason, the Iraqi air force would play no part in the war. A fundamental principle of modern conventional warfare is that a successful land battle requires air support and the presence or absence of such support *ceteris paribus* will very likely determine its outcome. The absence of an Iraqi air capability over the combat zone meant either that they would not fight a ground war when it came to it or the ground war would be very short indeed. In the event it turned out to be a combination of the two.

The role of aerial bombardment as a means of undermining the morale of civilian populations and in turn undermining the military capacity to prosecute the war is still a pertinent issue. It seems to be an almost unshakeable *a priori* conviction among many people that such a strategy must be effective. But all the evidence suggests that air bombardment has little effect in destroying the morale of the civilian population; indeed there is considerable evidence that it has the opposite effect – that is, in strengthening the determination to resist. There were two issues concerning this in the Gulf campaign. One concerned the 'real' accuracy of the Allied weapons – that is whether they were as accurate as claimed; with the implication that a great deal of so-called collateral damage in terms of human lives and property was in fact being caused. The other concerned the claim that one of the *objectives* of the air campaign was to undermine the civilian support for the Iraqi leadership and make it more difficult for them to continue the war – the implication being that the Coalition was deliberately targeting civilians or at least not trying over much to avoid them.

On the question of physical damage, though clearly not all the precision-guided ammunition reached their designated targets, there is little evidence to suggest that there was widespread non-target damage in any of the Iraqi towns and cities attacked. Indeed John Simpson, the BBC television reporter who was in Baghdad during and after the war, says that in Baghdad, for example, there were about thirty buildings destroyed, most or all were direct targets and all with little or no surrounding damage.[6] On the question of civilian bombing casualties, there is little direct evidence of numbers. However, it is significant that the only major incidents in which the Iraqis allowed 'free' television coverage showing civilian deaths were the Amiraya shelter, where there were some 300 hundred civilian casualties, and the market in Al Fallujah, where there were also substantial civilian deaths. It might be a reasonable deduction that if there had been mass civilian casualties the Iraqis would have used the fact more effectively for propaganda purposes. Of the two major incidents cited above, only the second was due to inaccuracy when one of the bombs in a raid on a bridge went astray and landed on a nearby market.

Aside from a lack of evidence of deliberate targeting of civilian populations there would have been little strategic rationale in such a policy since the Iraqi regime, as it has demonstrated over many years, does not rely on the support of the civilian population for its continuance in office, and moreover the prosecution of the war, in the short term at least, did not depend upon the support of the civilian population. Such a strategy would only be relevant if at all in a long war of attrition involving the whole population. Moreover a policy of civilian strategic bombing would certainly not have been politically feasible and may well have broken up the coalition. If there was a 'psychological objective' of deep air interdiction it would have been to destabilise the resolve of the Iraqi administrative and military leadership by the sheer accuracy and destructive power of the bombardment; perhaps even to convince Saddam Hussein's military commanders to overthrow him and sue for peace.

IRAQI STRATEGY

It is a conventional wisdom that defence is the stronger form of warfare than offence, leading to calculations about the numerical superiority of offensive capability over that of the defence necessary in order to prevail. It is usually held that the offence needs a superiority over the defence of between three and five to one. Superior technology and professionalism can offset this ratio to some extent, and in any case the validity of the ratio does depend upon the particular circumstances. The qualifying condition that Clausewitz makes in discussing this issue is that the defence should not be entirely immobile. He says that although the characteristic feature of the defence is 'awaiting the blow', the essential concept of defence is the 'parrying of a blow'.[7] Thus awaiting the blow is not sufficient, however well dug in you are, and unless you have the capability of parrying the blow you are not really engaged in warfare, you are merely waiting to be overrun.

This was a significant feature of the Iraqi land strategy and one of the major uncertainties facing the Coalition powers. The Iraqis were clearly well dug in – certainly along the front line on the Kuwait–Saudi border, and even the Republican Guard to the rear and inside southern Iraq were dug in such that the Allies found it difficult to accurately pin-point their positions. The question was, if they were so well dug in what capability did they have for parrying the blow? It was the undermining of this capability that was the prime objective of the theatre air campaign which was increased when the deep interdiction phase of the air war had been effectively completed. It is difficult to know if the Iraqis really intended to fight and were essentially prevented from doing so firstly by the ferocity of the air bombardment and secondly by the rapidity and efficiency of the ground offensive. The land offensive was over so quickly and with such apparently little actual fighting on the part of the Iraqis that one wonders whether they had a realistic military strategy at all.

From the Iraqi rhetoric in the pre-war phase of the conflict it appears that Saddam Hussein was convinced that he could hold down the American-led Coalition force for months if not years. He seemed to think that the long years of attrition in the Iran–Iraq war could be repeated in Kuwait against the Americans. Flexibility and adaptability are key features of a successful strategy and qualities which the Coalition allies applied in order to deal with what was for them an unforeseen military operation. The over-centralised nature of Iraqi military organisation[8] entailed the absence of those very qualities of flexibility and innovation that ensured the strategic and tactical superiority of the Coalition commanders on the battlefield. The Iraqis adopted a strategy which had been applied in their only other large-scale military operation – that against Iran. The Iraqi strategy can be simply stated: a massive defence in depth with sand berms, trenches and minefields to channel the advancing enemy, which would then be destroyed by concentrated artillery fire followed up with attack by mobile reserves from the rear.[9] Even against the militarily unsophisticated Iranians this strategy was not entirely successful. Moreover there are two prerequisites for such a strategy to have even a chance of success. Firstly it assumes that you know from which direction the enemy will come, so that you can channel him at the appropriate places; secondly it assumes that you have air support, if not to supplement bombardment at points of concentration, then to disrupt the enemy's reinforcement and logistic support capabilities. The one dimension during the Iran–Iraq war which kept Iraq from defeat was that of air power. Despite superiority on virtually every dimension except numbers of men, the Iraqis still failed to defeat the Iranians and indeed came very close to being defeated themselves. So the Iran–Iraq war was perhaps a dangerous precedent for Saddam, not one that held much prospect of success against a vastly more advanced opponent.

This raises the intriguing and astonishing issue of the Iraqi air force. Saddam's apparent strategy for the Kuwait theatre of first awaiting and then parrying the blow (to use Clausewitzian terminology) required an air capability over the battlefield. If not superiority in the air then something like parity would be required to have even the remotest possibility of putting such a ground strategy into effect. The 'defection' of a major part of the Iraqi air capability to Iran and the hiding away of much of the rest suggests a number of alternative explanations. Firstly Saddam Hussein did not understand that such a strategy would require close air support – surely even a military incompetent such as Saddam could not make such a fundamental strategic error. Secondly the military rhetoric was just that, and Saddam Hussein had no intention of using his air capability to support a counter-offensive in Kuwait since he believed that the Coalition would exhaust itself against impregnable defensive positions, and in any case a long battle of attrition would become a political burden that the Allies would not be able to sustain. Thirdly he did not really believe that the Allies would mount such a powerful deep air interdiction operation, part of the objective of which would be to eliminate Iraq's air capability. This latter explanation seems unlikely given the small number of Iraqi aircraft actually destroyed at least during the early stages of the air campaign which suggests that he would have been expecting such an attack. It is likely that the 'lesson' of the Arab–Israeli war of 1967 in which 75 per cent of Egyptian aircraft were destroyed on the ground when the Israelis achieved complete surprise did not go unlearnt by the Iraqis. Fourthly he was so intimidated by the power and effectiveness of the air interdiction that he sent his air force away to protect it for future use. Fifthly that his air force commanders and/or pilots were themselves so intimidated that they really did defect with their aircraft to Iran thus depriving Saddam of the very capability that would make any sense at all of his Kuwaiti ground strategy. As a consequence they left the Iraqi front-line ground troops to the mercy of their enemy's air and ground forces. If this fifth point is the explanation then it demonstrates another of the crucial prerequisites of success and that is the close cooperation of the different branches of the armed forces. The overall strategy must be one that integrates all three services; the defection of the arm crucial to a successful 'parrying of the blow' was almost a guarantee of defeat. Such lack of cooperation in the Iraqi military would no doubt be a function of the domination of Saddam Hussein over the whole politico-military establishment and the ineptness of his strategic planning.

The other prerequisite mentioned above for the Iraqi strategy to have any validity was an accurate prediction of the direction from which the enemy would advance. It was here that Iraqi strategy was starkly inadequate. It was essentially a failure of military vision, a failure to think on the same scale as the enemy, that ensured that the Iraqis did not remotely conceive that there might be an attack from the west, deep into Iraq, as opposed to a merely frontal assault from the south and south-west together with an amph- ibious assault on Kuwait City. It was this Coalition land war strategy that delivered the *coup de grace* to the Iraqis after they had suffered weeks of air bombardment and logistic isolation.

Other aspects of both Iraqi and Coalition military strategy will be discussed in the following separate sections.

STRATEGIC SURPRISE

The achievement of strategic surprise in war effectively increases the relative degree of force used. Surprise has the effect of adding to the force of the one who surprises and reducing the force of the one who is surprised.[10] Surprise can be achieved through time of attack, the place and targets attacked, the method and speed of attack and the technology used in the attack. Perhaps the greatest degree of surprise of the whole Gulf conflict was achieved by Saddam Hussein himself in his invasion of Kuwait. The achievement of strategic surprise, particularly when achieved in relation to a superpower, is usually attributed to a failure of intelligence. Intelligence failures result either from a failure in intelligence collection or a failure of intelligence interpretation. The questions that arose after Iraq's invasion were firstly whether there were diplomatic signals effectively giving notice of what was to happen and, if there were, why were they missed. Secondly was there any satellite surveillance evidence that would have indicated the imminence of an invasion, and if so, why wasn't action taken as a result of it.

This issue is discussed in more detail in Chapter 2. All that is necessary here is to indicate that insofar as the United States was taken by surprise by Iraq's invasion of Kuwait, it was as a result of incorrectly interpreting the significance of both diplomatic and satellite intelligence. The fact is that when the invasion occurred the world was presented with a *fait accompli*. The Kuwaiti army had retreated within twenty-four hours and Hussein had set up a puppet government in Kuwait within forty-eight hours. Military and diplomatic surprise had been achieved. Indeed so complete was the degree of surprise that the Americans remained on the diplomatic defensive for most of 'crisis' period up to the Coalition counter-attack on 17 January 1991. It was only with the launch of the counter-offensive that the pattern of surprise was reversed.

The publicly stated UN deadline of 15 January 1991 constrained to some extent the Coalition's ability to achieve strategic surprise in their timing of the counter-offensive. The Allies could not act before 15 January; on the other hand they could not delay very long after that date if they were to complete military operations within the local 'weather window' and indeed within the parallel 'political window'. For the Allies a short, sharp military operation was imperative. But the Coalition did achieve a dramatic and overwhelming degree of surprise in both phases of the war. In the air-war phase the element of surprise was contained firstly in the timing of the air onslaught – it was initiated not on the first possible opportunity that is, in the early hours of 16 January, but on the second, in the early hours of 17 January; secondly in the sheer massiveness of the air attack, and thirdly in its early effectiveness in incapacitating Iraq's air defence system and its internal communications systems. It was this massive initial onslaught that knocked the opponent back on his heels and from which he never really recovered – particularly since the intensity of the aerial attacks was maintained over a period of weeks.

In the ground war, as we have already discussed above, surprise was achieved in the great western flanking movement which cut off the line of retreat of the Republican Guard. This was achieved first because the Iraqis had apparently discounted such a strategy as a possibility; and secondly the Allies had encouraged the Iraqis in their predisposed belief that there would be a northward frontal push combined with an amphibious assault on Kuwait City by a massive deception operation. This involved the construction of the illusion of a military city complete with fake communications patterns and troop movements, as well as air activity and naval activity in the Gulf. The 'location' of this phantom city together with all the other decoy activity was all consistent with a prospective northward and amphibious coalition assault which disguised the early deployment of a massive force far to the west of the Iraqi defensive line.

INTRA-WAR ESCALATION

Intra-war escalation is also used to achieve surprise, to change the parameters of the war and to indicate resolve – that is, a determination to continue hostilities over values to which you attach a high priority. Escalation can be achieved in many different ways – for example, in choosing particularly sensitive or important targets or using particular types of weapon or technology. The Iraqis had access to two major mechanisms of escalation – one they did use and one they did not.

'Scud politics'

The one mechanism of escalation the Iraqis did use, of course, was the Scud missile. But it was not only the type of weapon that indicated the Iraqi leadership's willingness to escalate the scale and nature of hostilities, but the fact that it was used deliberately to involve a third party thereby attempting to escalate the war geographically and perhaps above all politically. The attempt to involve Israel was a planned and declared strategy that perhaps Saddam Hussein set too much store by. During the diplomatic phase of the crisis the threat was no doubt designed as a deterrent to persuade the Coalition not to use military force. During the war itself it was really an attempt to widen the conflict from the specific issue of the invasion of Kuwait into an Arab–Israeli conflict and indeed into an Islamic–Western conflict. But because Israel was prevailed upon to refrain from responding to the missile attacks, they failed to achieve the escalation hoped for by the Iraqis.

Perhaps it ought to be said at this stage that probably the major factor in the Israeli agreement not to respond to the Scud attacks was the lack of strategic rationale for such an Israeli response. There were no targets that the Israelis were better placed to attack than the Coalition allies; it was unlikely that they had any more intelligence on the location of Scud launchers in western Iraq, and the only 'political' target that might have warranted an Israeli response would have been Saddam Hussein himself and it is unlikely that the Israelis were in any better position to target him than the Americans were.

In fact the Scud missile had more political significance than any strictly military use. Whether used against Israeli or Saudi cities or even coalition military bases the missile was so inaccurate, random almost, that it posed very little military threat. Indeed in one respect the Scud provided a vehicle for another apparent American technological victory – that of the Patriot anti-missile missile. Subsequent analysis suggests however that this missile was not as successful as believed at the time.[11] Indeed its failure led to the only 'success' of the Scud during the whole war – the direct hit on an American troop barracks at Dhahran. Nevertheless the belief in its success at the time was an important morale booster for the Americans that to some extent offset the anxiety caused by the Scuds.

Though the military significance of the Scud was not in terms of the amount of damage and destruction it caused, there were two ways in which it did have a military impact. The first was in the continued element of surprise that its use entailed. The uncertainty as to how many the Iraqis had left meant that each missile that was launched had its own element of surprise and had the effect of maintaining the psychological and political pressure on the Americans and her allies and increased the urgency to find them. That meant, secondly, that a lot of military resources had to be devoted to finding and eliminating them. This indeed was one of the most significant US intelligence failures of the war. The Americans believed the Iraqis had about thirty-five Scud missile launchers – in fact they had some 200.[12]

Chemical weapons

The other mechanism of potential escalation the Iraqis possessed was that of chemical weapons. The persistent uncertainty on the part of the Coalition as to whether the Iraqis would use them (or even had the technological capability to do so) in conjunction with Scud missiles was the source of political anxiety. Having succeeded in forestalling an Israeli response to inaccurate Scud attacks using conventional warheads it was less certain that the United States would be able to restrain them if chemical weapons were used against their cities. The fact that the Iraqis did not use chemical weapons on Israeli (or Saudi) cities was either due to a lack of capability to deliver them by Scud or it was an Iraqi policy decision not to do so for fear of both the political and the military consequences.

Another source of anxiety on the Coalition's part was the uncertainty as to whether the Iraqis would use chemical weapons on the battlefield once the land war had started. Indeed for the Iraqis this Coalition uncertainty was itself perhaps a more useful military asset than their actual use. The use of chemical weapons was itself full of uncertainties. Firstly was the problem of how they could be used on the battlefield and how successful they could be against an enemy force prepared for them. The Iraqis have used them both against civilians and against troops in the field; in neither case did their targets have protection. Not only was their tactical and operational use problematical but the military and political consequences were uncertain – potentially those consequences could have been counter-productive for the Iraqis, making the actual use of chemical weapons not worth the risk. The uncertainty however meant that the Allied forces had to prepare for their use anyway which would be another operational constraint. On the other hand we still do not know whether the decision not to use them was a decision of the Iraqi high command or merely a local operational command decision. It has been said that this was an area of disagreement between Saddam Hussein and his local commanders. It has also been implied that the expectation or possibility of the use by the Iraqis of chemical weapons was part of an American deception operation designed to exacerbate the negative image of Saddam and justify battlefield bombardment of Iraqi troops. It has however been reported that no chemical weapons were found in the Kuwaiti theatre subsequent to the war.[13] It is not known whether they were removed by the retreating Iraqis or were not there in the first place.

INTRA-WAR INTELLIGENCE: SUCCESS AND FAILURE

Accurate information regarding the enemy's capabilities, dispositions, intentions and his beliefs about your capabilities, dispositions and intentions is the central purpose of intelligence operations and gathering. Intelligence is the major mechanism used to penetrate what Clausewitz called the 'fog of war'. Its objective is to convert ignorance into knowledge, to make certain what is uncertain, to make clear what is ambiguous. But of course there is also a 'fog of intelligence'. Most crisis situations and wars are characterised not by a paucity of information but by a surfeit – the problems arise in deciding what is and is not relevant and evaluating its truth. The United States and her allies had access to probably more intelligence information about their enemy than has been possible in any previous war. The amount of electronic and visual information from satellites and airborne sources must have been phenomenal to the extent that one is led to wonder whether anything at all could have been hidden from American intelligence.

Overestimate of Iraqi military strength

We cannot here engage in an exhaustive study of intelligence in the Gulf War but we can consider some indications of intelligence failure on the part of the Coalition allies. One was the apparent overestimation of the strength of the Iraqi military force in the Kuwaiti Theatre of Operations (KTO). This could have been an intelligence failure and indeed could have been the result of a deliberate Iraqi deception operation designed to convince the Allies that they had a greater force than they really did have. The Iraqis were certainly skilled in the use of decoys – the use of dummy tanks, artillery, Scud launchers – deriving from their training by the Soviet military. One wonders what strategic value that would have been to the Iraqis given that it would have encouraged an even greater counter-force on the part of the Americans. It has been reported that estimates of Iraqi strength were based upon the nominal strengths of known divisions and units sent to the KTO. In fact apparently most of those units were substantially under strength.[14] On the other hand such over-estimation could have been a natural caution – related to the lesson of Vietnam (i.e. don't underestimate your enemy). Both Generals Schwarzkopf and Powell were Vietnam veterans and were clear that any military response to the Iraqi invasion would be massive and determined.[15] Even then the usually recommended offence/defence ratio of 3:1 would have entailed a Coalition force of something like 1.5 million men. It was no doubt calculated that Allied technology could offset this conventional ratio and allow essential parity. Indeed there lies another potential explanation – that the overestimation was a deliberate exercise in misinformation on the part of the United States in order to justify sending a very large force which otherwise would have attracted additional domestic criticism.

Al-Ameriya Bunker

Another probable intelligence failure was the bombing of the bunker at Al-Ameriya in which some 300 civilians were killed. Such world-wide condemnation as there was would have been a major disincentive for the Americans deliberately targeting civilians; indeed it has already been indicated that there would have been no strategic value in doing so. It has been reported that the Pentagon has now admitted that this was a 'military error'[16] and if so it was either an operational error (i.e. a malfunction) or a failure of intelligence. The Americans believed they had sufficient intelligence on military traffic flows to indicate that it was a command and control facility and as such a legitimate military target. If that information was inaccurate then that needs explaining; if the information was accurate then the next question is were the Americans the subject of an Iraqi deception operation designed to achieve just what happened – that is, a very visible demonstration that the Coalition air campaign was killing lots of civilians. Such an operation would have been entirely consistent with Iraqi practice of using civilian personnel and civilian urban areas to shield military facilities. The hostage policy was a case in point and of course many Iraqi aircraft were deliberately housed in villages where they would be protected by the Coalition prohibitions on attacks on such areas. (The legal aspects of this incident are discussed in Chapter 6).

Khafji

The last example we will mention here was the Iraqi capture of the Saudi town of Khafji. Here the Iraqis achieved a genuine element of surprise and induced some embarrassment on the part of the Coalition forces. Its purpose was not clear – unless merely to test the preparedness of the Coalition forces; in which case it certainly did that and probably ensured that such a lapse on the part of the Coalition command would not happen again. Having said that, however, it is likely that it appeared more of blunder than it actually was because of the tardiness of the Coalition response in retaking the town. It was the gap between the Iraqi capture of the town and the Allied response that led to speculation about the competence of the Coalition forces. In fact, however, the gap was not due to the incompetence of the major Allied forces but to the political decision that it should be seen to be an Arab force that retook Khafji rather than an American or European force. Thus the delay was caused by the need to bring up Saudi forces for them to lead the attack.[17] This was meant to be a symbol of the fact, lest anyone should forget, that they were engaged in an inter-Arab conflict not a western-Arab conflict.

THE VIETNAM SYNDROME

The Vietnam War played an important part in the perceptions of both sides in the Gulf conflict. For one side the Vietnam scenario was one to be avoided; for the other it was one to be recreated. Vietnam has become the archetype of an 'asymmetrical' war – a war between a superpower and a Third World state. The outcome in which the superpower, the United States, had to retire, severely bloodied having failed to achieve its objectives, has given rise to many myths about the ability of small states to confront and prevail over powerful ones. 'Lessons' of Vietnam have been drawn by many states not least the United States itself; but also by other small states whose leaders might have aspirations in the same direction.

The American administration's repeated declarations that the Gulf War would not be 'another Vietnam' suggests that the Americans feared that it might turn out to be just that, but it thus ensured their determination that it should not do so. The claim that the US response to the Iraqi invasion was determined by their

Vietnam experience – that the Gulf War was merely an opportunity for the Americans to expunge the memory of Vietnam – is
unlikely to be the case (see Chapter 4 for an analysis of the likely
causes of the US response). However, having made the decision to
respond militarily if necessary, then there is little doubt that the
Vietnam experience was an important factor in determining the
manner in which that decision was put into action. Two major
errors the Americans made in Vietnam they determined not to
make in the Gulf. One was underestimating the enemy and the
other was the piecemeal build-up of forces. After the decision to
reinforce (9th November 1990), the military build-up in the Gulf
was as rapid as the logistics would allow and there was an early
determination that a force of the appropriate size and firepower
with all the naval and air support necessary would be sent to
conduct an offensive military operation. The Americans were careful to do the Iraqis the military honour of taking them seriously as
military opponents both in terms of their professional expertise
(their experience in the war with Iran was often cited as something not to be taken lightly) and in terms of the qualitative and
quantitative dimensions of their military power. This was partly for
political purposes in order to justify the sending of such a large
force, but it was also a genuine recognition that it would require a
very large and technologically sophisticated force to dislodge the
Iraqis from Kuwait. As it turned out this actually resulted in an
overestimation of the Iraqi military capability and an overestimation of their military performance in the Iran–Iraq war.

If Saddam Hussein's rhetoric was any guide to his actual
perceptions (and this was a persistent problem for the Coalition
during both the diplomatic phase and the war phase of the Gulf
conflict) then perceptions of Vietnam also played an important
part in the Iraqi strategic planning. Saddam Hussein said on a
number of occasions that his forces could hold the United States
down in a long and bloody war of attrition which would enmesh
them again in a distant war which the Americans would not be
able to sustain politically. He appeared on a number of occasions
to be rather contemptuous in claiming that the Americans or 'the
democracies' could not tolerate heavy casualties which could
include 10,000 dead. This of course flies in the face of the
evidence of the 'pugilistic' nature of democracies and of course
seems to ignore the actual European and American experience

through two world wars, Korea, Vietnam and a host of small post-colonial conflicts.

Drawing the wrong lesson (1) from the importance of public opinion in democracies and (2) from the American 'failure' in Vietnam, Saddam Hussein surmised, as did many of the (British) press, that democratic public opinion would not allow their governments to expend large casualties in war. What the Iraqis failed to appreciate was that democratic publics only refuse to support their governments in war when the cause for which the war is being fought is perceived to be unjust or the return not consonant with the cost. The more Saddam Hussein demonstrated his unrealism, his irrationality, his arrogance, his barbarity, the more western publics (in particular the British and American) supported the use of force as the only solution. It was not the 'body bags' that forced the United States out of Vietnam. The American public became disaffected (1) because of the way the US forces appeared to be conducting a 'barbaric' war (another reason why deliberate civilian bombing in the Gulf conflict would not have been strategically or politically sensible), (2) because it became very clear that they did not really know what they were fighting for, and (3) were showing little progress in achieving whatever it was they were fighting for.

Another commonly perceived but largely false lesson of the Vietnam War is that ideological zeal and moral commitment to a cause or the defence of your homeland can outweigh the most apparently overwhelming military and technological superiority; that the reason the North Vietnamese prevailed was because they had a strong belief in what they were doing – the liberation of their country from foreign occupation. The fact is that the Americans failed to prevail in Vietnam not because Vietnamese morale overwhelmed American technology (Marshall Foch in the First World War discovered the fallacy of such a belief) but because of military and political constraints on American action. In any case the Iraqis, unlike the Vietnamese, were not fighting on behalf of a major liberationist ideology and they were not fighting for the liberation of their own country but for their continued subjugation of another.

Even assuming that the Iraqi leadership would be able to call on the morale of the Iraqi people (in fact extremely doubtful given the nature of the Ba'athist regime) they lacked other assets which largely accounted for the North Vietnamese victory. Firstly the terrain: on a desert battlefield the Iraqis could not employ guerrilla strategy. The age of 'Lawrence of Arabia' could not be rekindled in the age of such powerful air capability. Moreover the Iraqis do not have any expertise in guerrilla warfare and neither were 'the whole Iraqi people' involved – a necessary prerequisite for successful guerrilla strategy. The second important element was external replenishment and supply. This was a major factor (if not the major factor) in the Vietnamese victory. No matter what they did the Americans could not staunch that supply. The Iraqis on the other hand had no major external benefactor which could resupply and reinforce the Iraqi war effort. Thirdly the Iraqis had no major diplomatic allies – indeed virtually none at all. The Americans had lined up virtually the whole world diplomatically behind it. Vietnam was a guide neither to Iraqi performance in the war, nor to American, nor indeed to the nature of the war itself. If the Vietnam connection was anything more than rhetoric then it is just another example of the utterly unrealistic nature of Iraqi political and military analysis.

THE GROUND WAR, POLITICAL CONTROL AND WAR TERMINATION

The ground phase of the war was dreaded by all sides – by both Iraqis and Coalition forces alike, by both politicians and the military, by leaders and their publics. It was the phase which would be the ultimate test of all the respective strategies, because however much confidence is expressed in strategic predictions or rational calculations, they are always shrouded in uncertainty. The events quickly confirmed the demoralisation of the Iraqi front-line troops, where they had survived the devastating and prolonged air bombardment of the previous weeks. Events also confirmed that there was nothing mystical, or inscrutable about Iraqi 'strategy'. The incredulity prompted by the apparent Iraqi intention to fight a ground war in the desert without air cover was dissipated when it became immediately apparent that indeed they could not and for the most part would not fight such a war.

The major limitation of the Iraqi 'grand strategy' was its parochialism. It fell into, and indeed was encouraged into, a restricted vision of the strategic possibilities by the 'political geography' of the region. Its troop deployment in the Kuwaiti Theatre of Operations demonstrated its preparation for an assault which, it was assumed, would essentially come from the south – from Saudi Arabia directly north into Kuwait, and from the small area of Iraq where it adjoins both Saudi Arabia and Kuwait, and by amphibious assault from the northern Gulf. What the Iraqis had apparently not anticipated was the great sweep out through the Iraqi western desert that would outflank the Iraqi forces and bar the retreat of the Republican Guard - despite General Colin Powell's graphic description of that very manoeuvre on 23 January 1991, some four weeks before the Allied ground offensive began: 'Our strategy for dealing with this army is very, very simple. First we're going to cut it off, then we're going to kill it'.

Once the ground war had started, the central political/strategic problem was how should it end. Once more Clausewitz provides an incisive guide: he cautions that it is imperative 'not to take the first step (in war) without considering the last'.[18] In other words war termination is an intrinsic part of the conduct of war. He further says that:

> No one starts a war – or rather, no one in his senses ought to do so – without first being clear in his mind what he intends to achieve by that war and how he intends to conduct it. [19]

Thus there is an intrinsic link between the beginning of war and its end, and that link depends upon the clarity of the political objective, the strategic means to achieve it and the proper balance between the two. It is the difficulty of ensuring the link between strategic means and political objective that gives rise to the clichéd observation that it is easier to start a war than to end it. Judging when the objective has been achieved is not necessarily, or even often, a straightforward matter; the problem is exacerbated of course if there are mutually incompatible objectives or perhaps where there is a lack of clarity about the specific nature of the objectives.

The formal political and military objectives of the Coalition allies were laid down in Security Council Resolution 678, which incorporated also Resolution 660. The resolutions contained both tangible and intangible objectives. The tangible objectives were the removal of Iraqi forces from Kuwait and specifically their removal to their locations as at 1 August 1990. As military object-ives the first was reasonable and plausible – the second was not. Insofar as the objective of relocating Iraqi troops to their positions as at 1 August 1990 was the limit stipulated for military action then it was unreasonable and unrealistic since the Allies could not be sure exactly where they were at that time. But even given that this is a pedantic point, the fact is that these are tangible objectives – it is possible to say when they have been achieved. It was clearly possible to determine when Iraqi troops had been driven out of Kuwait. What was less clear was to determine (1) when the Iraqi forces had been defeated and (2) when 'peace and security' had been established in the area. With regard to (1) it might seem to be another paradox that there has to be a a degree of collusion between the two sides in a war in more or less agreeing what constitutes victory and what constitutes defeat. An agreement results in the surrender of the defeated party. This is partly a technical matter requiring a professional military assessment of the relative states of your own and of your opponent's military forces and their capacity to continue. But it is also a matter of psychology, because war termination also requires the ability to admit defeat. There was always the danger that Saddam Hussein's 'messianic rationality' would induce him to refuse to abide by the rules of military logic – as indeed his military strategy indicated he had already done – and refuse to concede defeat and leave his forces fighting against overwhelming odds. In these circumstances it would be left to the Coalition side to take the initiative and cease military operations themselves before a formal surrender from the Iraqis.

Unlike the removal of Iraqi troops or even military defeat, the establishment of 'peace and security' is an intangible objective with a consequent lack of clarity about how its achievement can be judged. The point has already been made elsewhere that the establishment of peace and security in the region was not compatible with merely ejecting Iraqi troops from Kuwait, which would leave a situation in which the invasion could occur again at any time – particularly after Coalition troops had left the region. More generally it could be said that 'peace and security' in the region could not be established without divesting Iraq of the military capability (and even the political will) for invading any of her neighbours in the region. This latter would entail a comprehensive military defeat of the Iraqi army and steps to drastically reduce Iraq's overall military capability. Given that the political will for external adventures emanates from Saddam Hussein himself, the implication entails his removal.

Thus it was a combination of these problems that made it likely that ending the war, at whatever stage that was done, would be controversial. The choice was an impossible one for the Coalition leader, the United States. Effectively the choice was between going too far, and not going far enough. For this war there was in a sense no right time to end it. To continue military operations until the Iraqi army had actually been destroyed would not be – and indeed in the event was not – politically acceptable; particularly in a situation where the Iraqi Commander-in-Chief ordered not surrender but merely 'withdrawal', which left his forces still within the bounds of legitimate military action. To stop short of its destruction would be to compromise the 'peace and security' objective and ensure the political survival of Saddam Hussein.

It was not that the 'intangible' political objective – the 'peace and security' objective – could not be achieved. It could have been achieved militarily quite plausibly by continuing to destroy the Republican Guard in southern Iraq, which had already been effectively routed. The closing of the pincer was indeed about to take place when the order from President Bush came to stop the action. Even a subsequent move on to Baghdad was well within the grasp of the front line and indeed the next logical military step. The political and military consequences of that for both the United States and indeed for the United Nations itself would have been politically unsustainable both in terms of the necessity for the occupation and administration of Iraq, and in terms of justifying such an action to popular or even to political constituencies, domestically and internationally.

In the light of subsequent events – the survival and revival of the Republican Guard and the re-establishment of Saddam Hussein's power and even credibility within Iraq – the controversy centres on whether military action was halted rather too soon and whether allowing it to proceed a little longer would have sufficiently weakened the Iraqi military as to have effectively undermined its use by Saddam to re-establish his position. Political control of military action is a fundamental principle of the conduct of war and Clausewitz among others points to the dire consequences of failing to observe it. But in practice it is sometimes difficult to distinguish between political control and political interference. Without adopting the MacArthurian principle that since war occurs as a result of the failure of politics the latter has no role to play in its conduct,[20] it is possible to say that not all political control is justifiable in military or even in political terms.

It may be that it is not merely a question of a conflict between political objectives and military objectives but also of possible conflict between one set of political objectives or constraints and another.

In this case intervention based upon one set of political criteria compromised the achievement of one of the political objectives for which the war was being fought. The political constraints on the American president to halt military operations sooner rather than later came from both domestic and international constituencies, both political and popular. There is no question that President Bush's decision to terminate military operations after 'one hundred hours,' as opposed to the five days favoured by General Schwarzkopf, was a reasonable one given the image of unnecessary slaughter being drawn by many of those who supported military action as well as those who had opposed it in the first place. Nevertheless the direct political consequence of that decision was the survival and later consolidation of Saddam Hussein's power in Iraq, possibly ensuring the realisation of yet another of Clau- sewitz's astute observations about war:

> even the ultimate outcome of a war is not always to be regarded as final. The defeated state often considers the outcome merely as a transitory evil, for which a remedy may still be found in political conditions at some later date.[21]

With the political demise of George Bush, Saddam Hussein might consider those political conditions are close to being realised.

Chapter 10

The aftermath

Wars and crises are often seen to be transitions between one type of international system and another, or a turning-point or watershed in relations between states. But often this can be determined only in retrospect. The two world wars of the twentieth century were very large-scale events involving the great powers of their respective times, and the changes that followed them were profound for the whole international system, representing in both cases a change between one age and another; or perhaps as two 'stepped' changes that brought the modern world into existence. There is not scope here for a lengthy discussion on the subject of whether these wars were in a sense the midwives of those profound systemic changes or indeed themselves a manifestation of those changes – suffice it to say that the causal relationship between these phenomena will not be simple or straightfoward.

Smaller-scale conflicts will have less drastic consequences but may still bring about or be the result of changes in regional structures and in relationships between individual states. For example, the Cuban missile crisis between the United States and the Soviet Union was a pivotal event in a number of respects and to a large extent determined the nature of their relationship for the rest of the Cold War. Because the superpower relationship affected virtually every aspect of the international system from 1945 to the late 1980s, the Cuban missile crisis had implications for the whole system. On the other hand a purely bilateral conflict such as the Falklands War constituted a watershed in little more than Anglo-Argentinian relations, and of course within Argentina itself, where it led to a transition to a more democratic political system. So when we consider the 'aftermath' of the Gulf conflict it will be necessary to examine its consequences within individual states, in bilateral relations between states, in regional and sub-regional structures, and in global or systemic structures and relationships. But it would be convenient to start at the state level and consider the impact of the conflict on Iraq and Kuwait.

IRAQ

The conventional wisdom is that in the case of Iraq itself there is not much difference between the situation before and that after the war. Because of the way the war ended, Saddam Hussein and the Ba'athist regime was able to remain in power. The period since the ceasefire has seen the regime gradually and effectively restore its grip on the country and essentially continue in the same brutal fashion that it did before. Iraq always has been a state on the edge of fragmentation because of its ethnic and religious cleavages; the war further undermined that integrity by encouraging the anti-Ba'athist and anti-centre forces to attempt to take advantage of Baghdad's weakness as a result of the war, either to enforce their autonomy or to topple Saddam Hussein. With the virtually explicit support and encouragement of President Bush their success was seen to be only a matter of time. At the time of writing, despite frequent predictions of his demise, Saddam Hussein looks still to be in control and may even be consolidating his power and regaining control of the dissident regions in both the Kurdish north and the Shi'a south of the country.

The fact that the hoped-for overthrow of Saddam did not take place is a manifestation of a number of factors. One is merely a confirmation of the long-standing truth about the state of Iraq that it is very difficult to disrupt the balance between the centre and the periphery. The virtually continuous state of incipient fragmentation suggests that the opposing centrifugal and centripetal forces are in balance making for a permanent state of what might be called 'stable instability'. That is, none of the forces is strong enough to bring about a 'resolution' one way or the other. However, it is true that in this respect the western Coalition failed in one of its implicit objectives – to destroy the military power-base of Saddam and the Ba'ath in Iraq. It is here that the ambiguity of American/western objectives can be seen. The American objectives can be summarised as follows:

1 Destroy Iraq's/Ba'ath/Saddam's expansionist capability and superpower aspirations.
2 Preserve the Iraqi military capability to defend itself from outside attack.
3 Preserve the military capability to continue to play an important role in Gulf sub-regional security structure.
4 Preserve the ability to maintain internal security and prevent the break-up of the Iraqi state.

It may be that to expect to achieve such a set of finely tuned objectives was unrealistic in the first place. The power to ensure the integrity of the state entails the ability to put down all threats to the regime. Thus these objectives were mutually incompatible. The Americans had to rely on a *coup d'état* within the military/Ba'ath nexus if Saddam Hussein were to be overthrown without risking the disintegration of the country. Clearly the balance between incentives and disincentives for any opposition to Saddam to emerge may not have changed sufficiently as a result of the war; certainly the ability of Saddam Hussein ruthlessly to dispense with any potential rival within the leadership seems undiminished. The problem is how to eliminate Ba'athism, and more importantly 'Saddamism', without destroying Iraq. This might be a much more difficult task than at first appears since the relationship between 'state' and 'regime' in Iraq is much more integrated than in more pluralist states and even more than most totalitarian states. The idea of the 'dissolution' of the Iraqi popular identity as a result of the violence and brutality of 'Saddamism' is a potent explanation of the absence of a 'connection between military failure and the withholding of political allegiance' in Iraq.[1] Clearly a similar phenomenon can now be seen in the aftermath of the Gulf War. The Iraqi people seem trapped in the violent and megalomaniacal dreams and fantasies of Saddam Hussein and it seems unlikely that his demise will come from popular disaffection. The only power capable of bringing his overthrow is precluded from doing such by the massive international political consequences that would ensue and increasingly the lack of domestic will to take on such a task. The United States, even in the face of very serious problems on the international political horizon, is now likely to turn inwards to attempt to deal with the cohesion of its own political structure. Saddam Hussein is likely to be a beneficiary of that development. Indeed his persistent and increasing determination to test the will of the United States and the United Nations by obstructing UN weapons inspectors and by breaking the terms of the ceasefire resolution in both northern and southern Iraq is an indication of the Iraqi view of the constraints operating on the major western allies.

One of the lessons of the Gulf War is that there are limits on the use of even the most massive power capabilities. The unwillingness of the Americans to impose a 'solution' to the Iraqi problem is a manifestation of their ultimate inability to do so. To establish a Kurdish 'autonomous zone' in northern Iraq and to actively support a Shi'a uprising in the south seemed the obvious means by which the western powers could foster the downfall of Saddam. But ultimately, unless there are sufficient local forces to bring about a resolution, then the only way that outside intervention could achieve it would be through massive military aid, probably including not only air support but ground troops as well. Effectively such a scenario would be a resumption of the war but this time inside Iraq – north and south – with the objective of moving on and taking Baghdad. If such massive outside intervention was necessary to bring a new regime to power, it is likely that a large-scale presence would be necessary to sustain it in power for some time to come. This would open the probability of a long-term and massive western (probably Anglo-American) presence in Iraq – an eventuality utterly out of the question for any western power. Thus it can be seen that often states are confined to using their power to prevent the emergence of situations they do not want rather than bringing into existence situations they do want.

For the western powers the crucial value for which they were prepared to use their massive military capability was, perhaps rather cynically but nevertheless realistically, not human rights inside Iraq but the prevention of the breakdown of the balance of power in the Gulf region; or more precisely the prevention of the emergence of an Iraqi hegemony in the Gulf region and ultimately in the Middle East as a whole. That has been achieved in the short term at least; what has not been eliminated is the source of the desire for an Iraqi hegemony, that is, – Saddam Hussein and the Ba'ath. While they remain, the problem remains. The paradox is of course that a moderate, even democratic, regime in Iraq would be the condition necessary to attempt to construct an Iraqi unity by consent; but one of the ways in which it would have to demonstrate its democratic credentials would be to grant Kurdish autonomy, which in turn would be to grant that very fragmentation that successive repressive regimes have been trying to prevent. It is an irony that the persistent survival of Saddam Hussein may drive the former Coalition allies to conclude that the only way of getting rid of him would be to allow or even foster the break-up of Iraq into its regional parts based upon the Ottoman provinces of Mosul, Baghdad and Basra.

Democracy would not easily solve the problem that is Iraq – even assuming that democracy is a possibility in Iraq. The war would indeed prove to have been a turning-point if ultimately its conclusion presages a democratic revolution. It has been said that Iraq is the most fertile socio-political soil for the establishment of democracy in the Middle East and superficially at least one can understand the basis of that claim. But perhaps it is not saying much for the prospects of democracy in the Islamic world. It is not racist to query whether democracy is a possibility in any Arab/ Islamic society[2] (see below). To take the naïve view that a political structure and set of philosophical principles can merely be plucked out of their cultural and historical context and plunged into an entirely different one and be expected to survive and prosper may be expecting rather too much. Moreover, to be so confident of the moral and political probity of such a procedure to advocate that it should be imposed by external force is to show either arrogance or ignorance – neither of which should be the basis for conduct on the international stage. A western-imposed and -sustained democratic regime in Iraq would be unlikely to be able to rebut the charge of being merely an agent of western imperialism and would be unlikely to appeal to the undemocratic regimes to the south, to the east or to the west. It is likely that western political democracy will be more difficult to export than western economic industrial development. It is also likely that the one will not be possible without the other; though it must be said that one does not necessarily entail the other. For example, the democratic revolution in the former Soviet Union and Eastern Europe may ultimately founder upon the failure of the economic revolution. We may yet see the 'Saddamist' model spread to other ethnically fragmenting regions, particularly in former southern and central Asian Soviet republics. The bloody break-up of Yugoslavia and incipient disintegration in other parts of Eastern Europe suggests that such a model might well gain a re-entry into the European system.

KUWAIT

The restoration of Kuwaiti sovereignty was, from the legal and UN point of view, the central *raison d'être* of the war. It did not 'restore democracy to Kuwait' firstly because, despite President Bush's rhetoric, the Americans could not and did not have the objective of restoring democracy in Kuwait; and secondly of course Kuwait never had democracy in the first place, so it was rather a gloss on events to suggest that the Iraqi invasion overthrew democracy. In any case democracy could not be imposed from outside. The Kuwaiti regime is somewhat less undemocratic than Iraq itself and even the undemocratic aspects could be regarded as less malignant than the repression by the Iraqi Ba'ath. But the problem of democracy in the Middle East as a whole is a very deep one and a central uncertainty regarding the nature of the Middle East in the longer term is the extent to which western democratic ideas and ideals can become guiding principles in the future of Islamic political culture. An 'Islamic democracy' would have to be the result of organic growth, which is why external intervention in the region can only be in response to the external consequences of internal structures, rather than be an attempt to change those internal structures themselves.

In many respects the war has led to the persistence of undemocratic practices in Kuwait in the period immediately after the war with the apparent determination of the al-Sabah rulers to root out all those individuals who might have collaborated with the Iraqis during the occupation and the expulsion of all 'non-Kuwaitis' (especially Palestinians) from the country. This will entail either a stricter control over non-Kuwaiti workers or residents in the country in the future, or the Kuwaitis themselves will have to be prepared to take on the jobs for which in the past they have recruited some half million foreign workers. Thus the experience of the Iraqi invasion may well bring about some deep changes in Kuwaiti society and even perhaps in the definition of Kuwaiti nationality. It is possible that in the absence of plans for large-scale industrialisation the Kuwaiti economy will be able to cope with the absence of a large body of immigrant labour. On the other hand a reducing fertility rate among Kuwaiti nationals may be an issue that continues to concern the government.[3]

The war has also ensured the continued existence of Kuwait and has effectively ensured that any Iraqi territorial claims against

Kuwait, whether legitimate or not, will not be entertained by the international community. It may now be unlikely that any future Iraqi regime of whatever colour will comtemplate pressing such claims, and of course the war has confirmed Kuwait in its future determination to see that these claims are permanently erased from the political agenda of intra-Gulf relations. It must be said, however, that this is likely to exacerbate the problem in the future, of allowing some Iraqi presence on Warbah Island in the interests of being able to defend its access to the Persian Gulf, particularly if Iraq is at some stage to resume a legitimate role in a Gulf security structure. Indeed the United Nations Commission established after the ceasefire is seeking to fix once and for all the east–west stretch of the Iraq–Kuwait border. Basing its recommendations on less than clear historical documentation, the Commission is likely to fix the border somewhat north of the present border. The effect of this would be to divest Iraq of a number of oil wells in the Rumaila field over which Iraq has felt particularly strongly as well as depriving it of a large part of its Umm Qasr naval base.[4]

Though the war restored Kuwaiti sovereignty, it did nothing to alter its viability as a state; indeed it drew attention to its fragility. Its territory and population are so small that it cannot be self-reliant in defence terms; the restoration of its legal sovereignty has not given it the autonomy it has always lacked. However much oil wealth Kuwait has it will always be dependent upon external support for its independence. Since its existence the United Kingdom has performed that role. The post-war situation now raises the question whether Kuwait's viability will in future be guaranteed by extra-regional forces – notably the United States, which has now inherited Britain's role – or by forces within the Middle East region or within the Gulf sub-region. It may well be that its local integrity will be ensured by the presence of other Arab troops – for example, Egyptian, Syrian or Saudi Arabia, or any combination of these three. Whichever Arab forces perform such a function they will effectively be acting as proxies of the United States and other western states. For ultimately Kuwait's integrity will be of the highest interest for America not for its own sake but as a derivative of the political and economic value of Saudi Arabia for western interests in general and American interests in particular.

GULF SECURITY

It may be wishful thinking to hope or expect that the war will lead either to more pluralism in Middle Eastern internal politics or to more cooperation between states in establishing regional security structures. That the war did not solve many problems is no surprise; as discussed above, however, it did solve the major problem it was directed to. Or more accurately it solved part of that major problem. The part that it did not solve – and indeed a part which was provided for in the UN Resolution 678 – was the establishment of peace and security in the region. Peace, perhaps, of a sort. Security is a more difficult prospect. The war may have eliminated Iraq's capability to dominate the Gulf region but it has not re-established a self-sustaining balance in the sub-region. Indeed, while Iraq remains effectively a non-participant in regional or world affairs that balance cannot be restored. The status of the three key elements – Iraq, Iran and Saudi Arabia – and the relationship between them is still sufficiently uncertain as to make it likely that the establishment of a stable security structure for the Gulf region might take some time to bring about. As already suggested, radical changes will have to ensue inside Iraq before it will be ready to resume a legitimate and responsible role in the region – and one of course that the other states are likely to trust and accept. That essentially entails a new regime, ideally one which is not tainted by either Saddam or the Ba'ath – a tall order perhaps.

Both the other members of the Gulf 'security trio' – Saudi Arabia and Iran – have now suffered from the ambitions of an expansionist Iraq and will have a joint interest in curbing or balancing Iraqi power in the future. Their contrasting ideologies and allegiances however will not make this easy. But there are incentives on both sides to collaborate in restoring a power balance in the Gulf. Despite post-war moves to substantially enhance her military capability, Saudi Arabia remains vulnerable and it is unlikely that the Saudi government will relinquish its ultimate reliance on protection from the United States. But of course reliance on the United States for ultimate defence is itself a source of vulnerability in political and ideological terms both to radical Arab states and to the forces of Islamic fundamentalism, of which Iran is the legitimising source.

However, Iran's neutrality during the war itself was a relief to the Coalition and was an indication that even the presence of 'the Great Satan' in the region would not persuade the Iranians to 'let bygones be bygones' as far as Iraq was concerned. But it also signalled at least the temporary supremacy of the realists or 'participationists' within the Iranian regime, who recognise the importance for Iran of a rapprochment with the western powers for economic purposes. But overall with such unstable domestic situations in both Iraq and Iran and potentially even in Saudi Arabia, where political change will have to be given scope at some stage in the future, it is unlikely that a self-sustaining security structure can be established in the short or even medium term. Moreover the prospects for Iranian and fundamentalist influence may well increase in scope and direction given the the emergence of 'free-floating' Islamic republics as a result of the break-up of the Soviet Empire. The changed and changing political geography of South-West and Central Asia gives Iran a quite new and even pivotal geopolitical signficance in the region. Thus, though she cannot afford to turn away from an interest in the Gulf, there will be preoccupations to the north that will now complicate her regional role.

The implication of this is that the prospect of external intervention is likely to continue to be the ultimate arbiter of stability and balance in the Gulf region. However, it is a moot point as to whether the war has made the United States less or more willing to intervene in the future. The Americans have certainly now demonstrated their ability and willingness to protect their interests in the region; that in itself may be a sobering influence. However, domestic economic, political and social preoccupations may in the short to medium term inhibit America's willingness and perhaps ability to engage in large-scale conflicts overseas.

THE MIDDLE EAST IN GENERAL

It must be a source of regret among many in the Arab world that such a strutting, brutal, self-indulgent fantasist was allowed to become the repository, in the popular Arab mind and on the world stage, of Arab integrity and aspirations. Apart from the power-political consequences of the Iraqi defeat it was a public relations disaster for the Arab cause, despite the fact that three of the most prominent Arab states were members of the anti-Iraq Coalition. Far from demonstrating that the west did not understand the Arab mind, it appears, in superficial terms at least, to demonstrate that the west understands the Arab mind all too well. It appears to demonstrate that the western judgement of the Arabs, through Saddam Hussein, was accurate. The danger is that these simplistic perceptions and judgements are now reinforced and become the conventional wisdom untempered by caution against oversimplification.

The defining idea of 'Arab unity' seems to have been the first major casualty of the war; and the idea that western intervention or interest in the Middle East is axiomatically 'imperialist' seems to be the second. The attempt by Iraq, Iran, the Yemen and others to characterise the war as a war by western imperialists against Arabs or against Muslims has hidden the traumatic truth for the Arab world that the war was in fact a war of Arabs against Arabs – in terms of the concept of the Arab nationality, it was an Arab civil war. The fact that Arabs have now encountered Arabs on opposite sides of a major war within the Middle East and that three major Arab powers found themselves fighting in support of an external power against 'brother' Arabs has seriously compromised the validity of both these ideas. Indeed the war may have generated yet a new cleavage in the Arab/Islamic world (see Chapter 1).

But such profound changes may not be easily detected in the short term and may be seen to have resulted from the Gulf War only in retrospect. It is only by accepting statism (even though it might be a western idea in the contemporary international system) that the very notion of Arab unity or Arab solidarity can be put into practical effect. A mythical idea of Arabism which tended to see the possibility of one gigantic Arab nation-state was essentially a rhetorical device and as such was a hindrance to Arab political development rather than a realistic objective. What needs to be done is to graft the underlying notion of Arab brotherhood onto the reality of a regional nation-state system to lubricate the wheels of political cooperation.

The fact that the Arabs can be seen as incapable themselves of dealing with a major crisis among Arab states is no doubt a source of humiliation and will stimulate either a sober reflection of its implications for regional relationships or a further desire for revenge. For Arab governments in an ironic way the war may well have helped them to come to terms with a post-Cold War world rather sooner than they might otherwise have done. America's ascendency in the region is now unquestioned for the foreseeable future; it is an early demonstration that there is now no balance to American power and that Arab governments now no longer have the option of manipulating superpower conflict for their own interests. If by strengthening US power in the region Israeli power has also been strengthened, it may be seen as a direct result of the actions of one of their own brother Arab leaders. But the ascendency of Israeli power in the region is not an automatic consequence of the war.

The effect of the war, and American victory, on the Arab–Israeli dispute is rather more ambiguous than might have at first seemed. It became apparent early on in the Gulf crisis that whatever its outcome the western powers, in particular the United States, would have to get to more serious grips with the Palestinian issue in the aftermath. Though Saddam Hussein's equation of Iraq's occupation of Kuwait with the Israeli occupation of the West Bank was a false one, at the superficial level there seemed to be some validity in it. The fact of the matter was that the equation was made which in itself would have forced the issue on to the post-war Middle East agenda. Secondly, of course, the war forced upon the Americans the real implications of supporting Israel come hell or high water. The sudden absence of superpower restraints in the region increased the possibility of a war into which Israel might drag the United States behind it. A Middle East war in which America intervened on behalf of Israel would be a very different war indeed from the war against Iraq and one that America, even with single superpower status, would not want to get involved in. Thus the end of the Cold War itself made an Arab–Israeli rapprochment more urgent for the Americans, and the Gulf War perhaps made them realise that, if they had to fight in any war in the Middle East, they would much prefer to fight in an Arab–Arab war than in an Arab–Israeli war.

The post-war leverage that the Americans were able to exert upon the Israelis was to some extent a product of the 'balance of political debt' between the two sides. Certainly the Israelis owed the Americans a heavy debt for eliminating the most serious immediate threat to Israel in the Arab world. On the other hand the Israelis allowed themselves finally to be prevailed upon to exercise an unaccustomed restraint in the face of Scud missile attacks from Iraq, and they no doubt would expect some political return for that. But also of course the Americans provided some protection against these attacks – albeit belatedly – in the form of the valiant

Patriot missile. However, it may be that the Patriot was in the event as much a political missile as was the Scud.

While at the time of writing the Arab–Israeli peace talks are in some jeopardy over the Israeli expulsion of 400 Palestinians, the fact that they started at all was a product partly of the Gulf War and partly of the changed regional balance of interests as a result of the demise of Soviet power. The America–Israel tie was already being loosened to some extent, which would make Israel contemplate more seriously the prospect of a longer-term future without an American connection. The recent change of government in Israel has given a further fillip to those internal Israeli forces which may be more flexible in the search for a solution to the Palestinian problem. The Syrians also had already begun to review their strategic interests after the decline of their benefactor, the Soviet Union. It was this factor that has prompted a Syrian desire for closer relations with the western powers, especially the United States, which has manifested itself in the startling sight of Syrian troops joining with American troops to fight against fellow Arabs. This was perhaps the most stark indication of the sea-change in Middle Eastern politics brought about by the Gulf War and the end of the Cold War.

However, the role of the Palestinians in the Gulf crisis might ultimately allow their interests to be sacrificed to the conclusion of a separate Arab–Israeli rapprochement. The craven and unhesitating rush of Yassir Arafat to the side and support of Saddam Hussein was incautious to say the least and may yet allow the Americans to countenance a Palestinian solution short of self-determination – particularly if the Israelis can offer a deal to the Syrians that they cannot resist, such as a deal on the Golan Heights. That would 'peel off' Syria from the Palestinian issue in the same way that Egypt was 'peeled off' in the Camp David Agreements of 1978. In this eventuality it is conceivable that far from providing the basis for a solution of the Palestinian issue the Gulf War may have made it possible for an Arab–Israeli rapprochement to receive a higher priority than the Palestinian issue. Such a scenario would reduce the incentive for the Israelis to make concessions to the Palestinians.

It is conceivable, however, that the ultimate 'loser' of the Gulf War will be the Jordanian monarchy. Ironically perhaps the most pro-western of Arab leaders, the Hashemite King Hussein, a British protégé in the post-1945 Middle East, may well be regarded as expendable in the interests of a solution to the Palestinian problem which may allow a skirting of the West Bank problem. Even before the Iraqi invasion of Kuwait Palestinians probably outnumbered Bedouin in Jordan's population. The Gulf War caused an exodus of half a million Palestinians from Kuwait of which some 300,000 have returned to Jordan, of which they are nominally citizens. The question within Jordan of the majority population group effectively being debarred from positions of power may now come onto the agenda. The logic, firmly resisted by King Hussein up to now, of a Jordanian solution to the Palestinian problem may well assume an irresistible momentum. For not only would this be in accordance with the demographic realities in Jordan but may also be the only solution in which the Israelis might be prepared to do a territorial deal on the West Bank or part of it. So King Hussein, who for long has been both a champion of the Palestinian cause and a victim of its violence may well lose his throne in its interests.

On the other hand, there is some longer-term incentive for the Israelis to want an overall settlement of both the Palestinian issue and the broader relationship with the Arab world. Israel needs to get a clear vision of her future place in the Middle East region. If her legitimate claim is that her Arab opponents should not continue to regard her as an external interloper in the Arab world then the Arabs can also claim that she should stop behaving like one. Integration of Israel into the Middle East is the only long-term solution in the interests of both sides. However, powerful militarily Israel is in the region, her existence is bound to remain tenuous in the absence of an overall settlement. In a world of nuclear proliferation, now almost irresistible despite attempts to denuclearise Saddam's Iraq, Israeli regional superpower status will not eliminate the nuclear threat – a threat particularly potent given the very small territorial space that is Israel. For the one thing that the war did demonstrate was the vulnerability of Israel to missile attack – a vulnerability to which the development of a missile defence system might well be a response, but to which it will not be the answer.

DEMOCRACY VERSUS ISLAM

The elimination of the 'Soviet alternative' has brought into sharper focus the choice or confrontation between Islam and democracy in the Middle East. The existence of the 'Soviet model' gave some ideological legitimation to a secularism which was non-democratic and indeed repressive. One of the dilemmas today arises from the question as to what extent a democratic choice can be given to 'the people' to choose a non-democratic government. In many respects Soviet material support and the provision of an ideological fig-leaf has in the past allowed the Islamic world to avoid the choice and has enabled traditional repression and despotism to be exercised and legitimised through Arab interpretations of socialistic ideologies like the Ba'ath Party and other Arab nationalisms. It has also allowed western support of equally undemocratic and traditionalist regimes effectively inhibiting the development of pluralist systems in both types of country.

The crisis in Algerian politics in 1991–2 was an important manifestation of this confrontation. It cannot be claimed that this crisis emanated directly from the consequences of the Gulf War, but it is not insignificant for this confrontation that those states providing the will, the skill and matériel to defeat Saddam Hussein were western democratic regimes, and that the Iraqi Ba'ath was the most brutal product of that very repressive, Soviet type of secularism. But it is the failure of repressive secularism (masquerading as western secularism, e.g. pre-revolutionary Iran) that has given rise to the revival of Islamic fundamentalism.

Islam and democracy are incompatible as political systems. The reason for this is simply that it can never be democratic to claim divine authority for human political judgements or political principles – even when it is the 'will of the people' that such claims are made. The limit of the 'sovereignty of the people' is their right to divest themselves of that sovereignty. To vote an undemocratic regime into power may be an exercise in democracy, but it is the last act of a democracy and the last act of the exercise of sovereignty, usually taken by a people for whom in any case sovereignty and 'democracy' are a sham. Thus to acclaim the voting into power of an Islamic fundamentalist government is not to eliminate the problem of the incompatibility of democracy and Islam. The rise of political Islamicism in the Middle East is a product of the failure of secularism to provide the answers many Arabs seek – but it has not been a western type of secularism that has failed. The intervention of the military in Algeria in order to prevent an elected Islamic party from forming a government is a direct manifestation of the dilemma presented by a democratically elected non-democratic regime. But events in Algeria may well form a template for events elsewhere in the Middle East where governing elites may now be converting to the necessity for a western type of secular democracy but whose 'underclass' draw quite other conclusions from the Gulf War. The end of the Cold War and the Gulf War itself may have had the effect of redrawing even more starkly the conflict between 'westernism' and 'Islamicism'; this may well be the dominant 'cleavage' in the Middle East in the medium term.

The Gulf War may indeed have widened the gap between governing elites, constrained by both domestic and international forces, and their peoples who now, perhaps ironically, look not to democracy for the fulfilment of their aspirations but to Islam. It may not be until the failure of political Islam to deliver the goods in material and political terms is demonstrated that the Middle East will be ripe for a democratic revolution.

OTHER EFFECTS

Despite the perception that nothing much has changed, war always produces a different situation. Things are never the same after a war. At the very least war produces a psychological effect; a war cannot be 'unhappened'. Some of the consequences of war are immediately apparent; many can only be detected in retro-spect, some time after the event. One fundamental 'lesson' of the Gulf conflict is that war has not been eliminated from the agenda of even liberal-democratic regimes. It has starkly demonstrated to many to whom it was not already apparent that although the western democracies have fashioned for themselves a system in which the use of force is no longer (for ever?) a legitimate instrument of state policy, they still maintain the will and the deadly capability to use it in the world at large where their interests are threatened. Moreover it is likely that in the new more fluid international system of the medium-term future they will need to remain prepared for such intervention.

Another 'general' lesson of the Gulf War is that victory may be as much to do with your opponent's political and military incom-petence as with the skill and courage of your own forces. For Iraq to have provoked a military confrontation with the Americans two years before becoming a nuclear power was, at least in terms of *machtpolitik*, daft. This is not to say that even Saddam Hussein would have relished nuclear war with the United States; but an Iraqi nuclear capability would have added a completely new and ominous dimension to the crisis diplomacy, and it is unlikely that in these circumstances war would have ensued at all. If that analysis is correct it has implications for other possible effects of the Gulf War.

One relates to the effect the war will have on other 'potential Saddams' – what 'lessons' will they draw from the war? American power and indeed political skill would no doubt have hugely impressed them. Thus lesson one: do not get into a war with the United States and her allies. But that does not mean that such individuals will conclude that it is not possible to challenge the United States. They will be concentrating on Saddam's failures rather than America's successes. Though Saddam's military failures were unmistakable, and indeed terminal, his political failures were perhaps the most important. The most abject failure was in allowing the construction of a political climate in which the United States was able to use force directly in the Middle East. A direct frontal military challenge to the most powerful state in the world no doubt served Saddam's deluded imagination, but it was an act of unrealism and an act of folly. But it was not only American military power that Saddam Hussein challenged; his challenge included some of the most fundamental principles of international law and the principles of the United Nations itself. Such a blatant disregard for principles which many of his erstwhile Third World supporters rely upon for their own independence and legitimacy compromised their potential support and forced them willy nilly into the American-led UN Coalition. So lesson number two is, if you are intent on challenging the United States, make sure that at least you are on the right side of the law; that at least would make the political balance of forces more equal.

Another way of being able to challenge 'the west' but at the same time reduce the likelihood of getting into a war with them would be for such 'potential Saddams' to 'go nuclear'. There are obvious risks in such a strategy but also potential benefits. The risks lie in the failure to avert a war and the possibility of the war itself going nuclear. After all, it is a convention among the western nuclear powers that they would not use nuclear weapons against a non-nuclear power. The implication being that such a prohibition would not apply to states possessing nuclear weapons if it really came to the pinch. But the effects of the nuclear dimension during crises in such circumstances would be to raise the war threshold and provide incentives for de-escalation short of war. The domestic constraints on western states were only just insufficient to prevent their governments going to war in the Gulf; the presence of a 'nuclear factor' is likely to have made it politically impossible (as well as militarily undesirable).

However, if a new wave of nuclear proliferation is now to take place in the non-western world, it is not likely to be in the context of their relations with the western nuclear powers but in the context of their own regional security systems. The fact that Iraq was regarded as being in the 'second echelon' of nuclear 'threshold' states suggests that those in the first echelon already effectively have a nuclear capability. Such states as Israel, South Africa, India, perhaps even Pakistan, are already regarded as nuclear states. States such as Brazil, North Korea, Argentina may be closely behind. The significance of Iraq's nuclear programme and the horror with which the world viewed it has certainly raised the profile of the nuclear issue in relation to non-western states. The difficulty of finding all the facilities and equipment relating to Iraq's nuclear programme and of preventing its revival – and by implication the spread of nuclear weapons elsewhere, – has demonstrated the essential ineffectiveness of a formal non-proliferation regime.

It has prompted more urgent thought about the problem, that strategic analysts have been considering for some time, of switching from reliance on prohibitions to proliferation to beginning to fashion a regime to manage nuclear weapons in the event that nuclear proliferation takes place. The fact that nuclear proliferation did not take place at the rate predicted in the late 1960s (President Johnson in 1969 predicted that there would be between twenty-five and thirty nuclear weapons states by 1980) and the pursuit of a policy of 'nuclear ambiguity' by the 'near nuclear' states has served to keep the emphasis on non-proliferation as a means of 'getting the genie back into the bottle' at the expense of investigating the way in which the genie might be made to serve the interests of regional and global security. It is likely that the problem of nuclear-proliferation will now assume a higher profile at the United Nations. But the danger is that there will be a revival of the emphasis on non-proliferation rather than paying attention to the structures of security, which is where the motivations for nuclear proliferation are to be found. It is arguable that just as much urgency should be directed to constructing a regime, or series of regimes, within which nuclear weapons can find a stable and legitimate status of 'non-use', as to preventing what is likely to be the inevitable process of proliferation.

THE GULF WAR AND THE PROLIFERATION OF MILITARY TECHNOLOGY

It has always been an explicit western strategy in the Cold War to compensate its quantitative military disadvantage with a qualitative advantage – at battlefield, theatre and strategic levels. Thus technological innovation developed mainly by the United States has always been the basis of NATO's confidence to confront the Warsaw Pact forces. The element of surprise in warfare as a 'force multiplier' has already been discussed (see Chapter 9); technological superiority performs the same sort of function. The emphasis in NATO was not to attempt to offset the three to one disadvantage in battlefield weapons by making them 'three times better' themselves, but to direct the technology to controlling the environment in which they operated, making them perhaps three times more effective in achieving their battlefield objectives.[5] In practice this refers to effectiveness in command, control and intelligence, and in being able to undermine your opponent's defensive systems, and his command and control systems. In the Gulf War the Americans were able to maintain a very high degree of control and coordination of all Coalition forces and gather crucial information about the strength and disposition of the opposing forces through the use of satellite systems as well as more conventional air surveillance, reconnaisance aircraft and ground surveillance devices. They were able to destroy much of Iraq's own defensive systems through the use of precision guidance weapons systems. The American-led Coalition forces achieved a remarkable understanding of the whole war environment ('situation awareness') which enabled them to use their own offensive capabilities to maximum effect but also enabled them to undermine totally (to all intents and purposes) the opponent's offensive and defensive capability.

The spectacular success of military and support technology in the Gulf War (some have even spoken of a thousand-to-one discrepancy)[6] will without doubt lead to something of a technological arms race among countries in regional security complexes. Indeed this aspect of the Gulf War had such an impact that there may well be a switch from a nuclear acquisition strategy to greater emphasis on a conventional technology acquisition strategy among the major Third World regional powers. The proliferation of this sort of technology is unlikely to be prevented because much, if not most, of the basis for it already exists in the public domain.[7] However, the less obvious point to be made about the use of such sophisticated technology to such devastating effect is that these technological systems do not consist merely of 'gadgets', 'devices', 'gizmoes' or hi-tech pieces of equipment; they are really a complex combination of technological and human systems. It is this fusion of technology and human control that is crucial to the effective use of such systems and it is the latter that is more difficult to acquire and develop than the former. For it was not only the technology that accounted for the Coalition's victory but its incorporation into an effective and efficiently implemented strategy. It is the proliferation of this human professional expertise that is likely to lag behind the proliferation of the technology itself which may inhibit, to some extent at least, the effective use of these systems by other, perhaps less-developed states.

However, that is not to say that the proliferation of a wider range of military weaponry will not be a serious problem in the future. There is a sense in which the Gulf War might have changed the status of nuclear weapons as a symbol of power. During the Cold War nuclear weapons (often for quite irrational reasons) acquired the symbolic status of power. The Gulf War has seen a nuclear superpower demonstrating that sophisticated conventional weapons can not only be a symbol of power but can be an effective instrument of power. One of the most important areas of military proliferation that indeed was gaining pace before the Gulf War but may now be given added impetus, is that of missile technology. Missiles can serve both nuclear and conventional aspirations and the prominence of both Scud and Patriot missiles during the war will focus minds not only on missiles as offensive weapons but also on the problem of missile defence. Even at the former superpower level there is now talk of the deliberate proliferation of missile defensive technology as part of a new security structure between the west and the former Soviet territories. Certainly missile defence systems which may not have been a credible or even desirable prospect under conditions of superpower strategic stability could indeed become credible under conditions of non-massive missile threat from Third World states.

Though the Scud missile had rather more political significance than military effectiveness during the Gulf War, the difficulty of locating and preventing missile launchers was a serious embarrassment for the Americans and their allies. That fact would have had far more serious military significance had the missiles themselves been more sophisticated and if their warheads had rather more lethal payloads. Clearly an air force is in principle more flexible and sustainable as an offensive instrument than a missile force. But in the Gulf War the vulnerability of the Iraqi air force both in the air and on the ground led it to flee the battlefield and the Scud missile played a much more prominent role. In the long term the expense of acquiring and protecting an air force of sophisticated aircraft may lead other Third World states to opt for the development or acquisition of solid-fuel, more accurate missiles capable of carrying a more destructive or more effective payload as a more cost-effective military investment.[8]

The signficance of these future trends will impinge much more on regional systems than on relations between regional states and the developed western world. However, the longer-term prospect of the acquisition by Third World states of *intercontinental* missile technology will entail for the developed world (and particularly the current western nuclear powers of the United States, Britain and France) a post-Cold War revision of their missile targeting strategy. This is not merely because in the absence of the Soviet enemy the military sectors of the western world have 'to search for other enemies to justify their existence'. It is precisely because the relaxation of superpower constraints on the Third World foreign-policy behaviour together with the prospect of their acquisition of technology that brings European and American population centres within range of Third World military capability actually makes them potential enemies.

IMPACT ON THE COHESION OF 'THE WEST'

In the most obvious sense the Gulf War and the spectacular military victory of the UN Coalition forces was a demonstration of American overwhelming power and leadership. At a less obvious level – and again this point has been made elsewhere – it was a manifestation of the limitations of American power. One of the imperatives for confronting Saddam Hussein's act of aggression was the necessity for fashioning a future international environment in which such acts are deterred. For not only would there be a reluctance on the part of large sections of American opinion to assume the role of world policeman, and the 'loneliness' and antagonism that such a role would entail, but the role would put such a strain on American resources and an already ailing economy, that the United States would not be strong enough to bear it.

So the Gulf War contributed to the already emerging tension in American attitudes between a post-Cold War triumphalism and a reversion to a traditional isolationism. Though victory in the Gulf can on the face of it be added to victory in the Cold War to confirm US supremacy in the world and her leadership of the western alliance, this is tempered to a considerable extent by the failure both of an internally coherent European policy in the crisis and one which provided a consistent support for American action. The United Kingdom stood out alone among the European powers in her direct and unhesitating firmness to confront Iraq and reverse its invasion of Kuwait. This was born of a number of factors. Firstly it was yet another demonstration of the intrinsic difficulty Britain has in distancing herself from the United States. The fact is she very often sees the world through very much the same set of lenses as the Americans, and there seems to be an inherent 'Anglo-Saxon' solidarity. Secondly there was no doubt an element of Margaret Thatcher's insistent emphasis on the Atlantic axis very often at the expense of cross-Channel links. Thirdly there is perhaps even a 'natural' (some say quite inappropriate) pugnacity of the British which leads not perhaps to an eagerness to get into a fight but a determination not to shirk one if unavoidable.

Among the major continental European powers, France and Germany, there was what might be called a 'reversion to type'. France pursued her well-practised diplomacy of keeping all options wide open by following an independent diplomatic and military line directed to distancing herself certainly from the 'Anglo-Saxon' alliance but also from the European Community. This was reflected throughout the crisis phase and particularly in her attempted independent last-minute diplomacy in Baghdad and the UN without consultation of any of her allies on either side of the Atlantic. Even her military involvement in the war was literally peripheral in her flamboyant participation in the great flanking movement through the western desert of Iraq to An Nasiryah on the River Euphrates.

The Germans found themselves preoccupied with reunification at the time of the Gulf conflict and perhaps had some difficulty in focusing on events remote from the revolution in their domestic affairs. Thus the emphasis given to the constitutional prohibitions on the use of German troops beyond their own borders showed not only a reluctance to be diverted from their domestic concerns but also perhaps a reluctance to contemplate the implications of once more becoming an 'ordinary' state, which would include the preparedness to use force if and when the need arises. This is an issue that goes right to the heart of the nature of the German nation and the German state. The wave of anxiety that swept the nation at the very thought of German troops being involved once again in war beyond its borders brought forth an irritation if not a resentment towards those who appeared to be demanding that Germany take on a military responsibility alongside her allies in the Gulf. On the other hand there was an almost immediate recognition that Germany cannot assume a 'paymaster' role in which other states would act as mercenaries fighting wars over issues in which Germany also has an interest.

Of course this issue is and will be a test indeed of Germany's 'ordinariness' in nation-state terms. The Gulf War will have had the effect of bringing forward the internal debate on these issues which would in any case have taken place at some stage in the future. Not to put too fine a point on it the Germans have to recognise that in military terms it must be possible for them to assume a role somewhere between Nazism and pacifism. The 'pacifist option' is a reflection of anxiety among Germans that they may not be able to trust themselves with military power, which in turn is to concede that militarism is somehow always waiting in the German soul to rise again. The real issue is whether military force can assume the same role in their inter-state relations, as it does for the other liberal democracies in the western world, as a legitimate instrument of foreign policy in those circumstances in which it is an appropriate option. In many ways this will be the only way in which Germany can exorcise the ghost of Nazism now that the post-Nazi structures of Europe, within which a new constitutional Germany was born, have disintegrated.

There is a tendency for continental Europeans (with the exception of Britain and France) to assume that the principle of non-violence, that has become the chief feature of the Euro-Atlantic system of inter-state relations since the Second World War, can be and should be equally applicable in the non-European world. Although the European Community assumed a diplomatic and economic role in the Gulf conflict – it imposed sanctions before the United Nations did and attempted a common response to the hostage issue and on the diplomatic premises issue[9] – its role was not prominent and its equivocation (to say the least) over the use of military force again raises questions about the seriousness of the European commitment to an Atlantic link and the credibility of the notion of a common European security structure. The EC stance on the Gulf conflict prompted two opposing responses on the issue of European security. One suggested that it demonstrated the need for a European security umbrella: 'defence is vital for Europe's political self-definition . . . we must reinforce the EC by giving it this role, for it will not be strong without a clear security dimension'.[10] The opposing response suggests that far from 'proving' the need for a common defence policy, it points up the essential implausibility of European Political Union (EPU). The argument is clear – you cannot have EPU without a common security policy; thus if a common security policy is not possible then neither is EPU.

What the pro-European security policy case is really saying is that a common security policy must be used as an instrument to force EPU. Those who oppose suggest that this is putting the cart before the horse – if there is not political unity there cannot be security unity. The Gulf conflict has played a part in clarifying these issues and in conjunction with the disintegration of Eastern Europe will have set back the cause of Western European political union.

THE NEW WORLD: ORDER AND DISORDER

It is a common misperception that 'stability' is synonymous with 'peace', that a stable system is a peaceful system, that an absence of conflict entails stability. Given that war is one of the ways of relieving the pressures in the system, of resolving underlying conflicts in the system, it can be regarded as one of the mechanisms for maintaining the stability and continuity of the system.

Popular unfamiliarity with this sort of mechanism may explain a common confusion regarding the nature of the Cold War system. Was it peace or was it war? Was it stable or was it unstable? The period since 1945 can hardly be described as 'peaceful' – and yet many analysts regarded it as an essentially stable system. Indeed many practitioners regarded it as their central task to maintain that stability. The very term itself, 'cold war', is filled with ambiguity. It is of course still a point of academic controversy as to whether the Cold War system was stable or not. But it is this author's contention at least that a plausible depiction of the Cold War is that of a system of 'stable conflict'. Indeed the superpowers went out of their way to ensure that the necessary conflict in the system was not pushed beyond certain limits or allowed to get out of control, and they were careful on the whole to draw boundaries round their respective behaviours so as not to push the system into instability. The whole theme of 'adversarial collaboration' is a fruitful approach to understanding the Cold War.

This is not to draw a naïve or oversimplified picture of the Cold War; it was obviously much more complicated than the superficial image conveyed by this argument. However, it serves the purpose of the point to be made about the importance of our conceptualisations of the international system. One of the features of the Cold War system making for its manageability was that at the macrolevel at least it was relatively easy to conceptualise the system. Our models of the world should not be confused with reality but it is important to recognise that we behave according to the models of reality we build and not to the reality itself. Thus our understanding of our picture of the nature and structure of the international system at any one time will to a large extent determine our behaviour in it. Clearly the extent to which reality is tractable enough to allow us to construct reasonably plausible or accurate models of its structures and processes, will contribute to our ability to do so. In this sense the Cold War system was a simple system. At the macro-level at least, the superpower bipolarity (however that is defined) was a simple, reasonably accurate and even comfortable and pleasing model. Clearly as time proceeded and as the system changed many complications of the system took place and bipolarity came increasingly under stress as an explanatory model of the post-war system. Indeed that system became a many-layered system with different configurations of power at different 'levels' of the system and in different 'issue areas', and so on. But so long as the two major actors remained superpowers (even if that status was more 'wish' than substance – it may even have been the 'myth' of superpower status that sustained the system – the analogy with the story of the emperor who had no clothes is an apt one) the belief in the essential bipolarity could be maintained. It was in part at least the ease of conceptualisation of the system that made it tractable in operation.

This line of discussion has important implications for the post-Cold War world. If the Cold War system was a system of stable conflict, the danger now is of a system of unstable conflict. The lack of an easily detectable overarching structure of the new system and our difficulty in constructing a plausible model of the new system will contribute to our difficulty in managing it; that is, since we do not at present understand the dynamics of the new system we will find it difficult to construct effective institutions for managing the system and maintaining its stability. Clearly the structure of any system cannot be divorced from the decisions that are made in it at the macro and at the micro levels. But we should be realistic about our room for manoeuvre. This brings us back to some of the ideas mentioned in the Introduction to this book – those of structures and contingencies; the idea that structures do not directly determine action and behaviour, they merely set down a set of propensities within which decisions are made and actions taken.

What we have witnessed over the past three or four years and are witnessing today is the breakdown of previously existing structures. There is an increasing fluidity at the structural level of the international system – there is more uncertainty, more complexity, blurring of old boundaries, more unpredictability. It is paradoxical that, as was mentioned earlier, in periods of 'structural flux', it is possible for individual decisions and actions to have a greater impact on events – in these circumstances there is increased scope for effective action; in these circumstances decisions taken now can determine or at least influence the nature of future structures. However, the paradox is that although there is more *scope* for action and effective decision-making, it is less clear what decisions or actions should be taken. Because in situations of structural flux and fluidity it is much more difficult to conceptualise or construct a new model of the system, it is therefore much more difficult to know what action to take.

The 'new world order' has more to do with the end of the Cold War than with the end of the Gulf War. The difficult question to address is what significance does the Gulf War have for the future world order. Was the Gulf conflict, both its cause and its solution, an exception or a precedent for the future? The point has already been made that one of the characteristic features of the Gulf crisis, and one that enabled such a coherent response to it, was the clarity and almost simplicity of the issues at stake. It is not likely that such clarity will be a typical feature of future crises, and there is unlikely to be such a wide or deep consensus about how they should be dealt with.

It is likely that because of the increasing incoherence of the international system itself, any new security threats or dangers will themselves be less coherent and thus less easy to counter. Firstly issues in any inter-state conflict are likely to be less clear-cut and subject to a wider range of interpretation. If there are any other 'Saddam Husseins' with similar ambitions, they are likely to be rather more circumspect in their behaviour, making it more difficult to achieve consensus over counter-action. Secondly it is in any case more likely that conflict in the future will be related to internal disruption, ethnic conflict and disintegration than to inter-state conflict of interests. It will thus be more difficult to clearly define the direct security threat beyond a general instability and chaos. The ethnic conflict in the wake of the break-up of Yugoslavia may suggest a pattern both of future conflict and also of a future general reluctance of external powers to intervene. The reluctance to intervene has been a manifestation of the failure of external states, both in Europe and outside, to define a direct interest which could justify the expenditure of resources and perhaps lives. The Yugoslav crisis, no less than the Gulf crisis, is a demonstration that humanitarian issues are not sufficient for states to use military force. Those who believe that the so-called new world order provides an opportunity for the ethos of the international system to change to one where states are as prepared to intervene to prevent suffering as to protect their interests may be in for a disappointment – callous as that may sound.

It is possible that there might be a move to inject into the United Nations a more pro-active dynamic in these circumstances, but it is likely that such an attempt will confront the reluctance of those states most able to provide the resources to put it into action. The formation of a 'UN military force' is no nearer now than it was in 1945, firstly because of the reluctance of states to contribute troops or to confer such 'independent' military power to a non-state entity; but secondly because such a body might actually cause more conflict than it brings to an end. It is likely in the absence of overwhelming force – necessary for the sort of action seen in the Gulf (or even in the former Yugoslavia) but unlikely to be put at the disposal of a UN force – intervention of a third-party force, particularly in Yugoslav-type conflicts, may actually prolong the conflict rather than end it.

But aside from the willingness and the individual practicalities of such intervention there is the problem of the overall capacity of any entity, world body or superpower, to cope with the vast potential for conflict manifest in the widespread propensity for fragmentation in the post-Cold War world. The end of the Cold War has seemed to threaten the integrity of many of the states formed in the twentieth and even nineteenth century. It is a plausible scenario that such fragmentation could actually threaten the integrity of the international system itself.

The fragmentation of the former Soviet Empire and of Yugoslavia may well have a 'demonstration effect'. Sub-sub-nationalisms may threaten the integrity of such states as Russia and Ukraine themselves and such extreme fragmentation may be reflected in other areas. For example, the unity of the Indian state – a post-colonial construction – is now coming under question. Pakistan has always been on the brink of fragmentation, which is only prevented by repressive centralising governments. The failure of the democratic reform movement in China in 1989 was surely only a temporary respite for the communist regime there. Radical political and economic change in China may well have similar effects to those in the Soviet Union. Regionalism based on the differential economic effects of the economic reforms in China are already detectable.

One picture of the future international system is of an ordered core and a disordered periphery. In such a picture war has essentially been eliminated as an instrument of policy among the members of the 'core'. It is assumed that the interdependent prosperity of the Euro-Atlantic community and the collective security structures they have developed have made war an unnecessary and inappropriate means of conflict resolution among its members. though upheaval in Eastern Europe, the changing status of Germany and the waning of the vision of European unity may well begin to destabilise a Europe still trying to ignore the fundamental changes that are taking place in the system. But one area of potential difference of both interest and perception is likely to be the distribution of responsibility in the future for maintaining the 'security and stability' of the global system as a whole. In particular this relates to the question as to whether the United States will continue to have the willingness and capability to maintain its leadership role in this respect. The United States is likely to experience a conflict between its euphoria at finding itself 'the only superpower left' after the Cold War and its frustration at its inability to exert that power in an unambiguous way. The world may not be as tractable as Americans might expect it to be in the absence of the Soviet 'evil empire'. This frustration in turn might give rise to a degree of resentment against other members of the 'core' – in particular Europe (especially Germany) and Japan. There will now be increasing pressure on these two 'economic superpowers' to take on the political and security responsibilities consonant with their economic power. Notwithstanding the conflicts they may already be feeling between internal domestic ambitions and external security responsibilities (the earlier German withdrawal from the European Fighter Aircraft project was a case in point), there will be increasing pressures for both of these economically powerful states to stop 'hiding behind' the post-Second World War constraints on their status and begin behaving as 'ordinary states'. So far from other states now assuming the benefits of low defence expenditure (assumed by many to be one of the reasons for their economic prosperity) the pressures will be in the other direction – of Germany and Japan now being expected to take on the economic cost and political responsibilities of playing a much more central role both in their own and in global security issues.

If this 'core–periphery' security model has any validity, one question that arises is to what extent will the core powers be able to ignore (or be less responsive to) events on the extreme periphery. What incentives will there be for the core powers to be concerned about conflict, for example, in Africa? Will they only be concerned about conflict that rests on their own 'doorstep' – in Eastern Europe for example? It may be that geographical proximity will dictate core-power (European and US) interest in Eastern Europe. Though even here issue-related concerns might be more important than mere geographical proximity. In this respect the Middle East commanded, and will continue to command, more core-power attention than Yugoslavia. However, what might drastically increase the saliency of the Balkans as an issue of concern for the core powers is the connection of the two areas. The Islamic dimension in the Balkans has the potential to see the first Muslim intervention in Europe since the Ottoman Empire.

The Gulf War was a manifestation of the political, economic and security importance of the Middle East. Neither the end of the Cold War nor the end of the Gulf War are likely to see that importance diminish, and conflict within the Middle East will continue to be of concern to the core powers in the future.

Appendices

  I Gazetteer of states involved in the Gulf crisis

 II Chronology of the Gulf conflict

III Maps

    1 Map showing the unclear historical designation of Koweit
      compared with Kuwait's present borders

    2 Areas under dispute as at 1 August 1991 and border
      revision post-Gulf War 1991

    3 Troop deployments and Iraqi military targets as at 16
      January 1991

    4 Disposition of Iraqi troops in the Kuwaiti Theatre of
      Operations as at 16 January 1991

    5 Ground operations of the Gulf land war between 24 and
      27 February 1991

    6 The Middle East, the Arab world and the Muslim diaspora

 IV Documents

  V Statistics of the Gulf War

APPENDIX I GAZETTEER OF STATES INVOLVED IN THE GULF CRISIS

Country	Capital	Area (,000 km²)[a]	Population (m)[a]	Muslim (%)[b]	GDP 1990/1 ($bn)[c]	Military forces 1990/1 (,000s)[c]	Military expenditure 1990/1 ($p.a.)[c]	Political regime[a]	UN status	Stance on Gulf
Afghanistan	Kabul	647.5	18.136	98	3.70	45	286.56 m (1986)	Limited presidential - military still influential - only limited democracy in practice	-	Not prominent (Mujahedeen opposition to Kabul govnt. sent troops to UN Coalition)
Algeria	Algiers	2,381.75	22.972	98	45.43	125.5	904 m	Limited presidential	-	Pro-Iraq, but low profile
Argentina	Buenos Aires	2,780.0	31.2	-	300.80	83 + 377 reserves	7.27 bn	Limited presidential	-	Contributed to Coalition naval force
Australia	Canberra	7,686.85	15.763	-	64.69	68 + 30 reserves	1.24 bn (1988)	Parliamentary executive	-	Contributed to Coalition naval force

Country	Capital	Area (,000 km²)[a]	Population (m)[a]	Muslim (%)[b]	GDP 1990/1 ($bn)[c]	Military forces 1990/1 (,000s)[c]	Military expenditure 1990/1 ($p.a.)[c]	Political regime[a]	UN status	Stance on Gulf
Austria	Vienna	83.85	7.546	-	157.48	44 + 242 reserves	1.61 bn	Parliamentary executive	Non-perm. member SC Jan. 1991–	Pro-Coalition but low profile
Bahrain	Manama	0.62	0.442	90+	4.01	7.5	184 m	Absolute monarchy	-	Contributed troops and aircraft to coalition force
Bangladesh	Dacca	144.0	104.1	80	20.34 (1989)	106.5	326.9 m	Limited presidential – military still influential – only limited democracy in practice	-	Sent troops to Coalition force
Belgium	Brussels	30.51	9.868	2.4	194.6	485.5 + 234 reserves	2.58 bn (1989)	Parliamentary executive	Non-perm. member SC Jan. 1991–	Sent naval contribution (under WEA command)

Country	Capital	Area (,000 km²)[a]	Population (m)[a]	Muslim (%)[b]	GDP 1990/1 ($bn)[c]	Military forces 1990/1 (,000s)[c]	Military expenditure 1990/1 ($p.a.)[c]	Political regime[a]	UN status	Stance on Gulf
Canada	Ottawa	9,975.22	25.625	-	591.98	86.6 + 30 reserves	9.4 bn (1989)	Parliamentary executive	Non-perm. member SC 1990	Sent naval contribution
China	Beijing	9,561.0	1050.0	1	363.8	3,030 + 1,200 reserves	5.86 bn (1988)	Communist executive	Permanent member SC	Acquiesced in US SC diplomacy; abstained on Res. 678
Cuba	Havana	114.5	10.2	-	33.84	180 + 135 reserves	1.83 bn (1989)	Communist executive	Non-perm. member SC 1990–1	Pro-Iraq; voted against SC Res. 678 but complied with SC sanctions order
Czechoslovakia	Prague	127.9	15.5	-	123.1 (1989)	198 + 295 reserves	2.94 bn (1989)	Limited presidential executive	-	Contributed troops to Coalition force

Country	Capital	Area (,000 km²)[a]	Population (m)[a]	Muslim (%)[b]	GDP 1990/1 ($bn)[c]	Military forces 1990/1 (,000s)[c]	Military expenditure 1990/1 ($p.a.)[c]	Political regime[a]	UN status	Stance on Gulf
Denmark	Copenhagen	43.1	5.09	0.6	130.89	29.4 + 72.7 reserves	2.6 bn	Parliamentary executive	-	Contributed a vessel to naval force
Egypt	Cairo	1,001.5	50.5	93	39.5 (1989)	420 + 604 reserves	4.27 bn	Limited presidential executive	-	Crucial Arab member of Coalition; contributed troops
France	Paris	547.03	55.4	3.0	1,187.15	453.1 + 419 reserves	28.58 bn (1989)	Dual executive	Perm. member of SC	Prominent member of Coalition forces; contribution to ground, air and naval forces
Germany	Bonn	375.0	78.4	2.1	1,499.54	469 + 853 reserves	31.02 bn	Parliamentary executive	-	Ships deployed in eastern Med.

Country	Capital	Area (,000 km²)[a]	Population (m)[a]	Muslim (%)[b]	GDP 1990/1 ($bn)[c]	Military forces 1990/1 (,000s)[c]	Military expenditure 1990/1 ($p.a.)[c]	Political regime[a]	UN status	Stance on Gulf
Greece	Athens	131.9	9.95	1.4	67.16	158 + 406 reserves	3.79 bn	Parliamentary executive	-	Contributed a vessel to naval force
India	New Delhi	3,287.6	785.0	11.3	272.88 (1989)	1,265 + 160 reserves	8.94 bn (1989)	Parliamentary executive	Non-perm. member SC 1991–2	Pro-Coalition but low profile
Iran	Teheran	1,648.0	46.6	99	59.49	528 + 350 reserves	3.77 bn	Unlimited presidential executive (legally pluralist but effectively one party)	-	Anti Iraq and anti US; wanted a 'regional solution'
Iraq	Baghdad	444.0	16.27	95	58.53 (1989)	382 + 650 reserves	12.8 bn (1988)	Unlimited presidential; effectively one-party 'socialist'	-	Major belligerent

Country	Capital	Area (,000 km²)[a]	Population (m)[a]	Muslim (%)[b]	GDP 1990/1 ($bn)[c]	Military forces 1990/1 (,000s)[c]	Military expenditure 1990/1 ($p.a.)[c]	Political regime[a]	UN status	Stance on Gulf
Israel	Jerusalem	20.70	4.21	16	51.22	141 + 504 reserves	6.16 bn	Parliamentary executive	-	Anti-Iraq; pro-Coalition, was prevailed upon by US not to get involved.
Italy	Rome	301.28	57.23	0.3	1090.75	361.4 + 504 reserves	18.97 bn	Parliamentary executive	-	Contributed air and naval forces to the Coalition
Japan	Tokyo	371.86	121.4	-	2,971.20	246 + 50 reserves	28.406 bn (1988)	Parliamentary executive	-	Pro-Coalition; but was reluctant to support military action. Paid for a large part of it!
Jordan	Amman	98.00	3.52	95	3.87	101 + 35 reserves	571.21 m	Absolute executive (monarchy)	-	Difficult situation, opposed invasion, had to be pro-Iraq

Country	Capital	Area (,000 km²)[a]	Population (m)[a]	Muslim (%)[b]	GDP 1990/1 ($bn)[c]	Military forces 1990/1 (,000s)[c]	Military expenditure 1990/1 ($p.a.)[c]	Political regime[a]	UN status	Stance on Gulf
Kuwait	Kuwait City	19.0	1.77	91	25.31	8.2	1.504 bn	Absolute executive (monarchy)	-	Victim of Iraqi aggression; contributed ground, air and naval forces
Libya	Tripoli	1,759.5	3.9	95	28.96	85 + 40 reserves	1.51 bn	Unlimited presidential executive	-	Pro-Iraq but kept low profile
Malaysia	Kuala Lumpur	332.4	15.82	55	41.26	128 + 40 reserves	2.0 bn	Parliamentary executive (constitutional monarchy)	Non perm. member SC 1989–90	Pro-Coalition but low profile
Morocco	Marrakesh	458.7	23.7	98	25.36	195 + 100 reserves	121 bn (1989)	Dual executive (monarch holds near absolute power)	-	Contributed troops

Country	Capital	Area (,000 km²)[a]	Population (m)[a]	Muslim (%)[b]	GDP 1990/1 ($bn)[c]	Military forces 1990/1 (,000s)[c]	Military expenditure 1990/1 ($p.a.)[c]	Political regime[a]	UN status	Stance on Gulf
Netherlands	The Hague	34.0	14.48	2.8	278.76	101.4 + 152.4 reserves	7.464 bn	Parliamentary executive	-	Contributed naval forces under WEU command
Niger	Niamiey	1,267.0	6.72	97	1.93 (1989)	3.3 + 3.3 reserves	17.21 m (1989)	Military executive	-	Contributed troops
Norway	Oslo	323.9	4.17	0.3	106.82	32.7 + 285 reserves	2.97 bn (1989)	Parliamentary executive (constitutional monarchy)	-	Contributed a naval vessel to Coalition
Oman	Abu Dhabi	212.0	1.27	91	9.16	30.4	1.44 bn	Absolute executive (monarchy)	-	Contributed troops and aircraft
Pakistan	Islamabad	803.9	102.2	95	39.73	565 + 513 reserves	2.91 bn	Parliamentary executive	-	Contributed troops

Country	Capital	Area (,000 km²)ᵃ	Population (m)ᵃ	Muslim (%)ᵇ	GDP 1990/1 ($bn)ᶜ	Military forces 1990/1 (,000s)ᶜ	Military expenditure 1990/1 ($p.a.)ᶜ	Political regimeᵃ	UN status	Stance on Gulf
Poland	Warsaw	312.68	37.5	0.04	172.78 (1989)	312 + 505 reserves	3.23 bn (1989)	Limited presidential executive	-	Contributed 2 vessels to Coalition naval forces
Portugal	Lisbon	92.1	16.6	0.2	59.85	61.8 + 190 reserves	1.25 bn (1989)	Dual executive	-	Contributed 1 vessel (under WEU command)
Qatar	Doha	11.44	0.31	91	7.05	7.5	934.07 m	Absolute executive (monarchy)	-	Contributed troops and aircraft to Coalition force
Saudi Arabia	Riyadh	2,150.0	11.52	99	87.97	76.5	14.69 bn (1989)	Absolute executive (monarchy)	-	Major Arab member of Coalition; contributed troops and aircraft

Country	Capital	Area (,000 km²)a	Population (m)a	Muslim (%)b	GDP 1990/1 ($bn)c	Military forces 1990/1 (,000s)c	Military expenditure 1990/1 ($p.a.)c	Political regimea	UN status	Stance on Gulf
Senegal	Dakar	197.0	6.90	91	4.63 (1989)	9.7	94.95 m (1989)	Unlimited presidential (legally pluralist but effectively one-party socialist)	-	Contributed troops
Spain	Madrid	504.9	39.07	0.03	484.54	257.4 + 2,400 reserves	6.91 bn (1989)	Parliamentary executive (constitutional monarchy)	-	Contributed to naval forces under WEU command
Sudan	Khartoum	2,505.8	22.07	73	11.03	71.5	460 m (1989)	Military executive	-	Pro-Iraq, but low profile.
Syria	Damascus	185.18	10.96	80	16.21 (1989)	404 + 400 reserves	1.62 bn (1989)	Unlimited presidential executive (legally pluralist, but effectively one-party socialist)	-	Important Arab member of Coalition; contributed troops

Country	Capital	Area (,000 km^2)[a]	Population (m)[a]	Muslim (%)[b]	GDP 1990/1 ($bn)[c]	Military forces 1990/1 (,000s)[c]	Military expenditure 1990/1 ($p.a.)[c]	Political regime[a]	UN status	Stance on Gulf
Tunisia	Tunis	164.15	7.26	90	12.42	35	400.77 m	Limited presidential executive	-	Pro-Coalition
Turkey	Ankara	779.45	51.819	95	114.29	647 + 1,107 reserves	2.10 bn (1989)	Limited presidential executive	-	Pro-Coalition (NATO member)
UAE	Abu Dhabi	83.60	1.33	91	27.27 (1989)	44	1.59 bn	Absolute executive (monarchy)	-	Contributed troops and aircraft
UK	London	244.1	56.5	1.4	986.72	306 + 340 reserves	31.6 bn (1989)	Parliamentary executive (constitutional monarchy)	Perm. member SC	Major Coalition partner of US; contributed ground, air and naval forces

Country	Capital	Area (,000 km²)[a]	Population (m)[a]	Muslim (%)[b]	GDP 1990/1 ($bn)[c]	Military forces 1990/1 (,000s)[c]	Military expenditure 1990/1 ($p.a.)[c]	Political regime[a]	UN status	Stance on Gulf
US	Washington DC	9,372.57	241.0	0.6	5,423.4	2,029 + 1,721 reserves	289.76 bn	Limited presidential executive	Perm. member SC	Coalition leader who shouldered vast proportion of Coalition military effort
USSR (as it then was)	Moscow	22,402	280.0	16.	2,105.88 (1989)	3,440 + 5,239 reserves	119.44 bn	Communist executive (at time of Gulf crisis)	Perm. member SC	Collaborated with US in security council diplomacy
Yemeni Republic	Aden	531.57	8.60	99	9.0 (Joint N and S Yemen)	65 + 40 reserves	1.00 bn	Limited presidential (in process of establishing democratic institutions)	Non-perm. member SC 1990–1	Pro-Iraq: voted against SC Res. 678, but complied with sanctions order

a Dennis Derbyshire and Ian Derbyshire, *World Political Systems: An Introduction to Comparative Government* (Edinburgh: Chambers, 1991).
b Mainly from Chris Harris and Peter Chippendale, *What is Islam?* (London: W.H. Allen, 1990); Ceri Peach, 'The New Islamic Presence in Europe', *Geography Preview* 5 (3), January 1992, pp. 2–6.
c International Institute for Strategic Studies, *Military Balance*, (London: IISS, 1992).

APPENDIX II CHRONOLOGY OF THE GULF CONFLICT

2 Aug. 1990	Iraq invades Kuwait under pretext of aiding Kuwaiti revolutionaries; UN Security Council condemns Iraq in Resolution 660; joint US–Soviet statement calling for Iraqi withdrawal; Iraqi and Kuwaiti overseas assets frozen by US, Britain and France; Soviet Union stops arms deliveries to Iraq.
3 Aug.	Iraqi troops on Kuwait–Saudi border; US naval force bound for Gulf; Arab League condemns Iraqi action at a meeting in Cairo in which five members abstained and Libya left the meeting; contingent of Egyptian troops sent to Saudi Arabia.
4 Aug.	Iraq moves seized British servicemen from Kuwait to Baghdad.
5 Aug.	President Bush declares Iraqi aggression 'will not stand'.
6 Aug.	UN Security Council Resolution 661 (mandatory sanctions on Iraq); Saddam Hussein says he has no intention of invading Saudi Arabia; US Defence Secretary Cheney meets King Fahd of Saudi Arabia urging him to request US troops.
7 Aug.	US troops and aircraft sent to Saudi Arabia; US agrees to write off Egypt's military debts to US; Israel warns Jordan of its response if Iraqi troops enter Jordan.
8 Aug.	Iraq annexes Kuwait as its nineteenth province; US reiterates the defensive role of US troops in Saudi Arabia.
9 Aug.	UN Security Council Resolution 662 declares annexation illegal.
10 Aug.	Saddam Hussein calls for an Arab/Islamic rising against foreign intervention in Saudi Arabia; majority of Arab League condemns Iraq and approves sending of Arab troops to help Saudi Arabia.

11 Aug.	First British force arrives in Saudi Arabia.
12 Aug.	Iraqi peace overtures to Iran; Saddam Hussein offers Iraqi withdrawal in context of general withdrawal of Israel from occupied Palestine and Syria from Lebanon; President Bush rejects offer.
14 Aug.	Iran and Iraq reach deal for exchange of prisoners, Iraqi withdrawal from Iranian territory.
17 Aug.	Iraq detains citizens of 'aggressive nations' – this includes western and Japanese nationals; western navies begin blockade of Iraq.
18 Aug.	Tariq Aziz, Iraqi Foreign Minister, says Iraq would use chemical weapons only if attacked with nuclear weapons; UN Resolution 664 demands release of 'hostages'; British nationals moved from Kuwait.
19 Aug.	Saddam Hussein attempts to bargain foreign nationals for American withdrawal from Saudi Arabia and pledge not to attack Iraq; Americans refuse.
21 Aug.	Syria declares it is sending troops to Saudi Arabia.
23 Aug.	Saddam Hussein offers release of hostages and withdrawal from Kuwait in return for lifting of blockade and access to islands of Warba and Bubiyan.
25 Aug.	UN Security Council Resolution 665 authorises 'commensurate measures' to enforce enconomic embargo on Iraq.
31 Aug.	Talks between Tariq Aziz and Perez de Cuellar, UN Secretary-General, are unproductive; Arab League meeting supports UN resolutions.
5 Sept	Saddam Hussein calls for holy war and overthrow of King Fahd of Saudi Arabia and President Mubarak of Egypt; Tariq Aziz meets President Gorbachev in Moscow.
6 Sept	Britain to send ground forces.

9 Sept	Joint Bush–Gorbachev demand for unconditional Iraqi withdrawal from Kuwait and release of hostages.
10 Sept	Saddam Hussein offers Third World countries free oil as long as they use their own transport.
16 Sept	UN Security Council resolution condemning Iraqi violation of diplomatic premises and personnel in Kuwait.
17 Sept	Iraq offers withdrawal for conference on Palestine problem.
23 Sept	Saddam Hussein issues threats against Middle East oil-fields and against Israel
25 Sept	UN Security Council Resolution 670 imposes air blockade; first indication that Soviet Union might support the use of force.
1 Oct.	President Bush, speaking at UN, declares US wants peaceful solution, saying that Iraqi withdrawal must come before any consideration of problems between Iraq and Kuwait.
3 Oct.	Soviet Union launches diplomatic efforts to resolve crisis.
5 Oct.	Yevgeny Primakov, Soviet envoy with long experience of Iraq, meets Saddam Hussein and says political solution is possible.
21 Oct.	Edward Heath, former British prime minister, secures release of elderly and sick British hostages.
25 Oct.	American Commander Schwarzkopf asks for doubling of US troops in Saudi Arabia.
29 Oct.	UN Security Council Resolution 674 holds Iraq responsible for any breaches of Geneva and Vienna Conventions.
4 Nov.	Secretary of State Baker tours Europe and Middle East to discuss military option.
6 Nov.	US mid-term elections.

8 Nov.	President Bush announces large troops reinforcements for Saudi Arabia, to bring strength to 430,000.
9 Nov.	Former German chancellor, Willy Brandt, secures release of some 206 western hostages.
15 Nov.	US–Saudi joint military manoeuvres south of Kuwait.
16 Nov.	Baker begins canvassing Security Council members on 'use of force' resolution.
18 Nov.	Saddam Hussein announces 'drip-feed' release of hostages over three-month period up to 25 March 1991.
19 Nov.	Iraq reinforces troops in KTO by 100,000.
21 Nov.	President Bush meets Kuwaiti leader Shaikh Jaber al Sabah and Saudi King Fahd in Saudi Arabia.
22 Nov.	President Bush visits US troops in Saudi Arabia; Britain announces troop reinforcements.
23 Nov.	President Bush meets President Mubarak of Egypt and President Assad of Syria.
26 Nov.	President Gorbachev urges Iraq to withdraw from Kuwait.
27 Nov.	President Gorbachev supports the use of force.
28 Nov.	Gulf states aid package for Soviet Union being negotiated in Moscow; Margaret Thatcher replaced by John Major as British prime minister.
29 Nov.	UN Security Council Resolution 678 authorises 'all necessary means' to secure Iraqi compliance with Security Council resolutions after 15 January 1991
30 Nov.	President Bush invites Iraqi Foreign Secretary to Washington for talks and suggests US Secretary of State goes to Baghdad for talks with Saddam Hussein.
1 Dec.	Iraq accepts US offer of talks.

6 Dec.	Saddam Hussein decides to release all hostages.
15 Dec.	Proposed meeting between James Baker and Tariq Aziz in Washington called off.
16 Dec.	Soviet Union arranges evacuation of all its personnel in Iraq.
17 Dec.	EC foreign ministers cancel invitation for talks with Tariq Aziz.
20 Dec.	Shevardnadze forced to resign as Soviet Foreign Minister by internal criticism of his Gulf stance.
24 Dec.	Saddam Hussein says Israel would be first target in event of war.
25 Dec.	Israeli prime minister, Shamir, promises severe retaliation if attacked by Iraq.
4 Jan.	Iraq agrees to Aziz–Baker talks in Geneva 9 January.
7 Jan.	Saddam Hussein predicts 'the Mother of Battles' in the event of war.
9 Jan.	Aziz–Baker talks fail.
10 Jan.	Baker tours capitals of Coalition allies confirming Coalition military action against Iraq soon after the expiry of the UN deadline of 15 January.
11 Jan.	US pressures Israel not to respond if attacked by Iraq.
12 Jan.	US Congress votes narrowly in favour of military action.
13 Jan.	UN Secretary-General Perez de Cuellar in Baghdad fails to persuade Saddam Hussein to withdraw from Kuwait.
14 Jan.	French decide not to respond to Saddam Hussein's invitation to French Foreign Minister to visit Baghdad for talks.
16 Jan.	UN deadline expires.
17 Jan.	Coalition air campaign begins. (0300 hrs local time)

18 Jan.	First Iraqi Scud missile attack on Israel.
20 Jan.	Iraq parades captured Coalition airmen on TV; US Defence Secretary Cheney declares US aim to force Iraqis out of Kuwait and to destroy Iraqi military capability.
23 Jan.	Iraq begins leaking oil into Persian Gulf.
28 Jan.	Iraqi air force begins evacuating to Iran.
29 Jan.	Iraqi assault on Khafji; French defence minister Chévènement resigns in protest at Coalition war aims.
1 Feb.	Iraqis forced out of Khafji; Iran declares it will fight with Iraq if Israel joins war.
2 Feb.	Egypt and Saudi Arabia agree that they will not take the war onto Iraqi territory.
6 Feb.	Iraq breaks off diplomatic relations with the major Coalition members.
12 Feb.	US aircraft bomb Amiriya bunker in Baghdad.
21 Feb.	Iraq 'accepts' Soviet peace plan.
22 Feb.	President Bush rejects Soviet peace plan and puts counter-proposal, which included complete Iraqi withdrawal within one week starting 1700 23 February, and no attacking withdrawing Iraqi troops.
23 Feb.	US and other major Coalition members reject Gorbachev request to delay ground offensive.
24 Feb.	Coalition ground offensive begins.
25 Feb.	Iraq Scud missile kills twenty-six US servicemen at Dhahran.
27 Feb.	Kuwait City liberated; retreating Iraqi troops pursued and attacked from the air; letter from Tariq Aziz to UN Security Council accepting Resolutions 660, 662 and 674; Security Council permanent members demand unconditional acceptance of all resolutions relevant to the crisis.

28 Feb.   Temporary cease-fire declared by US after Iraqi
             acceptance of conditions.

3 Mar.   Cease-fire talks held.

Sources: The Times; Bruce Watson, Bruce George, Peter Tsouras and
            B.L. Cyr, *Military Lessons of the Gulf War* (London: Greenhill
            Books, 1991); Dilip Hiro, *Desert Shield to Desert Storm* (London:
            Paladin, 1992).

APPENDIX III MAPS

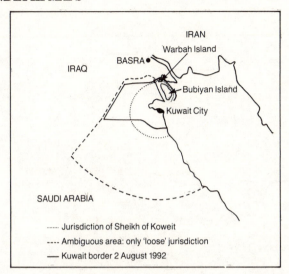

Map 1   Map showing the unclear historical designation of Koweit
compared with Kuwait's present boundaries. Adapted from
a map annexed to unratified convention of 1913

Source: E. Lauterpacht, J. Greenwood, M. Weller and D. Bethlehem (1991)
The Kuwait Crisis: Basic Documents, Cambridge: Grotius
Publications.

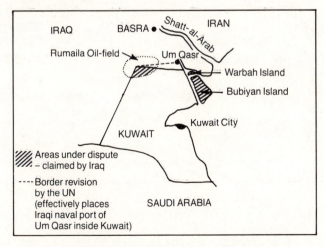

Map 2   Areas under dispute as at 1 August 1990 and border
revision post-Gulf War, 1991

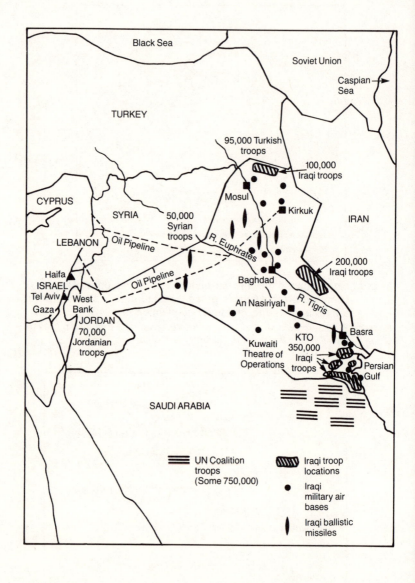

Map 3 Troop deployments and Iraqi military targets as at 16 January 1991

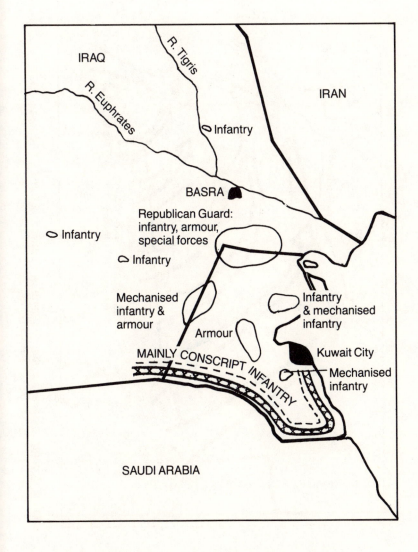

Map 4 Disposition of Iraqi troops in the Kuwaiti Theatre of
Operations as at 16 January 1991

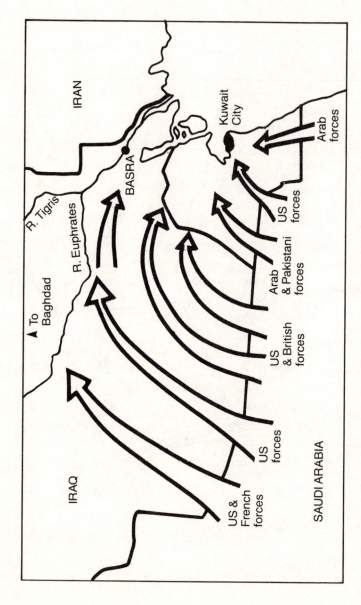

Map 5 Ground operations of the Gulf land war between 24 and 27 February 1991

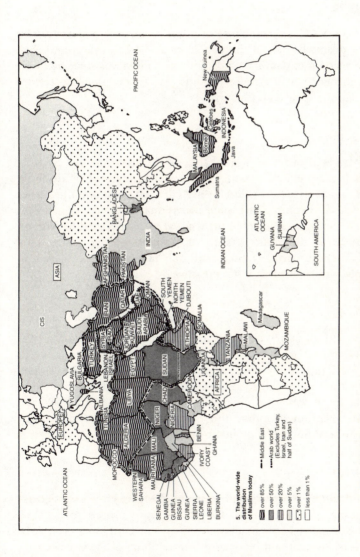

Map 6 The Middle East, the Arab World and the Muslim diaspora
Source: Figures for the Muslim diaspora are taken from M. Ruthven (1984) *Islam in the World*, Harmondsworth: Penguin.

APPENDIX IV DOCUMENTS

UN CHARTER CHAPTER VII: ACTION WITH RESPECT TO THREATS TO THE PEACE, BREACHES OF THE PEACE, AND ACTS OF AGGRESSION

Article 39

The Security Council shall determine the existence of any threat to the peace, breach of the peace, or act of aggression and shall make recommendations, or decide what measures shall be taken in accordance with Articles 41 and 42, to maintain or restore international peace and security.

Article 40

In order to prevent an aggravation of the situation, the Security Council may, before making the recommendations or deciding upon the measures provided for in Article 39, call upon the parties concerned to comply with such provisional measures as it deems necessary or desirable. Such provisional measures shall be without prejudice to the rights, claims or position of the parties concerned. The Security Council shall duly take account of failure to comply with such provisional measures.

Article 41

The Security Council may decide what measures not involving the use of armed force are to be employed to give effect to its decisions, and it may call upon the Members of the United Nations to apply such measures. These may include complete or partial interruption of economic relations and of rail, sea, air, postal, telegraphic, radio, and other means of communication, and the severance of diplomatic relations.

Article 42

Should the Security Council consider that measures provided for in Article 41 would be inadequate or have proved to be inadequate, it may take such action by air, sea or land forces as may be necessary to maintain or restore international peace and security.

Such action may include demonstrations, blockade, and other operations by air, sea or land forces of Members of the United Nations.

Article 43

1 All members of the United Nations, in order to contribute to the maintenance of international peace and security, undertake to make available to the Security Council, on its call and in accordance with a special agreement or agreements, armed forces, assistance and facilities, including rights of passage, necessary for the purpose of maintaining international peace and security.

2 Such agreement or agreements shall govern the numbers and types of forces, their degree of readiness and general location, and the nature of the facilities and assistance to be provided.

3 The agreement or agreements shall be negotiated as soon as possible on the initiative of the Security Council. They shall be concluded between the Security Council and members or between the Security Council and groups of Members and shall be subject to ratification by the signatory states in accordance with their respective constitutional processes.

Article 44

When the Security Council has decided to use force it shall, before calling upon a Member not represented on it to provide armed forces in fulfilment of the obligations assumed under Article 43, invite that Member, if the Member so desires, to participate in the decisions of the Security Council concerning the employment of contingents of that Member's armed forces.

Article 45

In order to enable the United Nations to take urgent military measures, Members shall hold immediately available national air-force contingents for combined international enforcement action. The strength and degree of readiness of these contingents and plans for their combined action shall be determined, within the limits laid down in the special agreement or agreements referred to in Article 43, by the Security Council with the assistance of the Military Staff Committee.

Article 46

Plans for the application of armed force shall be made by the Security Council with the assistance of the Military Staff Committee.

Article 47

1 There shall be established a Military Staff Committee to advise and assist the Security Council on all questions relating to the Security Council's military requirements for the maintenance of international peace and security, the employment and command of forces placed at its disposal, the regulation of armaments, and possible disarmament.

2 The Military Staff Committee shall consist of the Chiefs of Staff of the permanent members of the Security Council or their representatives. Any Member of the United Nations not permanently represented on the Committee shall be invited by the Committee to be associated with it when the efficient discharge of the Committee's responsibilities requires the participation of that Member in its work.

3 The Military Staff Committee shall be responsible under the Security Council for the strategic direction of any armed forces placed at the disposal of the Security Council. Questions relating to the command of such forces shall be worked out subsequently.

4 The Military Staff Committee, with the authorisation of the Security Council and after consultation with appropriate regional agencies, may establish regional sub-committees.

Article 48

1 The action required to carry out the decisions of the Security Council for the maintenance of international peace and security shall be taken by all the Members of the United Nations or by some of them, as the Security Council may determine.

2 Such decisions shall be carried out by the Members of the United Nations directly and through their action in the appropriate international agencies of which they are members.

Article 49

The Members of the United Nations shall join in affording mutual assistance in carrying out the measures decided upon by the Security Council.

Article 50

If preventive or enforcement measures against any state are taken by the Security Council, any other state, whether a Member of the United Nations or not, which finds itself confronted with special economic problems arising from the carrying out of those measures shall have the right to consult the Security Council with regard to a solution of those problems.

Article 51

Nothing in the present Charter shall impair the inherent right of individual or collective self-defence if an armed attack occurs against a Member of the United Nations, until the Security Council has taken the measures necessary to maintain international peace and security. Measures taken by Members in the exercise of this right of self-defence shall be immediately reported to the Security Council and shall not in any way affect the authority and responsibility of the Security Council under the present Charter to take at any time such action as it deems necessary in order to maintain or restore international peace and security.

SECURITY COUNCIL RESOLUTIONS RELATING TO THE GULF CONFLICT

Resolution 660: 2 August 1990

Defines the existence of a breach of international peace and security; condemns Iraq's invasion of Kuwait; demands Iraq withdraw forces to positions occupied on 1 August 1990; calls upon

Iraq and Kuwait to begin negotiation for resolution of their differences.

Resolution 661: 6 August 1990

Determines to end the Iraqi occupation of Kuwait and to restore
its sovereign independence; imposes mandatory sanctions against
Iraq and Kuwait; calls on members to protect Kuwaiti assets and
not to recognise any regime set up by the occupying power.

Resolution 662: 9 August 1990

Declares that Iraqi annexation of Kuwait has no legal validity and
demands that Iraq rescinds its act of annexation.

Resolution 664: 18 August 1990

Demands Iraq allows departure from Iraq and Kuwait of third-state
nationals and allows continuing access of consular officials to such
nationals.

Resolution 665: 25 August 1990

Expresses alarm at Iraq's continuing refusal to comply with previous resolutions; calls upon member states having maritime forces
in the area to take commensurate measures to stop inward and
outward shipping to Iraq and Kuwait.

Resolution 666: 13 September 1990

Establishes Iraq's responsibilities under international humanitarian law towards third-state nationals; makes provision for
humanitarian supplies to Iraq and Kuwait if necessary.

Resolution 667: 16 September 1990

Condemns and expresses outrage at Iraqi violations of diplomatic
premises and abduction of diplomats and foreign nationals in
Kuwait; holds Iraq responsible for acts of violence against such
persons and premises; demands release of foreign nationals and
Iraqi protection of diplomatic personnel and premises.

Resolution 669: 24 September 1990

Makes provision for assisting member states who suffer economic costs as a result of implementing Resolution 661 on mandatory sanctions.

Resolution 670: 25 September 1990

Reinforces the provisions of Resolution 661 and extends the blockade to air as well as land and sea access to Iraq and Kuwait; reminds states of their obligations under Resolution 661.

Resolution 674: 20 October 1990

Demands Iraq ceases taking Kuwaiti and third-state nationals as hostages; reminds Iraq of its liabilities under international law for loss, damage and injury as a result of the invasion and occupation of Kuwait.

Resolution 677: 28 November 1990

Mandates the Secretary-General of the United Nations to take possession of a copy of the Kuwaiti register of population (in order to substantiate in due course disappearance of Kuwaitis or the influx of non-Kuwaitis as a result of Iraqi policy while in occupation of Kuwait).

Resolution 678: 29 November 1990

Sets down a deadline of 15 January 1991 by which time 'all necessary means' may be used to implement Resolution 660 and to restore international peace and security in the area

Resolution 686: 2 March 1991

Notes the suspension of offensive combat operations by the UN Coalition members; asserts the importance of Iraq taking the measures necessary to bring about a 'definitive end to the hostilities'; sets down the conditions of the cease-fire and reaffirms the continued effectiveness of the provisions of Resolution 678 (all necessary means) while those conditions have not been met.

Resolution 687: 3 April 1991

Inter alia sets up commission to demarcate the Iraq–Kuwait border; guarantees the inviolability of the resultant boundary; establishes a UN observer unit; provides for the withdrawal of member states' military presence in Iraq; requests Iraqi reaffirmation of their obligations under the Geneva Protocol regarding chemical and biological weapons; provides for the destruction of such weapons, research programmes and manufacturing capabilities related to them; provides for the destruction of Iraqi ballistic missiles with a range greater than 150 kilometres together with relevant production facilities; provides the mechanism by which this destruction shall take place; demands unconditional Iraqi agreement not to use, develop, construct or acquire any of these weapons; requires unconditional Iraqi agreement not to acquire or develop nuclear weapons; provides for on-site inspection to ensure Iraqi compliance; sets up compensation fund for victims of Iraqi invasion and occupation of Kuwait; declares the issue remains on the agenda of the Security Council and establishes its willingness to take such further steps as may be required for the implementation of this resolution and to secure peace and security in the area.

Resolution 689: 9 April 1991

Provides for the review of the continuation of the UN observer unit every six months.

APPENDIX V STATISTICS OF THE GULF WAR

Contributions to Coalition ground forces

Afghanistan	300 mujahedin (i.e. the anti-government guerrilla movement)
Bahrain	3,500 troops
Bangladesh	2,000 troops
Czechoslovakia	350 men in chemical protection unit + 170 army troops
Egypt	40,000 troops; 400 tanks; 300 artillery pieces
France	13,500 troops; 110 tanks; 2,500 vehicles; 120 helicopters
Kuwait	7,000 troops
Morocco	2,000 troops
Niger	400 troops
Oman	2,500 troops
Pakistan	10,000 troops
Qatar	4,000 troops; 24 tanks
Saudi Arabia	95,000 troops; 550 tanks
Senegal	500 troops
Syria	20,000 troops
UAE	4,000 troops
United Kingdom	35,000 troops; 300 tanks; including extensive artillery, specialist, logistic and support personnel and equipment
United States	532,000 troops; 2,000 tanks; including very extensive artillery, specialist, logistic and support personnel and equipment

Coalition ground force losses

United States	148 killed
	458 wounded
United Kingdom	47 killed
	43 wounded
France	2 killed
	25 wounded
Egypt	14 killed
	120 wounded

Contributions to Coalition air forces combat aircraft

Bahrain	24	
Canada	24	
France	42	
Italy	10	
Kuwait	18	
Oman	20	
Qatar	12	
Saudi Arabia	175	
UAE	50	
United Kingdom	69	
Total non-US		444
United States	1,376	1,376
TOTAL		1,820

Coalition aircraft losses:

Combat losses	43
Non-combat losses	18

Contributions to Coalition naval forces

United States	8 aircraft carriers
	5 submarines
	2 battleships
	20 cruisers
	20 destroyers
	22 frigates
	35 amphibious ships
	4 mine warfare ships
	56 auxiliaries
	numerous aircraft squadrons
United Kingdom	5 destroyers
	6 frigates
	8 minehunters
	5 logistics landing ships
	2 ocean survey ships
	6 replenishment ships
	6 air squadrons
	3 helicopter groups

France	13 ships including 1 aircraft carrier, 2 destroyers, 4 frigates (under WEU command)
Italy	9 ships (under WEU command)
Australia	4 ships
Argentina	2 ships
Belgium	5 ships (under WEU command)
Canada	3 ships
Denmark	1 ship
Gemany	19 ships (in Mediterranean)
Greece	1 ship
Kuwait	3 sea craft
Netherlands	5 ships (under WEU command)
Norway	1 ship
Poland	2 ships
Portugal	1 ship (under WEU command)
Spain	3 ships (under WEU command)

Coalition naval losses

No Coalition ships were destroyed but two US ships were damaged by mines.

Iraqi ground forces in Kuwait Theatre of Operations (KTO)

It was originally estimated that over half a million Iraqi troops had been moved into the KTO but subsequent re-estimates put the figure closer to 300,000; some 1,000 tanks plus extensive artillery, support and specialist personnel and equipment.

Iraqi ground force losses

It is estimated that between 60,000 and 100,000 Iraqi military personnel were killed or wounded in action.

Iraqi combat air forces

16 bombers
647 fighters/ground attack/reconnaissance

Iraqi air losses

Of the total above, 127 were confirmed destroyed, 141 were estimated destroyed and 148 were flown to Iran.

Iraqi naval vessels

Some 87 vessels in all comprising one frigate, 7 missile attack boats, 3 submarine chasers, 6 fast attack boats, 32 patrol boats, 9 minesweepers, 3 landing ships, 3 cargo ships.

Iraqi naval losses

Many of these vessels were very heavily damaged or destroyed during hostilities.

Source: All of these figures have been derived from Bruce Watson, Bruce George, Peter Tsouras and B.L. Cyr, *Military Lessons of the Gulf War* (London: Greenhill Books, 1991), Appendices D, E and F.

Notes

INTRODUCTION

1 Michael Howard, *The Causes of War* (London: Unwin, 1984), pp. 7–22.
2 Karl Popper, *A World of Propensities* (Bristol: Thoemmes, 1990).
3 Kwame Nkrumah, the first president of the newly-independent Ghana was among the first to use the term in his book *Neo-Colonialism: The Last Stage of Imperialism* (London: Nelson, 1965).
4 Edward Said, *Orientalism: Western Concepts of the Orient* (London: Routledge & Kegan Paul, 1978); Rana Kabbani, *Europe's Myths of the Orient: Devise and Rule* (London: Macmillan, 1978).
5 Said, *op cit.*, pp. 223–4.
6 See, for example, Bryan Wilson (ed.), *Rationality* (Oxford: Basil Blackwell, 1970); Martin Hollis and Steven Lukes (eds), *Rationality and Relativism* (Oxford: Basil Blackwell, 1982); Ernest Gellner, *Legitimation of Belief* (Cambridge: Cambridge University Press, 1974); Alasdair Macintyre, 'Is a Science of Comparative Politics Possible?' in Alan Ryan (ed.), *The Philosophy of Social Explanation* (Oxford: Oxford University Press, 1973).
7 For example, John Stoessinger, *Why Nations Go to War*, 5th edn. (New York: St Martin's Press, 1990), pp. 213–14.

1 THE MIDDLE EAST IN HISTORICAL CONTEXT

1 Richard Burton and Charles Doughty are perhaps the most prominent but by no means the only nineteenth-century European travellers whose writings have formed the basis of the western idea of the Arabs, Islam and the Middle East. T.E. Lawrence ('Lawrence of Arabia') and Wilfred Thesiger may be regarded as the twentieth-century inheritors of the Burton/Doughty tradition.
2 Malise Ruthven, *Islam in the World*, 2nd edn, (Harmondsworth: Penguin Books, 1991).
3 Chris Horrie and Peter Chippindale, *What is Islam?* (London: W.H. Allen/The Observer, 1990).
4 Horrie and Chippindale, *op cit.*, p. 160.

5 Ernest Gellner, 'Islam and Marxism' *International Affairs* 67(1), January 1991, p.2.
6 There is a distinct literature in political science and political sociology on 'charismatic leadership'. For example, Jean Lacouture, *Demi-Gods: Charismatic Leadership in the Third World* (London: Secker & Warburg, 1971).
7 An excellent recent treatment is Anthony Smith, *National Identity* (Harmondsworth: Penguin Books, 1991).
8 See Fouad Ajemi, 'The Summer of Arab Discontent', *Foreign Affairs*, Winter 1990/1., pp. 1–20.
9 Hedley Bull and Adam Watson (eds), *The Expansion of International Society* (Oxford: Clarendon Press, 1984).
10 Iliya Harik, 'The Origins of the Arab State System', in Giacomo Luciani (ed.), *The Arab State* (London: Routledge, 1990).
11 Michael Hudson, *Arab Politics: The Search for Legitimacy* (London: Yale University Press, 1978), p. 272.
12 *Ibid.*
13 Peter Mansfield, *The Arabs* (Harmondsworth: Penguin Books, 1985), pp. 219–20.
14 Sir Anthony Eden, *Memoirs: Full Circle* (London: Cassell, 1960), pp. 423–4.
15 L. Carl Brown, *Intenational Politics and the Middle East: Old Rules Dangerous Game* (London: Princeton University Press, 1984), p. 150.
16 An introductory treatment of the European 'imperial retreat' is R.F. Holland, *European Decolonisation 1918–1981: An Introductory Survey* (Basingstoke: Macmillan, 1985)
17 Hugh Thomas, *The Suez Affair* (London: Weidenfeld & Nicolson, 1967).
18 Francis Fukuyama, *The End of History and the Last Man* (New York: Free Press, 1992).

2 CRISIS: THE PROVOCATION AND THE PROTAGONISTS

1 Michael Hudson, *Arab Politics: The Search for Legitimacy* (London: Yale Unversity Press, 1978), p.268.
2 Samir al-Khalil, *Republic Of Fear* (London: Hutchinson Radius, 1989), p. 149.
3 Hudson, *op cit*, p. 263.
4 *Ibid.*, p. 265–6.
5 *Ibid.*
6 Elizabeth Picard, 'Arab Military Politics: From Revolutionary Plot to Authoritarian State' in Giacomo Luciani (ed.), *The Arab State* (London: Routledge, 1991).
7 Fouad Ajemi, 'The Summer of Arab Discontent', *Foreign Affairs*, Winter 1990–1, p. 11.
8 Kiren Aziz Chaudhry, 'On the Way to the Market: Economic Liberalisation and Iraq's Invasion of Kuwait', *Middle East Report*, May–June 1991, pp. 14–23.

9 *Ibid.*
10 Gamal Abdul Nasser, *Nasser Speaks: Basic Documents,* translated by E. S. Farag, (London: The Morssett Press, 1972), p. 142.
11 Peter Mansfield, *The Arabs,* 2nd ed (Harmondsworth: Penguin Books, 1985), p. 390.
12 Picard, *op cit.,* p. 205.
13 See, for example, Peter Mansfield, 'Saddam Hussein's Political Thinking: The Comparison with Nasser', in Tim Niblock (ed.), *Iraq: The Contemporary State* (London: Croom Helm, 1982), pp. 62–73.
14 *Economist,* 29 September 1990, p. 19.
15 See Michael Handel, *War, Strategy and Intelligence* (London: Frank Cass, 1989).
16 *Economist,* 29 September 1990, p. 19.
17 See, for example, Conor Cruise O'Brien, *Times,* 19 September 1991, pp. 19–20.
18 See Glenn Paige, *Korean Decision* (London: Collier-Macmillan, 1967).
19 T. M. Franck and E. Weisband, *Word Politics: Verbal Strategy among the Superpowers* (New York: Oxford University Press, 1972).
20 *Newsweek,* 17 September 1990, pp. 10–12.
21 Ajemi, *op cit.*
22 Ian Black, *Guardian,* 27 August 1992.
23 Ajemi, *op cit.*
24 *Economist,* 25 August 1990, pp. 11 and 48.
25 *Ibid.* p. 49.
26 Dilip Hiro, *Desert Storm to Desert Shield* (London: Paladin, 1992), p. 255.

3 THE UNITED NATIONS AND THE GULF CONFLICT

1 H.G. Nicholas, *The United Nations as a Political Institution,* 4th edn (Oxford: Oxford University Press, 1971), p. 51.
2 Article 39 of the Charter reads: 'The Security Council shall determine the existence of any threat to the peace, breach of the peace, or act of aggression and shall make recommendations, or decide what measures shall be taken in accordance with Articles 41 and 42, to maintain or restore international peace and security'.
3 *Keesings Archives* 37641 36(7–8) (Cambridge: Longman, 1990), August 1990.
4 D.C. Watt, *Succeeding John Bull* (Cambridge: Cambridge University Press, 1984).

4 THE DIPLOMACY OF CRISIS

1 See among others: Glenn H. Snyder and P. Diesing, *Conflict among Nations* (Princeton, NJ: Princeton University Press, 1977); O.R. Young, *The Politics of Force: Bargaining During International Crises* (Princeton, NJ: Princeton University Press, 1968); R.N. Lebow, *Between Peace and War* (Baltimore: Johns Hopkins University Press, 1981).
2 Thomas C. Schelling, *Arms and Influence* (New Haven and London: Yale University Press, 1966), p. 97.

3 Snyder and Diesing, *op cit.*, p. 9.
4 See the analogy with the definition of war in Chapter 9.
5 Snyder and Diesing, *op cit.*, p. 13.
6 *Ibid.*, p. 7.
7 See for example, Ben Brown and David Schukman, *All Necessary Means: Inside the Gulf War* (London: BBC Books, 1991) p. 11.
8 Snyder and Diesing, *op cit.*, p. 15.
9 Schelling, *op cit.*, pp. 69ff.
10 *Ibid.*
11 For example: J. De Rivera, *The Psychological Dimension of Foreign Policy* (Columbus, Ohio: Merrill, 1968); R. Jervis, *Perception and Misperception in International Politics* (Princeton, NJ: Princeton University Press, 1976);I.L. Janis, *Victims of Groupthink* (Boston, Mass: Houghton Mifflin, 1972); F.I. Greenstein, 'The Impact of Personality on Politics', *American Political Science Review* 61(3), September 1967.
12 President Bush's 'popularity rating' fell from some 76 per cent in August 1990 to some 58 per cent in October 1990. (Source: *Congressional Quarterly*, 9 March 1991, p. 7).
13 See John Steinbruner, *The Cybernetic Theory of Decision* (Princeton, NJ: Princeton University Press, 1974), p. 340.
14 See, for example, Samir al-Khalil, *Republic of Fear* (London: Hutchinson, 1990); Peter Mansfield, 'Saddam Hussein's Political Thinking' in Tim Niblock (ed.), *Iraq: The Contemporary State*, (London: Croom Helm, 1982), pp. 62–73; Marion Farouk-Sluglett and Peter Sluglett, *Iraq since 1958: From Revolution to Dictatorship* (London: I B Taurus, 1990), pp. 205–13, 269–82.
15 John Bulloch and Harvey Morris, *Saddam's War* (London: Faber & Faber, 1991), p. 29
16 Richard Ned Lebow, *Between Peace and War: The Nature of International Crisis* (Baltimore and London: Johns Hopkins University Press, 1981), pp. 111–15.
17 Ole R. Holsti, 'Theories of Crisis Decision-making', in Paul Gordon Lauren (ed.), *Diplomacy: New Approaches in History, Theory and Policy* (New York: The Free Press, 1979), p. 107.
18 Lebow, *op cit.*, p 114.

5 THE GULF CONFLICT AND INTERNATIONAL LAW

1 A good basic text is Louis Henken, *How Nations Behave: Law and Foreign Policy* 2nd edn (New York: Praeger, 1979).
2 See Helen Milner, 'The Assumption of Anarchy in International Relations Theory: A Critique', *International Studies* (17) 1991, pp. 67–85.
3 The documents upon which the following analysis is based are contained in E. Lauterpacht, C.J. Greenwood, Marc Weller and Daniel Bethlehem (eds), *Kuwait Crisis: Basic Documents* (Cambridge: Grotius Publications, 1991).
4 Lauterpacht *et al.*, *op cit.*, p. 38.

5 Iliya Harik, 'The Origins of the Arab State System', in Giacomo Luciano (ed.), *The Arab State* (London: Routledge, 1990).
6 Lauterpacht *et al.*, *op cit.*, pp. 9–10.
7 *Ibid*, pp. 10–17.
8 Marquess of Landesdowne's letter to Antropoulo Pasha, Ottoman Ambassador in London, 11 September 1901, *ibid.*, p. 11.
9 Foreign Office memorandum 29 October 1901, *ibid.*, p. 13.
10 *Ibid.*, p. 12.
11 *Ibid.*
12 Memorandum by Marquess of Landesdowne, 21 March 1902, *ibid.*, p. 17.
13 *Ibid.*, pp. 33–5.
14 Article 2 of the unratified Convention of 1913, *ibid.*, p. 33.
15 *Ibid.*, p. 37.
16 Letter from the Prime Minister of Iraq to Sir F. Humphreys, 21 July 1932, *ibid.*, pp. 49–50.
17 Record of meeting between Iraqi and Kuwaiti delegations in Baghdad, 4 October 1963, ibid., pp. 56–7.
18 *Vienna Convention on Law of Treaties*, 1969 Art. 46, United Nations Doc. A/Conf. 39/29, 1969.
19 United Nations Treaty Series No. 345, quoted in Ian Brownlie, *International Law and the Use of Force by States* (Oxford: Clarendon Press, 1963), p. 253.
20 See W.T. Greenwood, 'Iraq's Invasion of Kuwait: Some Legal Issues', *World Today* 47(3), March 1991, pp. 39–43.
21 See Appendix 4 of this book for Chapter VII of the United Nations Charter.
22 For a good analysis of the record of economic sanctions as an instrument of coercion, see M.S. Daoudi and K.S. Dajani, *Economic Sanctions: Ideals and Experience* (London: Routledge & Kegan Paul, 1983).

6 THE LAWS OF WAR AND THE GULF CONFLICT

1 Carl von Clausewitz, *On War* edited and translated by Michael Howard and Peter Paret (Princeton, NJ: Princeton University Press, 1976) – Book One, Chapter 7, 'Friction in War', and Book Eight, Chapter 6B, 'War is an Instrument of Policy'; see also on the controllability of war, Michael Howard (ed.), *Restraints on War: Studies in the Limitation of Armed Conflicts* (Oxford: Oxford University Press, 1979).
2 The most accessible treatment of the development of the laws of war is Geoffrey Best, *Humanity in Warfare: The Modern History of International Law of Armed Conflicts* (London: Weidenfeld & Nicolson, 1980; Methuen, 1983).
3 Georg Schwarzenberger, *A Manual of International Law*, 5th edn (London: Stevens & Son, 1967), p. 195.
4 See, for example, Adam Roberts, *The Independent*, 23 August 1990.
5 All the relevant conventions, rules, protocols, and so on, governing

behaviour in warfare can be seen in Adam Roberts and Richard Guelff (eds) *Documents on the Laws of War* (Oxford: Clarendon Press, 1982).

6 *Ibid.*, p. 286.
7 *Ibid.*, p. 284.
8 *Ibid.*
9 *Ibid.*, p. 274.
10 Professor Rowe, letter to *The Times*, 19 January 1991.
11 Roberts and Guelff, *op cit.*, p. 222.
12 *Ibid.*, p. 380.
13 For example, the 1977 Geneva Protocol I on International Armed Conflicts Art. 55, Roberts and Guelff, *op cit.*, p. 418.
14 *Ibid.*
15 Schwarzenberger, *op cit.*, p. 197.
16 See, for example, Ingrid Detter De Lupis, *The Law of War* (Cambridge: Cambridge University Press, 1987). pp. 332–7.
17 Roberts and Guelff, *op cit.*, pp. 417–18.
18 Archer Jones, *The Art of War in the Western World*, (New York and Oxford: Oxford University Press, 1989), p. 692.
19 Bruce Watson, Bruce George, Peter Tzouras and B.L. Cyr, *Military Lessons of the Gulf War* (London: Greenhill Books, 1991), p. 115.
20 Detter De Lupis, *op cit.*, p. 273.
21 See Roberts and Guelff, *op cit.*, pp. 121–35.
22 *Ibid.*
23 *Ibid.*, p. 122.
24 *Ibid.*, p. 462.
25 *Ibid.*, pp. 419–20.
26 For example, John Simpson, BBC TV Foreign Editor, *Late Show: Gulf Journalists*, BBC2 broadcast, 6 June 1991.
27 Watson *et al.*, *op cit.*, p. 75.
28 Detter De Lupis, *op cit.*, p. 194; Roberts and Guelff, *op cit.*, pp. 467–8.
29 Roberts and Guelff, *op cit.*, p. 409.
30 *Sunday Times*, 3 February 1991.
31 Roberts and Guelff, *op cit.*, p. 410.
32 See Ben Brown and David Shukman, *All Necessary Means: Inside the Gulf War* (London: BBC Publications, 1991), pp. 154–5.
33 See Detter De Lupis, *op cit.*, pp. 254–8.
34 *Ibid.*, pp. 352–3.
35 See Robert K. Woetzel, *The Nuremberg Trials in International Law* (London and New York: Stevens/Praeger, 1962), pp. 232–3.

7 MORALITY AND THE GULF CONFLICT

1 Geoffrey Goodwin, 'An International Morality', in B. Parekh and R. N. Berki (eds), *The Morality of Politics* (London: Allen & Unwin, 1972).
2 *Ibid.*, pp. 110–11.
3 Carl von Clausewitz, *On War*, edited and translated by Michael Howard and Peter Paret (Princeton, NJ: Princeton University Press,

1976), Book Six, Ch. 5.

4 For example, Rown Williams in *The Guardian*, 1 November 1990, p. 19, talks of 'a war against Iraq started by the US and its allies'.

5 For example, J.E. Hare and Carey Joynt, *Ethics and International Affairs* (New York: St Martins Press, 1982), pp. 57–64.

6 Charis Waddy, *The Muslim Mind* (London: Longman, 1982), p. 101.

7 *Ibid.*, p. 100.

8 The Koran (2:190, The Cow).

9 R.W. Tucker, *The Just War: A Study in Contemporary American Doctrine* (Baltimore: Johns Hopkins University Press, 1960), p. 199.

10 For example, John Simpson, BBC TV Foreign Editor, *Late Show: Gulf Journalists*, BBC2 broadcast, 6 June 1991.

11 For example, Paul Rogers and Malcolm Dando, *A Violent Peace: Global Security after the Cold War* (London: Brassey's, 1992), Ch. 9.

8 THE ECONOMIC DIMENSION OF THE GULF CONFLICT

1 Peter Oppenheimer, 'The New Europe and the Middle East', *Energy Policy*, November 1990.

2 Stephen Gill and David Law, *The Global Political Economy: Perspectives, Problems and Policies* (Hemel Hempstead: Harvester/Wheatsheaf, 1988), p. 258.

3 Peter Mansfield, *The Arabs* (Harmondsworth: Penguin Books, 1985), p. 483.

4 Mansfield, *op cit.*, p. 482.

5 Robert Gilpin, *The Political Economy of International Relations* (Princeton, NJ: Princeton University Press, 1987), p. 297.

6 Gill and Law, *op cit.*, p. 262.

7 *Ibid.*, p. 261.

8 Mansfield, *op cit.*, p. 486.

9 *Economist*, 12 January 1991, pp. 84–5.

10 Gill and Law, *op cit.*, p. 263.

11 *Ibid.*, p. 264.

12 Pierre Terzian, 'The Gulf Crisis: the Oil Factor', *Journal of Palestinian Studies* XX(2), Winter 1991, p. 105

13 *Economist Book of Vital World Statistics* (London: Hutchinson, 1990), p. 83.

14 Terzian, *op cit.*, p. 101.

15 *Economist*, 12 January 1991, pp. 84–5.

16 *Financial Times*, 16/17 February 1991 and 14 January 1991.

17 *Ibid.*, 16/17 February 1991.

18 A very useful guide to the costing of the war and the basis of this section is Alan Ingham, 'Costing the Gulf War', *Economic Review*, May 1991, pp. 7–9.

19 Michael Prowse, *The Financial Times*, 25 January 1991, p. 16g.

20 Ingham, *op cit.*, p. 8.

21 *Financial Times*, 25 January 1991, p. 4a.

22 *Ibid.*

23 *Ibid.*, 18 January 1991, p. 4d.
24 Prowse, *op cit.*
25 *Economist*, 9 March 1991, p. 36.
26 *Financial Times*, 4 February 1991, p. 2.
27 *Ibid.*
28 *Ibid.*, 25 January 1991, p. 4b.
29 Prowse, *op cit.*
30 *Financial Times*, 26/7 January 1991, p. 3a.
31 *Economist*, 2 March 1991, p. 30.
32 For example, Fred Halliday, 'The Gulf War and Its Aftermath', *International Affairs* 67(2), April 1991.
33 *Financial Times*, 14 October 1991.
34 *Financial Times*, 25 January 1991, p. 4.
35 Michael Field, 'Business Prospects in the 1990s', *Regional Surveys of the World: The Middle East & North Africa*, 38th edn (London: Europa Publications, 1991), pp. 13–17.
36 *Sunday Times*, 4 October 1992, p. 16.
37 *Financial Times*, 15 February 1991, p. 3; Field, *op cit.*
38 *Economist*, 6 April 1991, p. 67.

9 WAR, STRATEGY AND THE GULF CONFLICT

1 Thomas C. Schelling, *Arms and Influence* (New Haven and London: Yale University Press, 1966), pp. 36–43; Herman Kahn, *On Thermonuclear War* (Princeton, NJ: Princeton University Press, 1960), pp. 291–5.
2 See discussion of the game of 'chicken' in, for example, James Dougherty and Robert L. Pfaltzgraff Jr, *Contending Theories of International Relations*, 3rd edn (New York and London: Harper & Row, 1990).
3 For example Peter Mansfield, 'Saddam Hussein's Political Thinking: The Comparison with Nasser', in Tim Niblock (ed.), *Iraq: The Contemporary State* (London: Croom Helm, 1982).
4 Mansfield, *op cit.*
5 John Kenneth Galbraith, *A Life in Our Time: Memoirs* (London: André Deutsch, 1981; Corgi Books, 1983), p. 218.
6 John Simpson, BBC TV Foreign Editor, *Late Show: Gulf Journalists*, BBC2 broadcast, 6 June 1991.
7 Carl von Clausewitz, *On War*, edited and translated by Michael Howard and Peter Paret (Princeton, NJ: Princeton University Press, 1976), p. 357.
8 Robert Harkavy and Stephanie Neuman, *Lessons of Recent Wars in the Third World* (Lexington, Mass.: Lexington Books, 1985). p. 287.
9 See David Segal, 'The Iran–Iraq War: A Military Analysis,' *Foreign Affairs*, Summer 1988.
10 See Michael Handel, *War, Strategy and Intelligence* (London: Frank Cass, 1989).
11 See Theodore A. Postol, 'Lessons of the Gulf War Experience with

Patriot', *International Security* 16(3), Winter 1991/2, pp. 119–71.

12 Bruce Watson, Bruce George, Peter Tsouras and B. L. Cyr, *Military Lessons of the Gulf War* (London: Greenhill Books, 1991), p. 154.

13 *Ibid.*

14 Watson, *et al., op cit.*

15 Pierre Salinger with Eric Laurent, *Secret Dossier: The Hidden Agenda behind the Gulf War* (Harmondsworth: Penguin Books, 1991).

16 Nick Gowing, *World Today*, June 1991.

17 See Watson *et al., op cit.,* pp 93–4; Ben Brown and David Shukman, *All Necessary Means* (London: BBC Books, 1991), pp. 73–6.

18 Carl von Clausewitz, *op cit.*, p. 584.

19 Carl von Clausewitz, *op cit.*, p. 579.

20 See Michael Howard, 'War as an Instrument of Policy', in Herbert Butterfield and Martin Wight, *Diplomatic Investigations* (London: George Allen & Unwin, 1966).

21 Clausewitz, *op cit.*, p. 80.

10 THE AFTERMATH

1 See Samir al-Khalil, *Republic of Fear: Saddam's Iraq* (London: Hutchinson Radius, 1989), p. 275.

2 See Martin Woollacott, *Guardian*, 29 July 1991, p. 19.

3 *Geofile*, no, 48 January 1985 (London: Mary Glasgow Publications).

4 *Financial Times*, 19 February 1992, p. 4.

5 William J. Perry, 'Desert Storm and Deterrence', *Foreign Affairs*, Summer 1991, p. 73.

6 *Ibid.*, p. 67.

7 *Ibid.*, p. 81.

8 W. Seth Carus, 'Missiles in the Third World: The 1991 Gulf War', *Orbis*, Spring 1991.

9 Adrian Hyde-Price, *European Security beyond the Cold War: Four Scenarios for the year 2010* (London: RIIA/Sage), p. 244.

10 Dominique Moisi, quoted in Hyde-Price, *op cit.*, pp. 244–5.

Index

Abyssinia 144, 160
Acheson, Dean 49, 50
Aden 27
Afghanistan 15, 144, 282, 313
Aflaq, Michel 36
Africa 15, 25, 27, 145, 268, 279
aggression 43, 61, 70, 74, 90, 95,
    108, 109, 112, 118, 139–41,
    143, 145, 162, 168, 172, 173,
    175, 176, 178, 179, 181–4, 186,
    187, 188, 209, 224, 225, 228,
    272
Ajemi, Fouad 318, 319
Alawite 16
Algeria 15, 18, 23, 24, 30, 265,
    266, 282
Algerian War 30
'all necessary means' 74, 78, 79,
    82, 105, 111, 142, 177, 227
American ambassador to
    Baghdad (see Glaspie)
Amiriya 163, 243
Anglo–Iranian Oil Company 194
Arab nationalism 20, 23, 29, 31,
    34, 65
Arab League 64, 74, 138
Arab al-Shimal 40
Arab al-Khalij 40
Arab mind 6, 260, 261
Arabism 21, 22, 26, 35, 38, 43, 261
Arafat 56, 57, 263
Argentina 98, 252, 282, 315
Asia 12, 15, 18, 25, 81, 260
Assad 16, 39, 66, 67
Ataturk, Mustapha Kemal 29

authority 19, 21, 38
authority, divine 265
authority, legal 88, 126, 127, 141,
    227, 228
Australia 282, 315
Austria 283
Aziz, Tariq 106

Ba'ath (Party, Ba'athists) 19, 35,
    37–9, 41, 42, 43, 46, 48, 66,
    143, 148, 164, 187, 201, 219,
    220, 246, 253–5, 257, 259, 265
Baghdad Pact 29, 34
Baghdad 6, 16, 29, 34, 40, 47, 57,
    81, 84, 96, 133, 147, 153, 162,
    163, 190, 231, 233, 250, 253,
    255, 272
Baghdad railway 134
Baghdad Radio 6
Bahrain 283, 313–14
Baker, US Secretary of State
    James 79, 106
balance of power 92, 98, 99, 184,
    192, 202, 255
Balkan 18, 21
Baltic states, Soviet annexation of
    131
Bangladesh 15, 283, 313
Basra 35, 132, 133, 136, 256
Bazoft 47
BBC 233
Beira 145
Belgium 283, 315
Belief system 125
Berki, N. 322

Best, Geoffrey 321
Bethlehem, Daniel 320, 321
Black, Ian 319
Brazil 268
Brown, Carl L. 318
Brown, Ben 320, 322, 325
Brownlie, Ian 321
Bubiyan 44, 49, 136, 138
Bull, Hedley 318
Bulloch, John 320
Burton, Richard 6, 317
Bush, President George 3, 85,
    102, 119–21, 142, 168, 177,
    250, 251, 253, 257; 'second
    term factor' 119–20; 'wimp
    factor' 120–1; 'vietnam
    syndrome' 121–2; foreign
    policy experience 120–1
Butterfield, Herbert 325

Cairo 40, 64, 66
Canada 196, 284, 314–15
Carus, W. Seth 325
CBW 156, 157
Chamberlain, Neville 160
Chaudhry, Kiren Aziz 318
chemical weapons 47, 164, 165,
    190, 241, 242
Cheney, US Secretary of Defence
    Richard 65
China 9, 12, 30, 34, 60, 71, 77,
    82, 83, 88, 131, 160, 185, 278,
    284
Chippindale, Peter 317
Christianity 21, 43, 67, 149, 176,
    185
CIA 120
Clausewitz, Carl von 172, 234,
    242, 248, 250, 251, 321, 323,
    324, 325
coercion 37, 43, 59, 75, 76, 94,
    104, 106, 108, 109, 119, 181,
    182, 187, 195, 201
coercive diplomacy 11, 62, 94,
    107, 111, 112, 152
cognitive factors 11, 123
cognitive rigidity 124, 125
Cold War 9, 13, 14, 18, 23, 24, 29,
    31, 32, 34, 36, 39, 51–3, 59, 65,

66, 71, 72, 80–3, 86, 87, 93, 94,
    96, 98, 99, 108, 120, 121, 129,
    131, 139, 172, 175, 184, 189,
    193, 206, 252, 261, 262, 263,
    266, 269–72, 274–6, 278–80
Cold War, and Middle East 51–3
collateral 158, 188, 189, 233
communist 19, 20, 29, 53, 54, 57,
    62, 71, 72, 80–3, 131, 278
'compellence' 104, 105, 109, 110
Congo 70–3, 140
Congress 43, 120, 127, 177, 178
Congressional elections 104, 120,
    142
conspiracy theory 48
crisis diplomacy 53, 58, 62, 80, 87,
    92–4, 110, 128, 180, 203, 267
crisis (see also Gulf crisis)
    characteristics of 91–3; and
    decision-making pathologies
    123–5; diplomacy and force
    181–3; escalation in 224–7;
    face-saving in 93; goals and
    objectives in 93–4; instruments
    of coercion in 108–12;
    precipitation of 94–7;
    management 94, 107–13;
    structure of 99–102 (diagram);
    thresholds 100, 101, 102; time
    and 92, 104–5, 106, 110–13;
    'war avoidance' versus
    'winning' in 93–4, 107–8
Cuba 54, 57, 77, 78, 284
Cuban missile crisis 93, 252
Cyprus 184
Cyr, B. L. 300, 316, 322, 325
Czechoslovakia 284, 313

Dajani, K. S. 321
Dando, Malcom 323
Daoudi, M. S. 321
de Rivera, J. 320
deadline 105–7, 110–13, 178, 227,
    238
declaration of war 151, 177
decolonisation 9, 25, 31, 193
democracy (democratic) 9, 20,
    21, 29, 49, 116, 118, 119, 122,
    125, 144, 187, 209, 246, 252,

255, 256, 257, 265, 266, 278
Denmark 196, 285, 315
deterrence 108, 109, 113, 181,
    188, 189, 219
Detter de Lupis, Ingrid 322
Dhahran 162, 240
Diesing, P. 319, 320
'double standards' 171, 173–5, 184
Dougherty, James 324
Doughty, Charles 6, 317
Dulles, John Foster 172

East Timor 185
Eastern Europe 4, 32, 256, 274,
    278, 279
EC 274
economic effects of Gulf War (*see*
    Gulf War, economic effects,
    quantifiable costs)
economic sanctions (*see* sanctions)
economic dimension, (*see* Gulf
    conflict)
Eden, Sir Anthony 29, 31, 121,
    318
Egypt 24, 27, 29, 30, 51, 63–6,
    117, 212, 214, 226, 263, 285,
    313
environmental damage caused by
    war, legal provisions 155–6
'end of history' 32
estoppel 137, 140, 141
ethnocentrism 7, 8, 10, 124
Euphrates 232, 273
European Community 18, 61,
    272, 274
European Political Union 274
European Court of Human
    Rights 170
European mind 12, 115

Faisal 29
Falklands conflict 50, 85, 93–5,
    139, 225, 252
Farag, E. S. 319
Farouk-Sluglett, Marion 320
fatwa 16
Field, Michael 324
First World War 27–9, 132, 135,
    230, 246

Foch, Marshall 246
France 15, 27, 30, 34, 61, 62, 84,
    129, 194, 271, 273, 285, 313–15
Franck, T. M. 319
French 19, 22, 27, 30, 31, 65, 84,
    107
Fukuyama, Francis 318

Galbraith, John Kenneth 232, 324
Galtieri, General 182
Gellner, Ernest 317, 318
General Assembly 70, 74, 168
Geneva Conventions 149, 152–4,
    159
Geneva Protocol 155, 156, 160,
    161, 163, 165, 166
Geneva talks 106, 228
George, Bruce 300, 316, 322, 325
Germany 54, 61, 134, 160, 177,
    199, 205, 209–210, 212, 215,
    272, 273, 278, 279, 285, 315
Gill, Stephen 198, 323
Gilpin, Robert 323
Glaspie, Ambassador 47, 49, 97
Golan Heights 263
Goodwin, Geoffrey 322
Gorbachev, Mikhail 4, 54, 79–83,
    105
Gowing, Nick 325
Greece 286, 315
Greenspan, Alan 211
Greenstein, F. I. 320
Greenwood, W. T. 321
Greenwood, C. J. 320, 321
Grenada 85, 174
Guelff, Richard 322
Gulf crisis, asymmetry in 94–5;
    and President Bush 119–22;
    and coaltion management
    58–63; characteristics of 91–3;
    and China 82–3; coalition
    outcome priorities 224
    (diagram); clarity of issues 277;
    and Cold War 24, 53; crisis
    diplomacy 91–125 passim; crisis
    management in 107–113; and
    cultural relativism 9, 10; and
    Egypt 65–6; escalation towards
    war in 225–7; explanation for

outcome 118–25; face-saving in
225; force versus sanctions
182–3, 188; and France 84; and
Germany 61–2; and hostages
114–16; idiosyncratic
(personality) factor in 118–25;
imperatives to war 225; initial
act of aggression 95–8;
instruments of coercion
107–113; and Iran 24; and
international law 128–9,
139–148, 149–69; (see
international law); Iraqi
coercive strategy in 113–17;
Iraqi outcome priorities 220–3,
220 (table); Iraqi scorched
earth threat in 114; Iraqi use of
hostages as coercive instrument
114–16; Iraqi use of the
'Vietnam factor' 116–17; Iraqi
threats against Israel 117; and
Jordan 55–6, 263–4;
management of 107–113;
market irrationality and 202–3;
negotiation as an instrument of
coercion in 106, 111–13;
nuclear dimension 108; and
'orientalism' 3, 6–8, 10; and
Palestinians 56–7, 263; and
personality 119–25; phases 102,
103–7; possible outcomes 222
(matrix diagram); precipitation
of 95–7; and 'public analysis'
1–2; and 'second term' factor
119–20; and Soviet Union 51–4
(see Soviet Union); attitudes of
Saddam Hussein 122–5, 219;
structure of 102 (diag), 99–107;
and Syria 24, 38–9, 66–8;
thresholds 100, 101, 102, 102
(diagram), 227; time factor and
103, 110, 111–13; and UK 62,
(see United Kingdom); and UN
(see United Nations); US
outcome priorities 223–4, 224
(table); and US (see United
States); Vietnam factor 121–2;
and 'western' attitudes 5; and
'wimp factor' 120–1; and

Yemen 57–8
Gulf conflict, aftermath 252–80
passim; and Arab schism 40;
and China 82–4; chronology
294–300; and civilians 159–64
passim; and coalition
management 58–63; and Cold
War 32; and conspiracy theory
48; and Cuban missile crisis 93;
economic dimension 191–214
passim; and end of Cold War
51–4; and Europe 273–4; and
Falklands conflict 94, 95; and
Germany 209–10, 273; and
international interests 175; and
Japan 209–11; and Jordan
55–6; and 'just war' principles
176–85; key stages in 228
(table); 'lessons' 266–7; and
morality 170–90 passim; and oil
market 202–4; possible
outcomes 222 (diagram); and
Saddam Hussein 23, 117 (see
Saddam Hussein); and
Secretary General of UN 73;
role of Soviet Union 51–4,
79–82 (see Soviet Union); and
strategic surprise 237; and Syria
66–8; as a 'resource war' 191–2;
strategic surprise in 237–8; and
UK 84–6 (see United
Kingdom); and UN 69–90
passim; and future role of UN
72; and 'Vietnam syndrome'
244–7; and definition of war
151; and Yemen 57–8

Gulf War 215–51, 313–16
(statistics); the aftermath of
252–8; in Iraq 253–6; in Kuwait
257–8; in Middle East 260–4;
cohesion of 'the west' 271–4; in
Europe 272–4;

Article 51 vs Article 47 150–2;
avoidability of 97; calculation
for war 218–24; 'centres of
gravity' in 229; chemical
weapons in 241–2; civilians as
targets in 233 (see also
international law);

Coalition air campaign 231–4;
   objectives of 231; 'collateral
   damage' and 233–4;
Coalition military strategy
   227–34, mobility in 230;
   three phases of 230–1;
   strategic surprise 238–9;
Coalition war aims 248–9;
   incompatibility of 227–9;
   Iraq's military defeat 180;
   'just peace' 178–80;
   liberation of Kuwait 178, 248;
   'peace and security' 249,120;
   and Cold War 23; costs of
   204–6; decision for war 215–18;
   and problem of declaration of
   war 176–8; discrimination and
   proportionality in 189–90;
   economic effects of 207–14;
   escalation in 224–7, 239–42;
   'Scud politics' 239–40;
   'expanding logic' of 229, 232;
   ground war 247–51, 304 (map);
   and intelligence 242–44;
   Iraqi military strategy 230,
   234–7; defensive nature of
   230, 235; chemical weapons
   in 241–2;
Iraqi troops in KTO 303
   (map); 'just war' principles
   applied to 176–85 (see also
   morality, international law);
   and the 'last resort' criterion
   182–3; 'lessons' of 266–8;
   military deployments and
   targets 302 (map); and military
   proliferation 269–71; and
   military technology 188–90;
   and the 'new world order'
   276–7; and oil 192, 199–200,
   201–2; and oil market 202–4;
   political control in 250–1;
   possible outcomes (matrix
   diagram) 222; as 'pre-paid' war
   208; when it began 153, 173; as
   resource war 191–2; and Soviet
   coup 1991, 54;
   strategic surprise in 237–9;
      chemical weapons as 241–2;

Scud missiles as 240;
   statistics of 313–16 (Appendix
   V); strategy 215–51 passim;
   Vietnam syndrome 244–7; war
   crimes 169; war termination in
   249–51; troop deployments in
   Gulf region 302 (map); and
   'the west' 271–4
Gulf Cooperation Council 41,
137, 200

Hague Draft Rules on Aerial
   Warfare 159–61
Hague Conventions 149, 154
Halliday, Fred 324
Handel, Michael 319, 324
Hare, J. E. 323
Harik, Iliya 318, 321
Harkavy, Robert 324
Hashemite 23, 28–30, 263
Hegel 171
Heikal, Mohammed 40
Hejaz 28
Henken, Louis 320
Hiro, Dilip 300, 319
Hobbes 170
Holland, R. F. 318
Hollis, Martin 317
Holsti, Ole R. 320
Holy war, (see jihad)
Horrie, Chris 317
hors de combat 159, 166
hostages 9, 24, 67, 114, 115, 153,
   168 (see international law,
   Saddam Hussein, Iraq); legal
   status of 152–4
Howard, Michael 317, 321, 323,
   324, 325
Hudson, Michael 318
human shields 115, 155
Humphreys, Sir F. 321
Hungary 144, 175
Hussein, King 55–7, 263, 264
Hussein, Saddam 3, 119, 261; and
   air campaign 234; and Amiriya
   bunker 164; attempts to
   overthrow 37, 253, 255; and
   Ba'athism 19, 36–9, 41–3;
   calculation and miscalculation

96–7, 217–20; character 44, 46, 50, 122, 221; and chemical weapons 164, 241; cognitive rigidity 125; decision for war 220–3; decision-making 122–5; defeat of 265; as charismatic leader 21; failures 267; foreign policy 44, 46, 48–9; and Glaspie 97; and Gulf security 259; and hostages 115–16, 153–4; and international law 128; intransigence 62; and invasion of Kuwait 33, 96, 97, 237, 238, 272; and Iran–Iraq war 123, 236; and Iraqi state 28; irrationality 124, 203, 218–19, 249, 254; and jihad 186; and Jordan 55–6; as a military target 240; military strategy 117, 235–7, 245; misperceptions 122–3, 124; model for other dictators 267, 277; and nuclear weapons 264, 266–7; objectives 182, 201, 230, 254; and oil 192, 201; and Palestine 262; and PLO 56–7; and Resolution 678 142–3; and 'Saddamism' 23; and sanctions 104, 148; and Saudi Arabia 210, 226; and 'scorched earth' policy 155, 157; and Scud missiles 239; and self-perception 43, 115, 123; and Soviet Union 54, 81–2; and superpowers 81; survival of 250–1, 254–6; and Syria 66–7; and United States 44–50, 96, 97, 106, 111, 116; and US public opinion 177; and Vietnam War 245–7; and war crimes 169

Hyde-Price, Adrian 325

India 12, 13, 15, 27, 30, 286
Indonesia 15
Ingham, Alan 323
intelligence 242; failures 46–50, 237–8, 242–4;
international relations 8

international law 126–48, 149–69; and the behaviour of states 126–8; behaviour of Iraq in relation to its claim against Kuwait 137–8; behaviour of other states in relation to Iraq's claim against Kuwait 138–9; civilians in war 159–64; consensual nature of 128; derogation from the rules of war 157–8; and domestic law 127–8; and economic sanctions 144–8; and *estoppel* 137; and the Gulf crisis 128–9; hostages 7, 152–4; and Iraqi claims against Kuwait 129–39; and law making 127; military necessity and 156–9, 162; use of obnoxious weapons 164–5; acts of 'perfidy' 165–6; prisoners of war 154–5; recognition of states and governments 130–1; and 'scorched earth' strategy 155–7; the United Nations and the Gulf crisis 139–44; of war 149–69; legal status of Gulf conflict as a war 151–2; war crimes 167–9; (*see also* Geneva Conventions, Geneva Protocols, Gulf War, Saddam Hussein)

International Energy Agency (IEA), 203

Iran 9, 16–20, 23, 24, 34, 39, 41, 43, 46, 81, 84, 123, 137, 146, 164, 179, 190, 194, 198, 200, 204, 235–7, 245, 259, 260, 265, 286

Iraq, Iraqis 286; airforce 271; al-Amiriya 163–4, 234; annexation of Kuwait 64, 76, 103, 131, 184–5, ba'ath(ism), 19, 21, 34, 35–9, 219, 253–4, 265; blockade against 74; and CENTO 29; and chemical weapons 156, 164, 231, 241–2; and China 83; and treatment of civilians 159–60; coercive threats 114–17; conflict outcome priorities 220 (table);

crisis decision-making 125, 222; crisis strategy 66, 108, 112–13; crisis talks 106; and Cuba 54; decision to invade 39–50, 44–50, 45 (diagram); decision for war 219–23; defensive strategy 230, 235; and democracy 256; diplomacy 6; economic impact of Gulf War 213; economy 40–3; as a fabricated state 28; and France 84; and aftermath of Gulf War 253–6; and Gulf security 259–60; and end of Gulf War 249–51; high command 231, 234; and Hashemites 29; and hostages 77, 114–15, 152–4; integrity of 28; and international law 77, 78, 79, 128–9, 131–2, 137–9, 143; and Iran 17; and Iran–Iraq war 16, 39, 200, 235, 245; and Israel 117; and Jordan 55–6; and Kurds 19; Kuwait 11, 34, 40–1, 42, 103, 137, 138; leadership 233; and Libya 55; as a mandated territory 28, 30; and Middle East balance of power 255; military centres of gravity 229; military forces and losses 315–16; military strategy 234–7, 247–8; military strength 242–3; Mutla Ridge 166–7; nature of 34–5, 253; and nuclear weapons 47, 156, 157, 264, 268; and oil 195, 199, 200, 201; and oil revenues 197–8, 201; and OPEC 192; and Ottoman Empire 132–3; and Ottoman succession 136–7; and pan-Arabism 43; 'passive deterrence' strategy 108; perceptions of Vietnam War 245–7; acts of 'perfidy' 166; potential breakup 256; and prisoners of war 154–5; and 'protected areas' 158; as radical state 23; Republican Guard 230; and 'Saddamism' 254;

sanctions against 74, 102, 104, 109–110, 145–8, 182; and 'scorched earth' strategy 155–6; Scud missile attacks 162, 239–40; security and strategic interests 43–4, 258; and Syria 38–9, 66–7; territorial claims against Kuwait 11, 34, 129–32, 132–7, 137–9, 144, 257–8; and military 29, 37; and Shi'a 16; and Soviet Union 53–4, 80, 81, 103, 145, 198; and statehood 26, 28, 253; and supergun 47; and strategic surprise 237, 244; and Third World 83; troops 102–3, 231, 248–9; fails to respond to ultimatum 151; and United Kingdom 28, 84–5; and UN 76; and UN Border Commission 258; and UN resolutions 145–6; and United States 44, 46–50, 80, 96–7, 98–9, 103, 123–4; and state of war with Coalition 154; and war crimes 168–9; war damage in 233; and Yemen 55, 57–8, 79

Iraqi invasion 33, 40, 42–4, 48, 54, 56, 60, 64, 66, 74, 76, 79, 80, 94, 98, 99, 103, 121, 140, 141, 175, 191, 192, 201, 203, 225, 226, 227, 228, 243, 244, 257, 264

Iraqi military 33, 35, 37, 105, 143, 159, 167, 227, 228, 230, 231, 232, 235, 237, 242, 245, 249, 250, 254

Islam 15, 19–21, 23, 38, 66, 115, 186, 264–6, 305 (map)

Islam and democracy 264–6

Islamic fundamentalism 23, 24, 64, 65, 81, 259, 265

Islamic diaspora 15

Islamicism 265, 266

Israel 14, 17, 22, 31, 32, 47, 52, 55–7, 63, 65–7, 98, 117, 144, 159, 162, 165, 179, 194, 239–40, 262–4, 287

Italy 144, 145, 160, 287, 314–15

Janis, I. L. 320
Japan 9, 98, 160, 196, 209, 210, 279, 287
Jerusalem 157
Jervis, R. 320
jihad 66, 171, 185, 186
Jones, Archer 322
Jordan 23, 24, 28, 55, 57, 147, 214, 264, 287
Joynt, Carey 323
jus ad bellum 149, 176
jus in bello 149, 152, 176
just war 2, 11, 149, 171, 176–9, 181, 185, 186, 189, 224 (*see also* Gulf War, international law)

Kahn, Herman 324
Karbala 16
KGB 81
Khafji 166, 244
al-Khalil, Samir 318, 320, 325
Khomeini, Ayatollah 16
Koran 186
Korea 49, 70, 71, 73, 97, 140, 208, 268
Koweit 133–6, 301 (map)
Kriegsraison 157
Krushchev, Nikita 4
Kurds 19, 35, 38, 39, 164, 253, 255, 256
Kuwait City 135, 167, 237, 239
Kuwait 288; and aftermath of war 257–8; annexation of 44, 49, 64, 76, 77, 84, 85, 97, 98, 103, 144, 184, 226; Coalition war aims 178; and democracy 257; economic impact of war on 213; economy 197, 199; financial contribution to allies 212; and France 84; independent status 138, 139; and Iraq 33, 34, 40–1, 46, 76, 103, 112, 137; Iraq–Kuwait border 41, 258; Iraqi antagonism towards 40–2; Iraqi invasion of 33, 47, 53, 54, 56, 58, 66, 96, 97, 98, 112, 139, 141, 143–4, 173, 186, 228 (table); Iraqi occupation of 10,

117, 140, 159, 162, 229, 262; Iraqi territorial claims against 11, 39, 43–4, 47, 57, 129–32, 136, 137–8, 139, 257–8; Iraq's scorched earth strategy 155, 157; and Jordan 214; liberation of 227, 232; military contribution 313–15; and oil 114, 199, 201, 203–4, 258; and OAPEC 198; and oil revenues 197–8, 200; and Ottoman Empire 132, 133–7; and Palestinians 214, 264; and Rumaila oil field 41; and Saddam Hussein 23, 49, 50; and Saudi Arabia 64; and Security Council Resolutions 674 and 677 76, 77; sovereignty 258; and Syria 66, 67; and Third World 83; and United Kingdom 75, 84–5, 134, 136, 141, 272; and UN 74, 137; and United States 49, 75, 96–7, 98, 102, 106, 141, 142, 173–4, 202, 258

Lacouture, Jean 318
Landesdowne, Marquess of 321
Lauren, Paul Gordon 320
Laurent, Eric 325
Lauterpacht, E. 320, 321
Law, David 198, 323
Lawrence, T. E. 247, 317
laws of war 11, 114, 149–51, 158, 159, 163, 164, 167, 171, 176
League of Nations 26, 27, 34, 131, 136, 144, 160
Lebanon 24, 39, 47, 67, 184
Lebow, R. N. 319, 320
legitimacy 16, 26, 28, 36–8, 41, 43, 58, 130, 131, 136, 137, 267
Lesseps, Ferdinand de 13
Libya 23, 288
Luciani, Giacomo 318, 321
Lukes, Steven 317

MacArthur, General Douglas 71, 250
MacIntyre, Alasdair 317

Malaysia 15, 288
Mansfield, Peter 197, 318, 319, 320, 323, 324
Marxism 3, 4, 9, 20, 21
Mecca 16, 66
Mesopotamia 133
Middle East 10, 11, 112, 115, 305 (map); balance of power in 98, 184; British policy in 29–30, 84–5; Cold War in 23–4, 31, 36, 52, 263; conflict in 117; conservativism vs. radicalism in 22–3; and cultural relativism 9–10; defined 12–14; democracy vs. Islam in 256, 257, 264–6; and Europe 12–14; and France 30, 62, 84; fundamentalism vs. secularism in 19–20, 186, 266; and imperialism 27, 31, 64, 261; and international relations 1–10; and Iraq 35; and Islam 15, 16; and Israel 264; non-Arabs in 17–19; and oil 192, 194, 203; and 'orientalism' 3, 6; pan-Arabism vs. statism in 21–2; and Soviet Union 36, 51–2, 66, 81–2; stability in 123; nature of state in 25–32; structual complexities of 14–25, 192; and superpowers 31; tourism in 212; and United States 60, 63; war in 262, 263; and 'the west' 5, 6, 8, 34, 261, 266, 279–80
Military Staff Committee 80, 86, 150
military necessity (*kriegsraison*), 156–8, 162, 168
military deception 165
military technology, proliferation of 269–71
Milner, Helen 320
misperception 8, 69, 96, 122, 123, 126, 274
Mitterand, President 84
Moisi, Dominique 325
morality 170–2, 174, 176, 185; and 'double standards' 173–5;

as foreign policy objective 172; and jihad 185–6; 'just war' principles (*see* war, just war); and military technology 188–90; 'proportionality' 183–5; and *raison d'etat* 171–3; of sanctions 187–8; and war 170–1
Morocco 15, 288, 313
Morris, Harvey 320
Mossadegh, Muhammed 193
Mosul 132, 133, 256
'mother of all battles' 124
Mozambique 145
Mubarak, President 226
Mubarakh, Sheikh 134
Muslim diaspora 15–16, 305 (map)
Muslims 15, 16, 18, 19, 35, 39, 81, 186, 261, 280
Mutla Ridge 166–7

Nasser, Gamal Abdul 24, 29–31, 34, 43, 51, 65, 123, 319
NATO 18, 34, 59, 145, 205, 269
neo-colonialism 6, 22
Netherlands 289, 315
Neuman, Stephanie 324
new world order 90, 274–80; intervention in 277–8; post Cold War structures 277–80
Niblock, Tim 319, 320, 324
Nicholas, H. G. 319
Niger 289, 313
Nkrumah, Kwame 317
Norway 196, 289, 315
nuclear deterrence 188, 189, 219
nuclear weapons 47, 52, 94, 108, 156, 157, 160, 165, 178, 179, 188–90, 198, 219, 231, 264, 266–71
nuclear proliferation 268–9

O'Brien, Conor Cruise 319
OAPEC 195, 198–200
occupied territories 56, 144, 153
OECD 196, 204
oil 11, 13, 18, 19, 23, 24, 34, 40–2, 55, 57, 64, 98, 102, 114,

135, 143, 145, 155, 184,
191–204, 207, 211–14, 258;
demand for 195–6; and dispute
between Iraq and Kuwait
199–201; exporters 200 (table);
market and the Gulf conflict
203–4; 'irrationality' of 202–4;
political economy of 191,
193–204; price 194, 195, 196,
198, 201–4; breakdown of
196–7 (table); producers 199
(table); as *raison de guerre*
191–2; revenues to members of
OPEC 197–8; 'shock' (1973)
194–5, 196; (1979) 197; and
western resonse to Iraqi
invasion 201–2
Oman 289, 313–14
OPEC 192, 194–201, 204
OPEC, conflict within 198
Oppenheimer, Peter 323
Organisation of Petroleum
Exporting Countries (*see* OPEC)
Organisation of Arab Petroleum
Exporting Countries (*see*
OAPEC)
orientalism 3, 6, 7, 10, 12
Ottoman Empire 18, 19, 22, 26–8,
132, 133, 135, 136, 256, 280

Pahlavi, Shah 17
Paige, Glenn 319
Pakistan 289, 313
Palestine, Palestinian 13, 17, 22,
26, 32, 52, 55–7, 112, 144, 214,
257, 262–4
pan-Arabism 21, 22, 26, 43
Parekh, B. 322
Paret, Peter 321, 323, 324
Pasha, Antropoulo 321
Patriot anti-missile missile 240,
263, 270
'peace and security' 74, 76, 78,
86, 87, 139, 140, 142, 143, 150,
228, 229, 249, 250, 259
Peking 131
Perestroika 53, 54
Perez de Cuellar 107
Perry, William J. 325

Persian Gulf 43, 133, 134, 146,
258; security in 261
Pfaltzgraff Jr., Robert L. 324
Picard, Elizabeth 318, 319
PLO 56, 57, 64, 65
Poland 290, 315
political science 1, 2, 4, 5, 7
political culture 26, 28, 31, 35, 36,
65, 85, 257
Popper, Karl 317
Portugal 290, 315
Postel, Theodore A. 325
Powell, General Colin 243, 248
prisoners of war, legal status
154–5 (*see* international law)
proportionality in war 156, 163,
183, 184, 189, 190
Prowse, Michael 323, 324
public opinion 115, 120, 153,
166, 172, 246

Qassim, Abdul Karim 30, 35, 138
Qatar 290, 313–14

rationality (and irrationality), 44,
109, 122, 124, 125, 195, 203,
216–21, 246, 247, 249, 270
Red Cross 152, 154
relativism 7, 9, 10
Renan, Ernest 13
reprisals 167
Republican Guard 248
Roberts, Adam 322
Rogers, Paul 323
Rowe, Professor 322
Rumaila 41, 49, 258
Rushdie 16
Ruthven, Malise 305, 317
Ryan, Alan 317

Sadat, Anwar 65
Saddamism 23, 254
Said, Edward 6, 7, 10, 317
al-Said, Nuri 29, 30
Saladin 43, 57, 123, 157
Salinger, Pierre 325
sanctions, morality of 187–8
sanctions 2, 74, 75, 77–80, 88,
102, 104, 109, 110, 114, 129,

140, 144, 145–8, 171, 182, 187, 188, 203, 206, 207, 213, 214, 220, 274

Saudi Arabia 16, 17, 24, 33, 40, 43, 44, 57, 64, 66, 67, 85, 99, 102, 103, 105, 117, 120, 139, 141, 142, 159, 162, 173, 192, 197, 198, 201, 203, 204, 213, 214, 225–9, 248, 258–60, 290, 313–14

Schelling, Thomas, C. 93, 104, 320, 324

Shukman, David 320, 322, 325

Schwarzenberger, Georg 321, 322

Schwarzkopf 166, 243, 251

'scorched earth strategy', 114, 155, 157 (see also Saddam Hussein, Gulf War)

Scud missile 55, 162, 164, 165, 239–241, 262, 263, 270, 271; political rather than military weapon 240; and military surprise 240

Second World War 6, 13, 34, 61, 85, 120, 131, 160, 172, 192, 193, 202, 208, 232, 274

secularism 18–23, 29, 36, 38–40, 172, 226, 265, 266

Segal, David 324

Senegal 291, 313

Shah of Iran (see Pahlavi)

Shevardnadze, Eduard 53, 54, 62, 79–81, 89, 90

Shi'a 16, 17, 19, 39, 255

Shi'ite 35

Sidqi, General Bakr 28, 29

Simpson, John 322, 323, 324

Sluglett, Peter 320

Smith, Anthony 318

Snyder Glenn H. 319, 320

South Africa 145

Southern Rhodesia 144, 145

Soviet Union 293; and Afghanistan 144; annexation of Baltic states 131; break-up of 4, 20, 65, 260, 263, 278; change of attitude 90; and China 83; and Cold War 14, 31–2, 34, 120; and Congo 73; and

Czechoslovakia 144; and Egypt 34; and use of force 88, 105; role in Gulf conflict 51–4, 60, 62, 79–82, 89, 263; and Hungary 144, 175; and Iraq 44, 145, 197–8, 242 (see Iraq); support Iraqi claims against Kuwait (1963), 138–9; and Korean War 71–2; and Middle East 23–4, 29, 34, 62, 81–2; and Military Staff Committee 86; and Muslims 15; and NATO 18; and secularism 20, 265; and Security Council 79, 80; and 'Soviet alternative' 264–5; and Syria 36, 66–7; US–Soviet solidarity 103; and Vietnam War 117

Spain 90, 291, 315

St Augustine 176

statism 21, 261

Status Quo Agreement 133, 134

Steinbruner, John 320

Stoessinger, John 317

strategic surprise 48, 237, 238

Sudan 291

Suez Canal 13, 27, 30, 31, 65, 213

Sunni 16, 19, 35, 39

supergun 47

superpowers 13, 31, 49, 52, 53, 65, 66, 72, 83, 93, 94, 99, 108, 131, 183, 189, 202, 209, 221, 237, 244, 252, 254, 262, 264, 270, 271, 275, 276, 278, 279

Surinam 15

Syria, Syrian 16, 18, 21, 23–5, 27, 28, 36, 38, 39, 43, 63, 64, 66, 67, 104, 133, 145, 263, 291, 313

Terzian, Pierre 323

Thatcher Margaret 85, 125, 168, 272

Thesiger, Wilfred 317

Third World 24, 27, 38, 51, 61, 79, 83, 95, 99, 183, 202, 209, 210, 218, 221, 244, 267, 270, 271

Thomas, Hugh 318

Tibet, Chinese annexation of 185

Transjordan 28, 140
Treaty of Brotherhood and
    Alliance 140
Tucker, R. W. 323
Tunisia 292
Turkey, Turkish 16–19, 29, 34,
    132, 133, 134, 166, 210, 292
Tsouras, Peter 300, 316, 322, 325

UAE 22, 197, 201, 292, 313–14
Umm Qasr 136, 258
United Kingdom, Britain, British
    292; and Arab nationalism 31;
    and Article 51 75, 141, 142,
    146, 150; and Baghdad Pact
    (1955) 34; and blockade of
    Iraq 146; and coalition forces
    61; and Falklands War (1982)
    85, 98, 139; financial cost of
    war 211–12; and France 61;
    and Geneva Protocol 156, 164;
    and hostage issue 153; and
    imperialism 27, 30, 193;
    interests in Gulf conflict 84–6;
    and Iraq 28–30, 34, 84–5; and
    Iraqi nuclear programme 47;
    and Koweit 133–6; and Kuwait
    84–5, 136, 258; and mandated
    territories 27–8; and Middle
    East 13, 22, 84, 193; military
    contribution 313–15; and
    Muslim migration 15; and oil
    34, 135, 193, 194, 196; and
    Ottoman Empire 27–8; and
    Persian Gulf 43, 134; political
    influence 209; and prisoners of
    war 155; and 'retreat from
    empire' 30; and Security
    Council 74, 78, 86, 141; seizure
    of British servicemen 103;
    sends troops to Saudi Arabia
    141; and Status Quo
    Agreement (1901) 133, 134;
    and Suez canal 27; and Suez
    crisis (1956) 13, 30, 31, 34–5,
    65; overthrow of Margaret
    Thatcher 125; and Turkey 134;
    and United States 31, 61, 62,
    85, 89, 99, 103, 209, 258, 272;

and state of war 154
United Nations 53, 69–90 passim;
    and action under Article 51
    140, 142, 150–2; and 'all
    necessary means' 142; and
    Article 47 150–2; and Charter
    69–70, 75, 130, 141, 142, 145;
    and China 82–3; and Congo
    70, 71–2, 73; and declaration of
    war 151–2; effectiveness of 73,
    89–90; ethos of 74–5; and
    France 61; and use of force
    104, 105; significance of Gulf
    conflict for 69; role of in Gulf
    crisis 10, 69, 72–8, 76; and
    international law 11, 127, 128,
    129, 139–44, 267; and Iraq 75,
    76, 137, 138; Iraq–Kuwait
    Border Commission 258; and
    Korean War 70–1, 73; and
    annexation of Kuwait 76; and
    Kuwait 136, 137, 138, 141, 257;
    and military coercion 76; and
    military conflict 69–72; and
    Military Staff Committee 86–7;
    and 'new world order' 89–90,
    129, 277–8; and
    non-interference 143; and
    nuclear proliferation 268; and
    peaceful resolution 70, 74, 139;
    public expectations of 70; and
    sanctions 104, 109, 145, 147;
    Secretary General 72, 73–4, 88,
    107; solidarity in 58, 113;
    schizophrenic nature of 73;
    and legitimacy of states 130–1,
    138; and territorial claims 131;
    and United Kingdom 61, 142;
    and United States 58, 87–9, 99,
    111, 122, 129, 141, 142; and
    war crimes 168, 169
United Nations Charter 69, 130,
    139, 140, 145; Article 2 147;
    Article 39 74, 306; Article 42
    76, 145, 152; Article 43 87, 307;
    Article 51 76, 88, 139, 141, 142,
    146; Chapter VII 143, 145, 152,
    306–9
United Nations Security Council

10, 11, 53–5, 57, 60–2, 70–83,
86–90, 102, 104, 109, 113, 128,
131, 136–42, 145, 146, 150,
151, 177, 178, 203, 221, 227,
248; Resolution 660 74, 77,
145, 221, 227, 309; Resolution
661 74, 75, 88, 102, 145, 146,
203, 310; Resolution 662 76,
310; Resolution 665 75, 88,
146, 310; Resolution 670 75,
147, 311; Resolution 674 76,
311; Resolution 678 74–7, 88,
105, 113, 142, 150, 151, 177,
227, 248, 259, 311
UN Coalition 5, 15, 48, 58–68;
and air war 115, 231–4; Arab
members of 63–8, 117; and
Article 51 141; authorisation
for military action 141; and
blockade 145, 146; balancing
costs 224; and chemical
weapons 241; counter-offensive
207; and Egypt 65–6; and
Europe 60–2; and France 84;
and Germany 209–10; ground
war 247; Iraq counter-threat to
114, 116–17; and Israel 63, 162;
and international law 129; and
Iraq 154; and Japan 209–19;
and jihad 186; and Jordan 55;
and Khafji 244; and Kuwait
213; military forces 33, 105,
112, 230; military strategy
227–34, 269; and 'mother of all
battles' 124; motivations 184;
nature of 59; 'nightmare
scenario' 221, 223; outcome
priorities 224; problems of
management 58–63 passim;
and Saddam Hussein 115,
124–5, 222, 223, 235, 245,
254–5, 256; and Saudi Arabia
63–5; Scud attacks 240; Security
Council mandate 151; and
Soviet Union 90; strategic
surprise 238–9; and Syria 38–9,
66–7; time constraints 225; and
Third World 83; and Turkey
145; US leadership 270, 271;
and use of force 148; victory
270, 271; war aims 229, 248–51
UN Convention on Prohibitions
165
United States, US, America,
Americans 114, 293, 293;
ambiguous role 87; al-Amiriya
bunker 243; and Article 47 142,
150; and Article 51 75, 76, 141,
150; and blockade of Iraq 146;
and President Bush 119–22;
calculation for war 224;
coalition management 58–63,
102, 104; and 'compellance'
104–5, 109; Congress 177–8,
298; Congressional elections
104, 296; and chemical
weapons 164, 241; and China
82–3; crisis strategy 103–7, 109,
110, 111; decision to use force
105; and declaration of war
177; on diplomatic defensive
94; and 'double standards'
173–5; economic effects in 207,
208–9, 211; and Egypt 65; and
France 84, 272; intelligence
242; and international law 129;
and Iraq 46,96, 266–7, 297; and
Iraqi threat to Israel 117; and
Israel 32, 262–3, 298; and
Jewish lobby 14; and Jordan
56–7; and just war principles
176–84 passim; and Korean
War 97; and Kuwait 64, 141,
197, 257–8; and Kuwaiti
reconstruction 213; lessons of
Gulf War 255, 262; limitations
of power 271; Middle East 14,
31, 98–9, 193, 260, 261–2;
military build-up 111, 294, 297;
military contribution 313–15;
and military control of UN
operation 150, 269; and
Military Staff Committee 86;
military strategy 227–31 passim;
and Mutla Ridge 166–7;
'nightmare scenario' 221; and
oil 193, 194, 196, 199, 202; and
negotiations with Iraq 106,

111–12; and Patriot missiles 240; preferred outcomes 223–4; and public opinion 115; response options 183; response to invasion of Kuwait 46, 94, 96, 98–9, 102, 103, 192, 202, 294; and Saddam Hussein 122–4, 219, 220, 223, 240, 254–5; and Saudi Arabia 64–5, 141–2, 258–9, 294, 297; and Soviet Union 62, 80–2, 103, 299; Strategic Bombing Survey (1945) 232; and 'structural imperatives' 125, 226–7; and Suez crisis 31; and Syria 66–7; time pressure on 182; and UN 58, 69, 87–90, 128, 142, 151; and UK 85–6, 209, 258, 272, (*see* United Kingdom); 'Vietnam factor' 116–17, 172, 243, 244–7; war aims 178–80, 253–4, 299; and attitude to war crimes 168–9; and War Powers Act (1973) 177; and world role 279

Ur 158

Vienna Convention on the Law of Treaties 138
Vienna Conventions 77
Vietnam 85, 99, 116, 117, 121, 122, 172, 208, 243–7
'Vietnam factor' 121, 122

Waddy, Charis 323
war; and aggression 140, 172–3; air power and 232–4; calculation for 218–24; cost–benefit analysis 216–18; crimes 160, 167–9; and crisis 11, 92–3, 94; damage 162–3; and decision 215–18; defensive strategy in 134–6, 234–5; definition 151, 172–3; escalation in 224–7, 239–42; explanation of 2–3, 5; holy war 2 (*see* jihad); imperative of 95, 108, 118, 224–5, 227; and intelligence 242–4; 'just war' principles 2, 11, 149, 176–85; as a 'last resort' 106, 181–3; and law 2, 11, 114, 149–69; and misperception 8; moral consequences of avoiding 180; and morality 11, 170–3; non-declaration of 151–2, 176–8; perceptions and rationality 218–24; proportionality and 183–5, 189–90; 'ruses' of (*see* international law, acts of 'perfidy'); and system change 252–3; technology and 188–90; termination 247–52; threshold 95, 107, 108; and UN 152
war threshold 95, 107, 108, 268
Warbah 44, 49, 258
Watson, Bruce 300, 316, 322, 325
Watson, Adam 318
Watt, D. C. 319
Weisband, E. 319
Weller, Marc 320, 321
Wight, Martin 325
Williams, Rowan 323
Wilson, Bryan 317
Woetzel, Robert K. 322
Woollacott, Martin 325
world government 127

Yemen 22, 24, 57, 58, 77–9, 261, 293
Young, O. R. 319
Yugoslavia 256, 277–9